LAND
OF THE
LUSTROUS
10

HARUKO ICHIKAWA

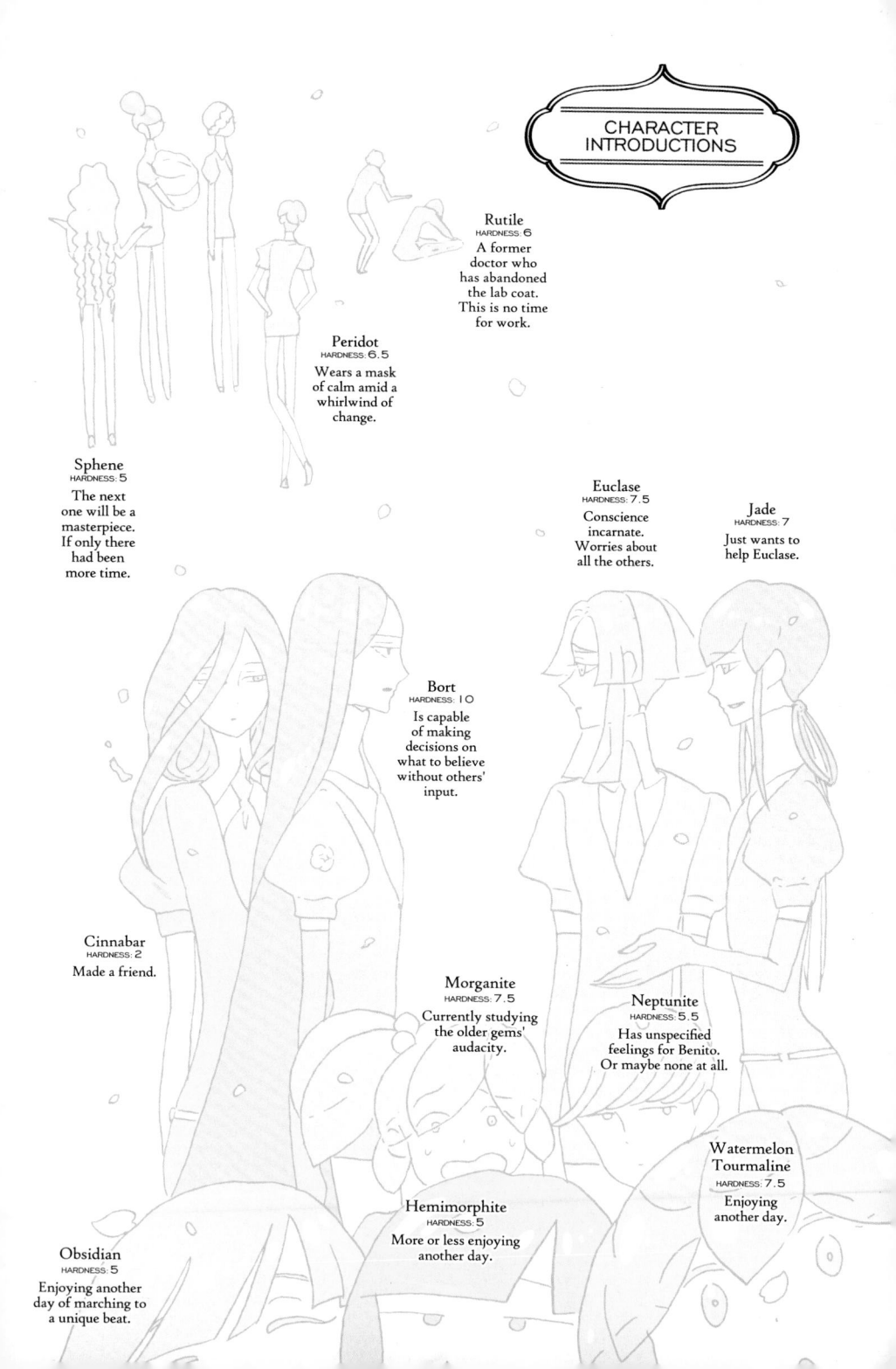

CHARACTER INTRODUCTIONS

Rutile
HARDNESS: 6
A former doctor who has abandoned the lab coat. This is no time for work.

Peridot
HARDNESS: 6.5
Wears a mask of calm amid a whirlwind of change.

Sphene
HARDNESS: 5
The next one will be a masterpiece. If only there had been more time.

Euclase
HARDNESS: 7.5
Conscience incarnate. Worries about all the others.

Jade
HARDNESS: 7
Just wants to help Euclase.

Bort
HARDNESS: 10
Is capable of making decisions on what to believe without others' input.

Cinnabar
HARDNESS: 2
Made a friend.

Morganite
HARDNESS: 7.5
Currently studying the older gems' audacity.

Neptunite
HARDNESS: 5.5
Has unspecified feelings for Benito. Or maybe none at all.

Watermelon Tourmaline
HARDNESS: 7.5
Enjoying another day.

Hemimorphite
HARDNESS: 5
More or less enjoying another day.

Obsidian
HARDNESS: 5
Enjoying another day of marching to a unique beat.

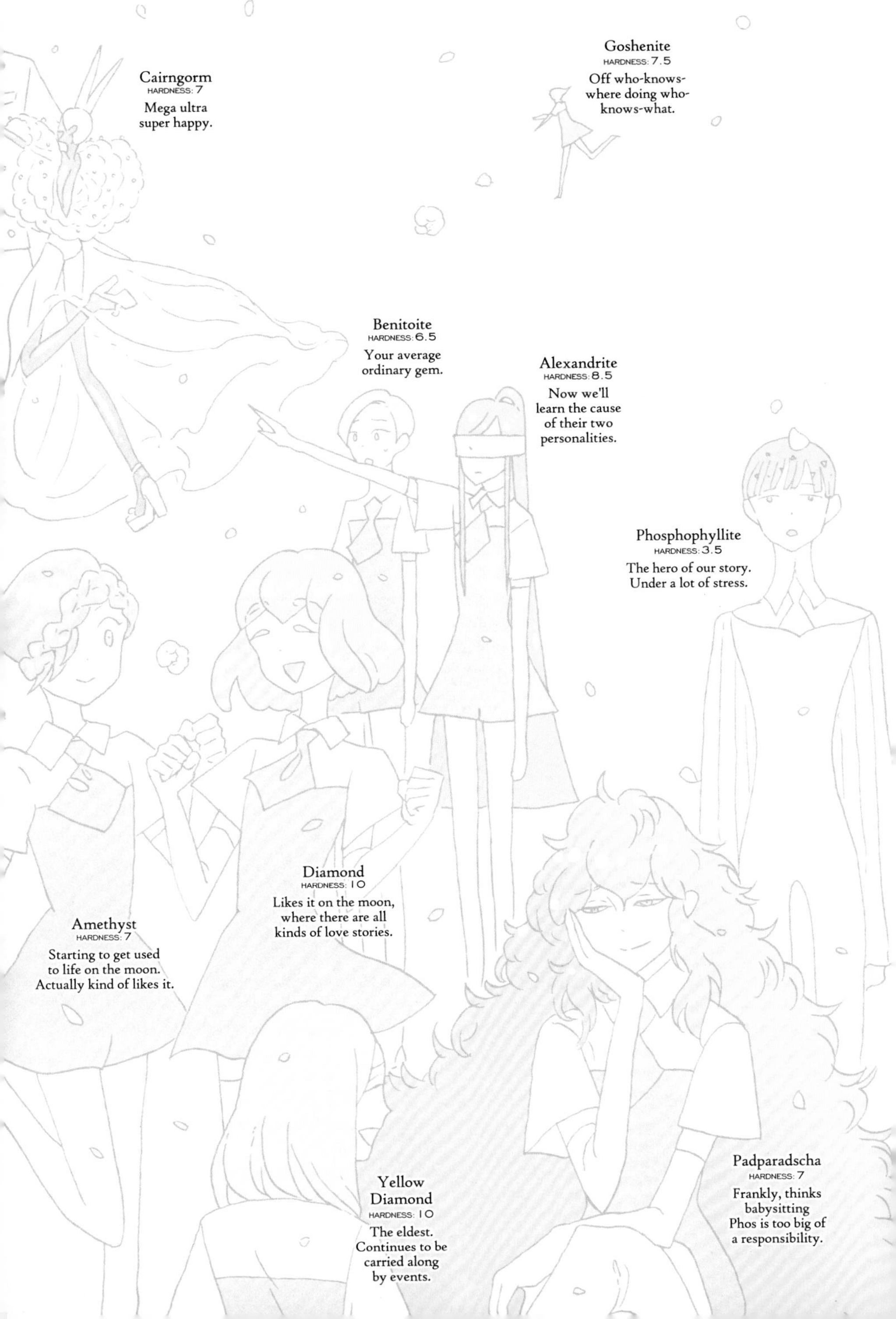
Goshenite
HARDNESS: 7.5
Off who-knows-where doing who-knows-what.
Cairngorm
HARDNESS: 7
Mega ultra super happy.
Alexandrite
HARDNESS: 8.5
Now we'll learn the cause of their two personalities.
Benitoite
HARDNESS: 6.5
Your average ordinary gem.
Phosphophyllite
HARDNESS: 3.5
The hero of our story. Under a lot of stress.
Diamond
HARDNESS: 10
Likes it on the moon, where there are all kinds of love stories.
Amethyst
HARDNESS: 7
Starting to get used to life on the moon. Actually kind of likes it.
Padparadscha
HARDNESS: 7
Frankly, thinks babysitting Phos is too big of a responsibility.
Yellow Diamond
HARDNESS: 10
The eldest. Continues to be carried along by events.

CONTENTS

CHAPTER 71: Failure — 5

CHAPTER 72: Savior — 25

CHAPTER 73: Choice — 45

CHAPTER 74: Ceremony — 65

CHAPTER 75: Wish — 85

CHAPTER 76: Admirabilis — 105

CHAPTER 77: Authentication — 131

CHAPTER 78: Passage — 151

CHAPTER 79: 220 Years — 171

Land of the Lavish Gowns — 195

CHAPTER 71:

Failure

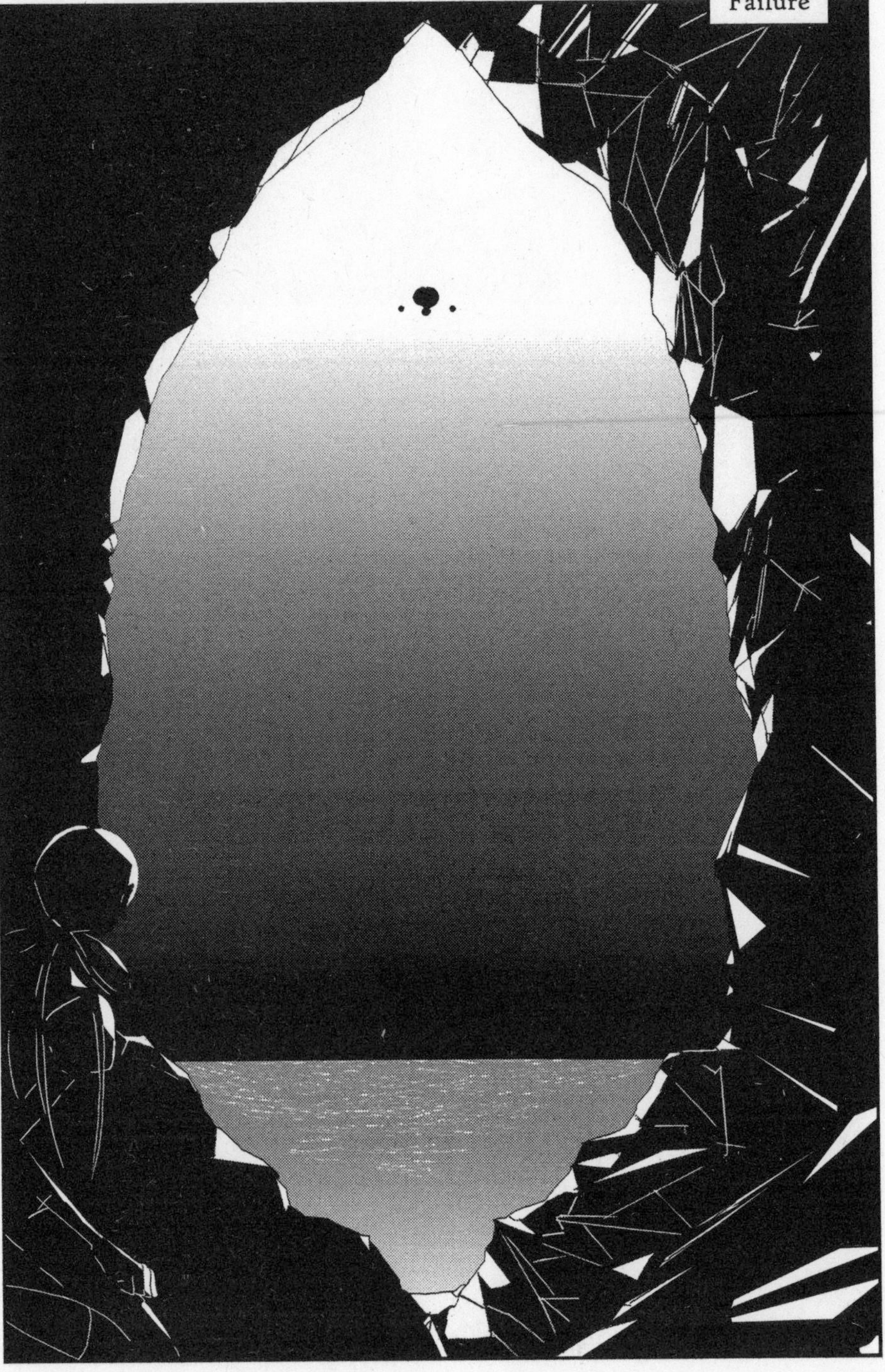

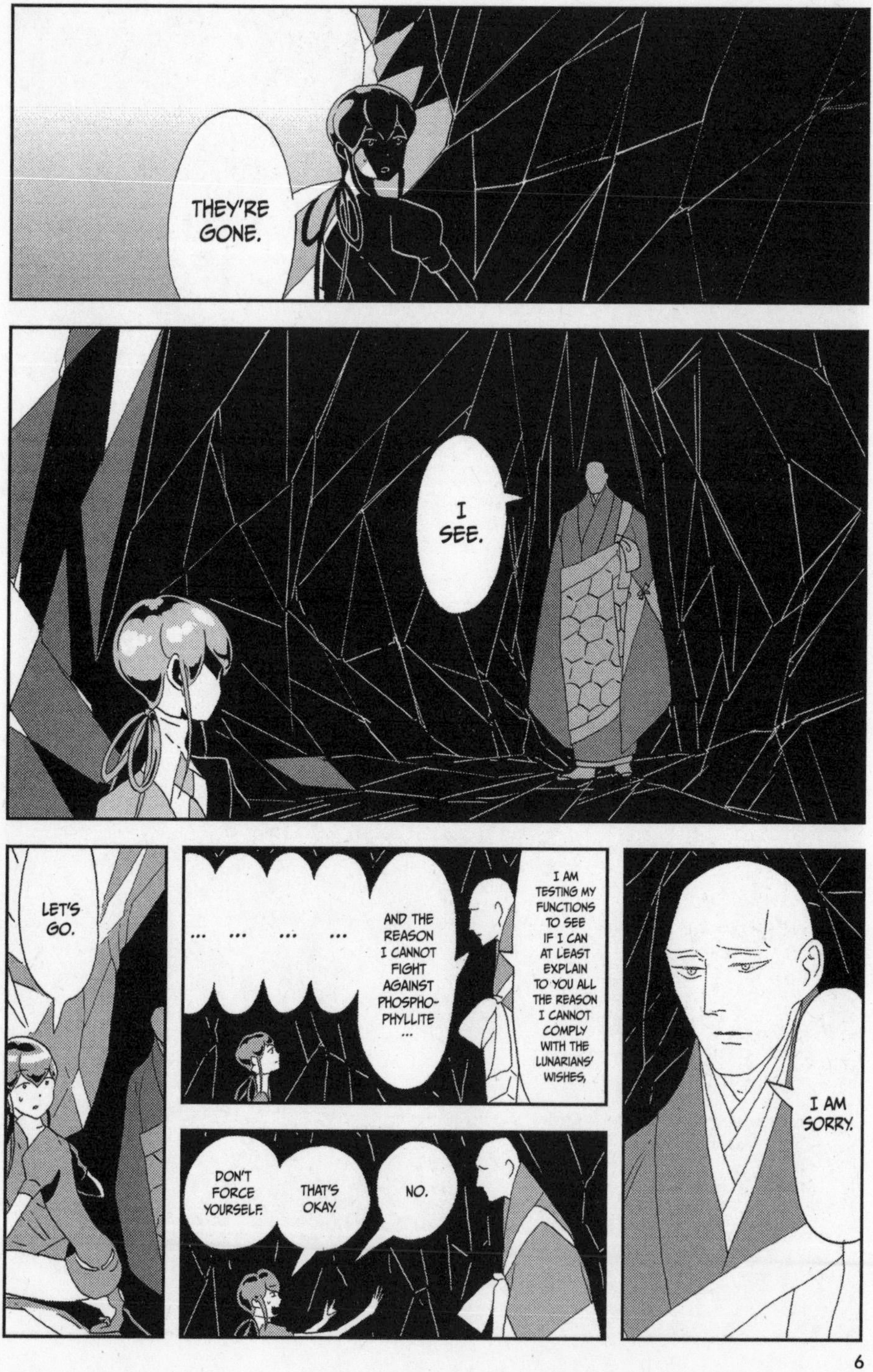

THEY'RE GONE.
I SEE.
I AM SORRY.
I AM TESTING MY FUNCTIONS TO SEE IF I CAN AT LEAST EXPLAIN TO YOU ALL THE REASON I CANNOT COMPLY WITH THE LUNARIANS' WISHES,
AND THE REASON I CANNOT FIGHT AGAINST PHOSPHO-PHYLLITE ...
...
...
...
...
NO.
THAT'S OKAY.
DON'T FORCE YOURSELF.
LET'S GO.

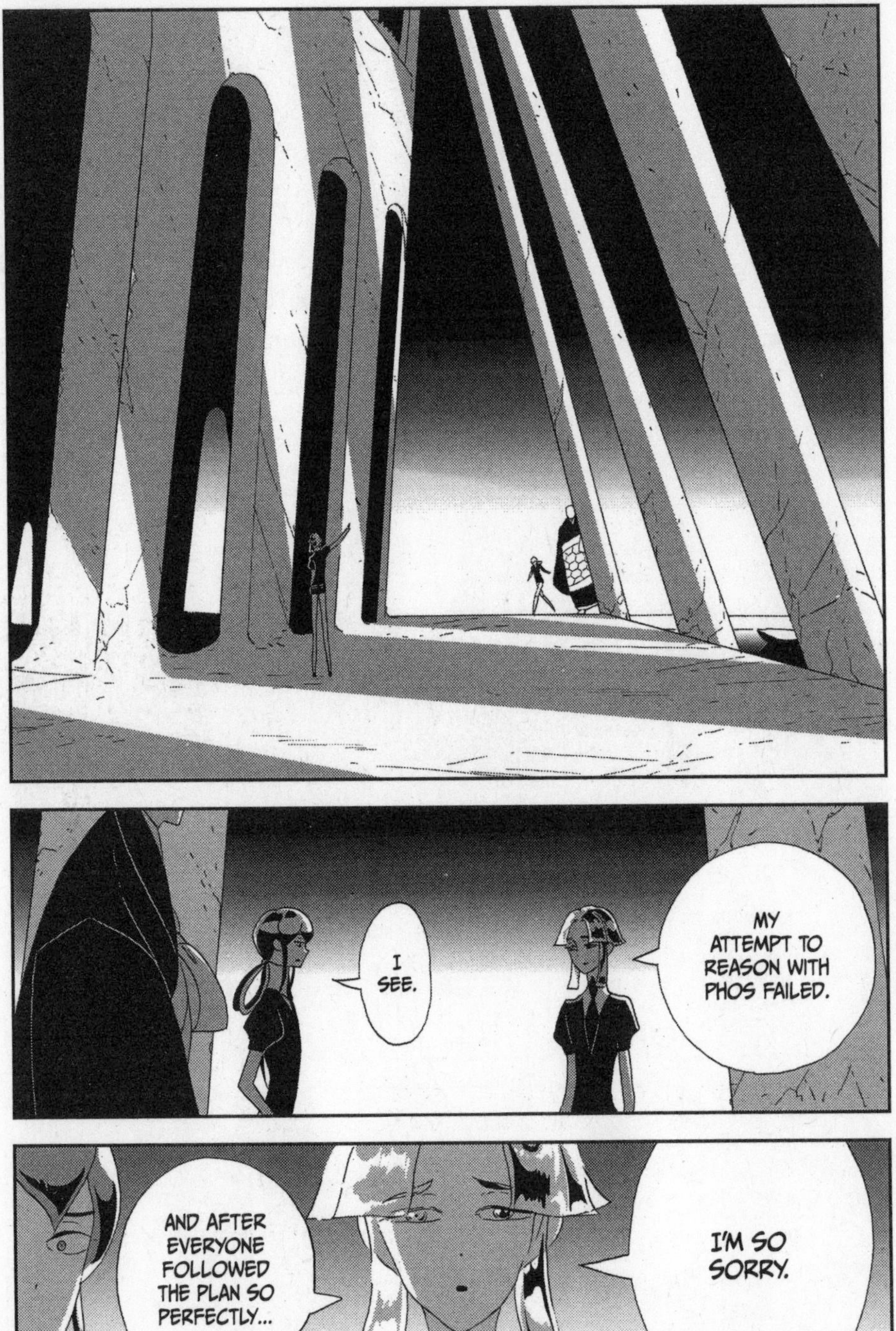
MY ATTEMPT TO REASON WITH PHOS FAILED.
I SEE.
I'M SO SORRY.
AND AFTER EVERYONE FOLLOWED THE PLAN SO PERFECTLY...

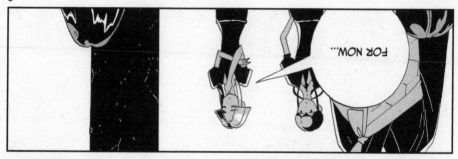

IT'S FINE.
WE PROTECTED KONGŌ.
THAT'S TRUE.
PHOS SUDDENLY STARTED TALKING ABOUT HARDNESS...
AND I DISCOVERED THAT PHOS *DOES* HAVE A WEAKNESS.
YELLOW SEEMED TO BE SANE...
BUT PADPARADSCHA WAS TOTALLY BONKERS. WHAT WAS THAT? IT WAS SUPER SCARY!
AND THAT LITTLE LUNARIAN...
FOR NOW...

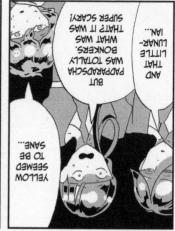

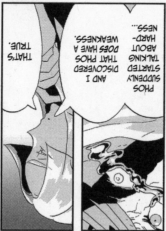

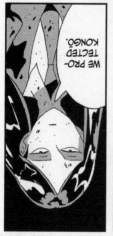

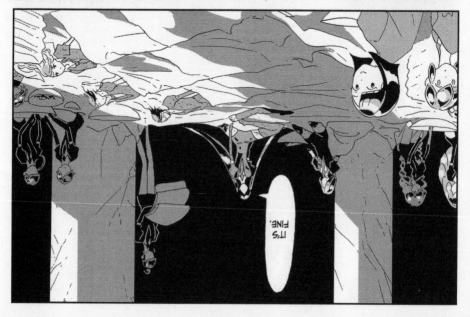

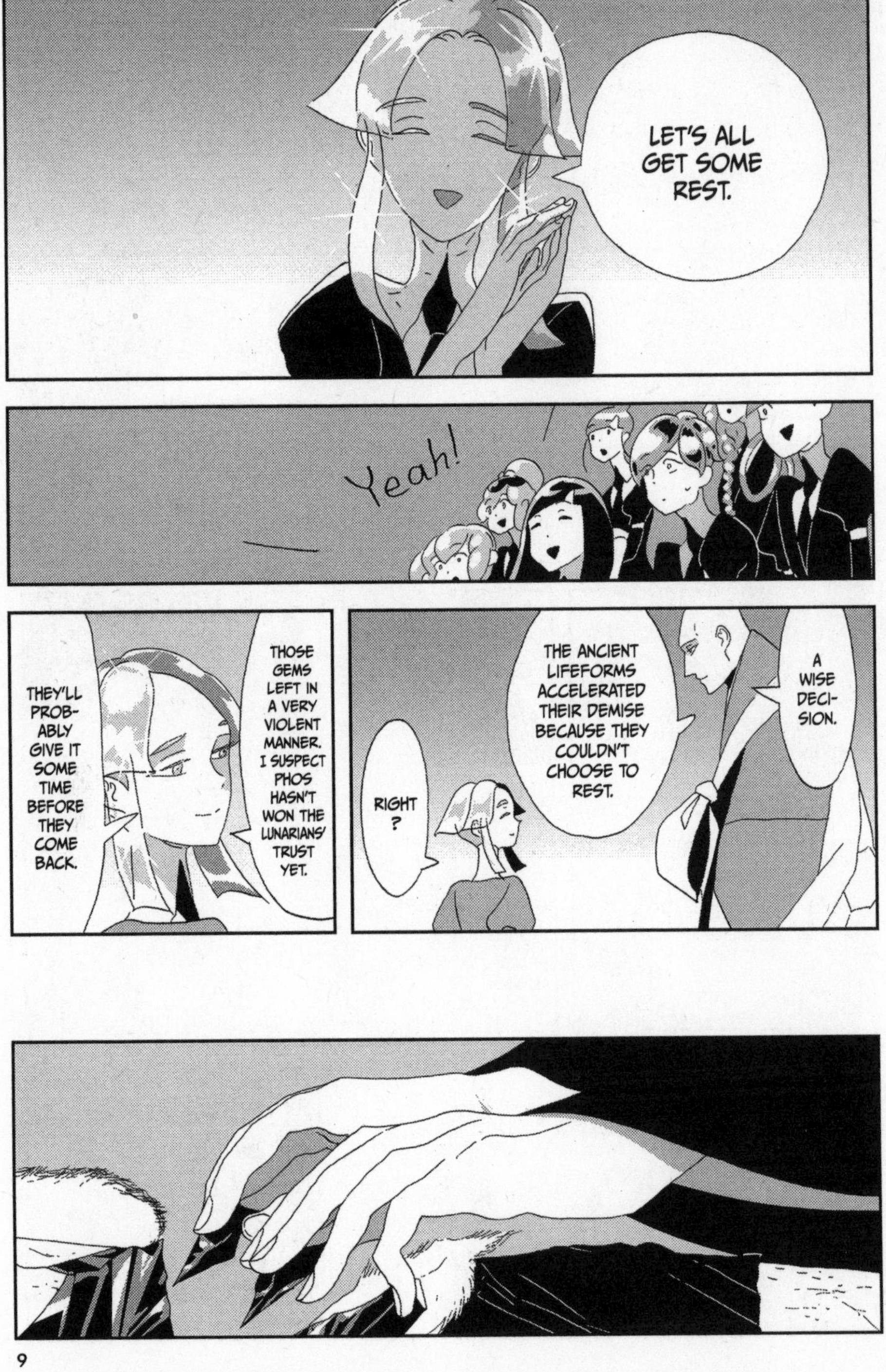
LET'S ALL GET SOME REST.
Yeah!
A WISE DECI-SION.
THE ANCIENT LIFEFORMS ACCELERATED THEIR DEMISE BECAUSE THEY COULDN'T CHOOSE TO REST.
RIGHT ?
THOSE GEMS LEFT IN A VERY VIOLENT MANNER. I SUSPECT PHOS HASN'T WON THE LUNARIANS' TRUST YET.
THEY'LL PROB-ABLY GIVE IT SOME TIME BEFORE THEY COME BACK.

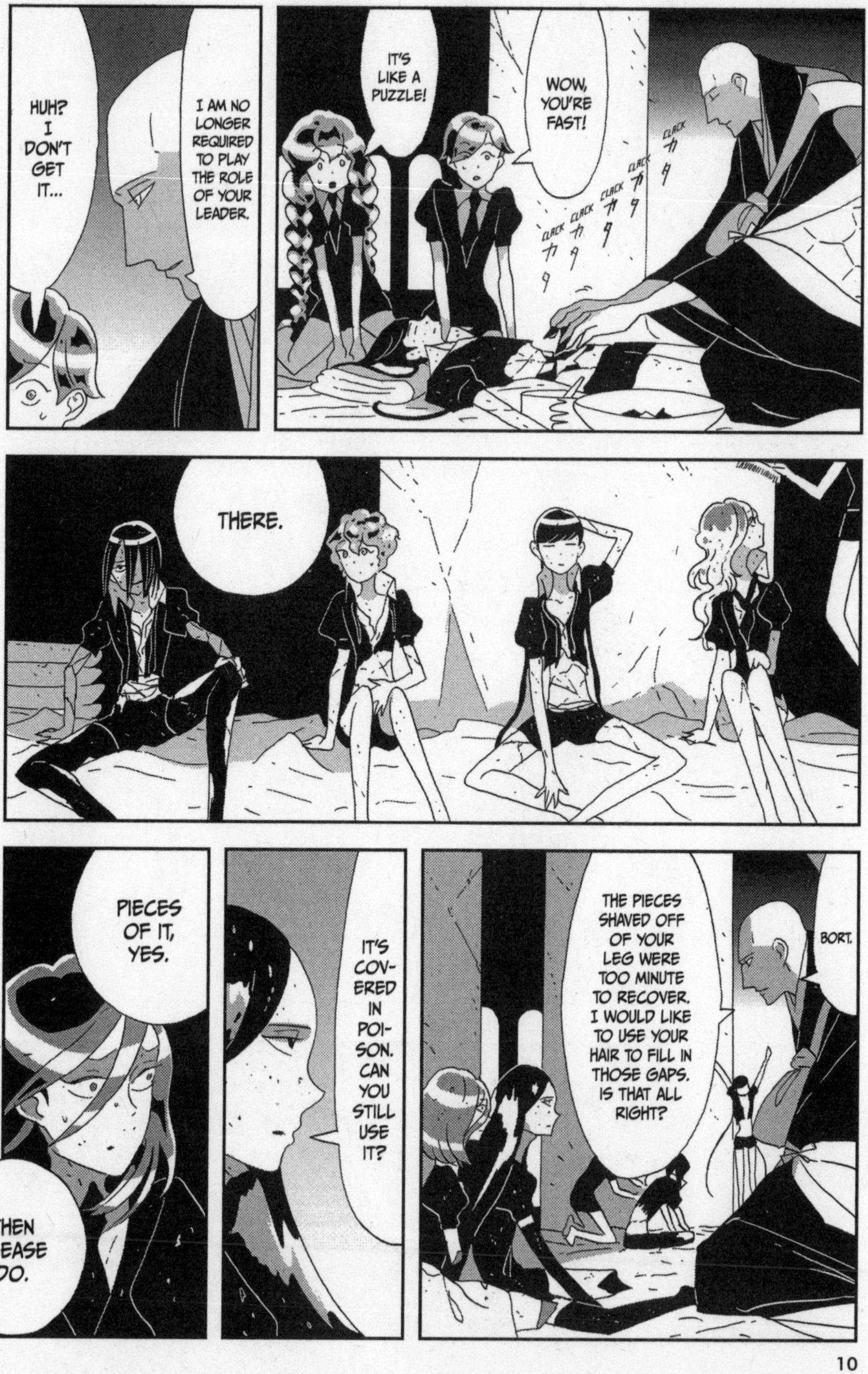
CLACK
CLACK
CLACK
CLACK
CLACK
WOW, YOU'RE FAST!
IT'S LIKE A PUZZLE!
I AM NO LONGER REQUIRED TO PLAY THE ROLE OF YOUR LEADER.
HUH? I DON'T GET IT...
THERE.
BORT.
THE PIECES SHAVED OFF OF YOUR LEG WERE TOO MINUTE TO RECOVER. I WOULD LIKE TO USE YOUR HAIR TO FILL IN THOSE GAPS. IS THAT ALL RIGHT?
IT'S COV-ERED IN POI-SON. CAN YOU STILL USE IT?
PIECES OF IT, YES.
THEN PLEASE DO.

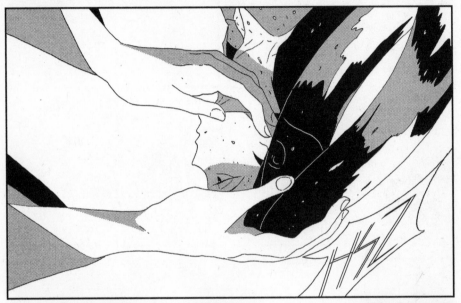

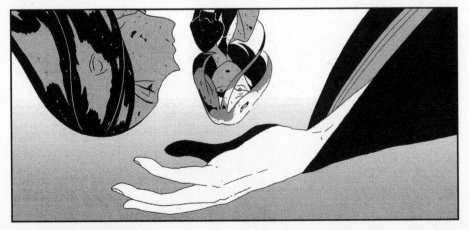

YOUR RIGHT HAND.

DON'T WORRY ABOUT IT.

...I'M SORRY.

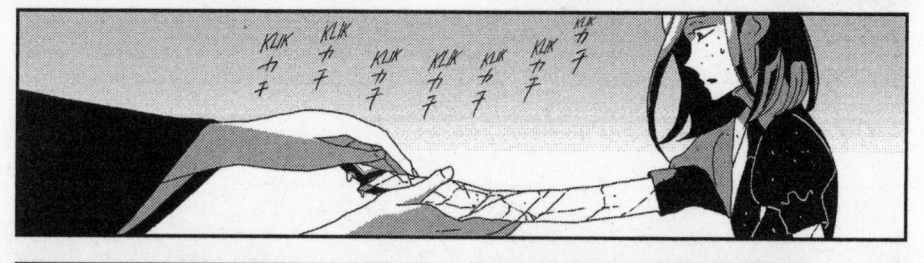

KLIK KLIK KLIK KLIK KLIK KLIK

IF THEY HAVE THE TECHNOLOGY TO GET PADPARADSCHA MOVING AGAIN, THEN THERE IS A GOOD CHANCE THAT THEY *CAN* REMOVE YOUR VENOM.

PHOSPHOPHYLLITE TOLD ME THAT, ON THE MOON, THEY CAN REMOVE THE POISON. DO YOU THINK PADPARADSCHA WILL REALLY BE OKAY?

I COVERED PADPAR-ADSCHA IN MY VENOM.

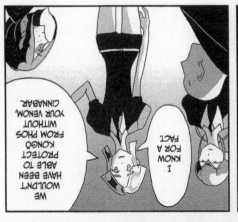

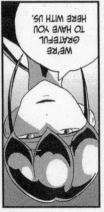

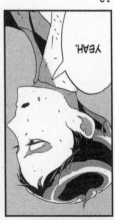

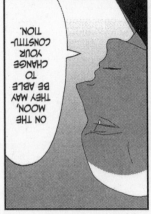

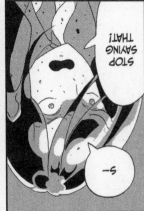

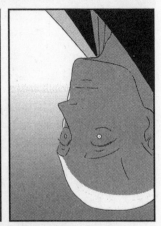

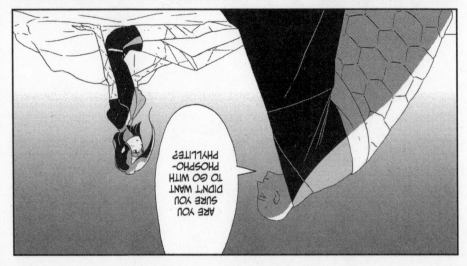

ARE YOU SURE YOU DIDN'T WANT TO GO WITH PHOSPHO-PHYLLITE?
ON THE MOON, THEY MAY BE ABLE TO CHANGE YOUR CONSTITU-TION.
S—
STOP SAYING THAT!
WE WOULDN'T HAVE BEEN ABLE TO PROTECT KONGŌ FROM PHOS WITHOUT YOUR VENOM, CINNABAR.
I KNOW FOR A FACT.
WE'RE GRATEFUL TO HAVE YOU HERE WITH US.
YEAH.

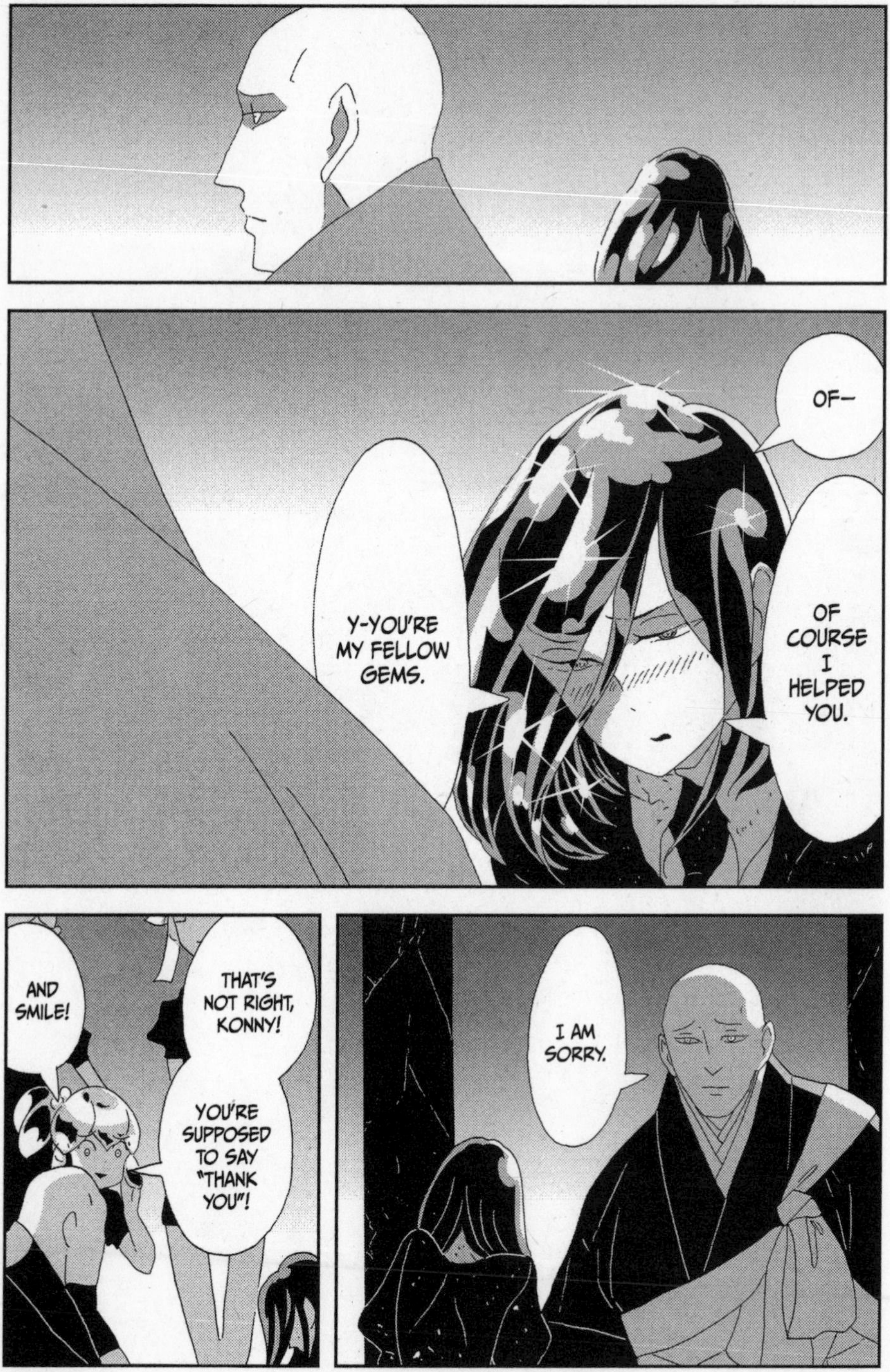
OF—
OF COURSE I HELPED YOU.
Y-YOU'RE MY FELLOW GEMS.
I AM SORRY.
THAT'S NOT RIGHT, KONNY!
YOU'RE SUPPOSED TO SAY "THANK YOU"!
AND SMILE!

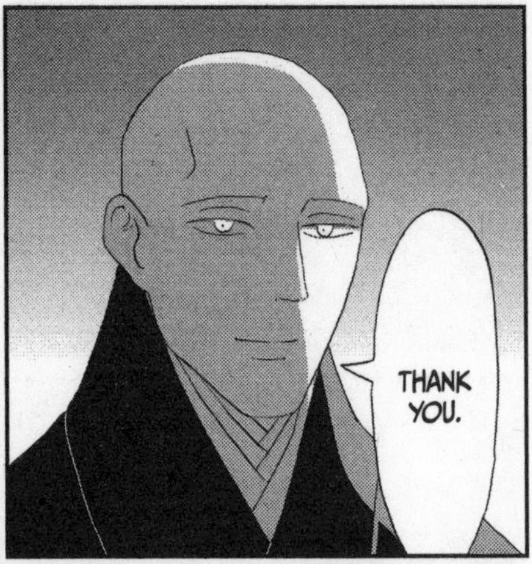
THANK YOU.
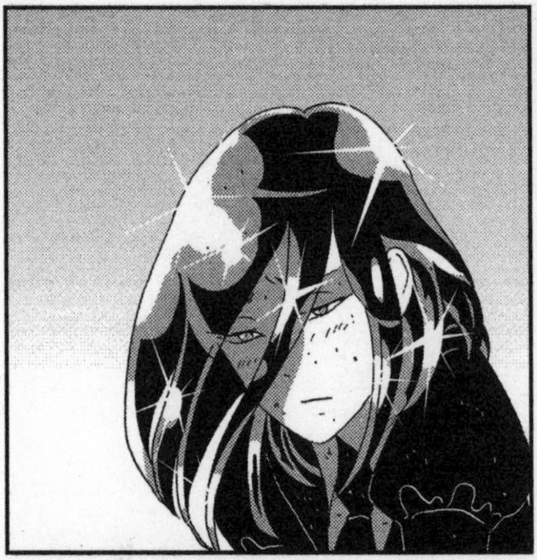
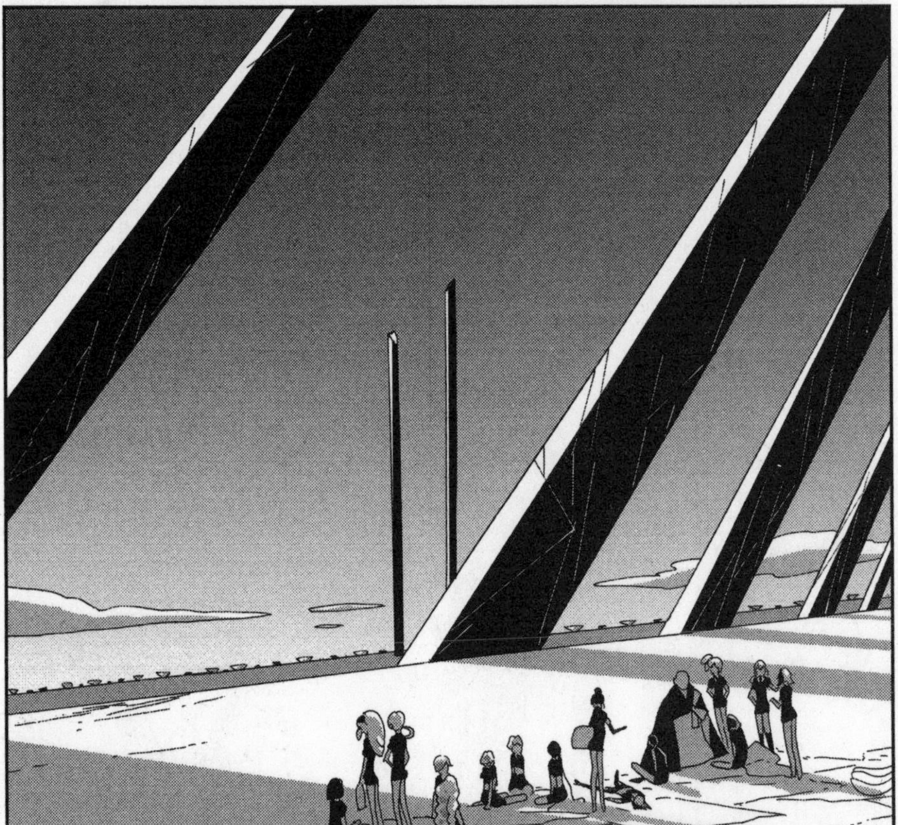

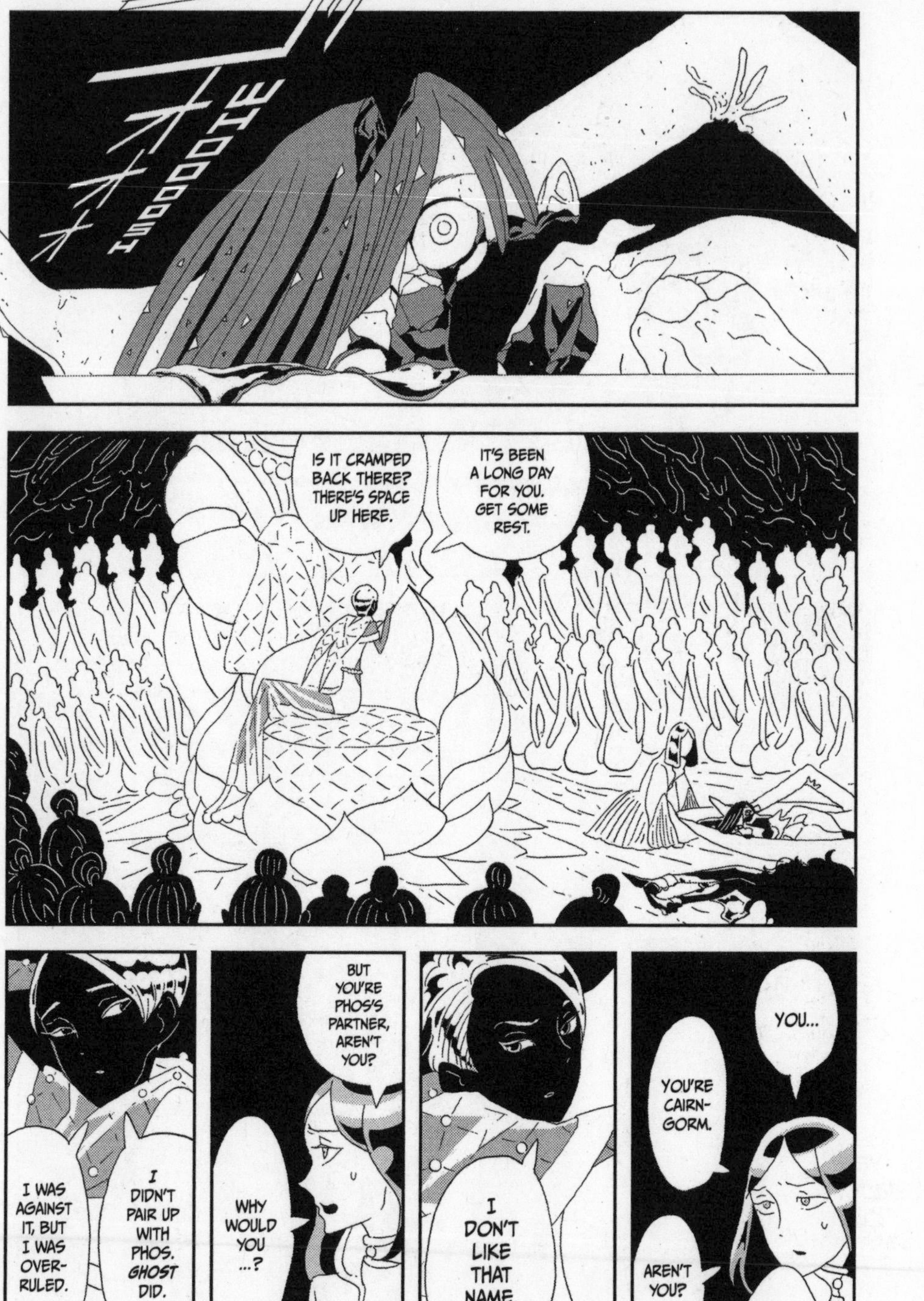
オオオオ
WHOOOOSH
IT'S BEEN A LONG DAY FOR YOU. GET SOME REST.
IS IT CRAMPED BACK THERE? THERE'S SPACE UP HERE.
YOU...
YOU'RE CAIRN-GORM.
AREN'T YOU?
I DON'T LIKE THAT NAME.
BUT YOU'RE PHOS'S PARTNER, AREN'T YOU?
WHY WOULD YOU ...?
I DIDN'T PAIR UP WITH PHOS. GHOST DID.
I WAS AGAINST IT, BUT I WAS OVER-RULED.

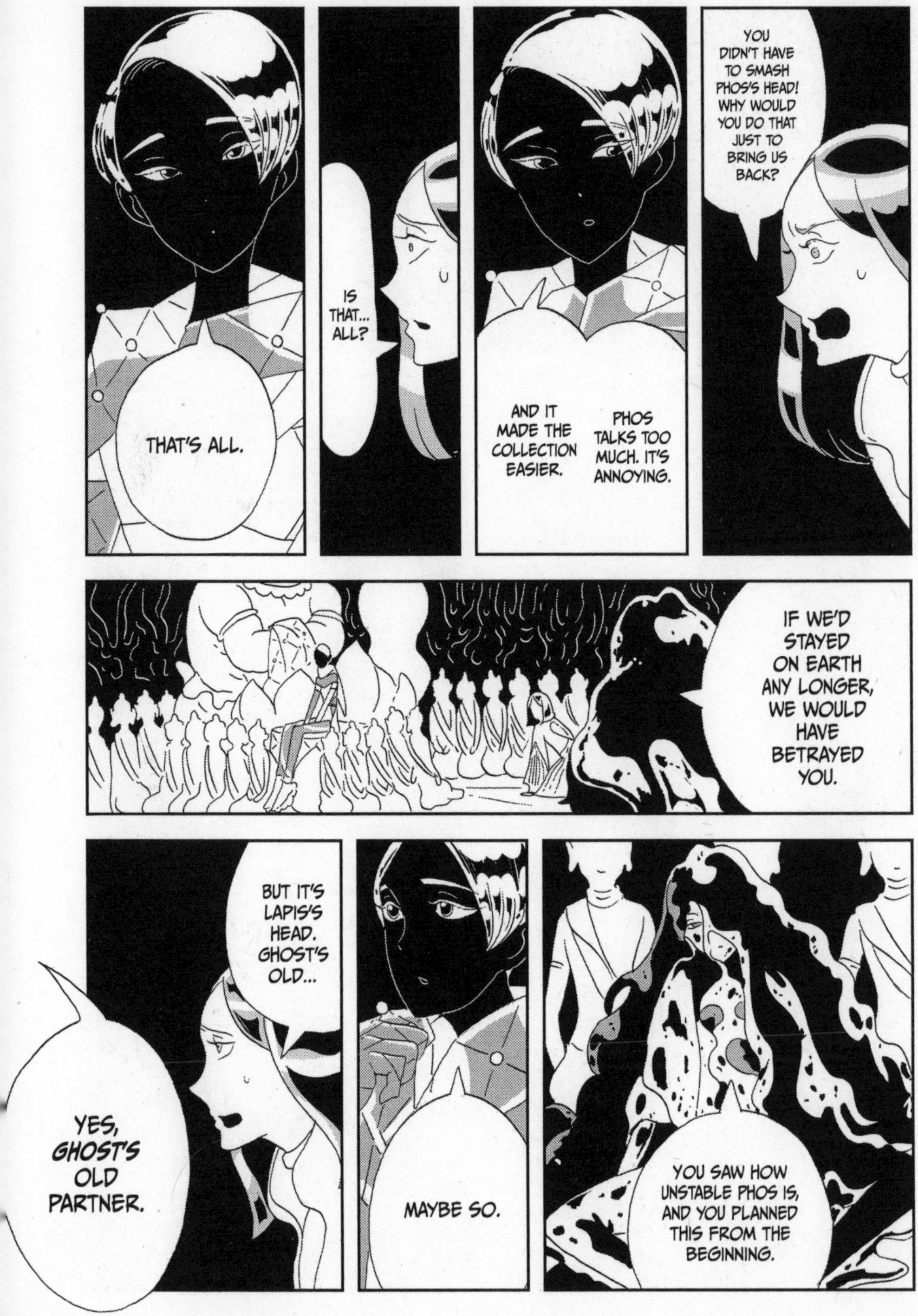
YOU DIDN'T HAVE TO SMASH PHOS'S HEAD! WHY WOULD YOU DO THAT JUST TO BRING US BACK?
PHOS TALKS TOO MUCH. IT'S ANNOYING.
AND IT MADE THE COLLECTION EASIER.
IS THAT... ALL?
THAT'S ALL.
IF WE'D STAYED ON EARTH ANY LONGER, WE WOULD HAVE BETRAYED YOU.
YOU SAW HOW UNSTABLE PHOS IS, AND YOU PLANNED THIS FROM THE BEGINNING.
MAYBE SO.
BUT IT'S LAPIS'S HEAD. GHOST'S OLD...
YES, GHOST'S OLD PARTNER.

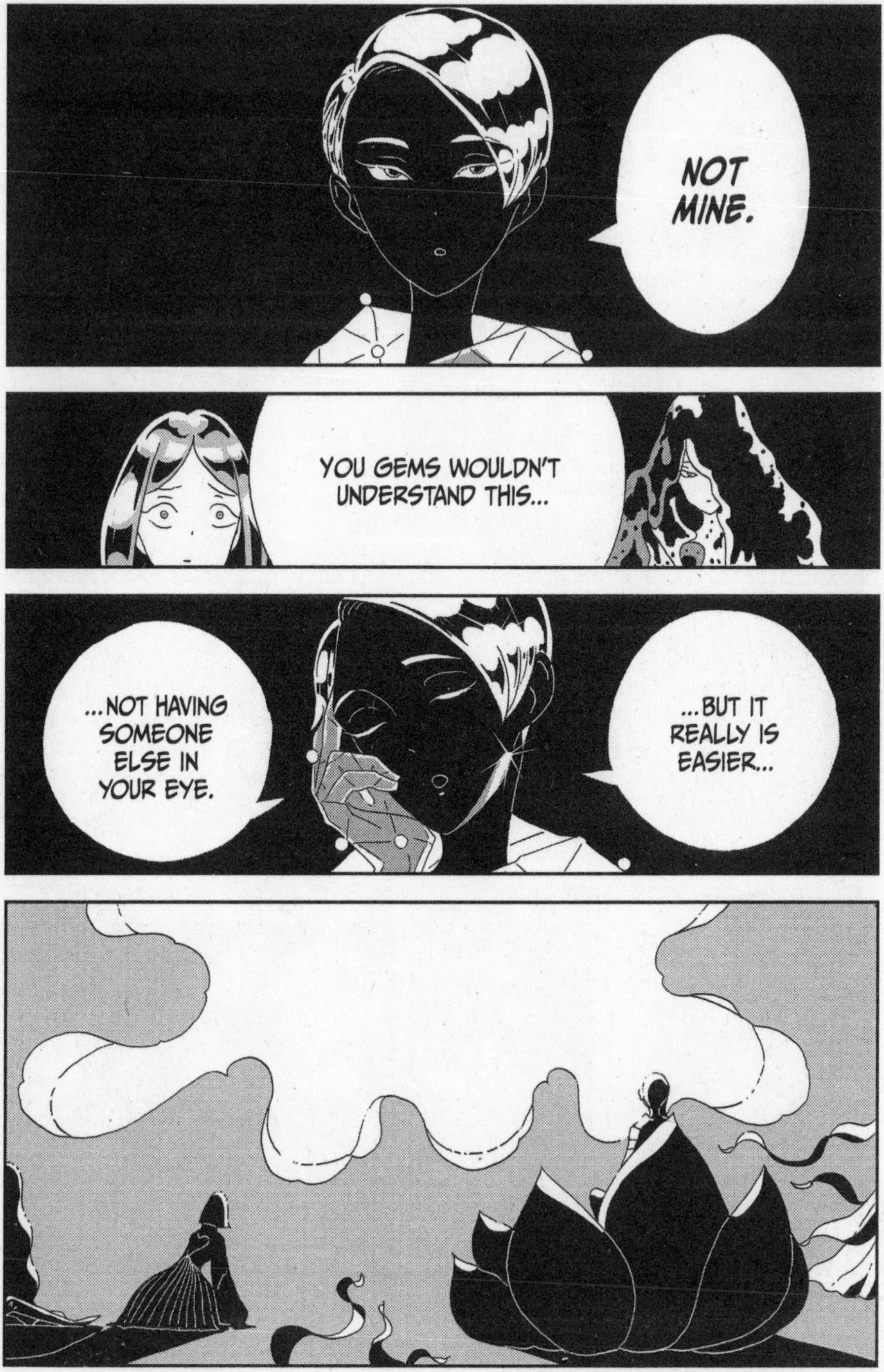
NOT MINE.
YOU GEMS WOULDN'T UNDERSTAND THIS...
...BUT IT REALLY IS EASIER...
...NOT HAVING SOMEONE ELSE IN YOUR EYE.

I'M HOME.

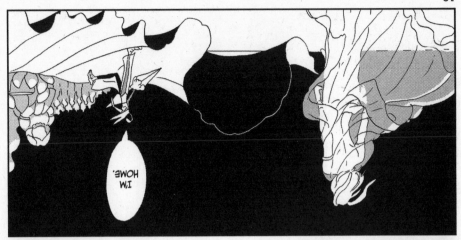

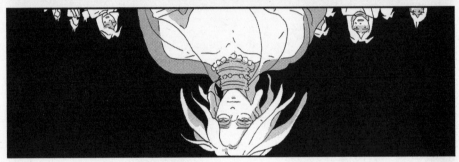

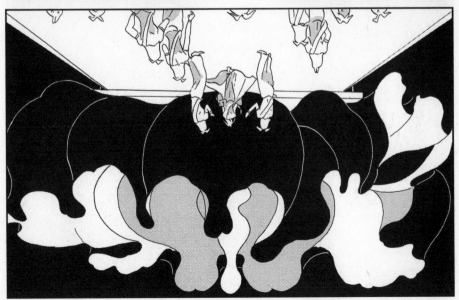

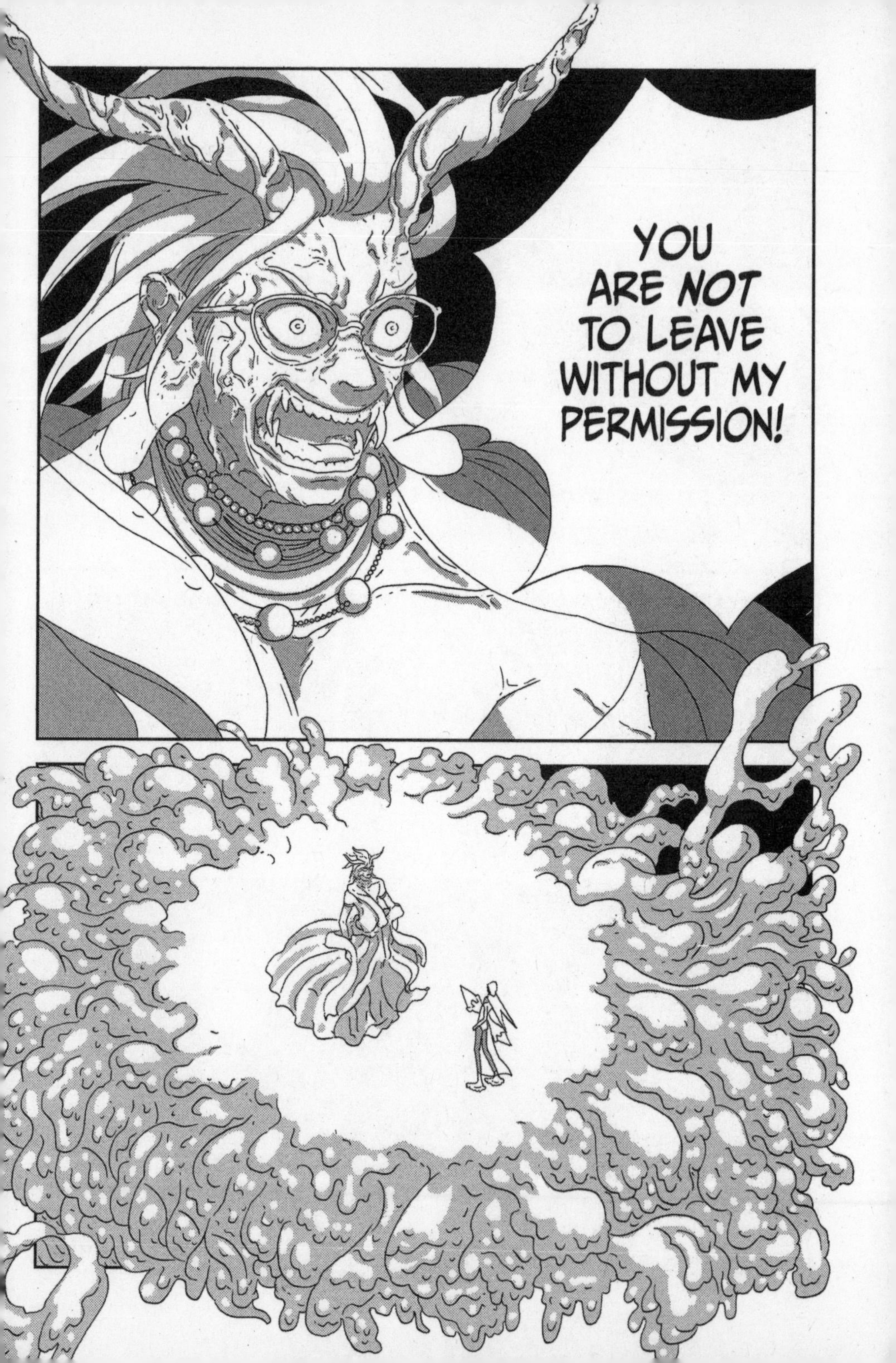
YOU ARE NOT TO LEAVE WITHOUT MY PERMISSION!

BUT—
DO YOU HAVE ANY IDEA HOW WORRIED I WAS?!

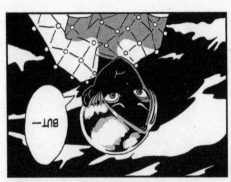

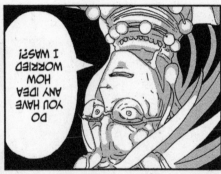

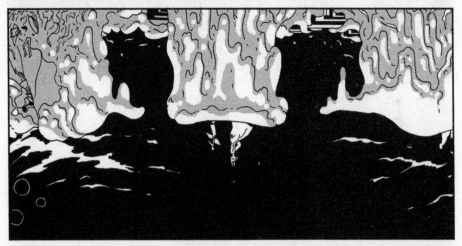

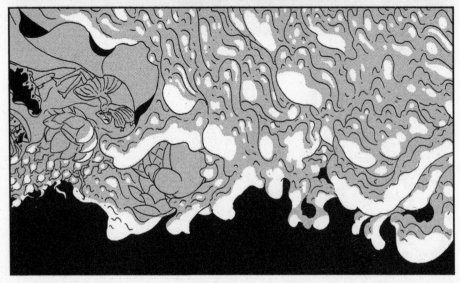

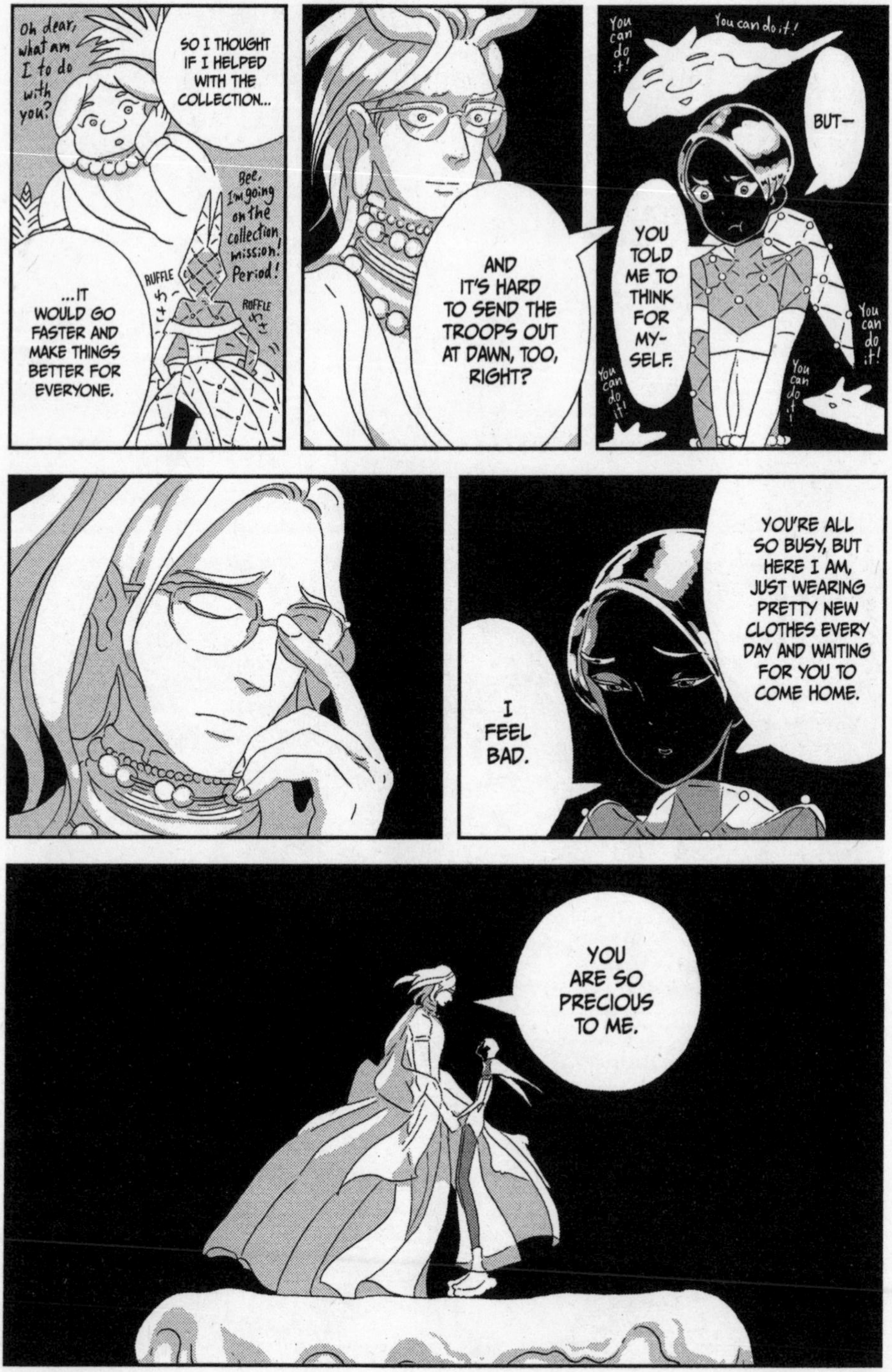
You can do it!
You can do it!
BUT—
YOU TOLD ME TO THINK FOR MY-SELF.
You can do it!
You can do it!
You can do it!
AND IT'S HARD TO SEND THE TROOPS OUT AT DAWN, TOO, RIGHT?
SO I THOUGHT IF I HELPED WITH THE COLLECTION...
Oh dear, what am I to do with you?
Bee, I'm going on the collection mission! Period!
RUFFLE わさ
RUFFLE わさ
...IT WOULD GO FASTER AND MAKE THINGS BETTER FOR EVERYONE.
YOU'RE ALL SO BUSY, BUT HERE I AM, JUST WEARING PRETTY NEW CLOTHES EVERY DAY AND WAITING FOR YOU TO COME HOME.
I FEEL BAD.
YOU ARE SO PRECIOUS TO ME.

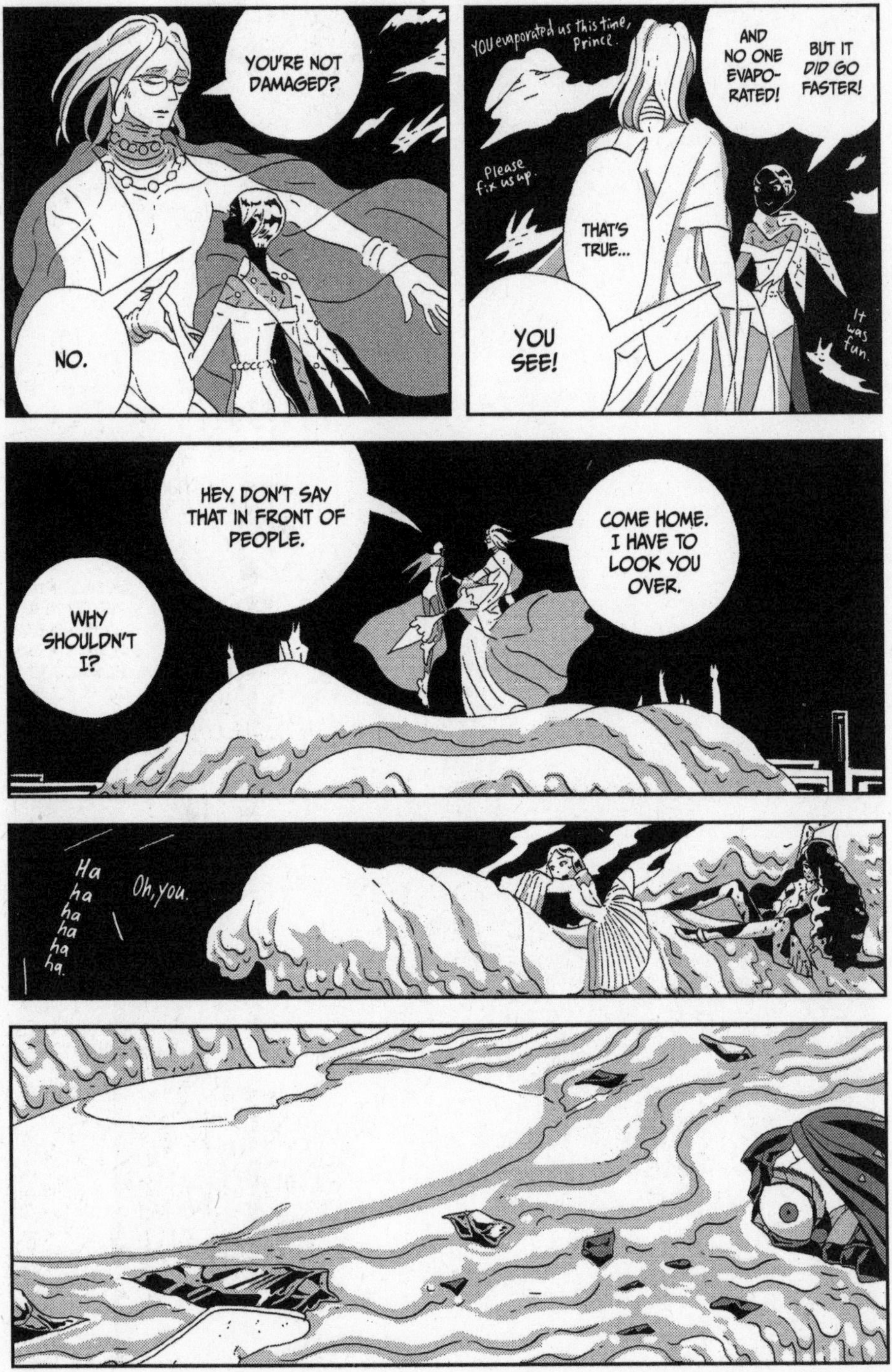
BUT IT DID GO FASTER!
AND NO ONE EVAPORATED!
YOU evaporated us this time, Prince.
Please fix us up.
THAT'S TRUE...
YOU SEE!
It was fun.
YOU'RE NOT DAMAGED?
NO.
COME HOME. I HAVE TO LOOK YOU OVER.
HEY. DON'T SAY THAT IN FRONT OF PEOPLE.
WHY SHOULDN'T I?
Oh, you.
Ha ha ha ha ha ha.

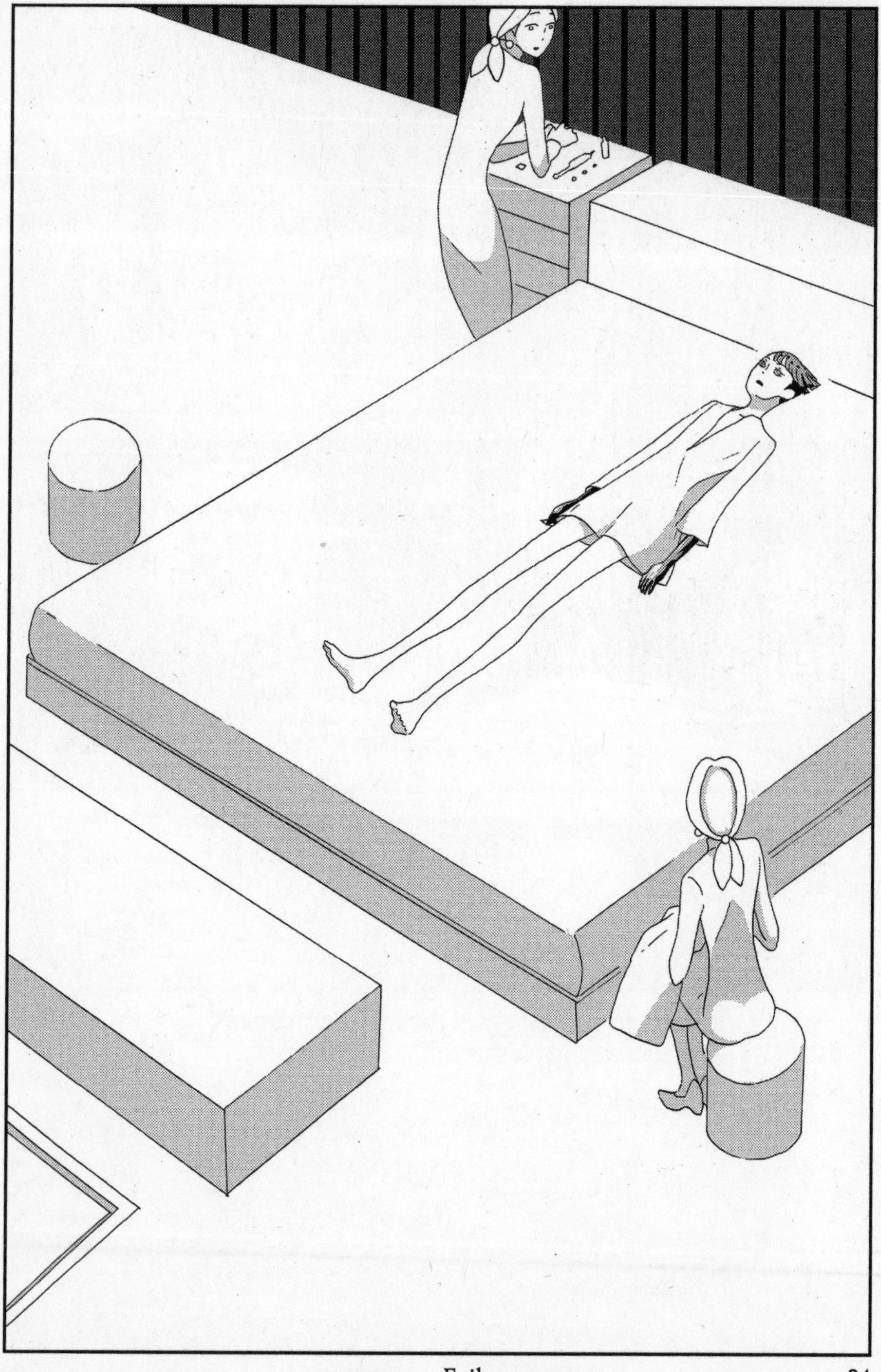

CHAPTER 71: Failure END

CHAPTER 72: Savior

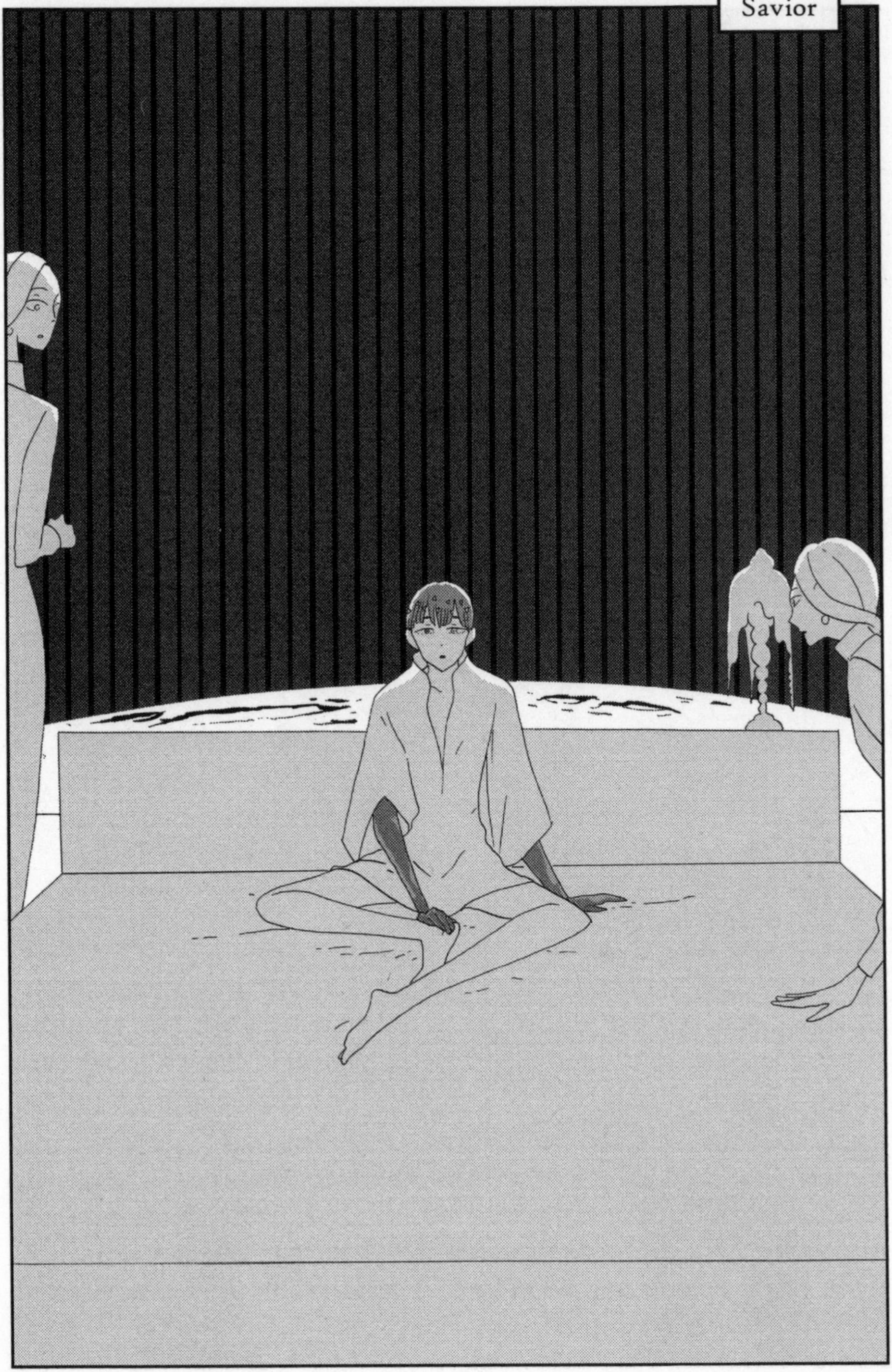

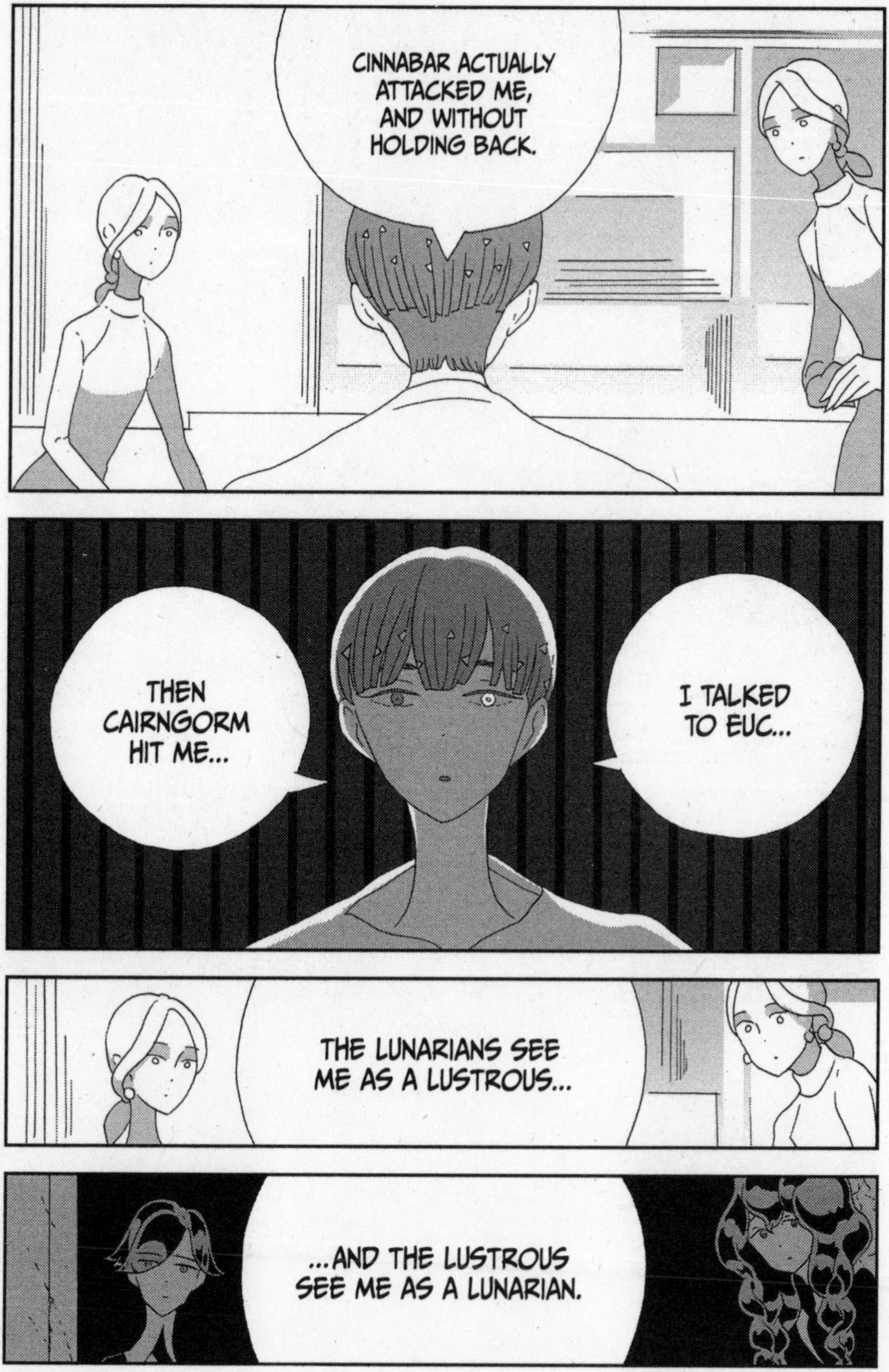
CINNABAR ACTUALLY ATTACKED ME, AND WITHOUT HOLDING BACK.
I TALKED TO EUC...
THEN CAIRNGORM HIT ME...
THE LUNARIANS SEE ME AS A LUSTROUS...
...AND THE LUSTROUS SEE ME AS A LUNARIAN.

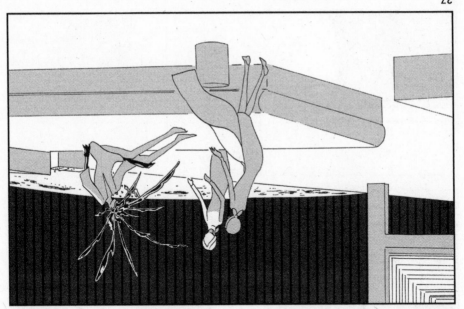

WHAT AM I?

YOU ARE PHOS-PHOPHYL-LITE.

THE HOPE OF THE LUNAR-IANS.

WHEN I DIDN'T EVEN GET A LOOK AT KONGŌ?

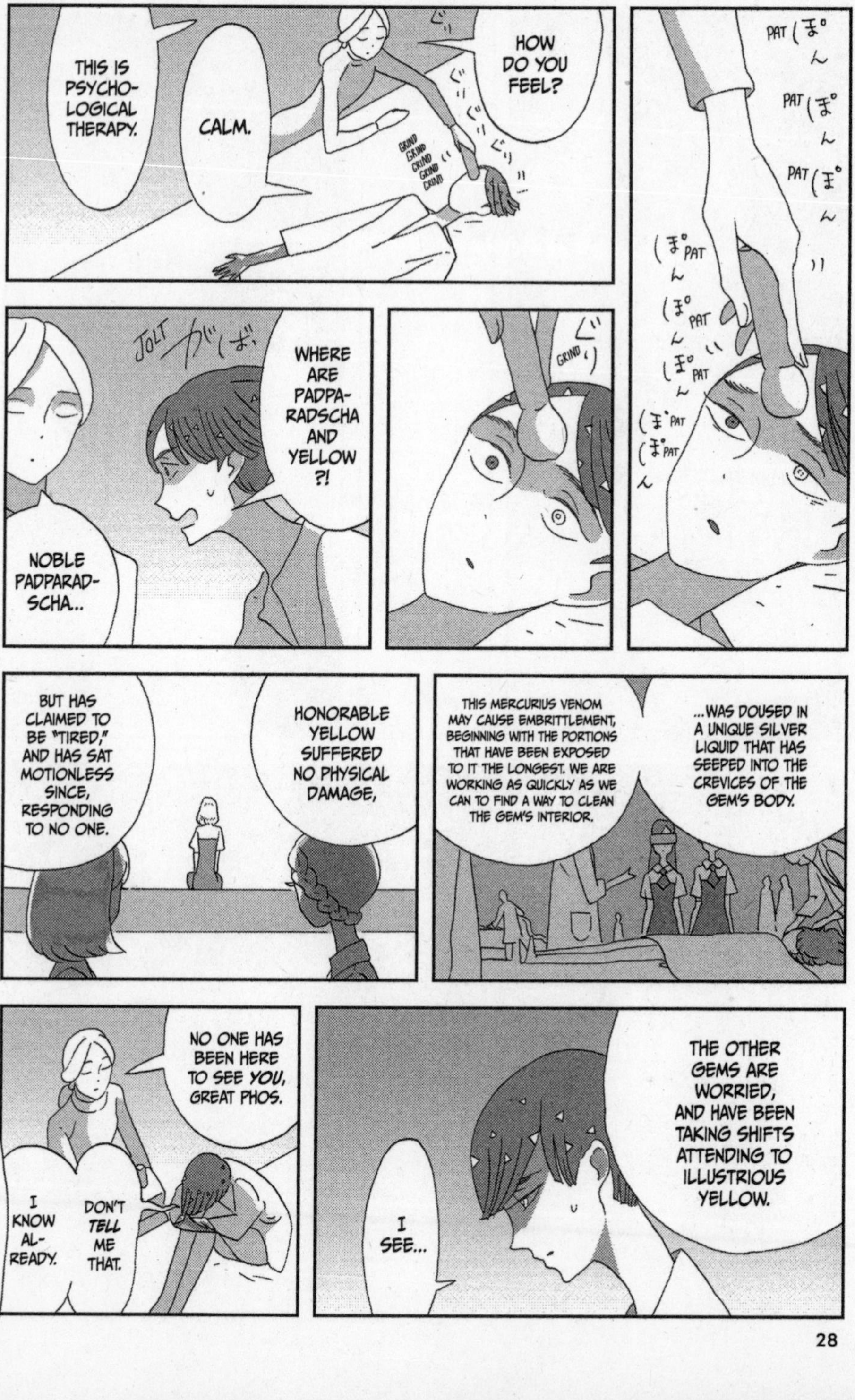
PAT
PAT
PAT
PAT
PAT
PAT
PAT
PAT
HOW DO YOU FEEL?
GRIND GRIND GRIND GRIND GRIND
CALM.
THIS IS PSYCHOLOGICAL THERAPY.
GRIND
WHERE ARE PADPARADSCHA AND YELLOW?!
JOLT
NOBLE PADPARADSCHA...
...WAS DOUSED IN A UNIQUE SILVER LIQUID THAT HAS SEEPED INTO THE CREVICES OF THE GEM'S BODY.
THIS MERCURIUS VENOM MAY CAUSE EMBRITTLEMENT, BEGINNING WITH THE PORTIONS THAT HAVE BEEN EXPOSED TO IT THE LONGEST. WE ARE WORKING AS QUICKLY AS WE CAN TO FIND A WAY TO CLEAN THE GEM'S INTERIOR.
HONORABLE YELLOW SUFFERED NO PHYSICAL DAMAGE,
BUT HAS CLAIMED TO BE "TIRED," AND HAS SAT MOTIONLESS SINCE, RESPONDING TO NO ONE.
THE OTHER GEMS ARE WORRIED, AND HAVE BEEN TAKING SHIFTS ATTENDING TO ILLUSTRIOUS YELLOW.
I SEE...
NO ONE HAS BEEN HERE TO SEE *YOU*, GREAT PHOS.
DON'T *TELL* ME THAT.
I KNOW ALREADY.

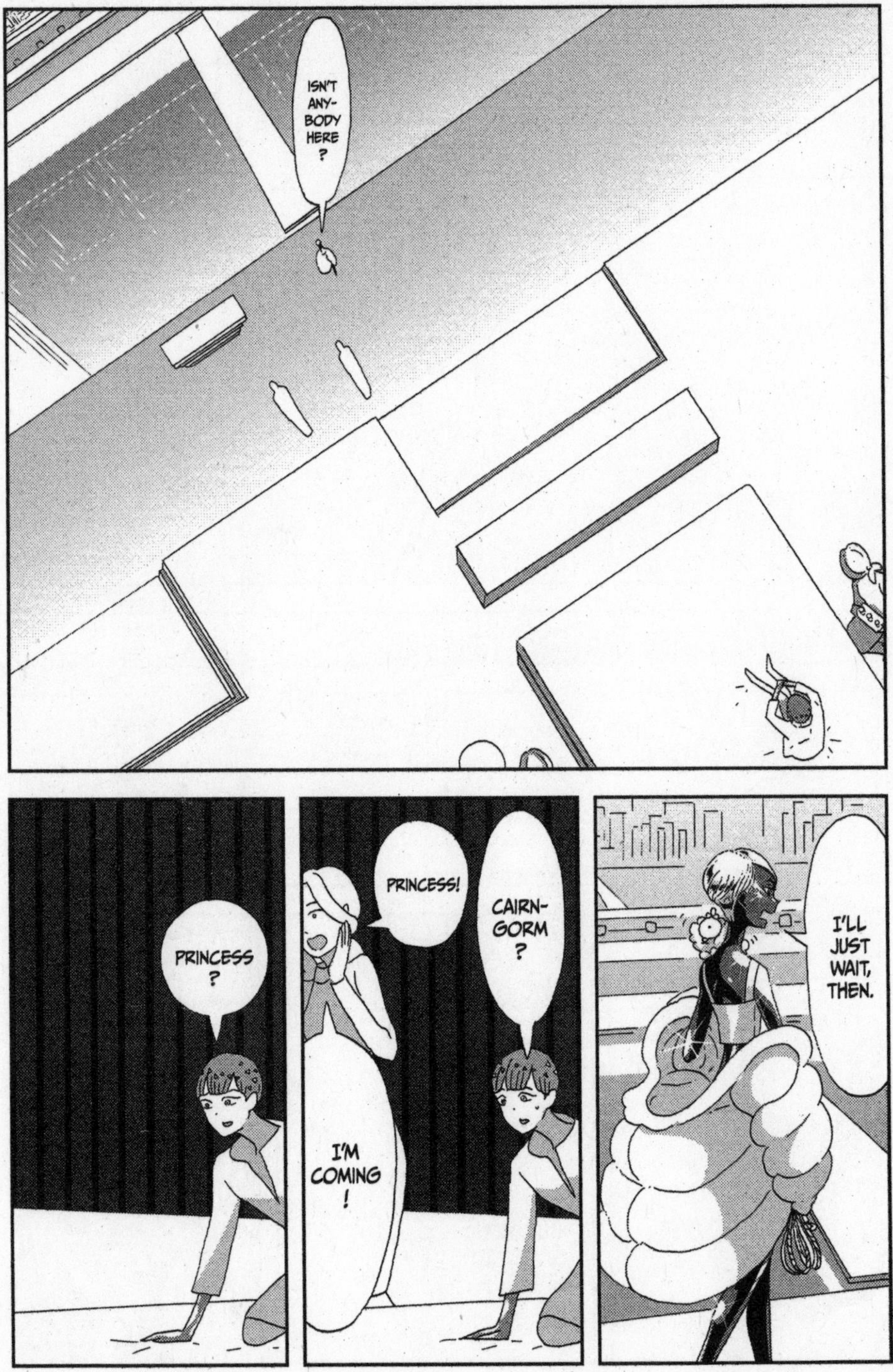
ISN'T ANY-BODY HERE ?
I'LL JUST WAIT, THEN.
CAIRN-GORM ?
PRINCESS!
I'M COMING !
PRINCESS ?

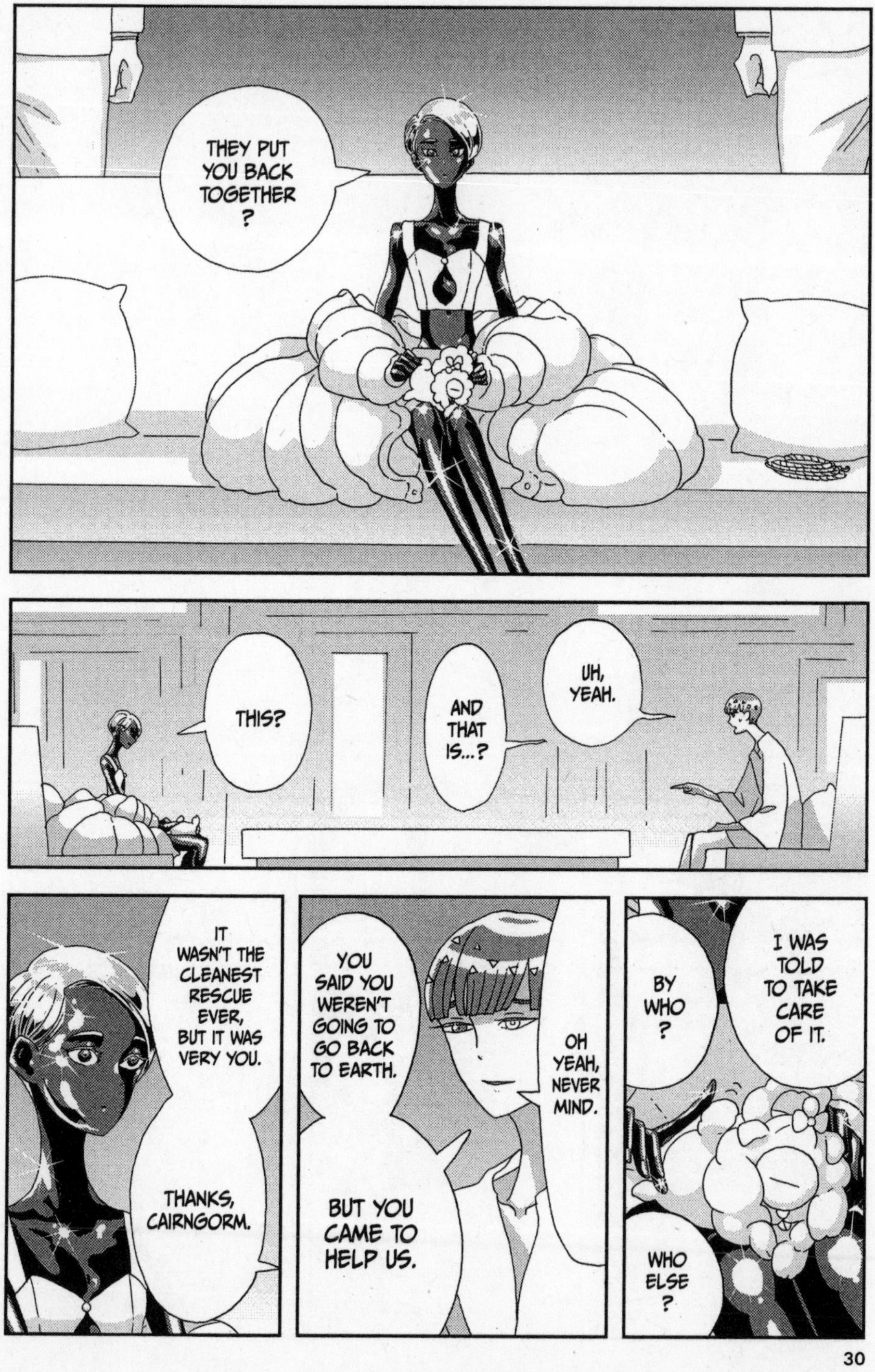
THEY PUT YOU BACK TOGETHER ?
UH, YEAH.
AND THAT IS...?
THIS?
I WAS TOLD TO TAKE CARE OF IT.
BY WHO ?
WHO ELSE ?
YOU SAID YOU WEREN'T GOING TO GO BACK TO EARTH.
OH YEAH, NEVER MIND.
BUT YOU CAME TO HELP US.
IT WASN'T THE CLEANEST RESCUE EVER, BUT IT WAS VERY YOU.
THANKS, CAIRNGORM.

I ALWAYS KNEW I COULD COUNT ON YOU THE MOST.
YOU'RE WRONG.

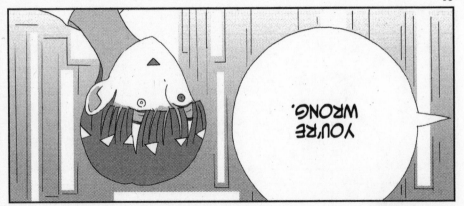

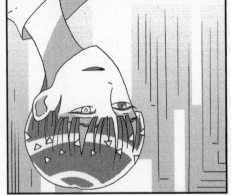

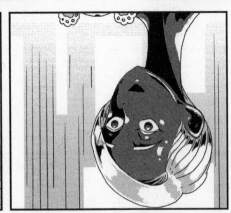

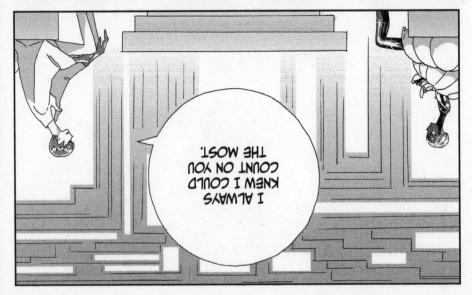

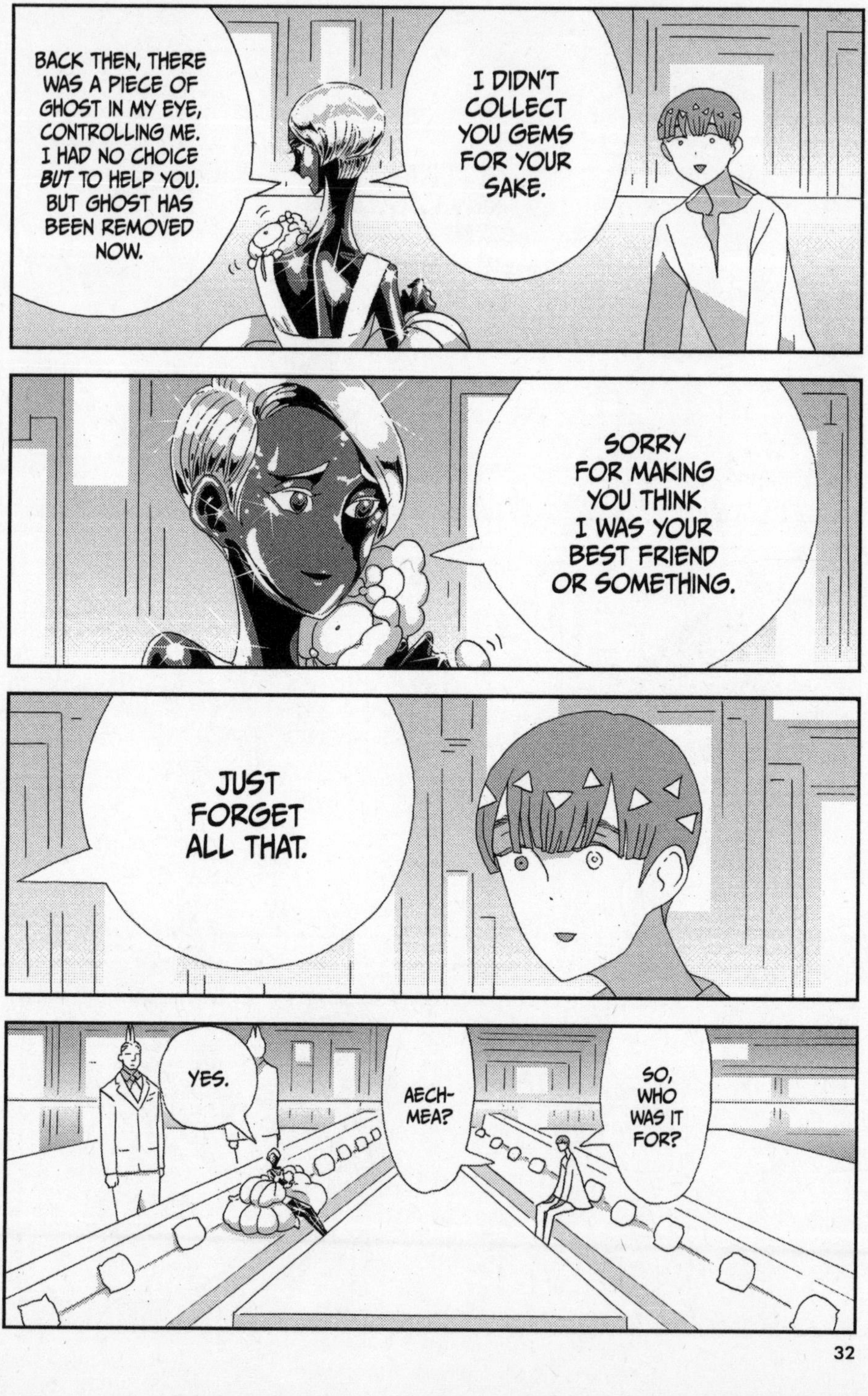
I DIDN'T COLLECT YOU GEMS FOR YOUR SAKE.
BACK THEN, THERE WAS A PIECE OF GHOST IN MY EYE, CONTROLLING ME. I HAD NO CHOICE *BUT* TO HELP YOU. BUT GHOST HAS BEEN REMOVED NOW.
SORRY FOR MAKING YOU THINK I WAS YOUR BEST FRIEND OR SOMETHING.
JUST FORGET ALL THAT.
SO, WHO WAS IT FOR?
AECH-MEA?
YES.

...OH NO.
DON'T TELL ME YOU ACTUALLY *LIKE* THAT JERK?
I DO.
TALK ABOUT BAD TASTE!
SHUT UP, YOU UGLY COMPOSITE STONE. YOU WANT ME TO BUST YOUR HEAD AGAIN ?
WHAT WAS THAT, UGLY DESTRUCTO?
DON'T GO BUSTING HEADS LIKE IT'S NO BIG DEAL.
ANYWAY,
YOU WOULDN'T UNDERSTAND THE PRINCE'S CHARMS.
WELL, DUH.
WHAT IS THERE TO LIKE ?
TEXTURE.
MY DARLING IS SOFT AND FLUFFY, SMELLS JUST LIKE A SUMMER'S EVENING, IS SMART— BUT ALSO SHY— AND IT'S CUTE HOW THEY NEVER STOP TALKING WHEN I'M THE ONLY ONE AROUND.
CUTE? *THAT* SNOB?
EWW!
SHUT UP, UGLY.
YOU'RE UGLY.

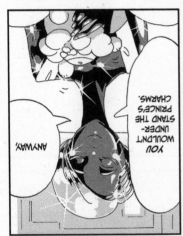

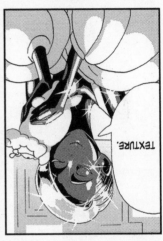

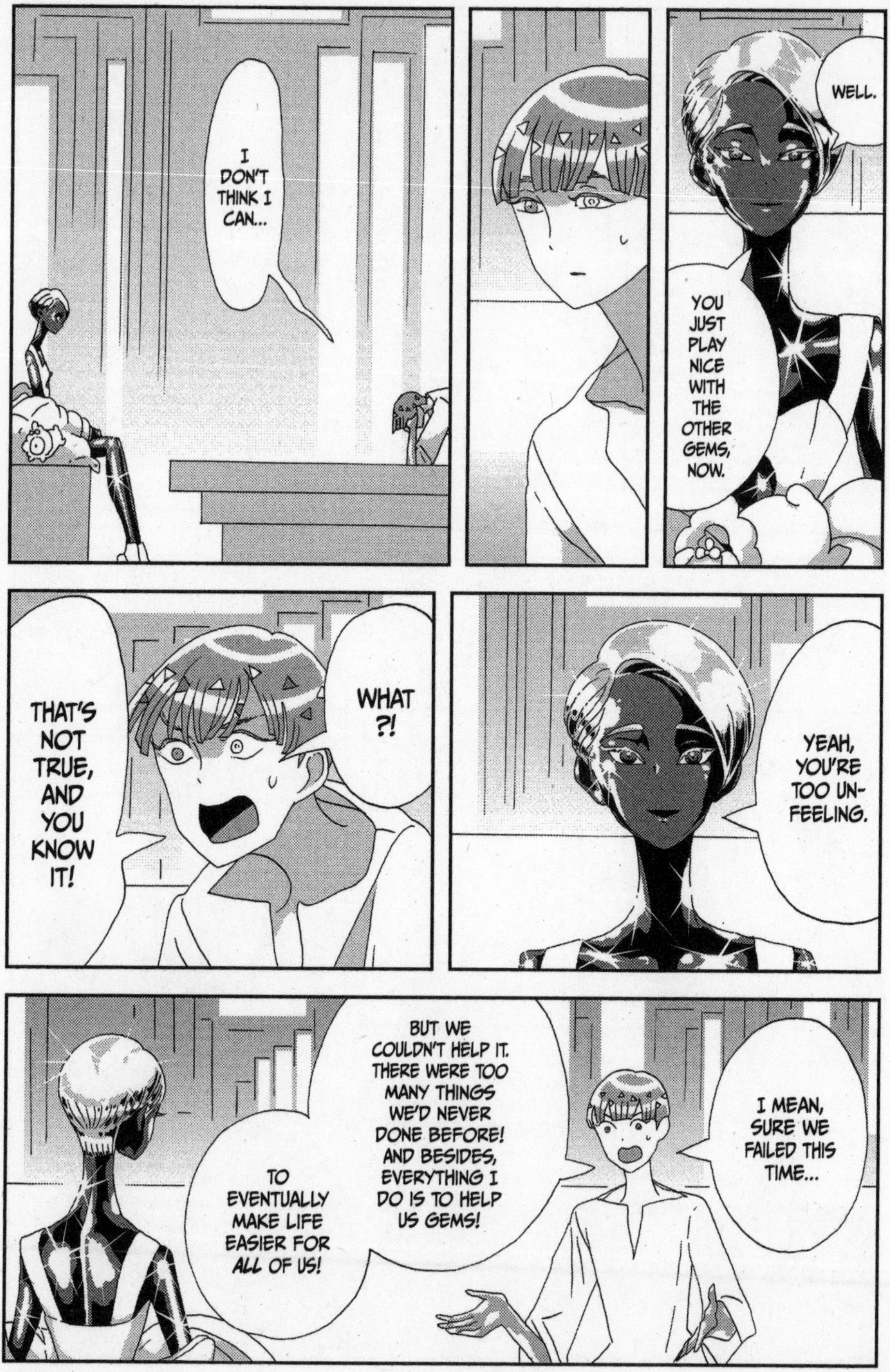
WELL.
YOU JUST PLAY NICE WITH THE OTHER GEMS, NOW.
I DON'T THINK I CAN...
YEAH, YOU'RE TOO UN-FEELING.
WHAT ?!
THAT'S NOT TRUE, AND YOU KNOW IT!
I MEAN, SURE WE FAILED THIS TIME...
BUT WE COULDN'T HELP IT. THERE WERE TOO MANY THINGS WE'D NEVER DONE BEFORE! AND BESIDES, EVERYTHING I DO IS TO HELP US GEMS!
TO EVENTUALLY MAKE LIFE EASIER FOR ALL OF US!

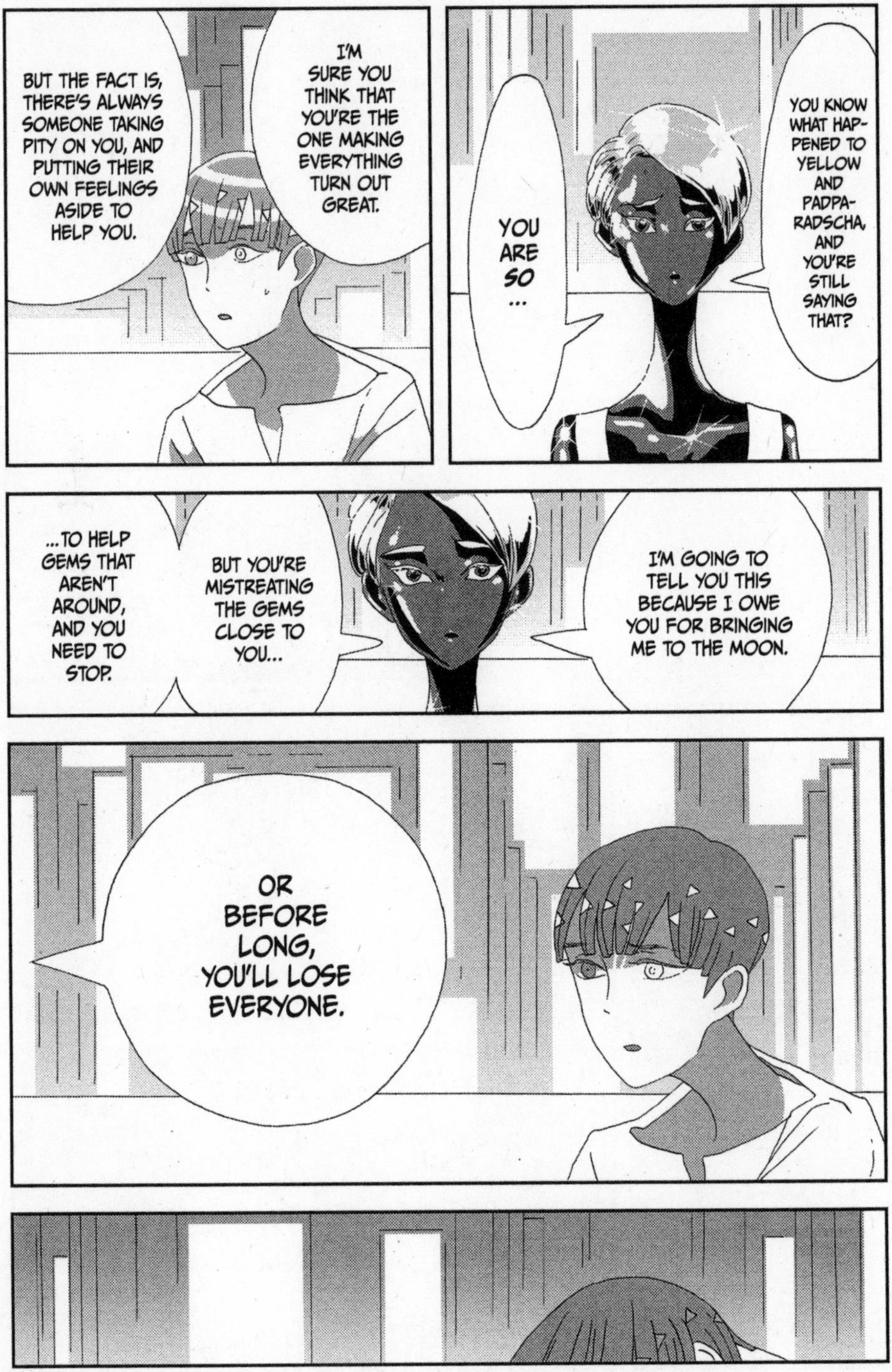
YOU KNOW WHAT HAP-PENED TO YELLOW AND PADPA-RADSCHA, AND YOU'RE STILL SAYING THAT?
YOU ARE SO ...
I'M SURE YOU THINK THAT YOU'RE THE ONE MAKING EVERYTHING TURN OUT GREAT.
BUT THE FACT IS, THERE'S ALWAYS SOMEONE TAKING PITY ON YOU, AND PUTTING THEIR OWN FEELINGS ASIDE TO HELP YOU.
I'M GOING TO TELL YOU THIS BECAUSE I OWE YOU FOR BRINGING ME TO THE MOON.
BUT YOU'RE MISTREATING THE GEMS CLOSE TO YOU...
...TO HELP GEMS THAT AREN'T AROUND, AND YOU NEED TO STOP.
OR BEFORE LONG, YOU'LL LOSE EVERYONE.

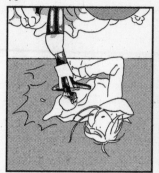

YOU'RE LATE!

SQUEEZE

SORRY TO KEEP YOU WAITING.

YOU'RE LATE!

SORRY TO KEEP YOU WAITING.

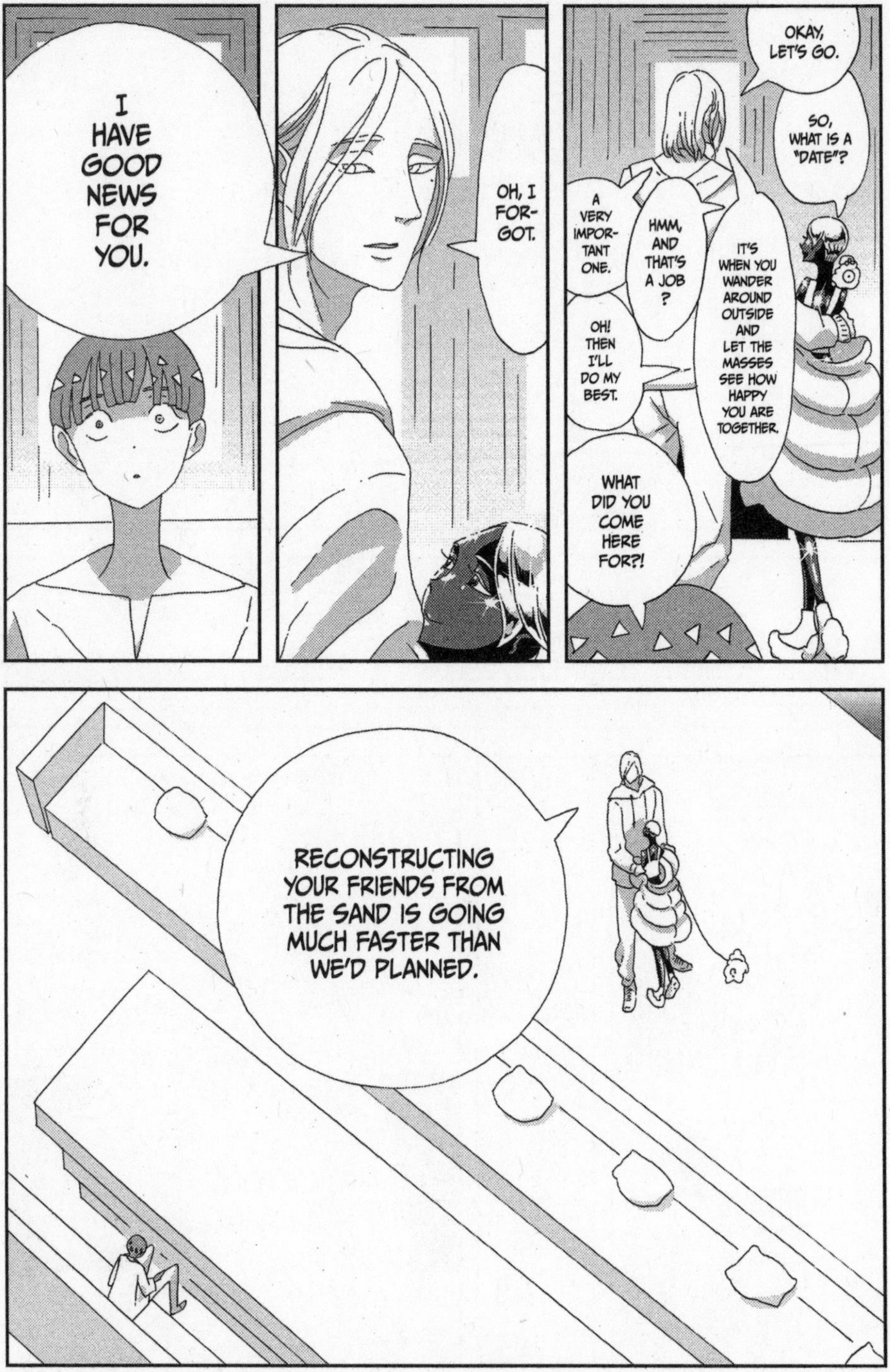
OKAY, LET'S GO.
SO, WHAT IS A "DATE"?
IT'S WHEN YOU WANDER AROUND OUTSIDE AND LET THE MASSES SEE HOW HAPPY YOU ARE TOGETHER.
HMM, AND THAT'S A JOB ?
A VERY IMPORTANT ONE.
OH! THEN I'LL DO MY BEST.
WHAT DID YOU COME HERE FOR?!
OH, I FORGOT.
I HAVE GOOD NEWS FOR YOU.
RECONSTRUCTING YOUR FRIENDS FROM THE SAND IS GOING MUCH FASTER THAN WE'D PLANNED.

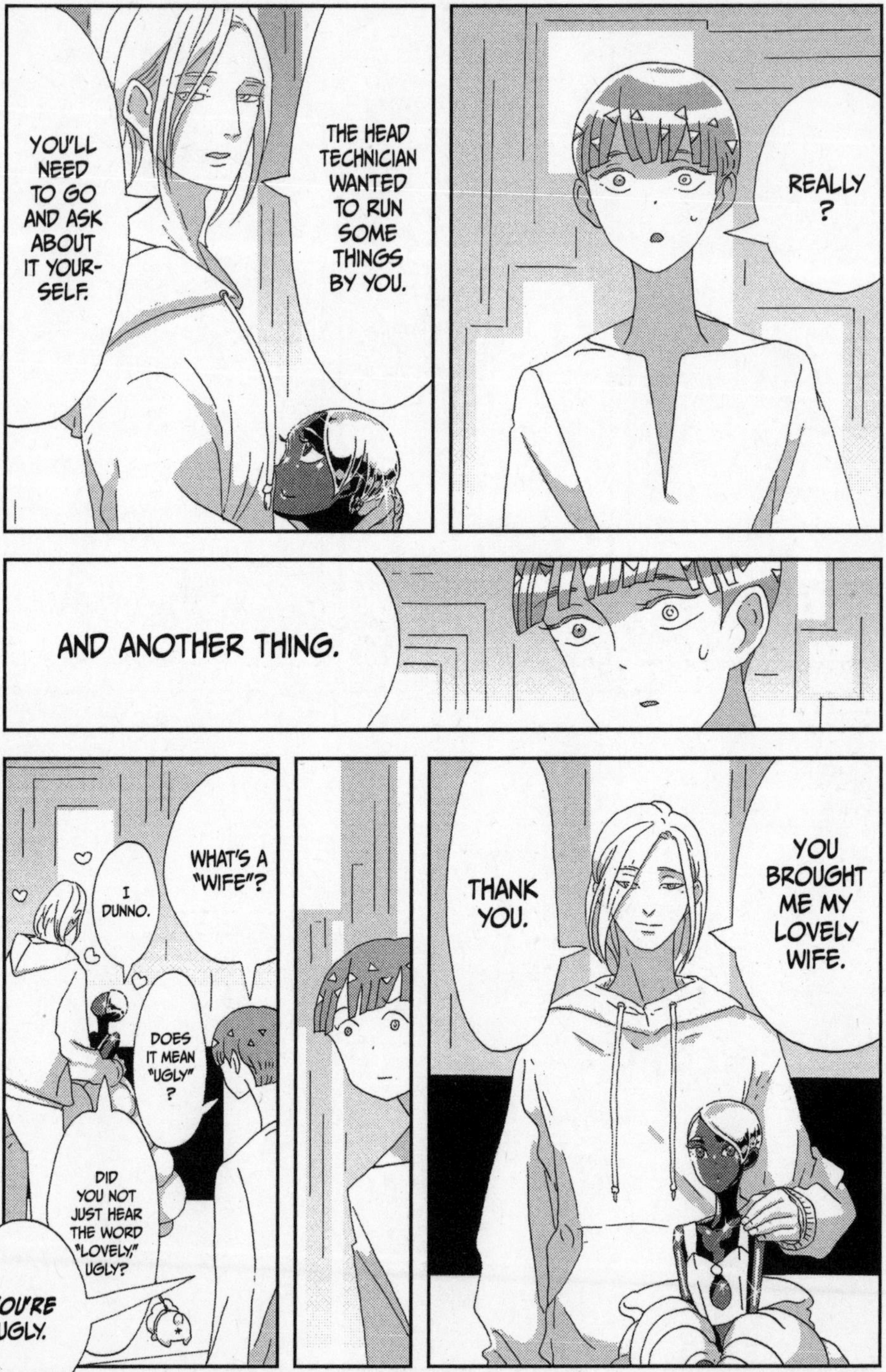
REALLY?
THE HEAD TECHNICIAN WANTED TO RUN SOME THINGS BY YOU.
YOU'LL NEED TO GO AND ASK ABOUT IT YOURSELF.
AND ANOTHER THING.
YOU BROUGHT ME MY LOVELY WIFE.
THANK YOU.
WHAT'S A "WIFE"?
I DUNNO.
DOES IT MEAN "UGLY"?
DID YOU NOT JUST HEAR THE WORD "LOVELY," UGLY?
YOU'RE UGLY.

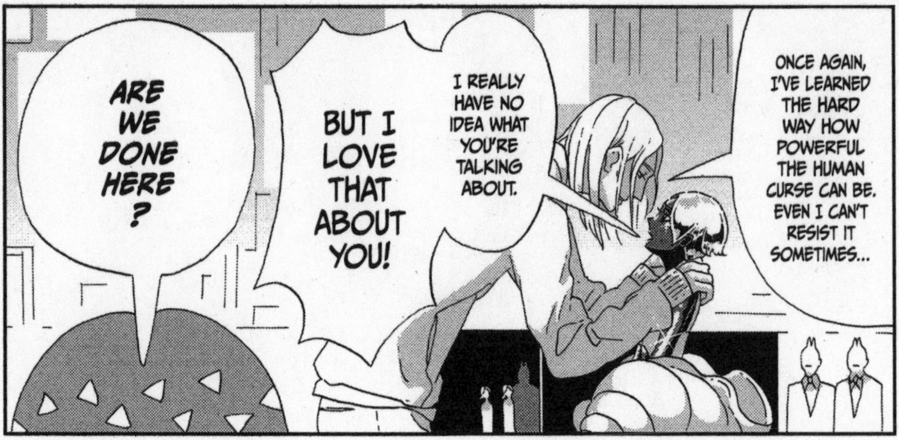
ONCE AGAIN, I'VE LEARNED THE HARD WAY HOW POWERFUL THE HUMAN CURSE CAN BE. EVEN I CAN'T RESIST IT SOMETIMES...
I REALLY HAVE NO IDEA WHAT YOU'RE TALKING ABOUT.
BUT I LOVE THAT ABOUT YOU!
ARE WE DONE HERE ?

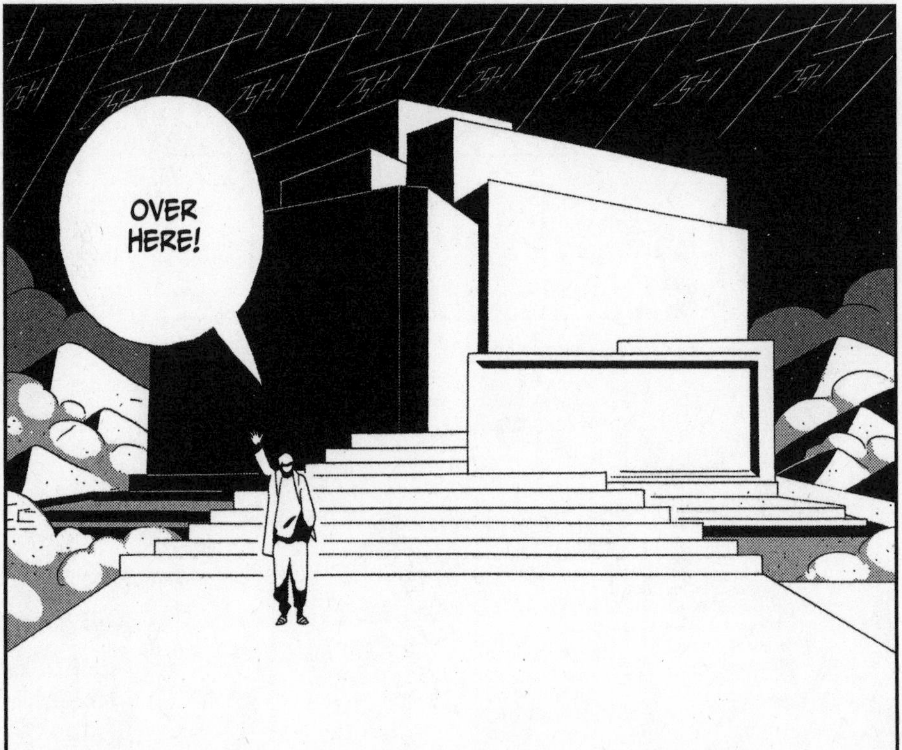
OVER HERE!

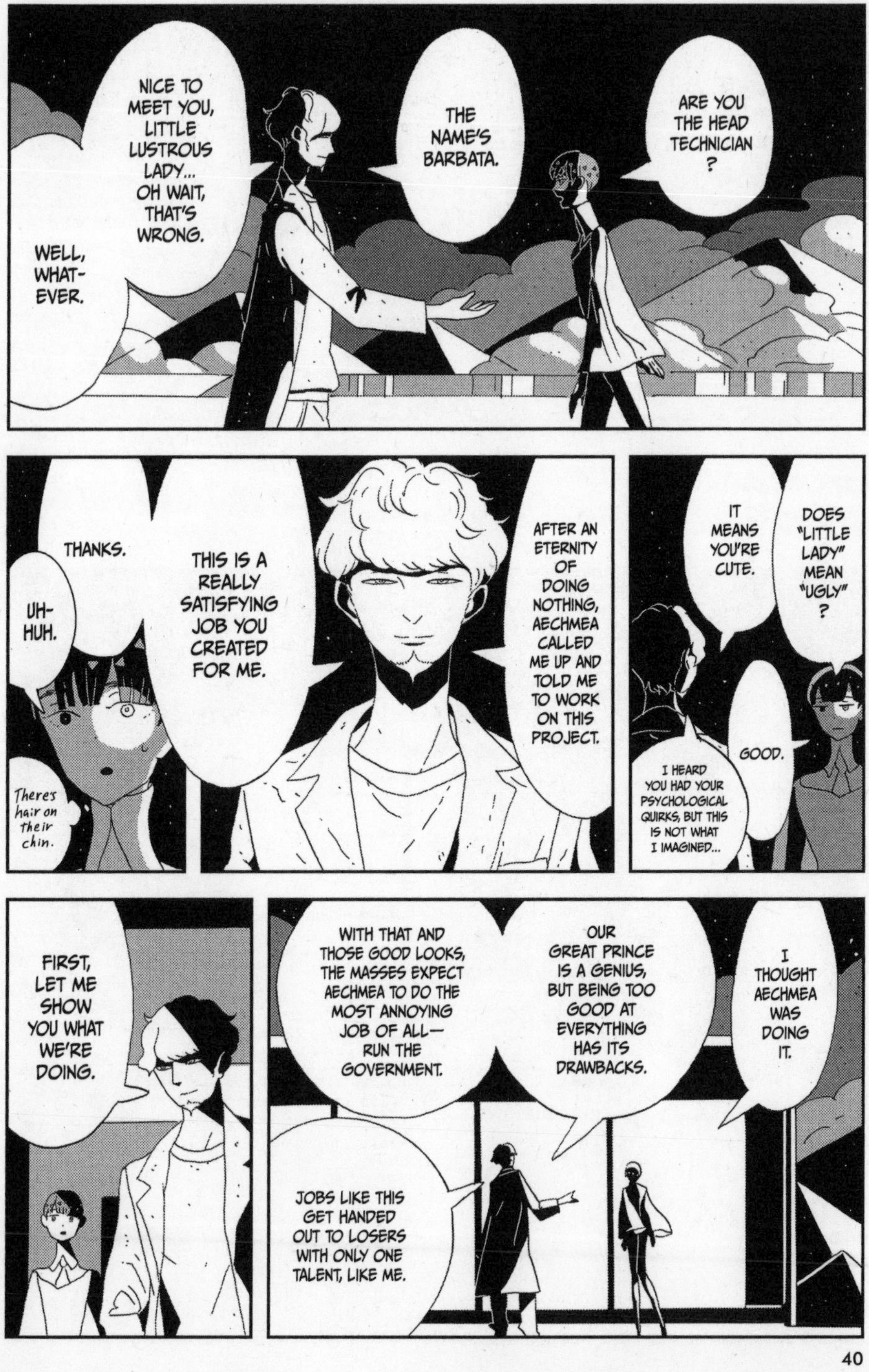
ARE YOU THE HEAD TECHNICIAN ?
THE NAME'S BARBATA.
NICE TO MEET YOU, LITTLE LUSTROUS LADY... OH WAIT, THAT'S WRONG.
WELL, WHAT-EVER.
DOES "LITTLE LADY" MEAN "UGLY" ?
IT MEANS YOU'RE CUTE.
GOOD.
I HEARD YOU HAD YOUR PSYCHOLOGICAL QUIRKS, BUT THIS IS NOT WHAT I IMAGINED...
AFTER AN ETERNITY OF DOING NOTHING, AECHMEA CALLED ME UP AND TOLD ME TO WORK ON THIS PROJECT.
THIS IS A REALLY SATISFYING JOB YOU CREATED FOR ME.
THANKS.
UH-HUH.
There's hair on their chin.
I THOUGHT AECHMEA WAS DOING IT.
OUR GREAT PRINCE IS A GENIUS, BUT BEING TOO GOOD AT EVERYTHING HAS ITS DRAWBACKS.
WITH THAT AND THOSE GOOD LOOKS, THE MASSES EXPECT AECHMEA TO DO THE MOST ANNOYING JOB OF ALL— RUN THE GOVERNMENT.
JOBS LIKE THIS GET HANDED OUT TO LOSERS WITH ONLY ONE TALENT, LIKE ME.
FIRST, LET ME SHOW YOU WHAT WE'RE DOING.

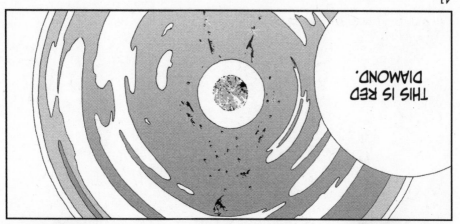

THIS IS RED
DIAMOND.

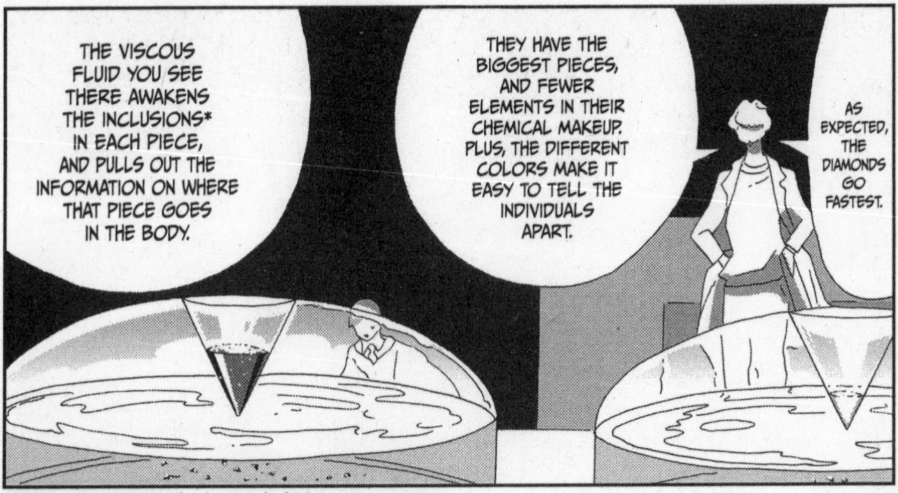
AS EXPECTED, THE DIAMONDS GO FASTEST.
THEY HAVE THE BIGGEST PIECES, AND FEWER ELEMENTS IN THEIR CHEMICAL MAKEUP. PLUS, THE DIFFERENT COLORS MAKE IT EASY TO TELL THE INDIVIDUALS APART.
THE VISCOUS FLUID YOU SEE THERE AWAKENS THE INCLUSIONS* IN EACH PIECE, AND PULLS OUT THE INFORMATION ON WHERE THAT PIECE GOES IN THE BODY.

*Microscopic organisms that live inside the Lustrous

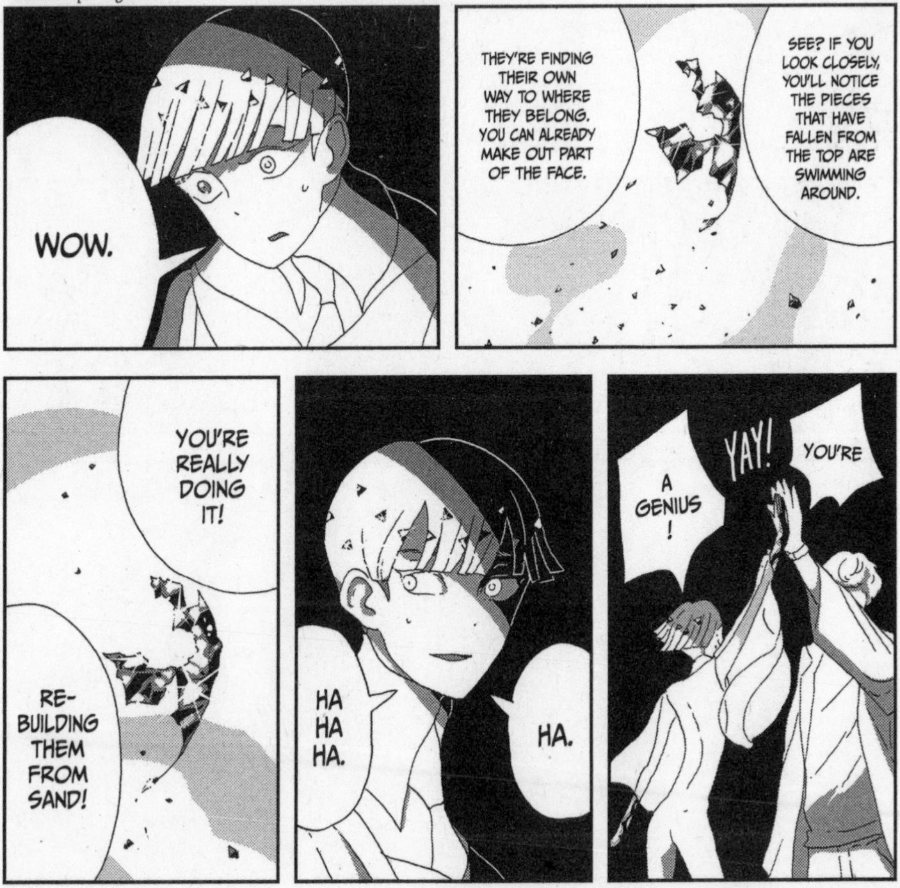
SEE? IF YOU LOOK CLOSELY, YOU'LL NOTICE THE PIECES THAT HAVE FALLEN FROM THE TOP ARE SWIMMING AROUND.
THEY'RE FINDING THEIR OWN WAY TO WHERE THEY BELONG. YOU CAN ALREADY MAKE OUT PART OF THE FACE.
WOW.
YOU'RE
YAY!
A GENIUS !
HA HA HA.
HA.
YOU'RE REALLY DOING IT!
RE-BUILDING THEM FROM SAND!

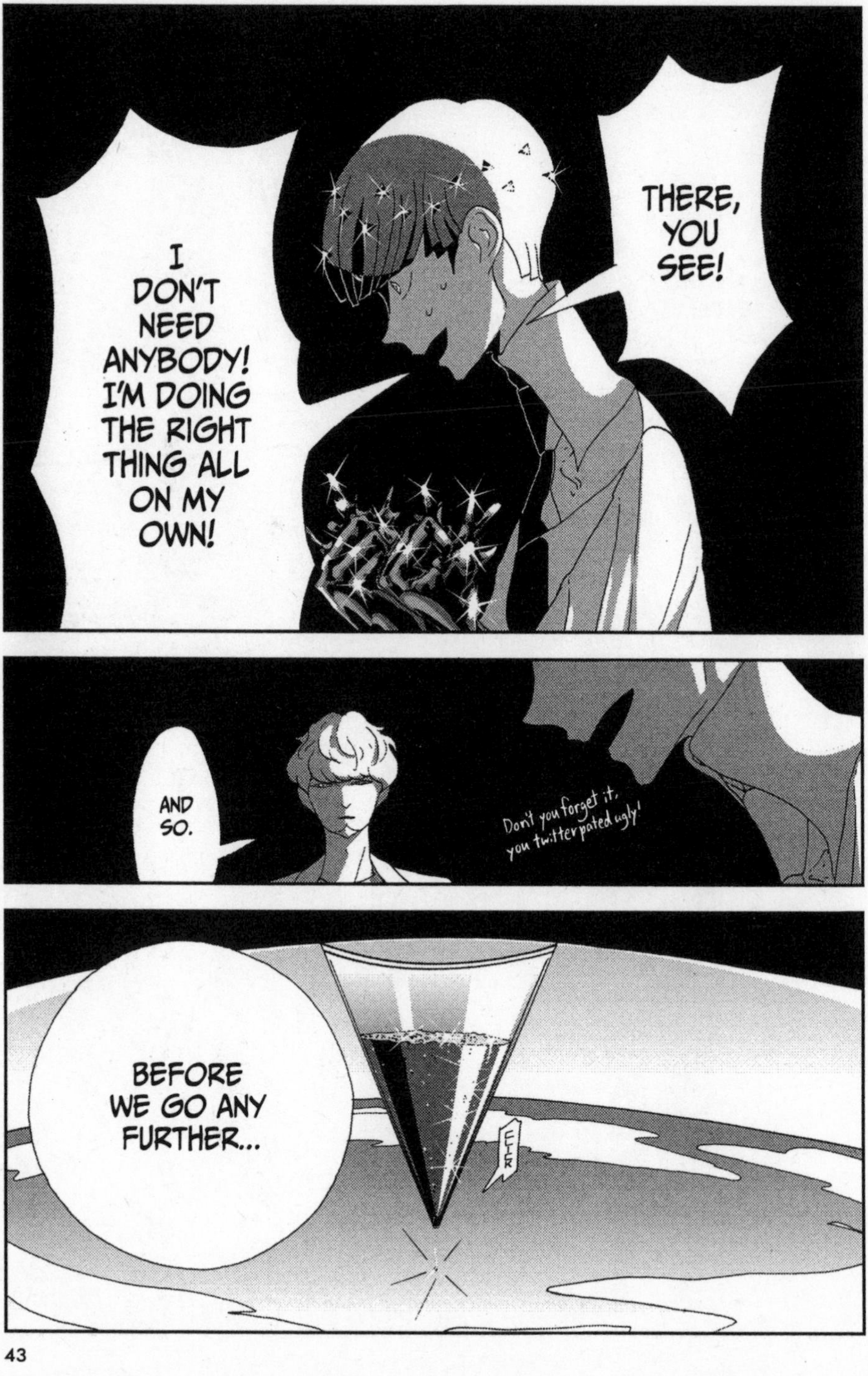
THERE, YOU SEE!
I DON'T NEED ANYBODY! I'M DOING THE RIGHT THING ALL ON MY OWN!
Don't you forget it, you twitterpated ugly!
AND SO.
BEFORE WE GO ANY FURTHER...
CLIK

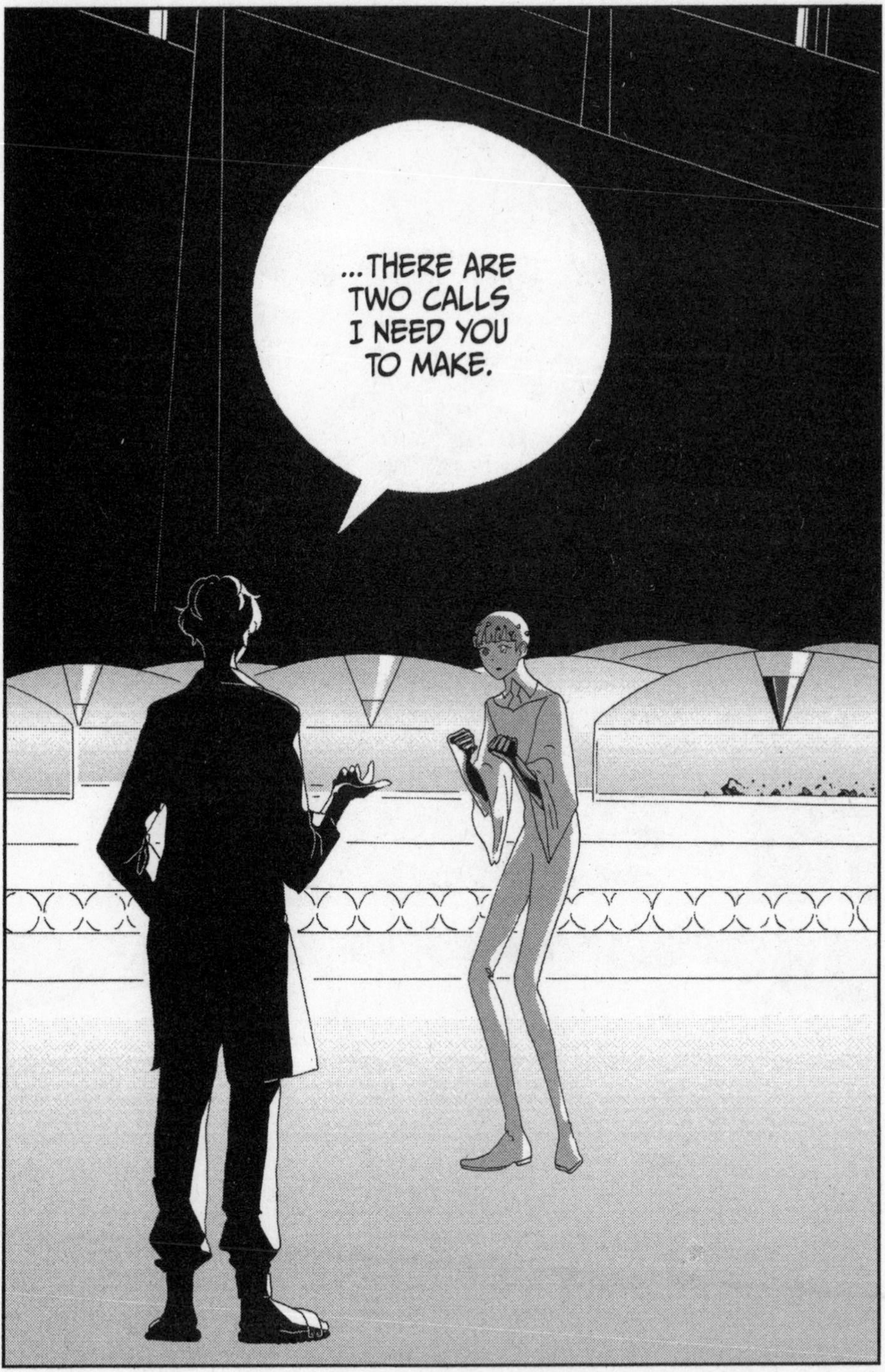
...THERE ARE TWO CALLS I NEED YOU TO MAKE.

CHAPTER 73:

Choice

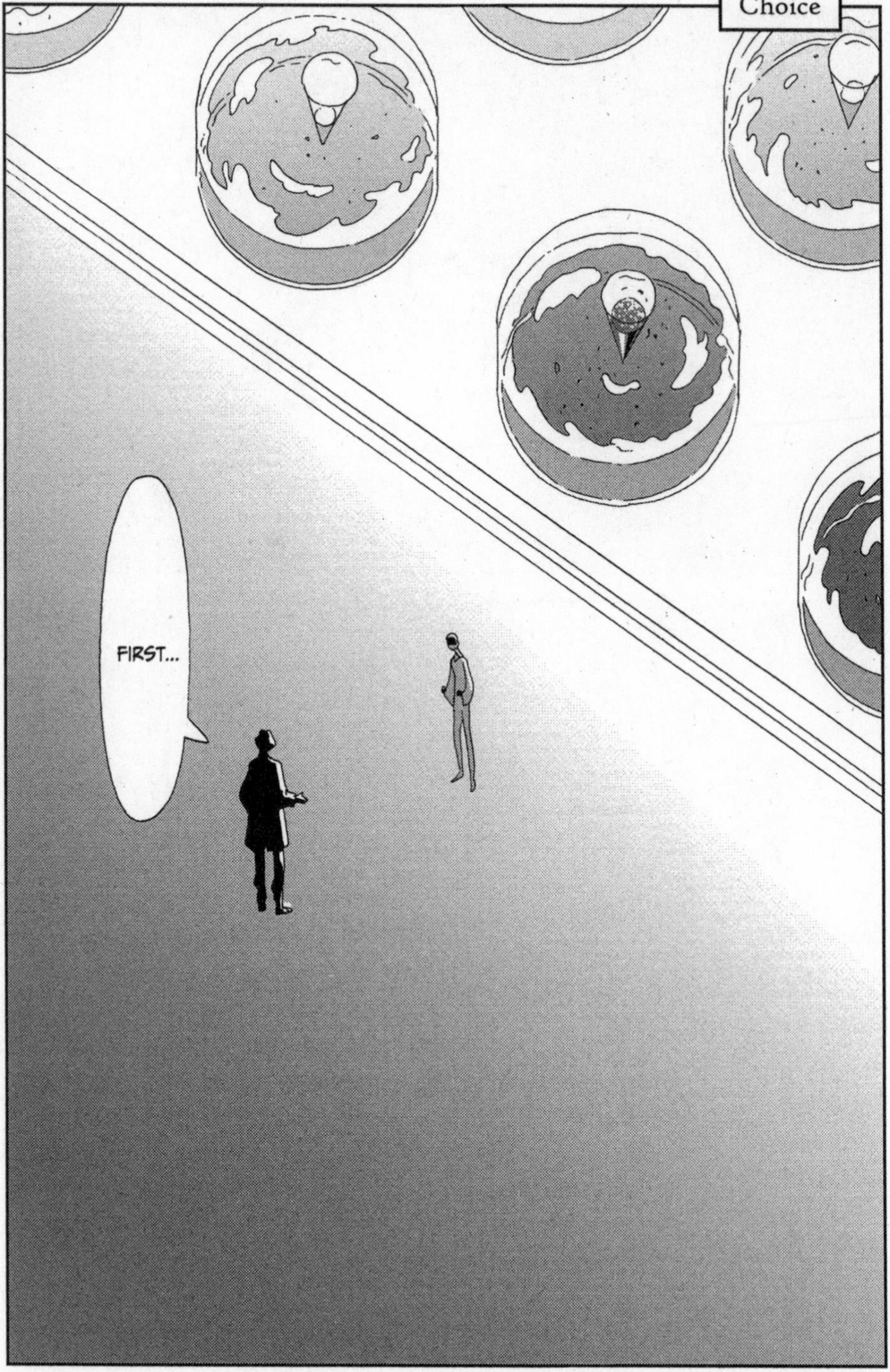
FIRST...

...WE CAN REBUILD THEIR BODIES, BUT NOT THEIR MEMORIES.
WHEN INCLUSIONS ARE CRUSHED INTO TINY PIECES, THEN EXPOSED TO THE OUT-SIDE AIR FOR A LONG TIME, THEY NEED TO SAVE ENERGY TO SAFEGUARD THE MOST IMPORTANT INFORMATION—THEIR POSITION IN THE BODY—SO THEY THROW OUT ALL OTHER INFORMATION AND GO INTO SUSPENDED ANIMATION.
AT THIS POINT IN TIME, WE HAVE NO PROSPECT OF EVER RESTORING THAT INFOR-MATION.
SO I DON'T REALLY NEED YOU TO MAKE A CALL ON THAT, JUST TO KNOW IT.
...
GOT IT.
THANKS.

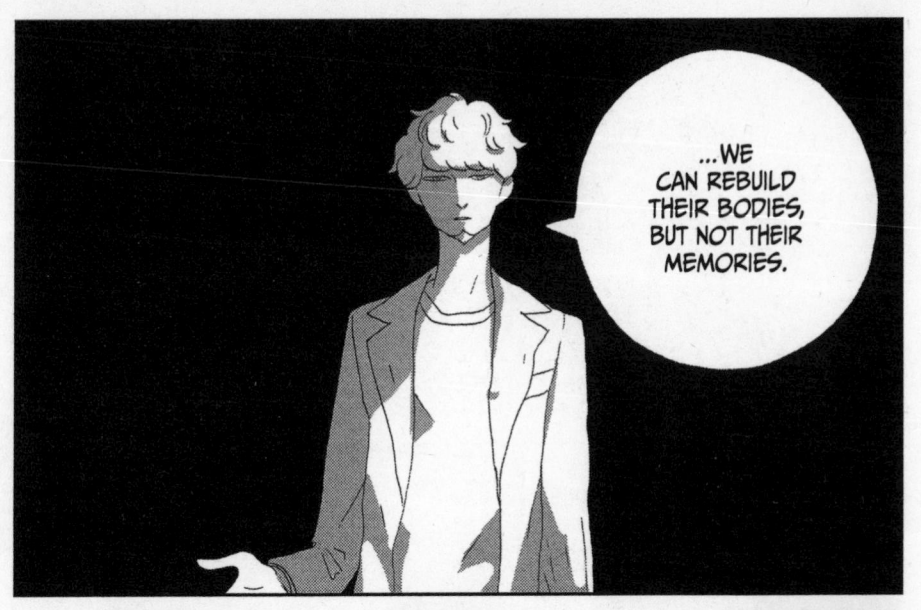

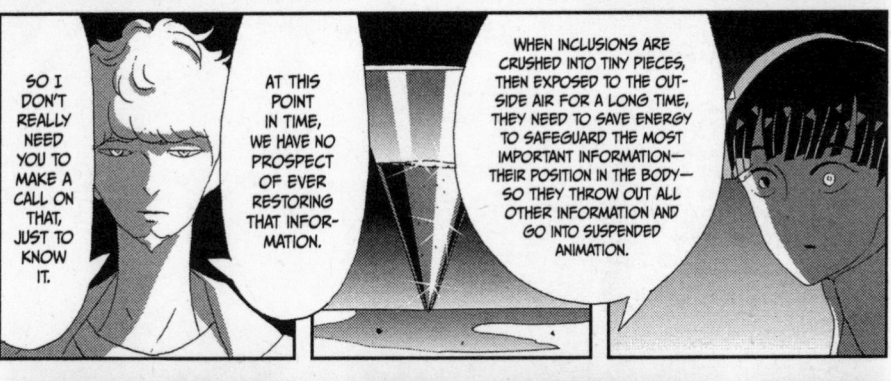

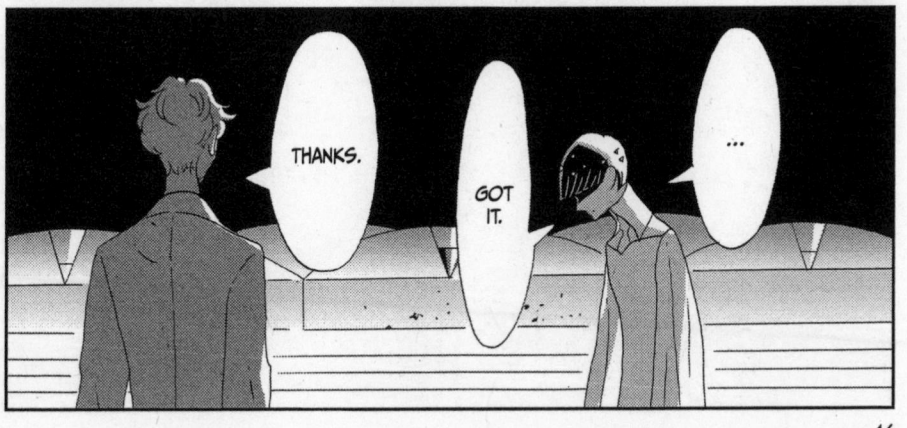

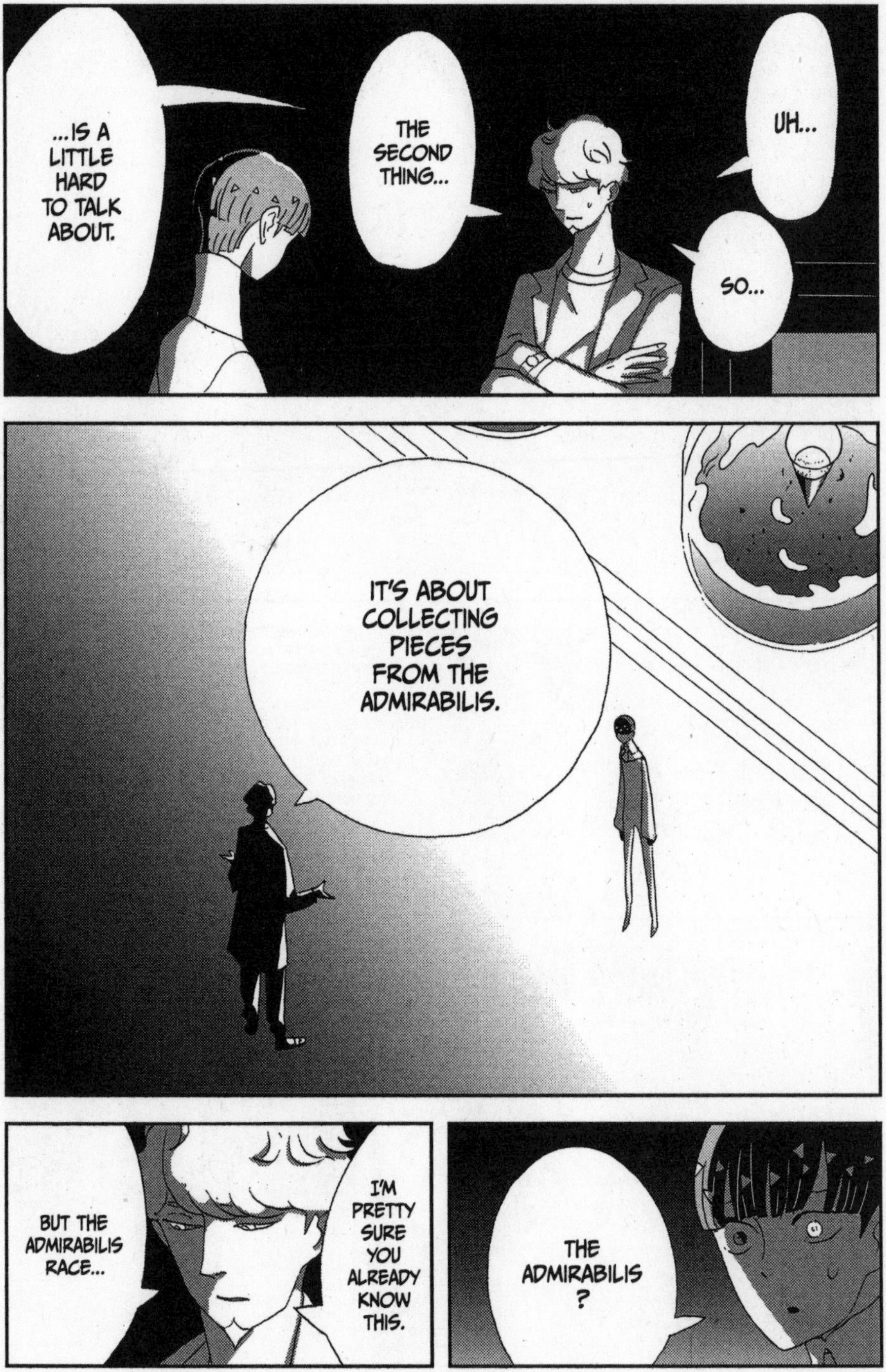
UH...
SO...
THE SECOND THING...
...IS A LITTLE HARD TO TALK ABOUT.
IT'S ABOUT COLLECTING PIECES FROM THE ADMIRABILIS.
THE ADMIRABILIS?
I'M PRETTY SURE YOU ALREADY KNOW THIS.
BUT THE ADMIRABILIS RACE...

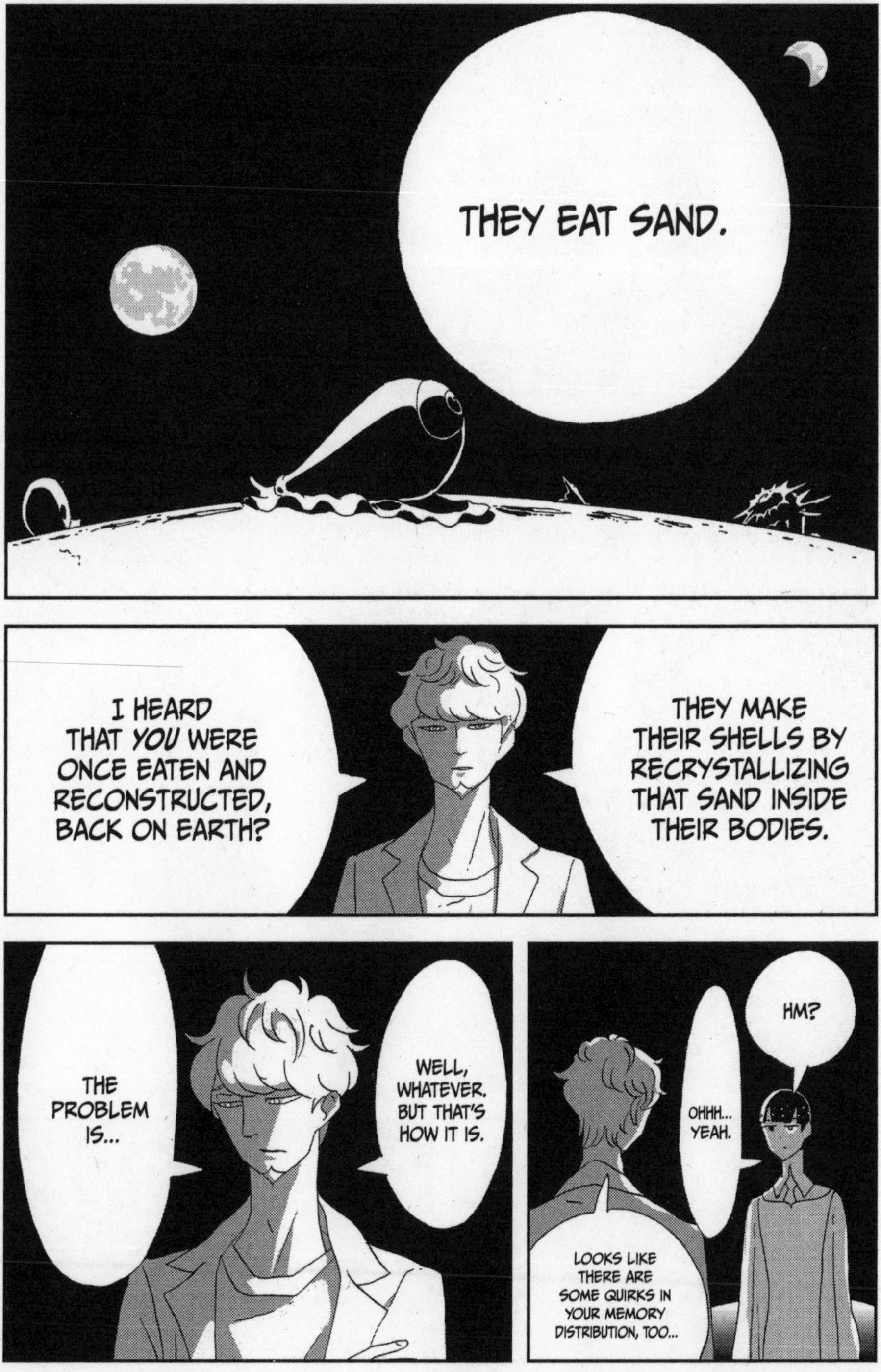
THEY EAT SAND.
THEY MAKE THEIR SHELLS BY RECRYSTALLIZING THAT SAND INSIDE THEIR BODIES.
I HEARD THAT YOU WERE ONCE EATEN AND RECONSTRUCTED, BACK ON EARTH?
HM?
OHHH... YEAH.
LOOKS LIKE THERE ARE SOME QUIRKS IN YOUR MEMORY DISTRIBUTION, TOO...
WELL, WHATEVER. BUT THAT'S HOW IT IS.
THE PROBLEM IS...

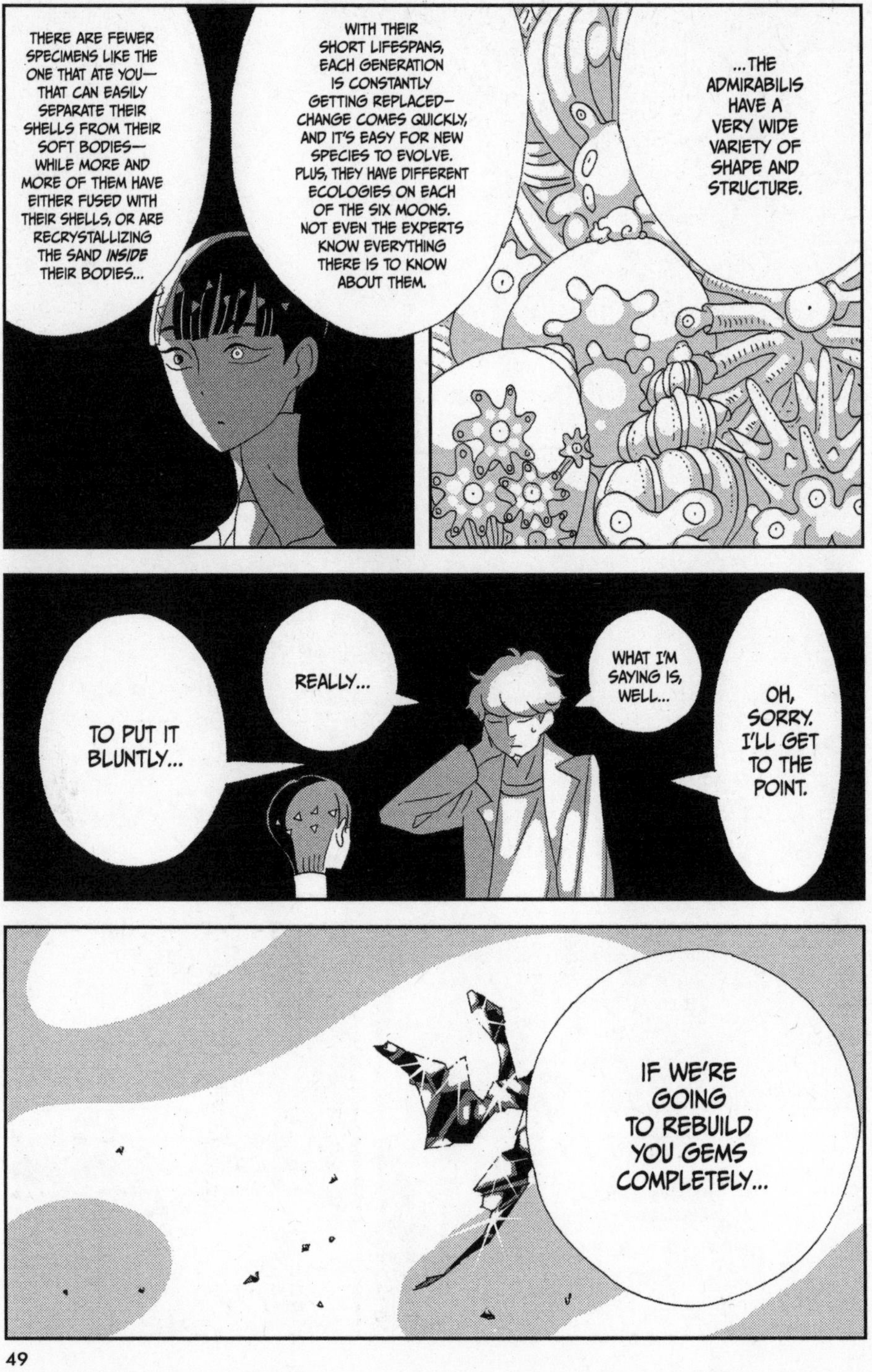
...THE ADMIRABILIS HAVE A VERY WIDE VARIETY OF SHAPE AND STRUCTURE.
WITH THEIR SHORT LIFESPANS, EACH GENERATION IS CONSTANTLY GETTING REPLACED—CHANGE COMES QUICKLY, AND IT'S EASY FOR NEW SPECIES TO EVOLVE. PLUS, THEY HAVE DIFFERENT ECOLOGIES ON EACH OF THE SIX MOONS. NOT EVEN THE EXPERTS KNOW EVERYTHING THERE IS TO KNOW ABOUT THEM.
THERE ARE FEWER SPECIMENS LIKE THE ONE THAT ATE YOU—THAT CAN EASILY SEPARATE THEIR SHELLS FROM THEIR SOFT BODIES—WHILE MORE AND MORE OF THEM HAVE EITHER FUSED WITH THEIR SHELLS, OR ARE RECRYSTALLIZING THE SAND *INSIDE* THEIR BODIES...
OH, SORRY. I'LL GET TO THE POINT.
WHAT I'M SAYING IS, WELL...
REALLY...
TO PUT IT BLUNTLY...
IF WE'RE GOING TO REBUILD YOU GEMS COMPLETELY...

WE'RE GOING TO HAVE TO KILL ALL THE ADMIRABILIS.
OH, WAIT, YOU DON'T REALLY KNOW THE WORD "KILL," DO YOU?
IT MEANS WE'LL TAKE THEM APART, AND THEY'LL BE LOST FOREVER.

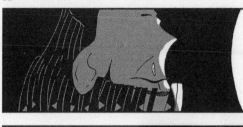

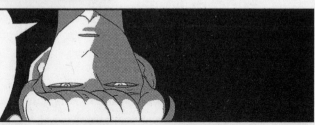

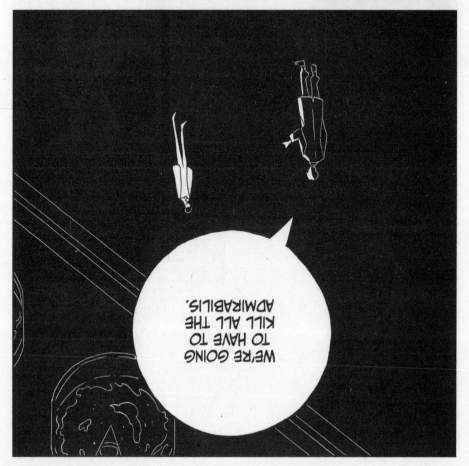

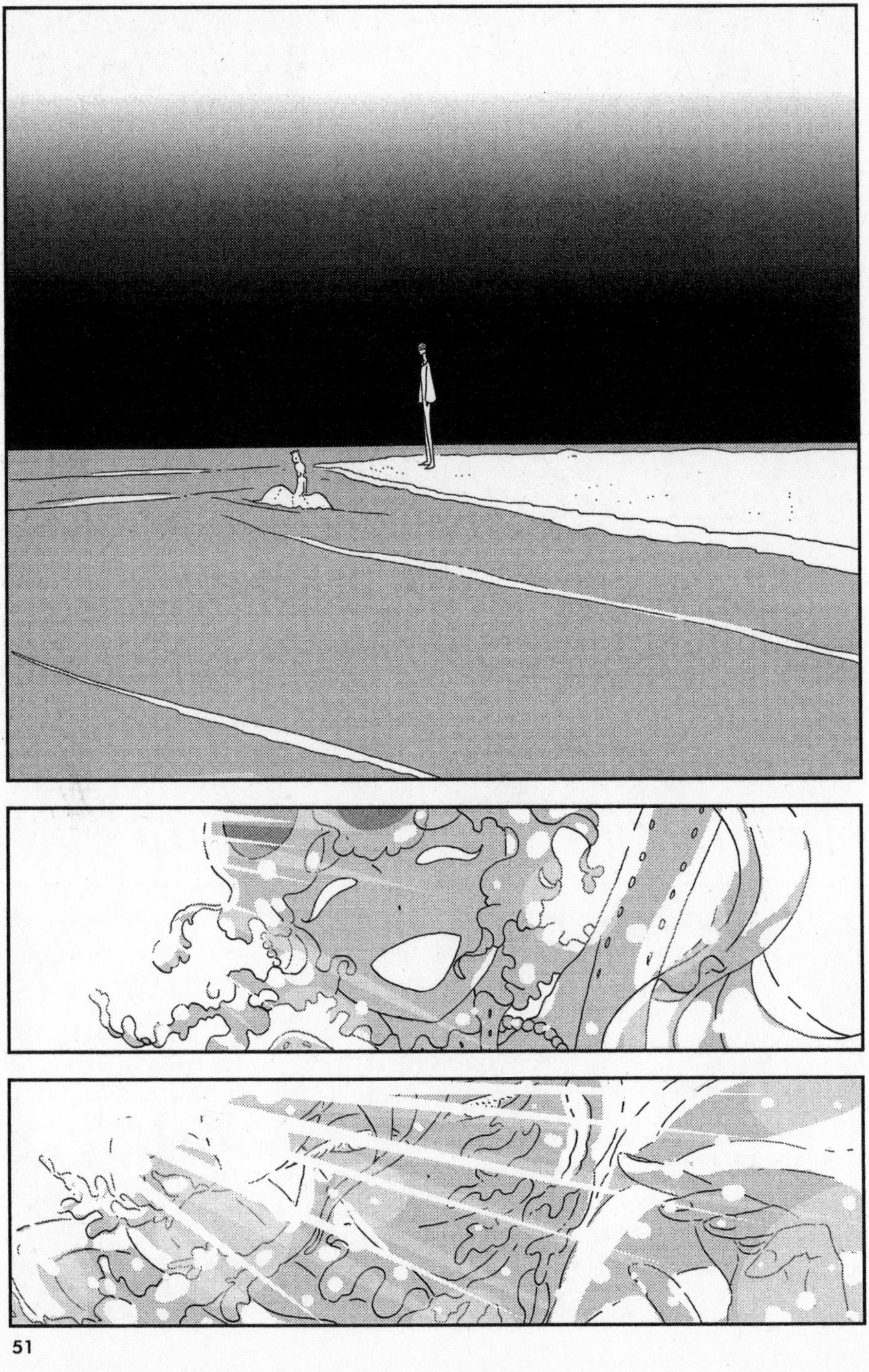

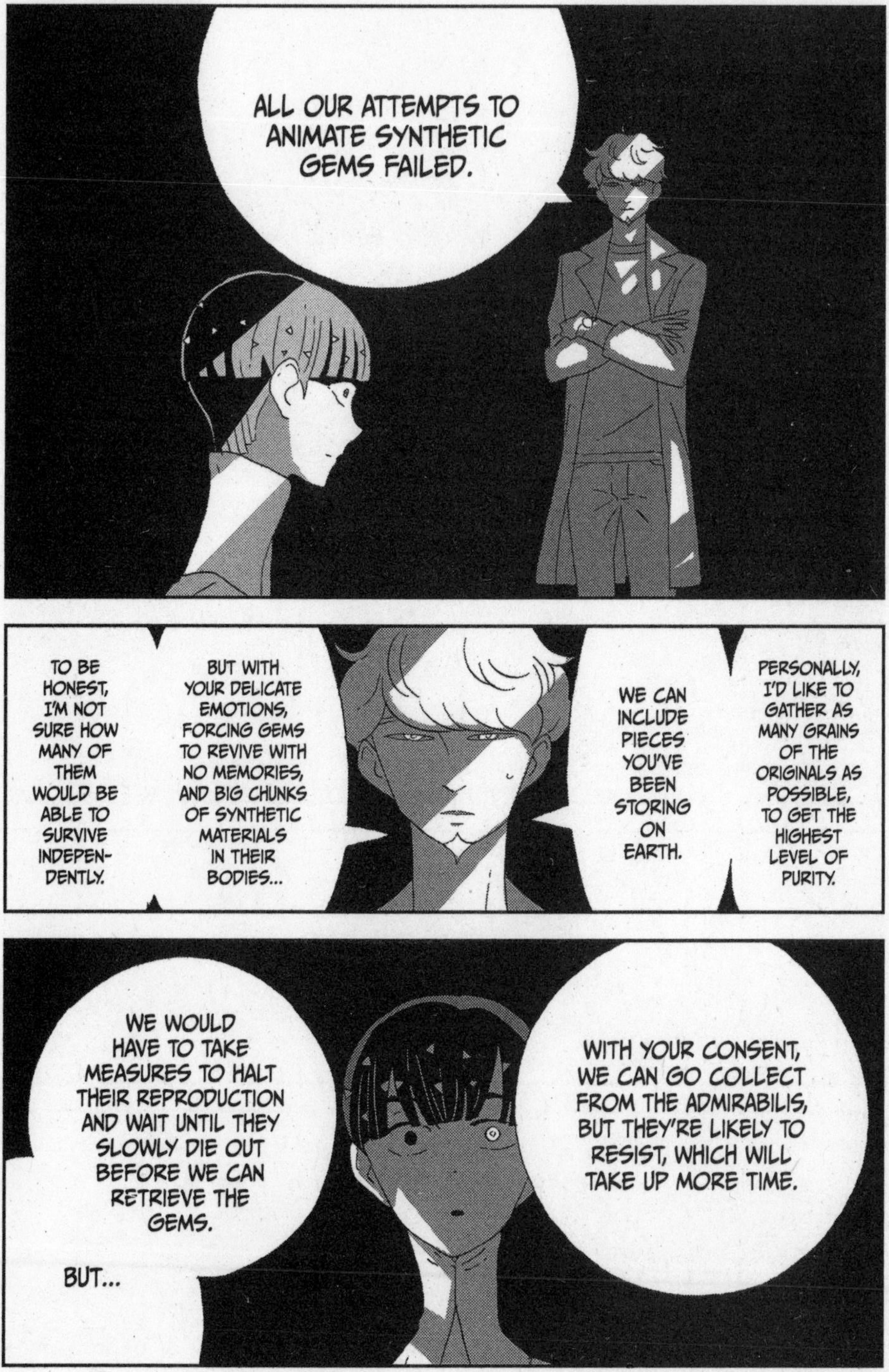
ALL OUR ATTEMPTS TO ANIMATE SYNTHETIC GEMS FAILED.
PERSONALLY, I'D LIKE TO GATHER AS MANY GRAINS OF THE ORIGINALS AS POSSIBLE, TO GET THE HIGHEST LEVEL OF PURITY.
WE CAN INCLUDE PIECES YOU'VE BEEN STORING ON EARTH.
BUT WITH YOUR DELICATE EMOTIONS, FORCING GEMS TO REVIVE WITH NO MEMORIES, AND BIG CHUNKS OF SYNTHETIC MATERIALS IN THEIR BODIES...
TO BE HONEST, I'M NOT SURE HOW MANY OF THEM WOULD BE ABLE TO SURVIVE INDEPEN-DENTLY.
WITH YOUR CONSENT, WE CAN GO COLLECT FROM THE ADMIRABILIS, BUT THEY'RE LIKELY TO RESIST, WHICH WILL TAKE UP MORE TIME.
WE WOULD HAVE TO TAKE MEASURES TO HALT THEIR REPRODUCTION AND WAIT UNTIL THEY SLOWLY DIE OUT BEFORE WE CAN RETRIEVE THE GEMS.
BUT...

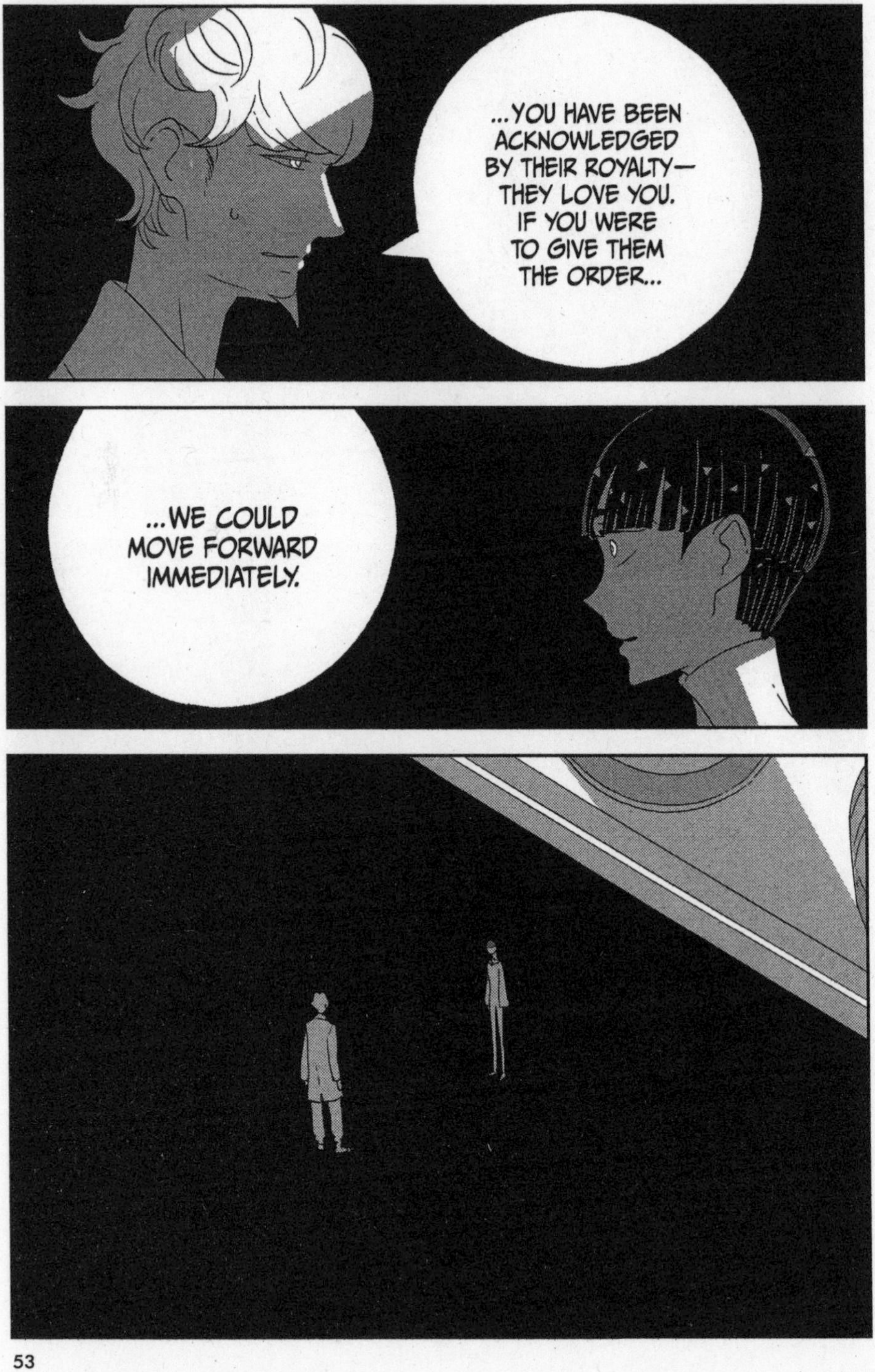
...YOU HAVE BEEN ACKNOWLEDGED BY THEIR ROYALTY—THEY LOVE YOU. IF YOU WERE TO GIVE THEM THE ORDER...
...WE COULD MOVE FORWARD IMMEDIATELY.

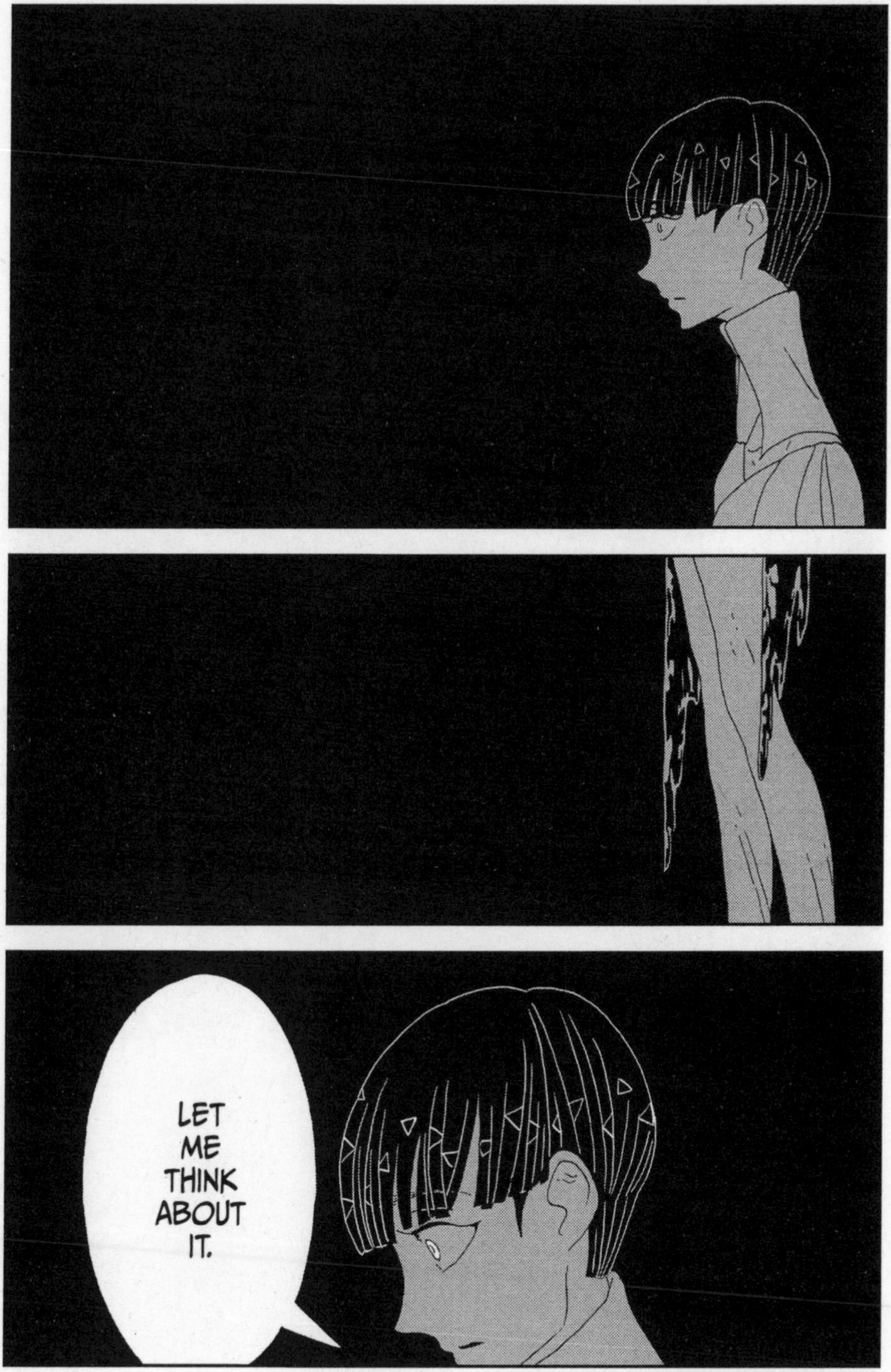
LET ME THINK ABOUT IT.

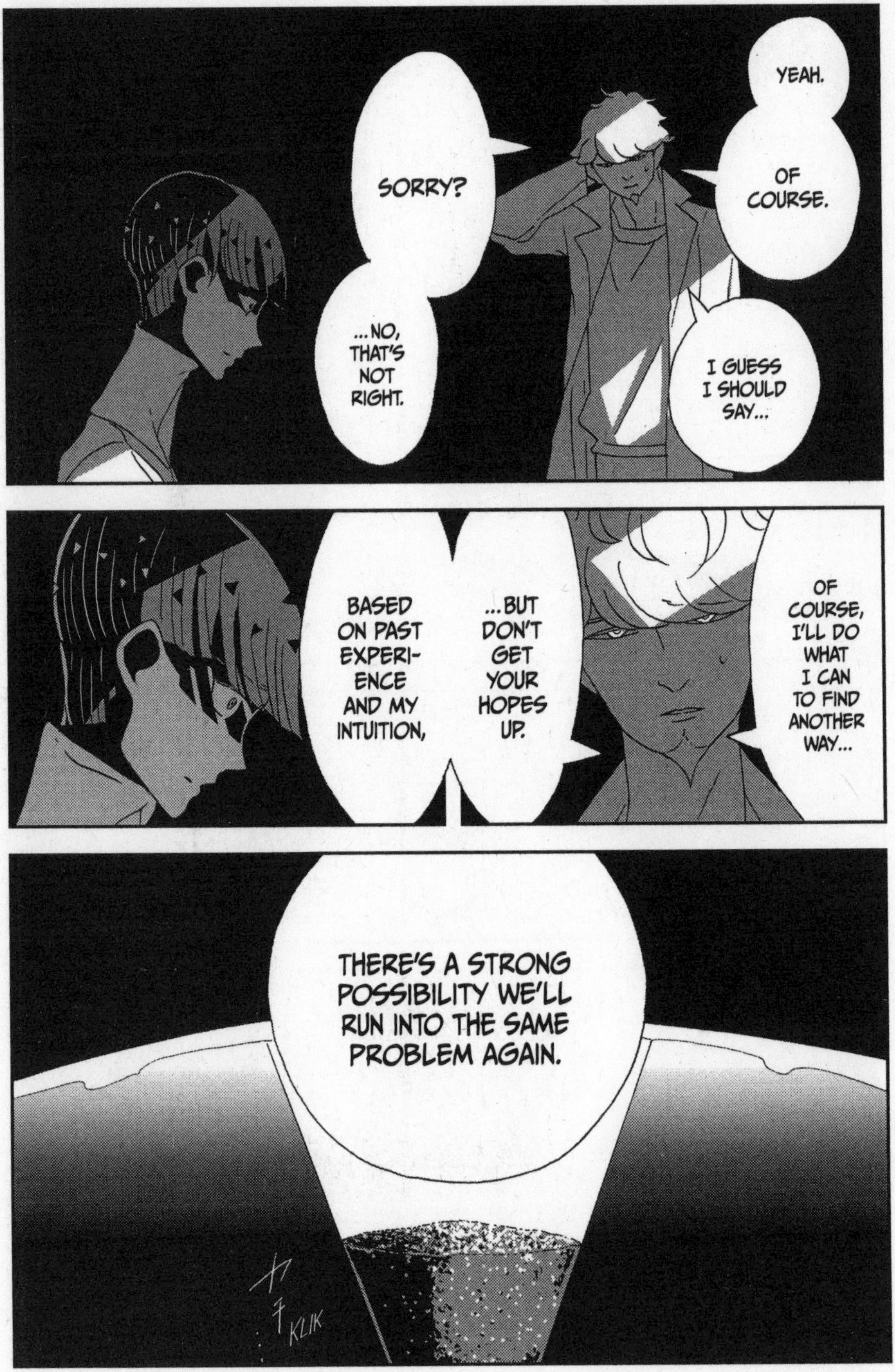
YEAH.
OF COURSE.
SORRY?
I GUESS I SHOULD SAY...
...NO, THAT'S NOT RIGHT.
OF COURSE, I'LL DO WHAT I CAN TO FIND ANOTHER WAY...
...BUT DON'T GET YOUR HOPES UP.
BASED ON PAST EXPERI-ENCE AND MY INTUITION,
THERE'S A STRONG POSSIBILITY WE'LL RUN INTO THE SAME PROBLEM AGAIN.
KLIK

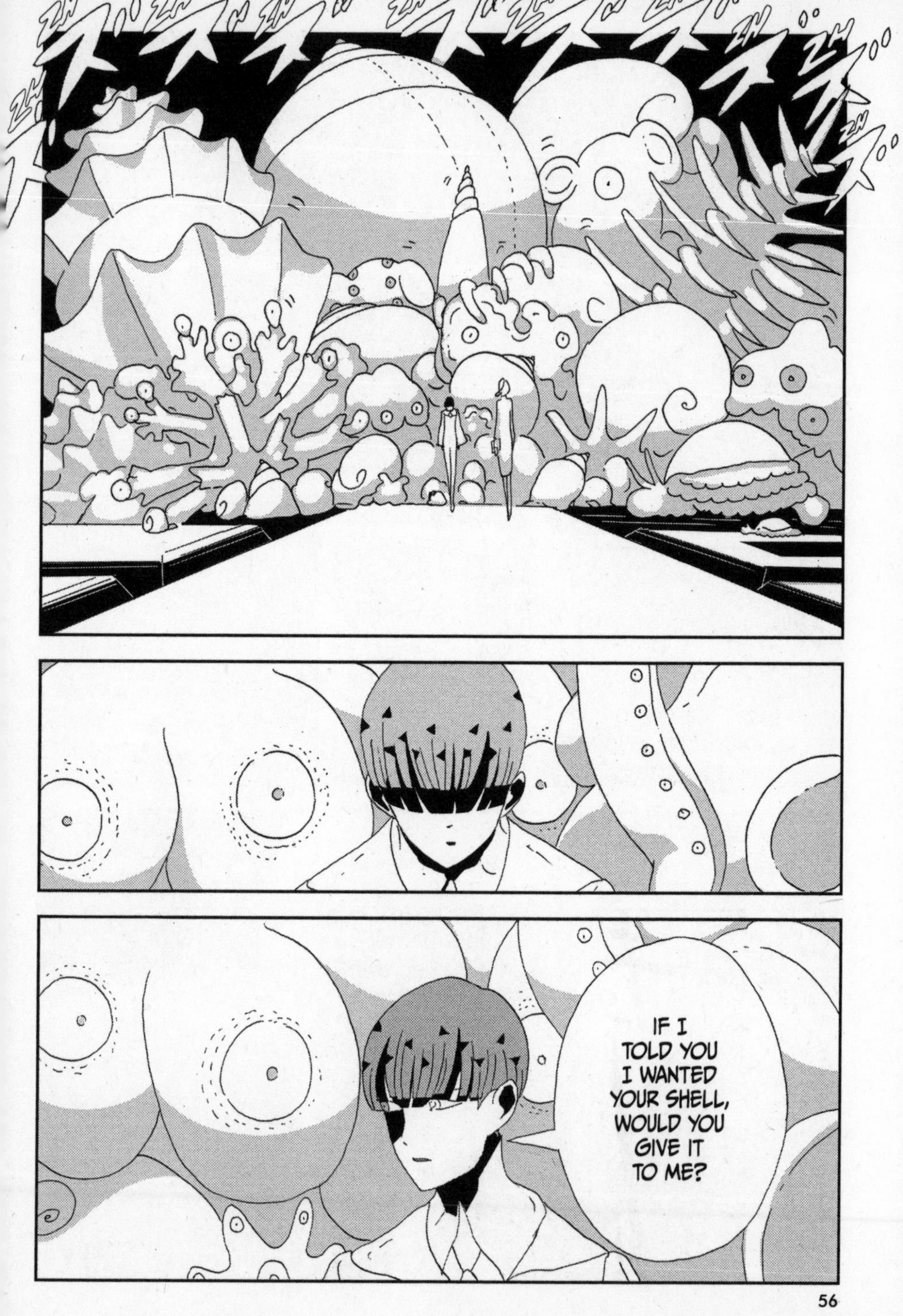
IF I TOLD YOU I WANTED YOUR SHELL, WOULD YOU GIVE IT TO ME?

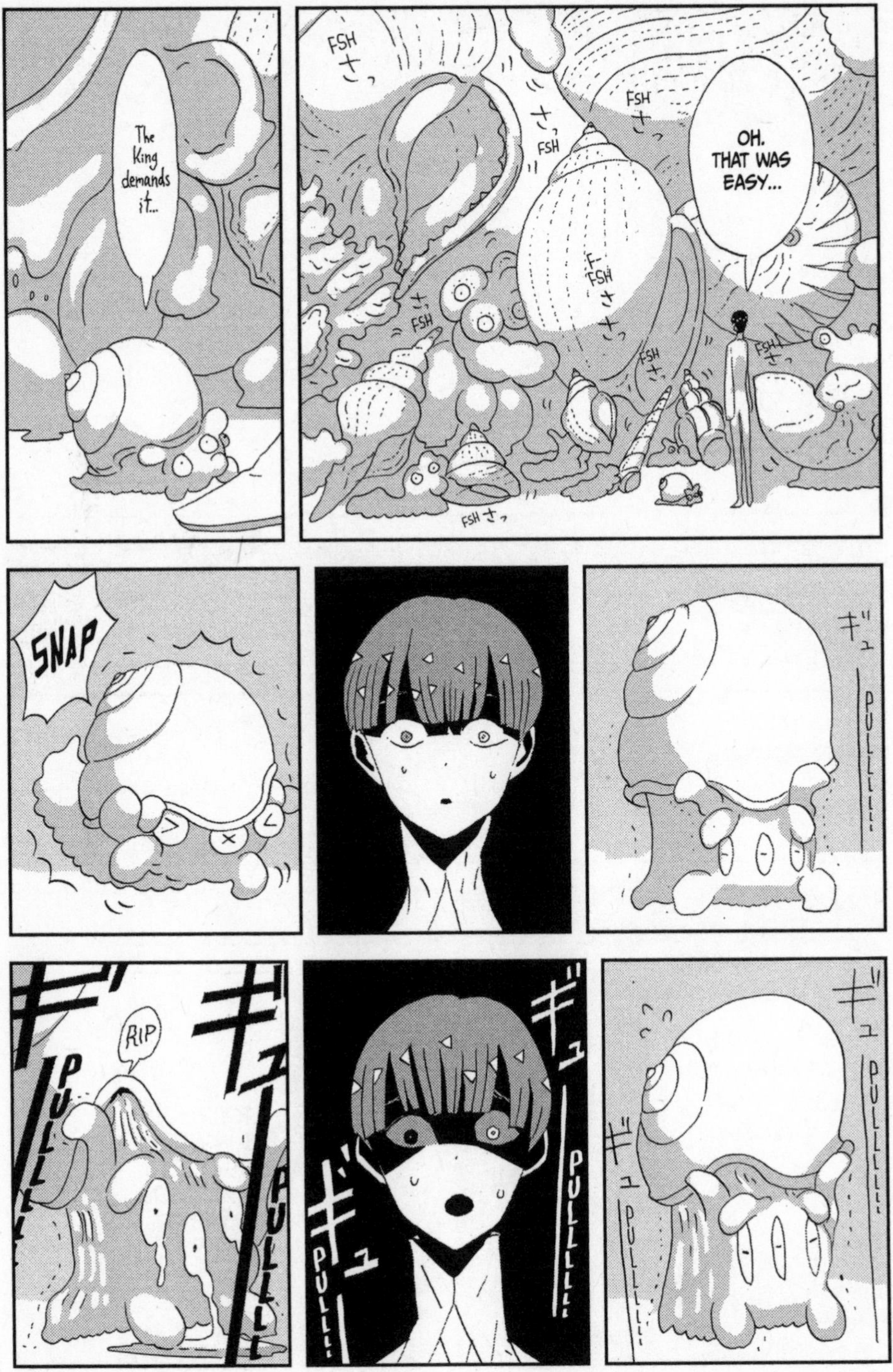
FSH さっ
FSH さっ
FSH さっ
OH. THAT WAS EASY...
F-FSH さっ
FSH さっ
FSH さっ
FSH さっ
FSH さっ
The King demands it...
ギュ
PULLLLL...
SNAP
ギュ
PULLLLL...
ギュ
PULLLLL...
ギュ
PULLLLL...
ギュ
PULLLL...
RIP
PULLLL
PULLLL
ギュ
ギュ

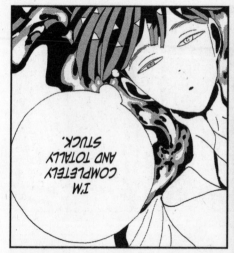

JUUUUST KIDDING!
YOU FELL FOR IT!
GRICH
GRICH
I'M COMPLETELY AND TOTALLY STUCK.
BUT MY HEAD WON'T STOP THINKING.

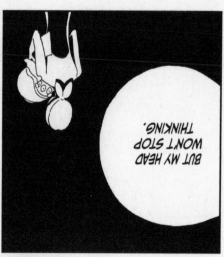

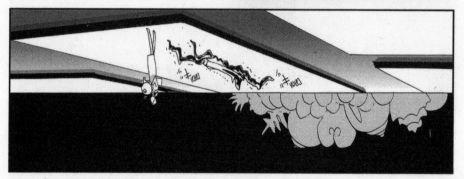

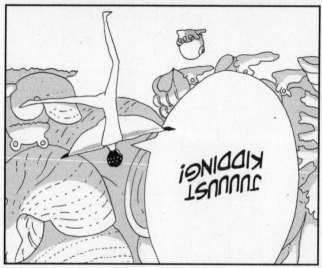

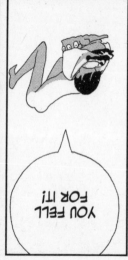

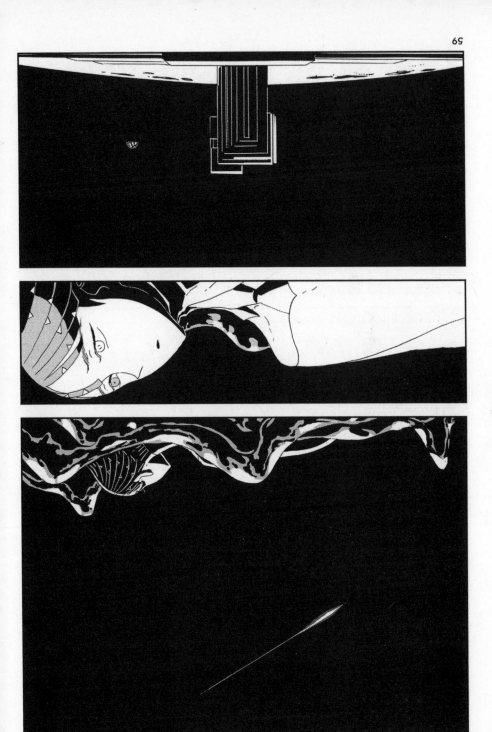

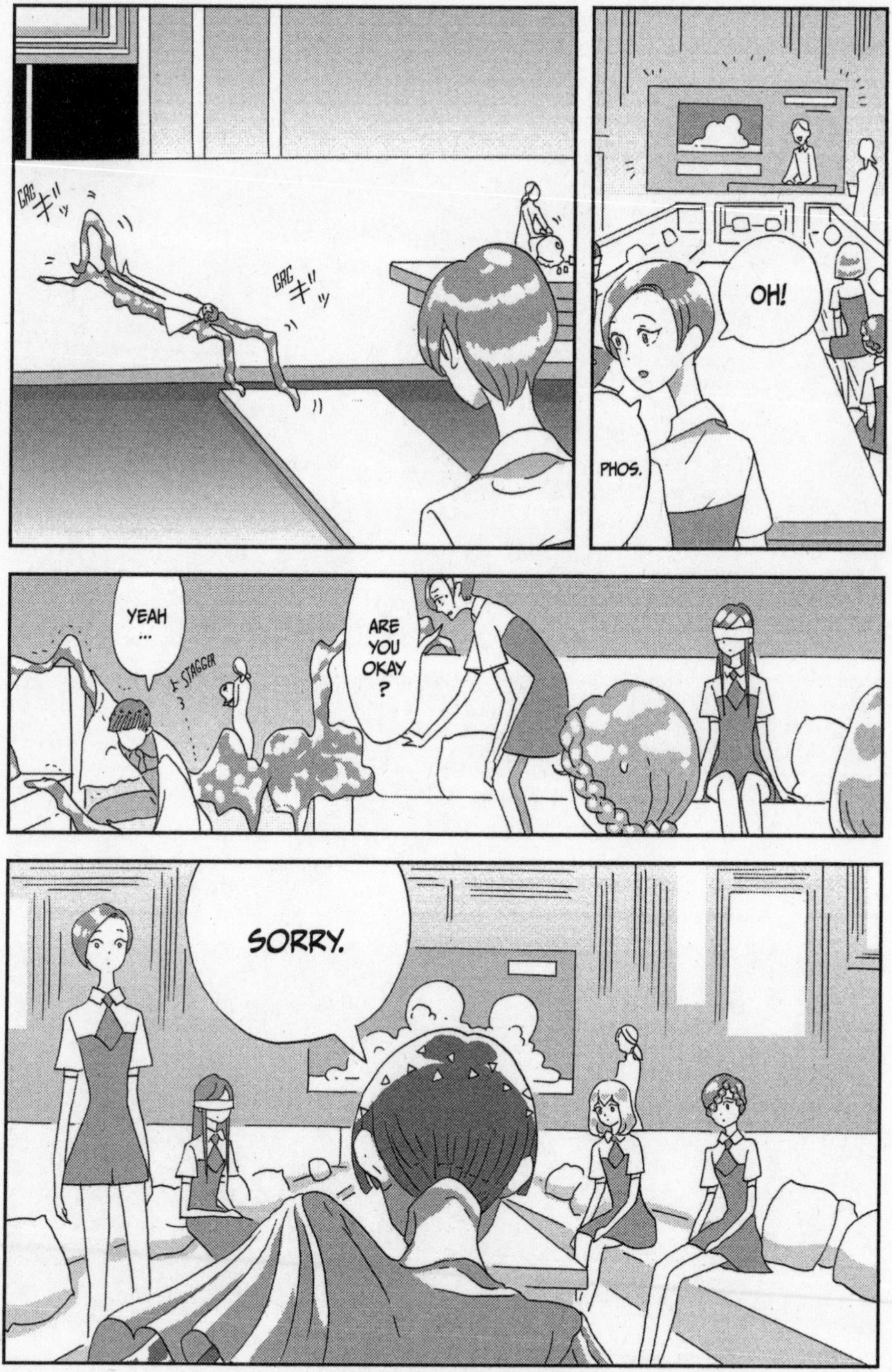
OH!
PHOS.
GRG ギッ
GRG ギッ
ARE YOU OKAY?
YEAH...
STAGGER
SORRY.

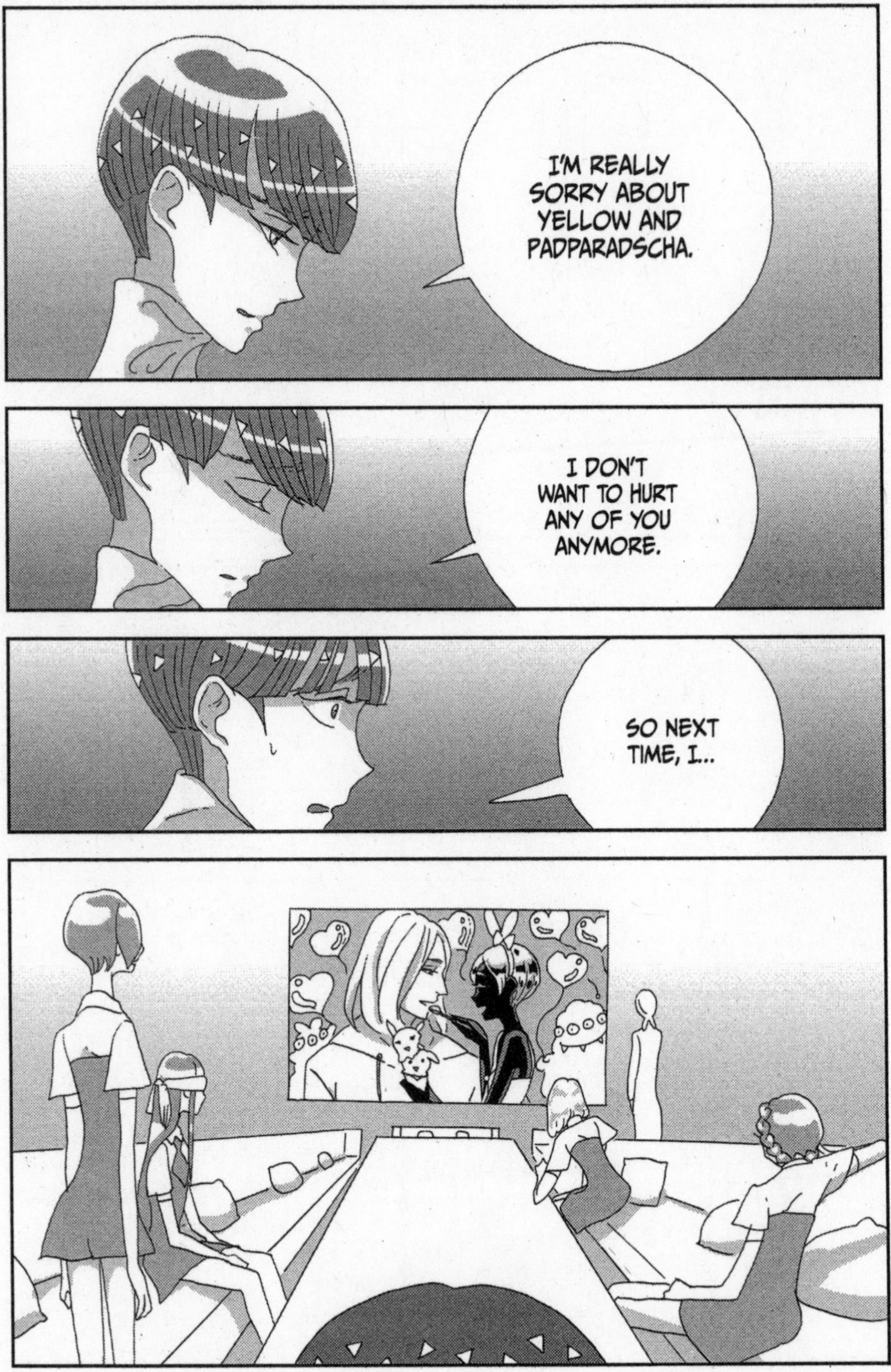
I'M REALLY SORRY ABOUT YELLOW AND PADPARADSCHA.
I DON'T WANT TO HURT ANY OF YOU ANYMORE.
SO NEXT TIME, I...

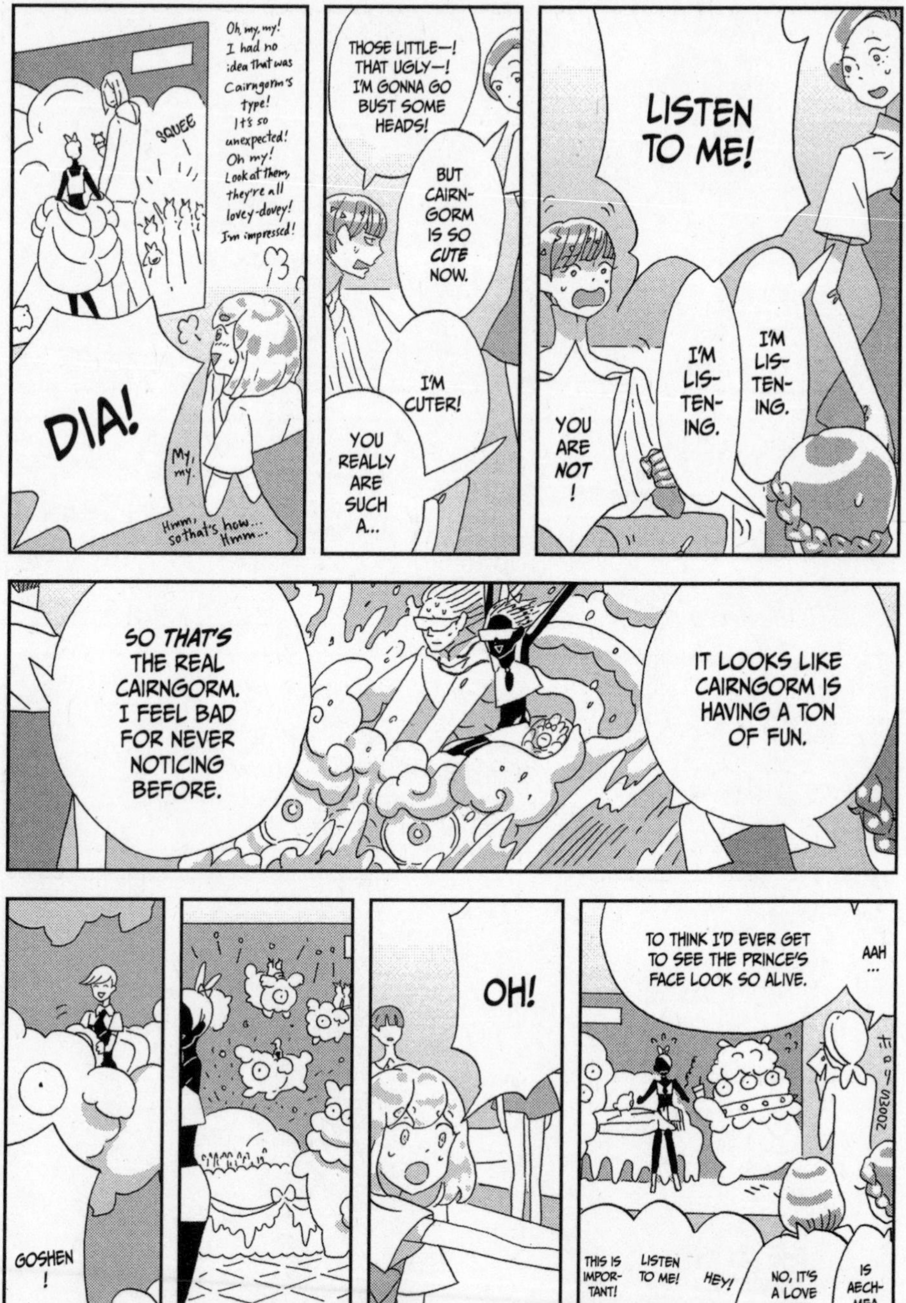
LISTEN TO ME!
I'M LIS-TEN-ING.
I'M LIS-TEN-ING.
YOU ARE NOT !
THOSE LITTLE—! THAT UGLY—! I'M GONNA GO BUST SOME HEADS!
BUT CAIRN-GORM IS SO CUTE NOW.
I'M CUTER!
YOU REALLY ARE SUCH A...
Oh, my, my! I had no idea that was Cairngorm's type! It's so unexpected! Oh my! Look at them, they're all lovey-dovey! I'm impressed!
SQUEE
DIA!
My, my.
Hmm, so that's how... Hmm...
IT LOOKS LIKE CAIRNGORM IS HAVING A TON OF FUN.
SO THAT'S THE REAL CAIRNGORM. I FEEL BAD FOR NEVER NOTICING BEFORE.
TO THINK I'D EVER GET TO SEE THE PRINCE'S FACE LOOK SO ALIVE.
AAH ...
IS AECH-MEA UNCON-SCIOUS ?
NO, IT'S A LOVE TACTIC. TO GET CAIRNGORM'S ATTENTION.
HEY!
LISTEN TO ME!
THIS IS IMPOR-TANT!
OH!
GOSHEN !

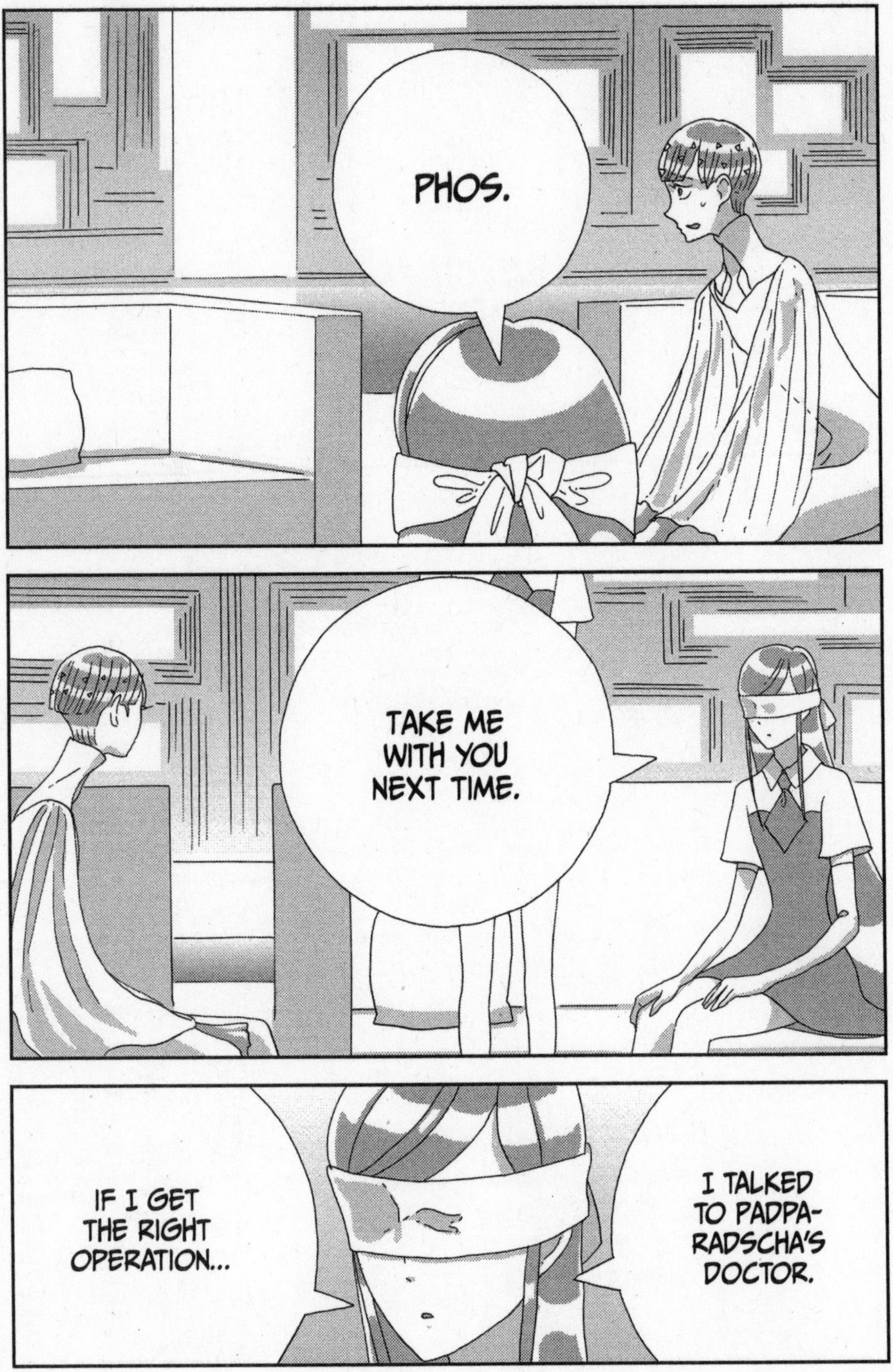
PHOS.
TAKE ME WITH YOU NEXT TIME.
I TALKED TO PADPA-RADSCHA'S DOCTOR.
IF I GET THE RIGHT OPERATION...

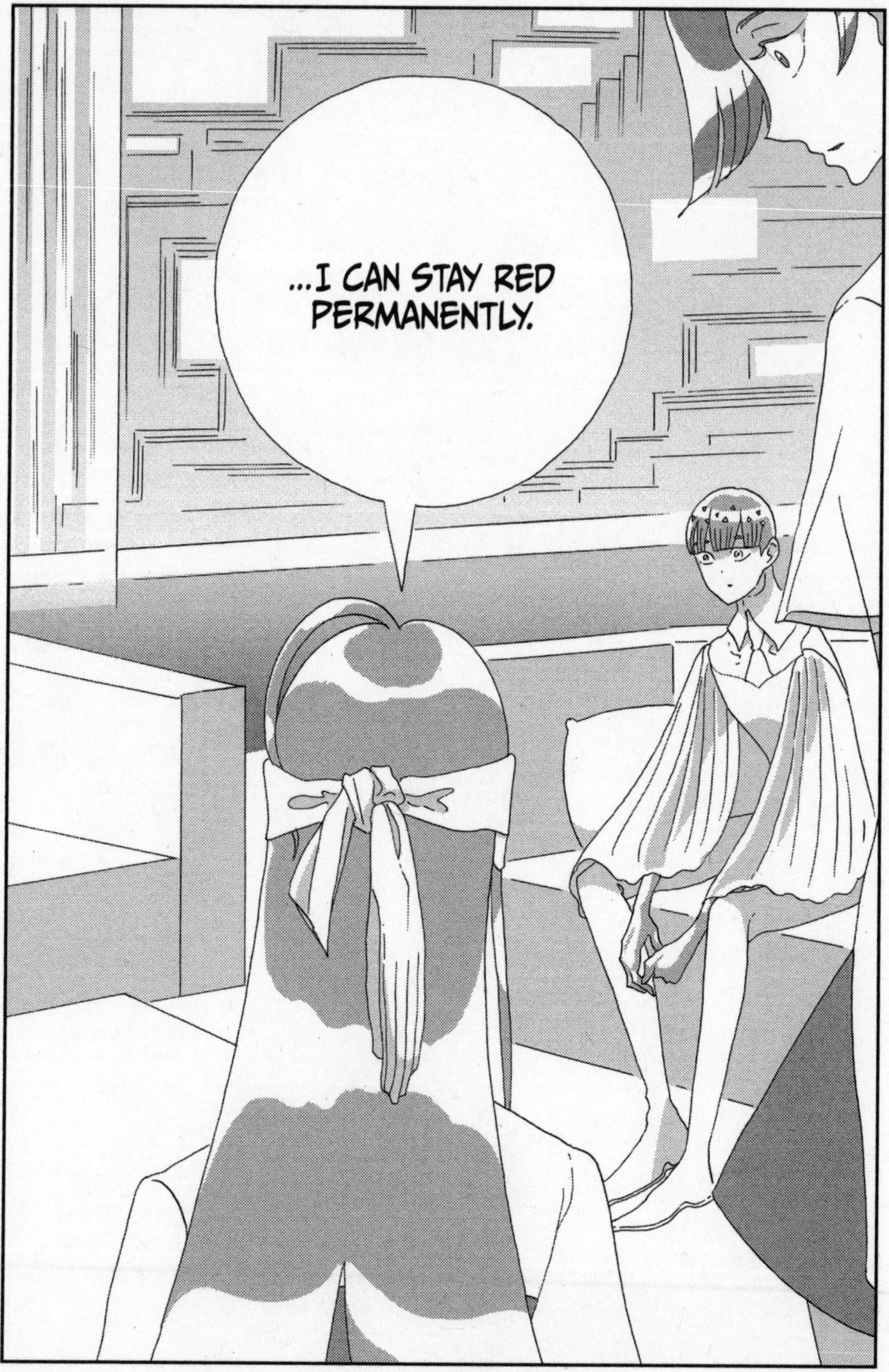
...I CAN STAY RED PERMANENTLY.

CHAPTER 73: Choice END

CHAPTER 74:
Ceremony

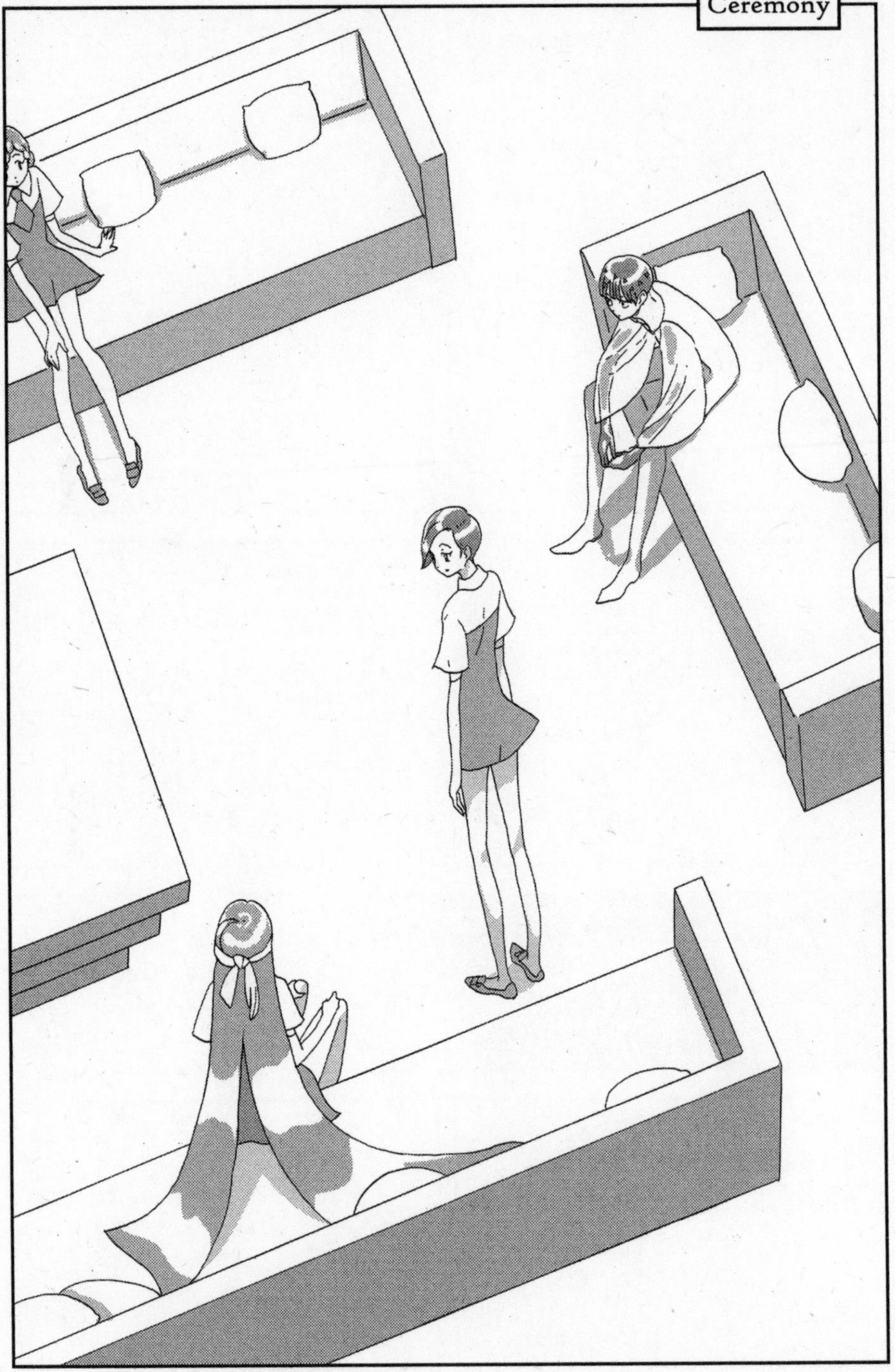

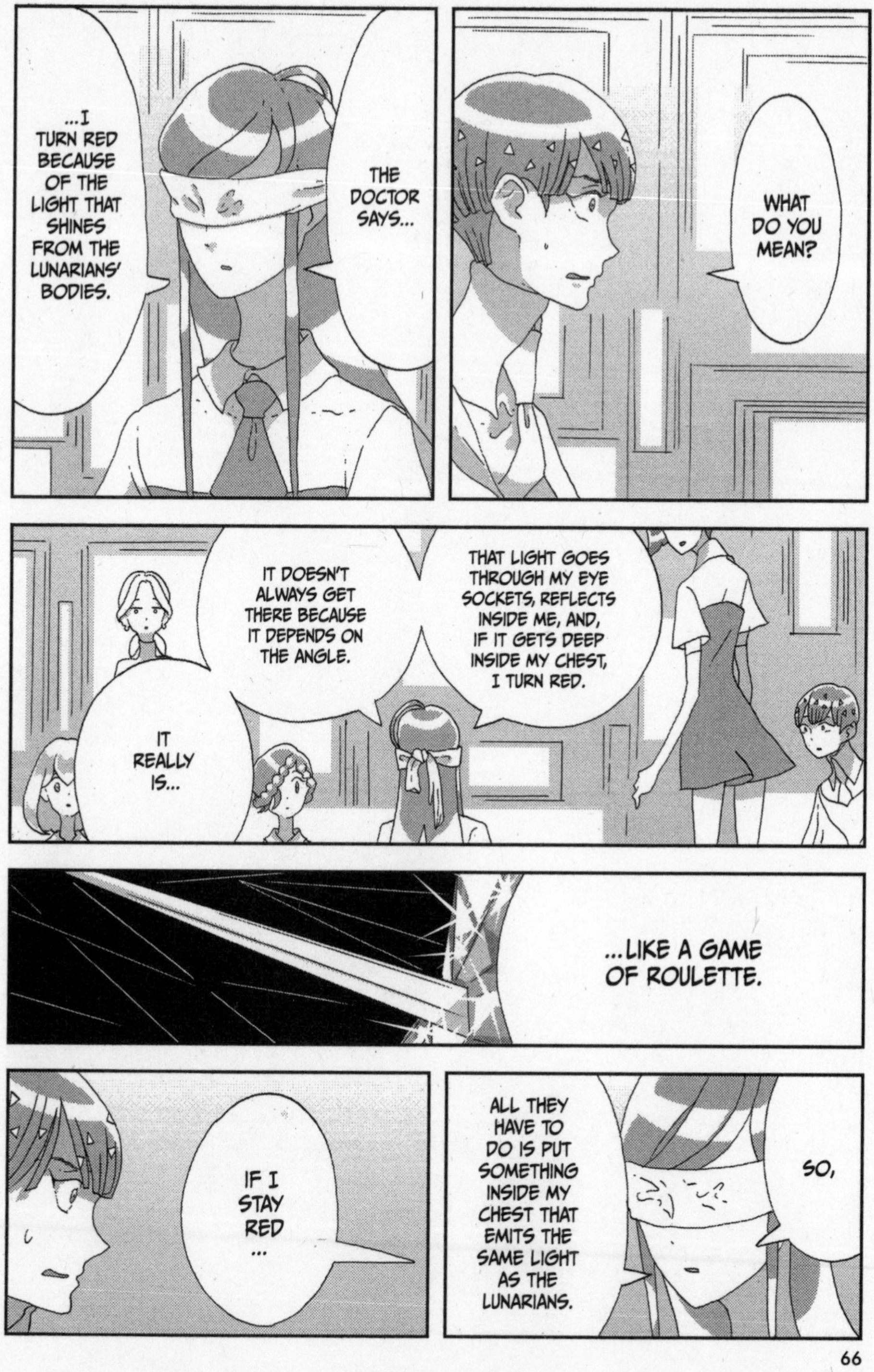
WHAT DO YOU MEAN?
THE DOCTOR SAYS...
...I TURN RED BECAUSE OF THE LIGHT THAT SHINES FROM THE LUNARIANS' BODIES.
THAT LIGHT GOES THROUGH MY EYE SOCKETS, REFLECTS INSIDE ME, AND, IF IT GETS DEEP INSIDE MY CHEST, I TURN RED.
IT DOESN'T ALWAYS GET THERE BECAUSE IT DEPENDS ON THE ANGLE.
IT REALLY IS...
...LIKE A GAME OF ROULETTE.
SO,
ALL THEY HAVE TO DO IS PUT SOMETHING INSIDE MY CHEST THAT EMITS THE SAME LIGHT AS THE LUNARIANS.
IF I STAY RED ...

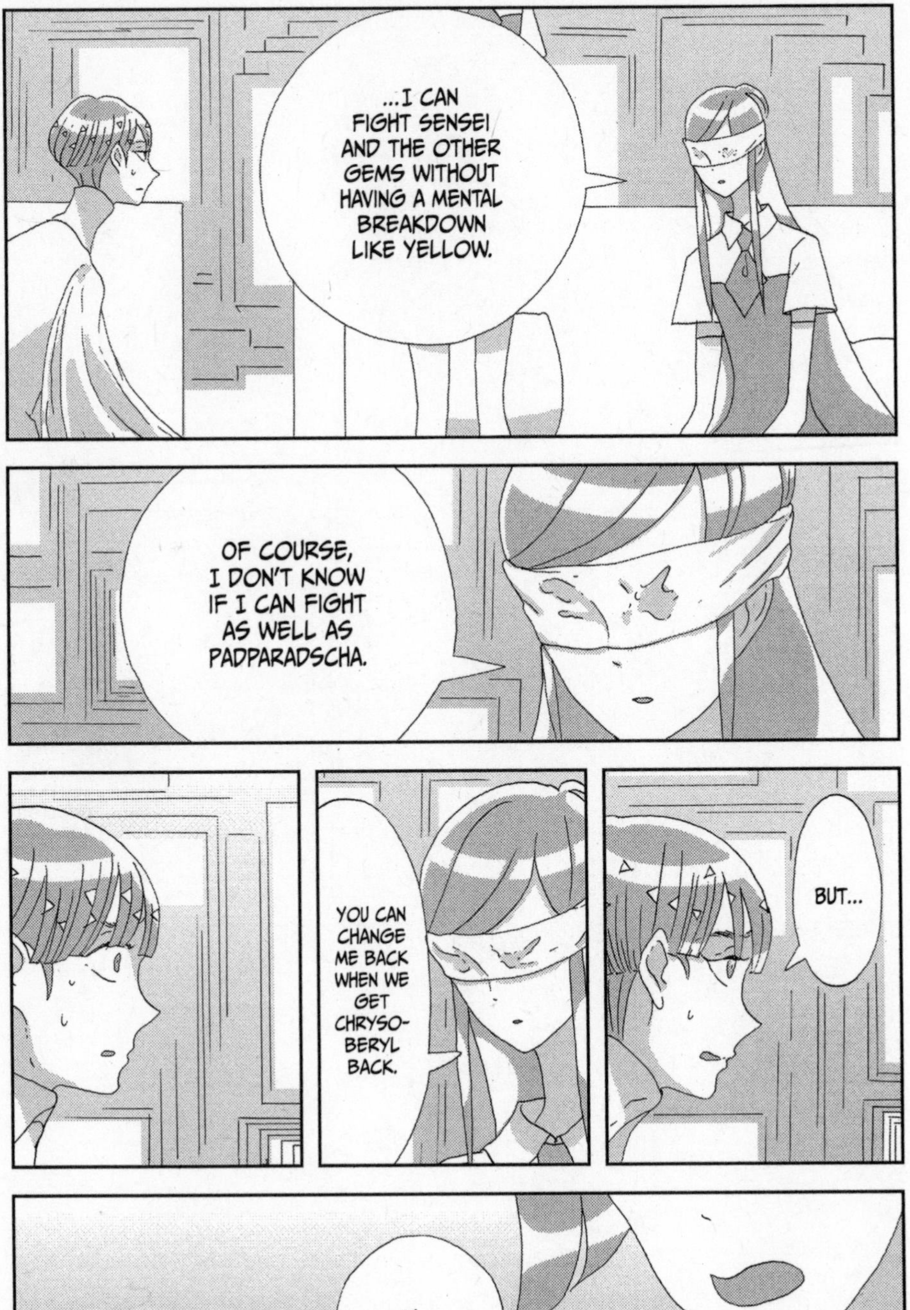
...I CAN FIGHT SENSEI AND THE OTHER GEMS WITHOUT HAVING A MENTAL BREAKDOWN LIKE YELLOW.
OF COURSE, I DON'T KNOW IF I CAN FIGHT AS WELL AS PADPARADSCHA.
BUT...
YOU CAN CHANGE ME BACK WHEN WE GET CHRYSO-BERYL BACK.
N—

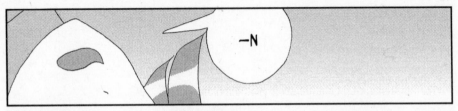

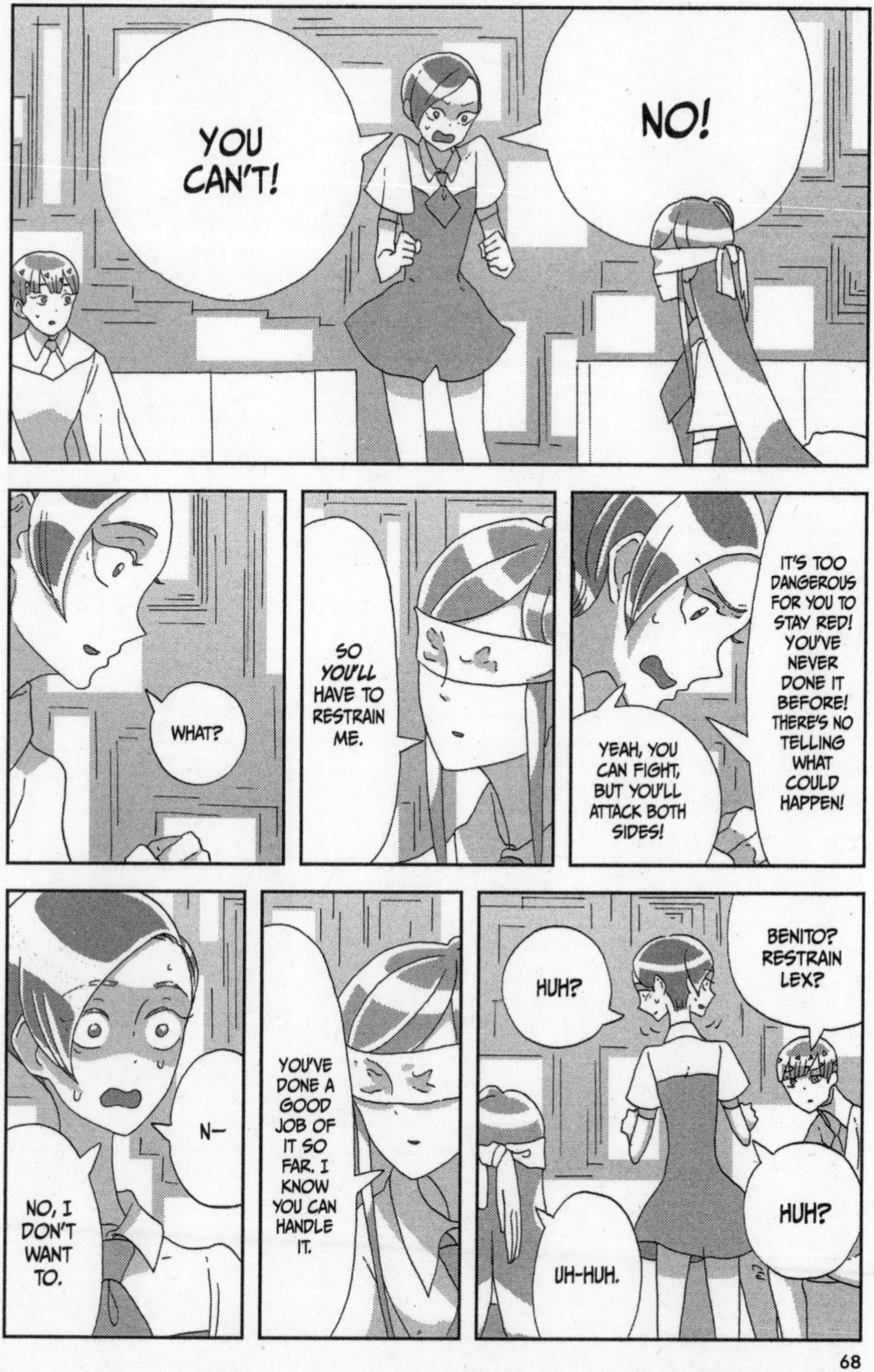
NO!
YOU CAN'T!
IT'S TOO DANGEROUS FOR YOU TO STAY RED! YOU'VE NEVER DONE IT BEFORE! THERE'S NO TELLING WHAT COULD HAPPEN!
YEAH, YOU CAN FIGHT, BUT YOU'LL ATTACK BOTH SIDES!
SO YOU'LL HAVE TO RESTRAIN ME.
WHAT?
BENITO? RESTRAIN LEX?
HUH?
HUH?
UH-HUH.
YOU'VE DONE A GOOD JOB OF IT SO FAR. I KNOW YOU CAN HANDLE IT.
N—
NO, I DON'T WANT TO.

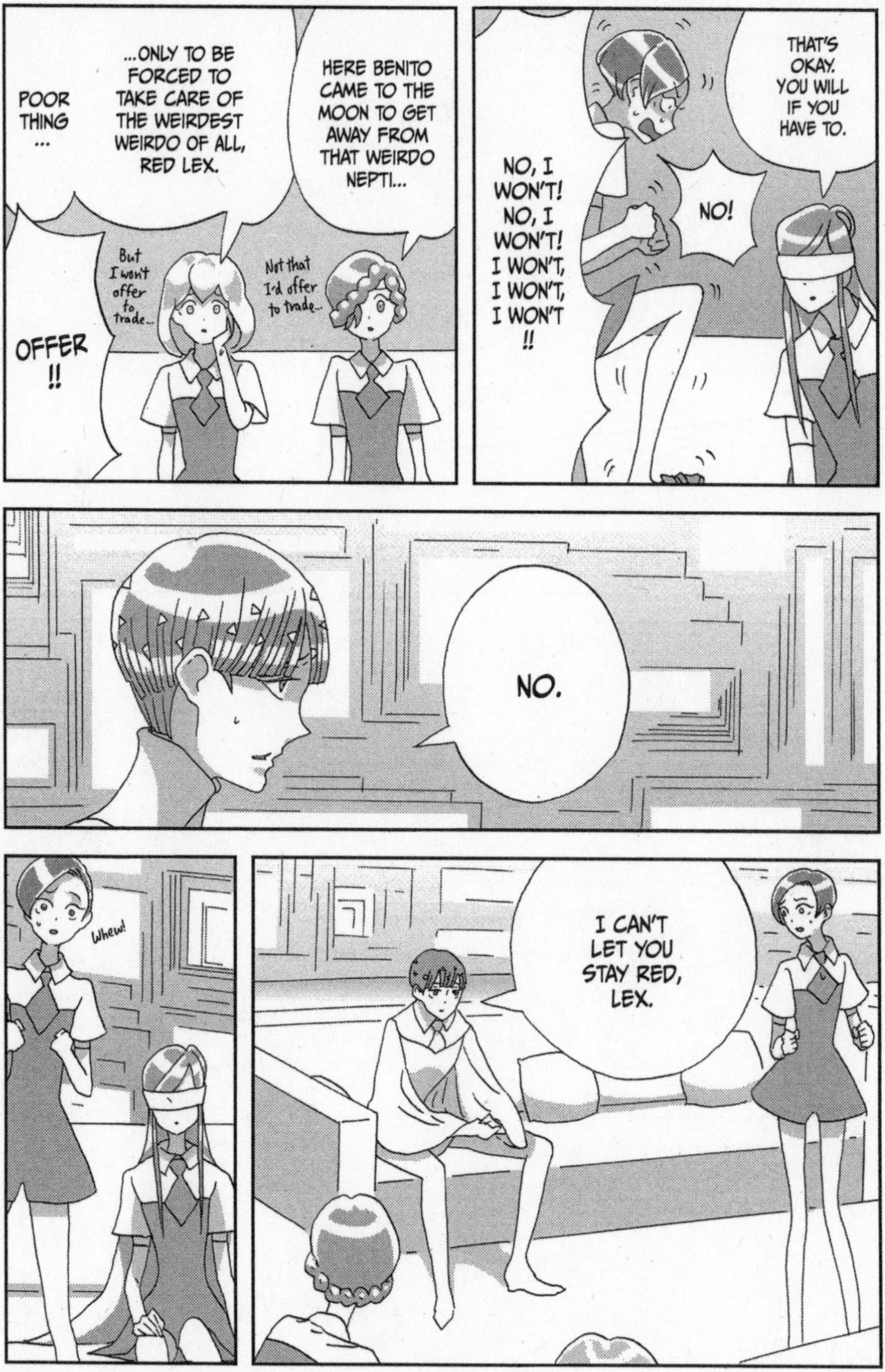
THAT'S OKAY. YOU WILL IF YOU HAVE TO.
NO!
NO, I WON'T! NO, I WON'T! I WON'T, I WON'T, I WON'T !!
HERE BENITO CAME TO THE MOON TO GET AWAY FROM THAT WEIRDO NEPTI...
Not that I'd offer to trade...
...ONLY TO BE FORCED TO TAKE CARE OF THE WEIRDEST WEIRDO OF ALL, RED LEX.
But I won't offer to trade...
POOR THING ...
OFFER !!
NO.
I CAN'T LET YOU STAY RED, LEX.
Whew!

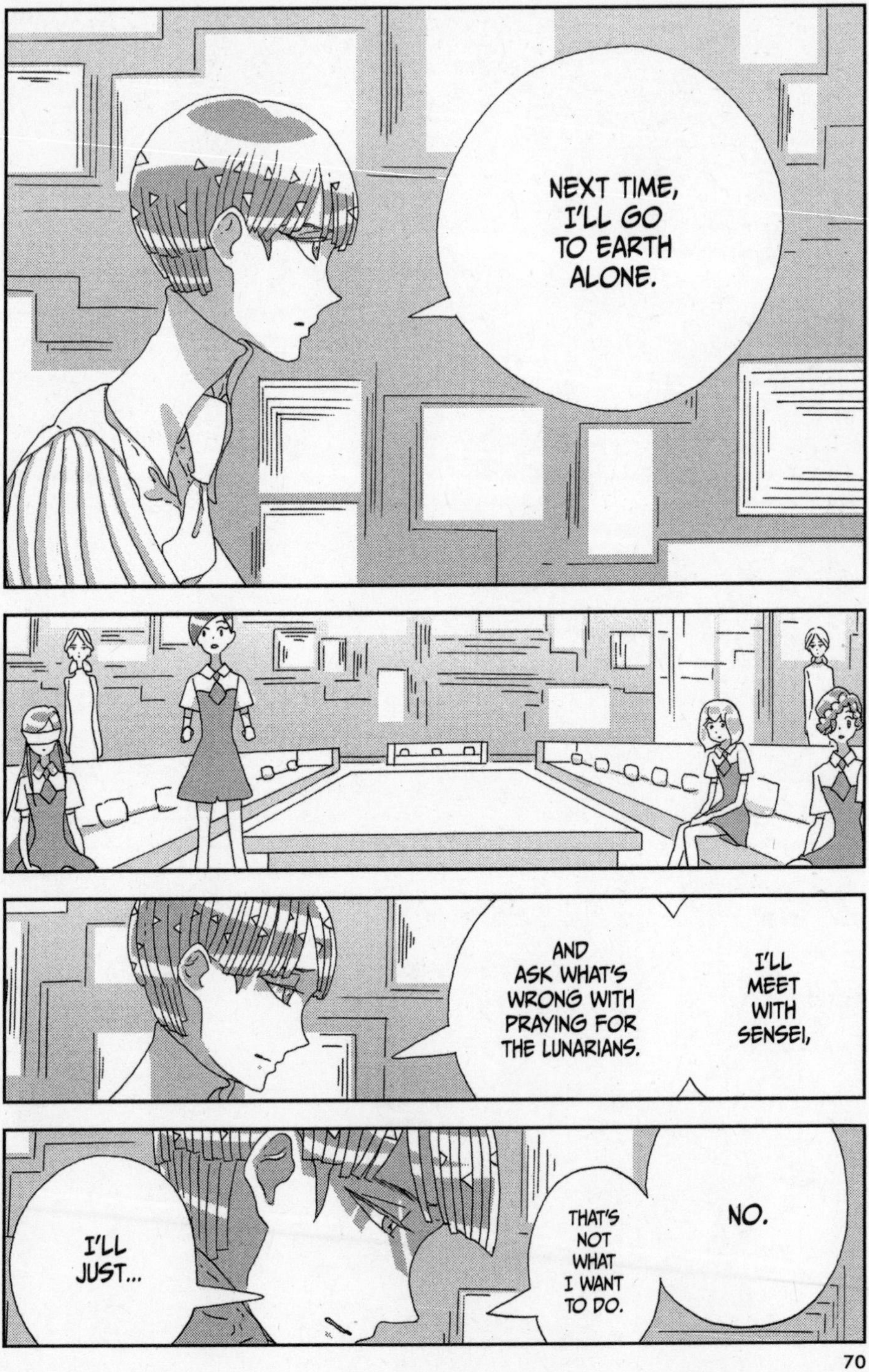
NEXT TIME, I'LL GO TO EARTH ALONE.
I'LL MEET WITH SENSEI,
AND ASK WHAT'S WRONG WITH PRAYING FOR THE LUNARIANS.
NO.
THAT'S NOT WHAT I WANT TO DO.
I'LL JUST...

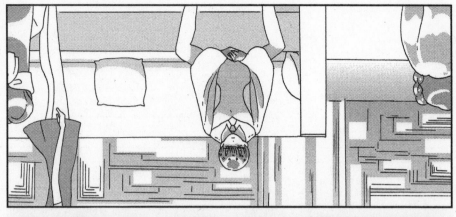

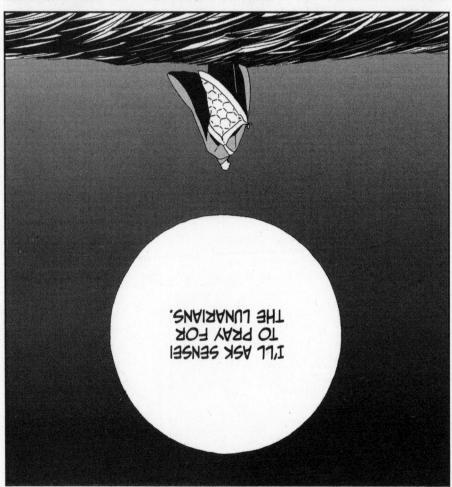

I'LL ASK SENSEI
TO PRAY FOR
THE LUNARIANS.

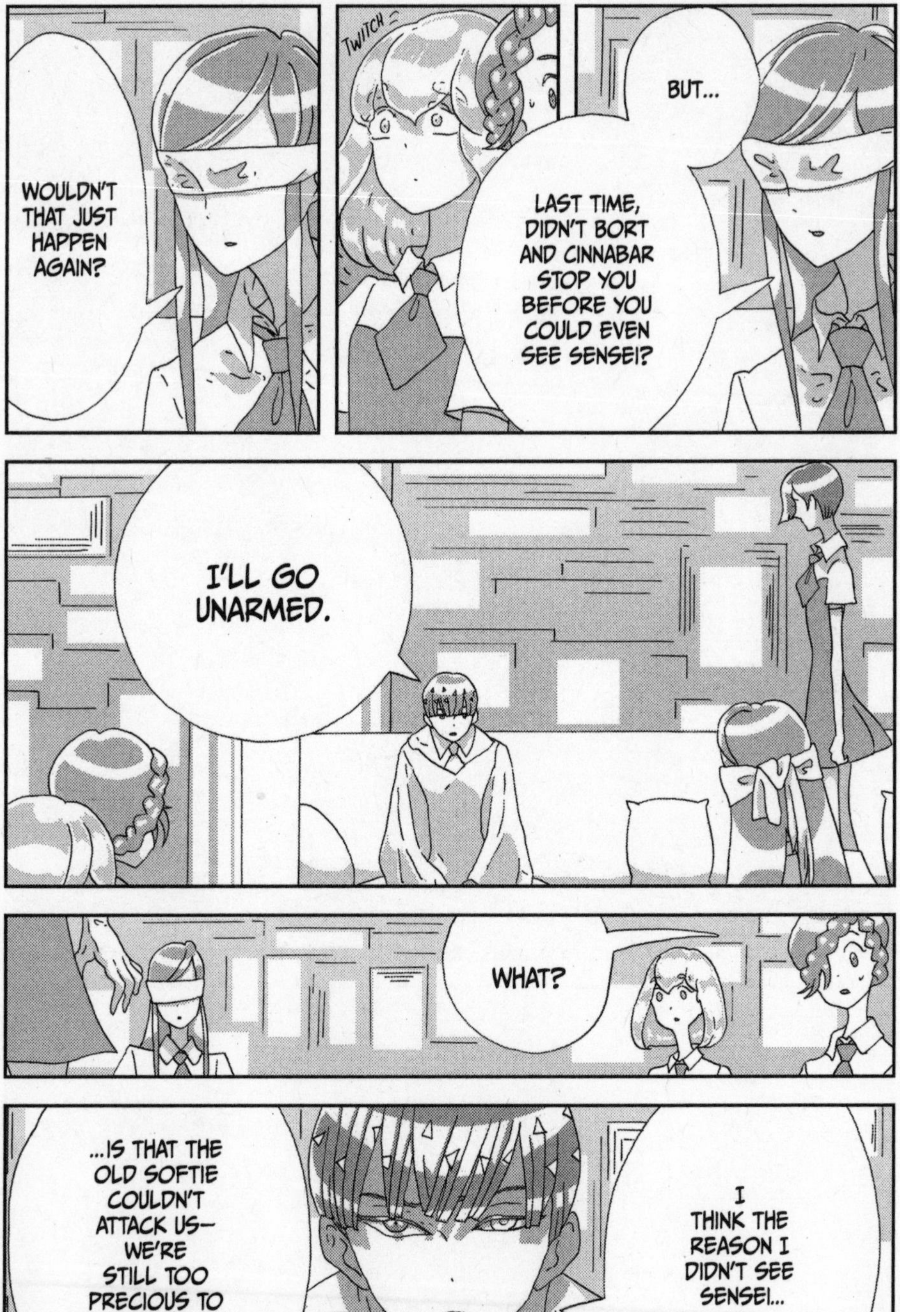
BUT...
LAST TIME, DIDN'T BORT AND CINNABAR STOP YOU BEFORE YOU COULD EVEN SEE SENSEI?
TWITCH
WOULDN'T THAT JUST HAPPEN AGAIN?
I'LL GO UNARMED.
WHAT?
I THINK THE REASON I DIDN'T SEE SENSEI...
...IS THAT THE OLD SOFTIE COULDN'T ATTACK US— WE'RE STILL TOO PRECIOUS TO OUR FORMER TEACHER.

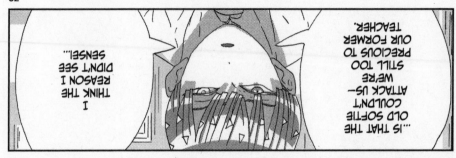

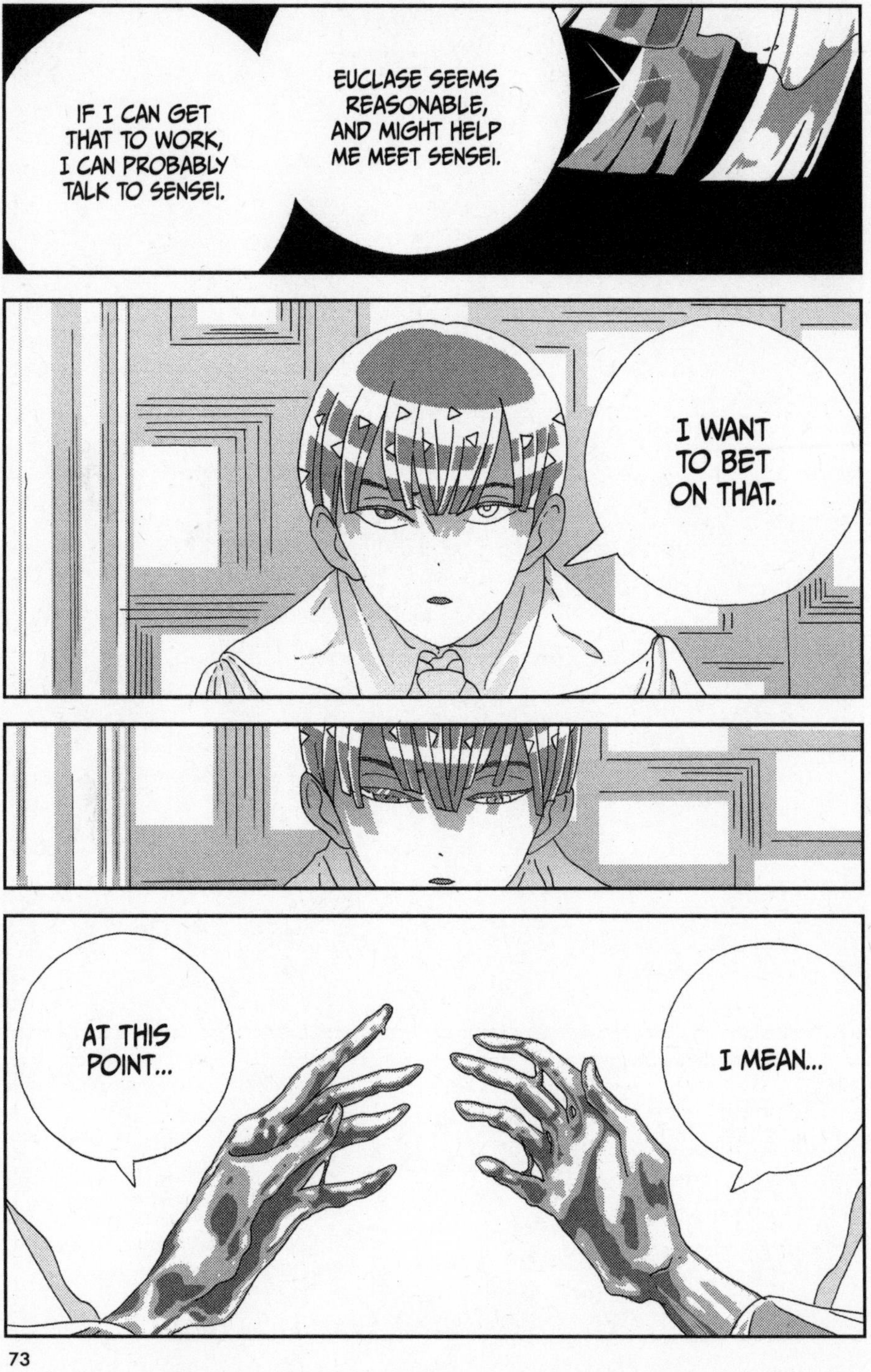
EUCLASE SEEMS REASONABLE, AND MIGHT HELP ME MEET SENSEI.
IF I CAN GET THAT TO WORK, I CAN PROBABLY TALK TO SENSEI.
I WANT TO BET ON THAT.
I MEAN...
AT THIS POINT...

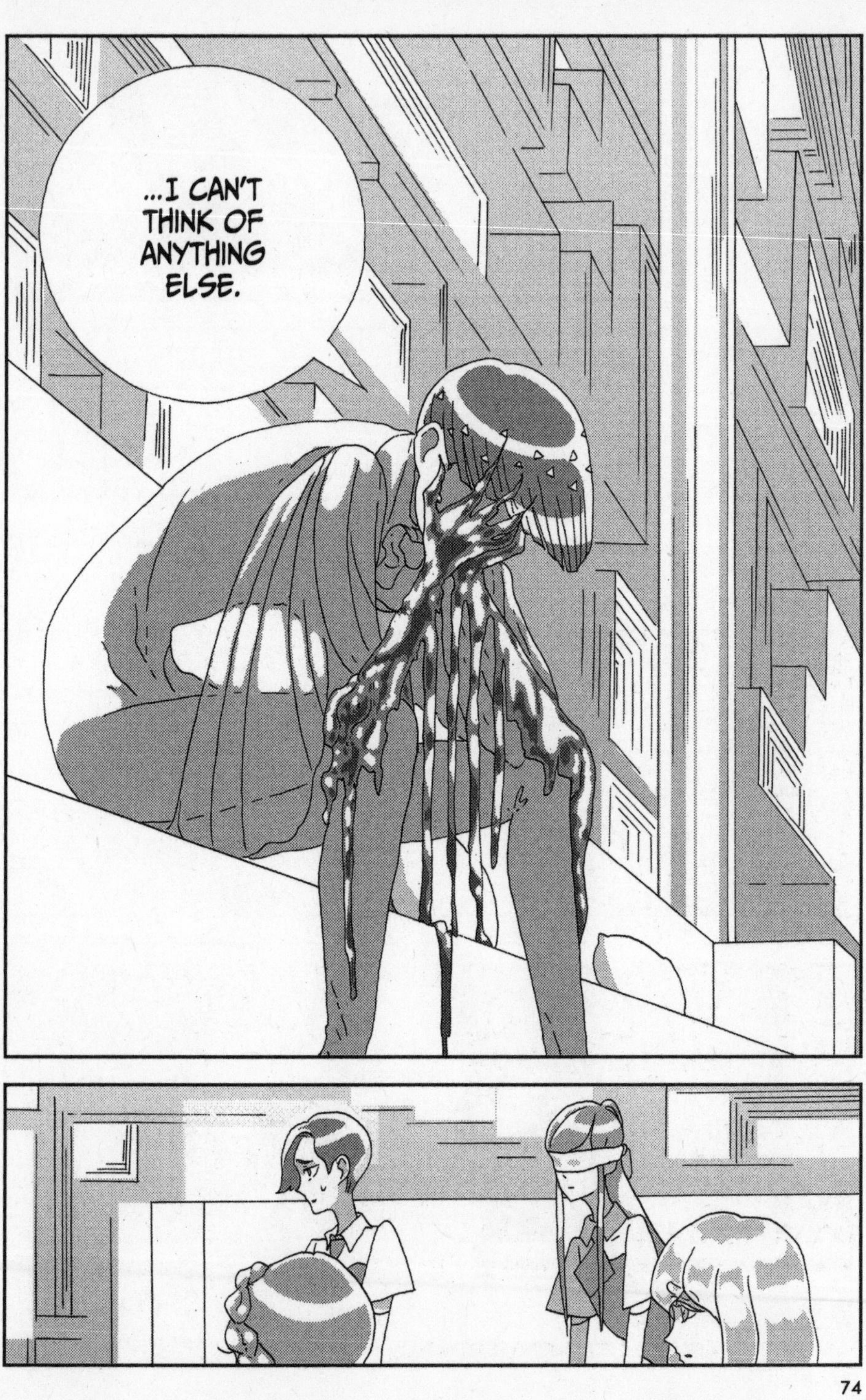
...I CAN'T THINK OF ANYTHING ELSE.

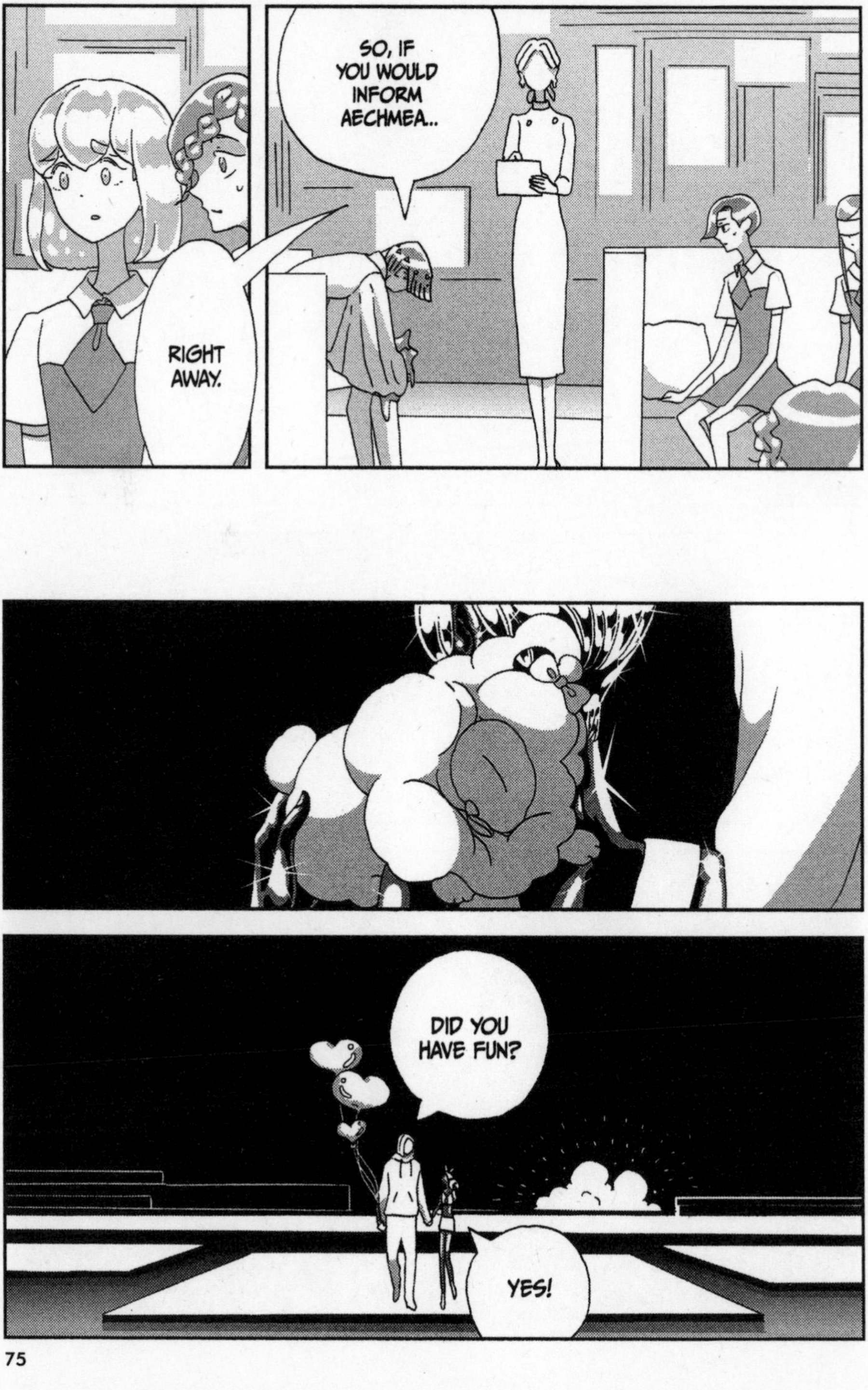
SO, IF YOU WOULD INFORM AECHMEA..
RIGHT AWAY.
DID YOU HAVE FUN?
YES!

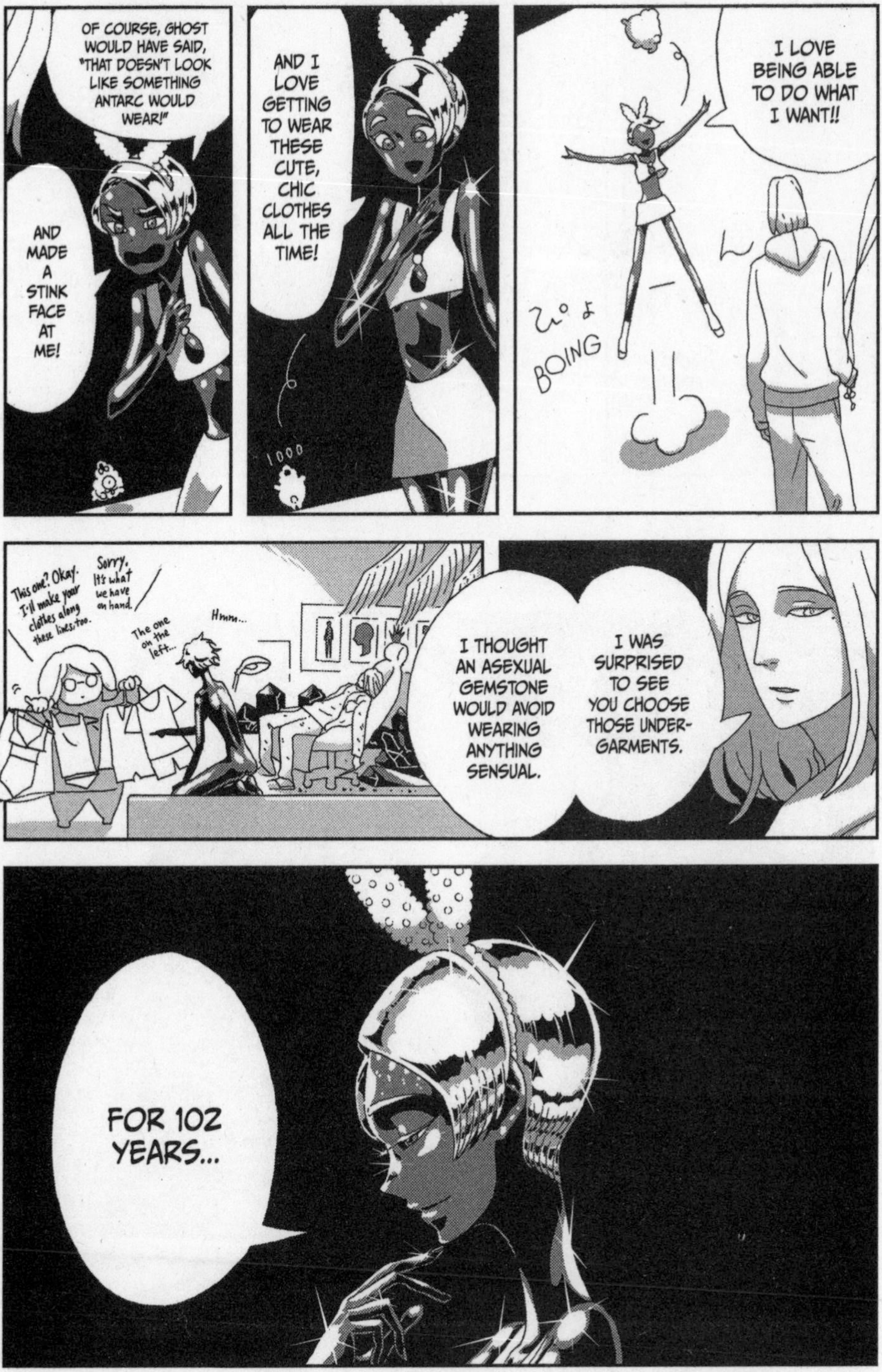
I LOVE BEING ABLE TO DO WHAT I WANT!!
BOING
AND I LOVE GETTING TO WEAR THESE CUTE, CHIC CLOTHES ALL THE TIME!
OF COURSE, GHOST WOULD HAVE SAID, "THAT DOESN'T LOOK LIKE SOMETHING ANTARC WOULD WEAR!"
AND MADE A STINK FACE AT ME!
I WAS SURPRISED TO SEE YOU CHOOSE THOSE UNDER-GARMENTS.
I THOUGHT AN ASEXUAL GEMSTONE WOULD AVOID WEARING ANYTHING SENSUAL.
Hmm...
The one on the left...
Sorry. It's what we have on hand.
This one? Okay. I'll make your clothes along these lines, too.
FOR 102 YEARS...

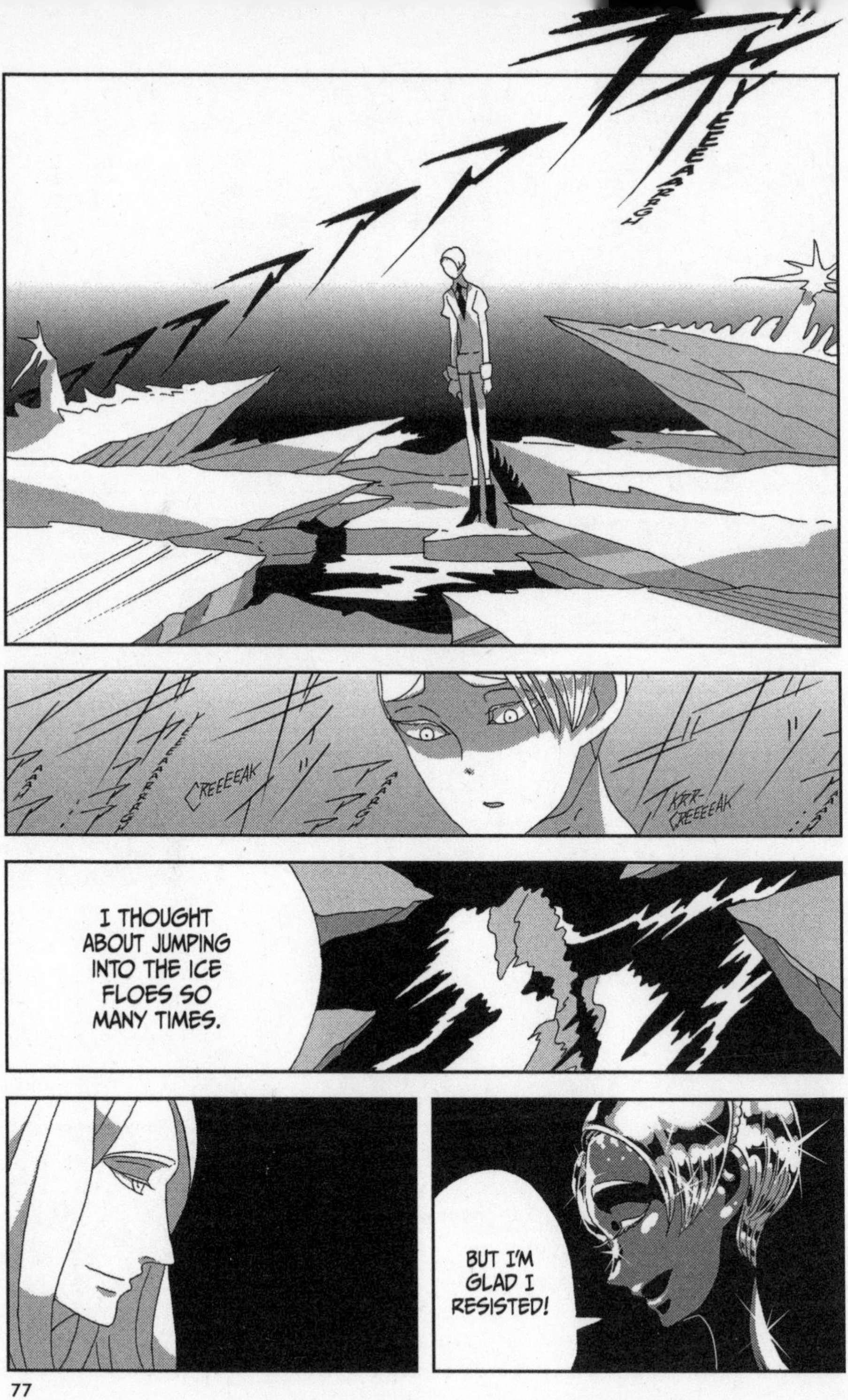

VEEEARRGH
CREEEEAK
KRR-CREEEEAK
I THOUGHT ABOUT JUMPING INTO THE ICE FLOES SO MANY TIMES.
BUT I'M GLAD I RESISTED!

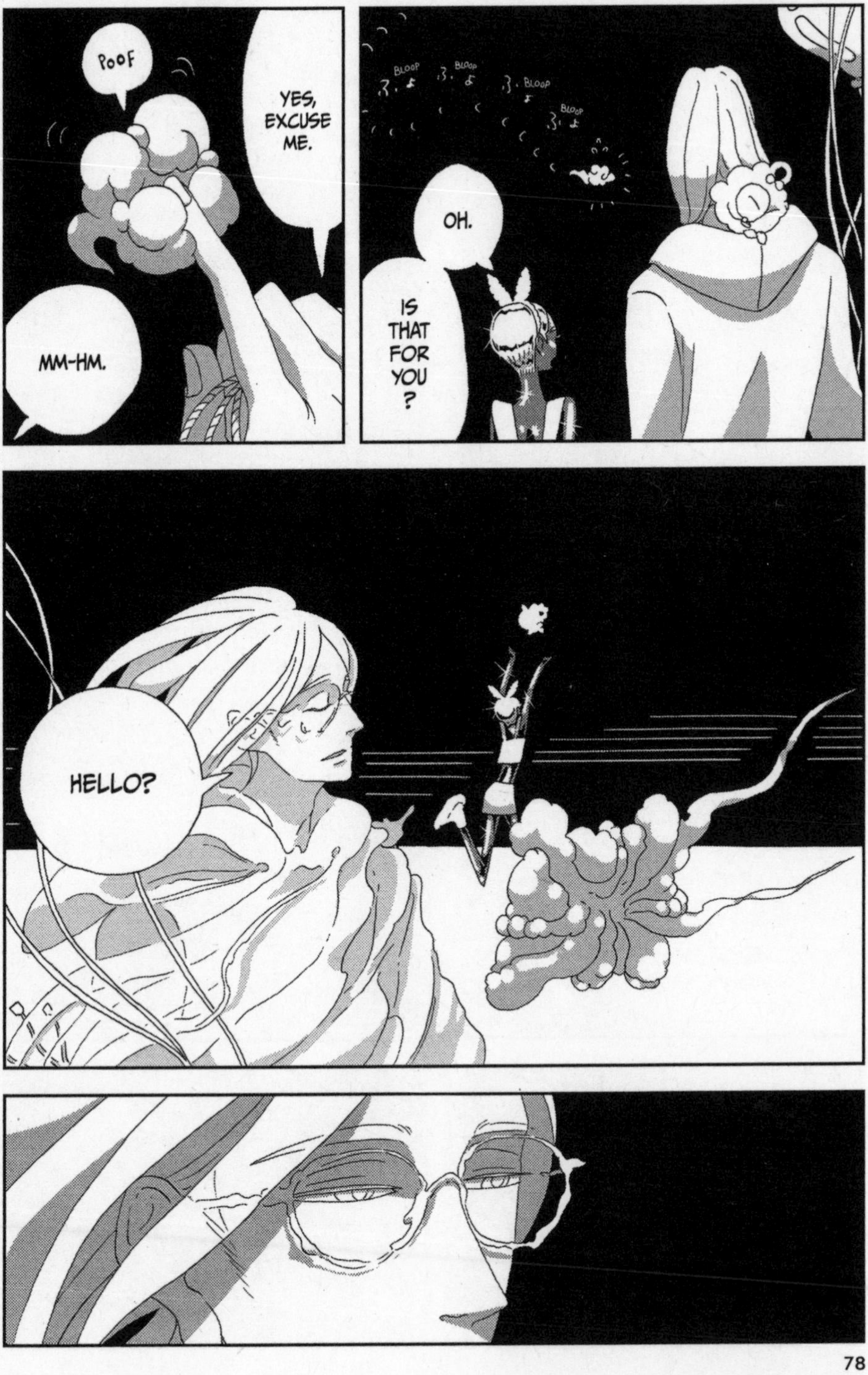
BLOOP
BLOOP
BLOOP
BLOOP
OH.
IS THAT FOR YOU?
YES, EXCUSE ME.
POOF
MM-HM.
HELLO?

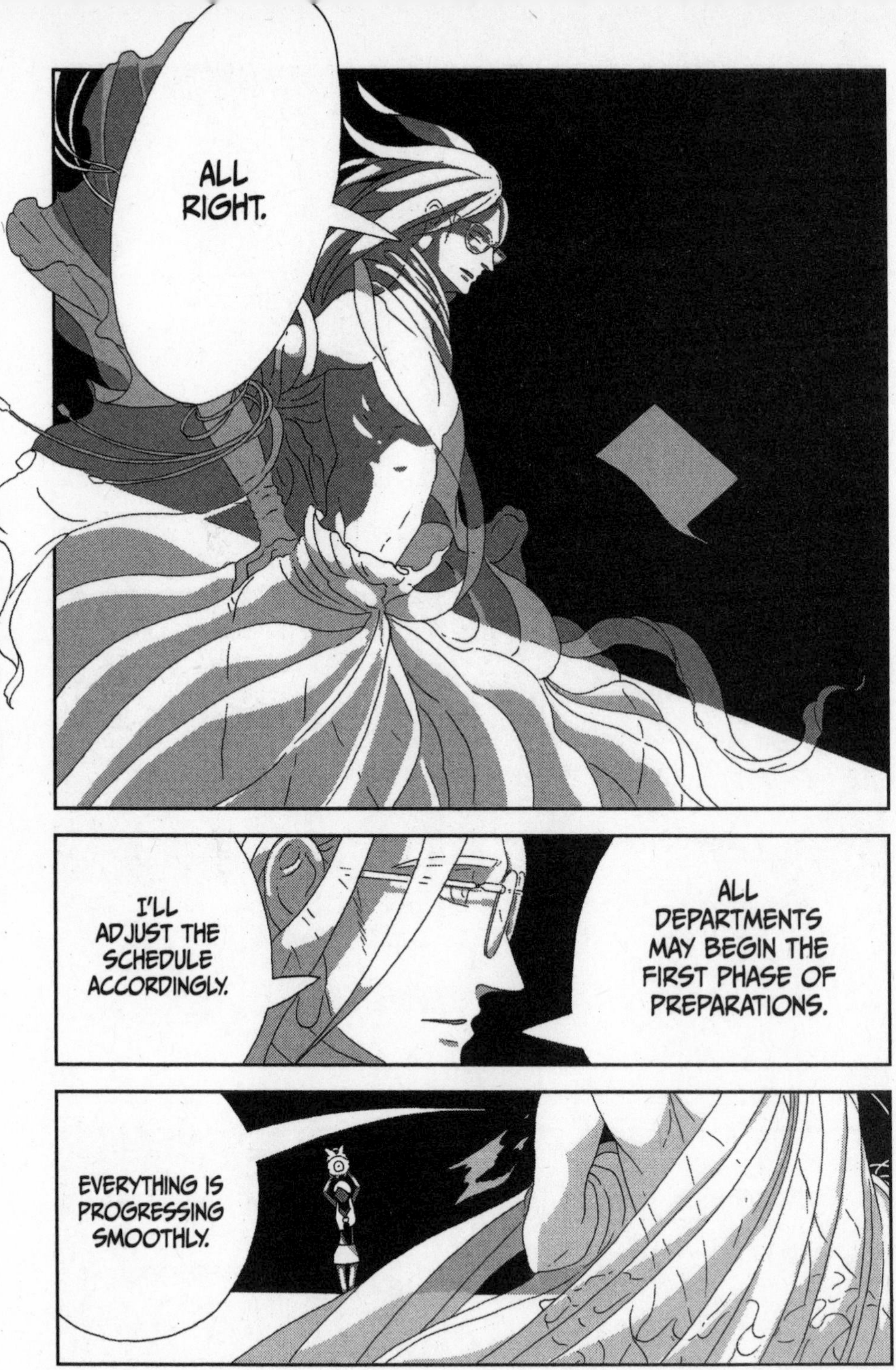
ALL RIGHT.
ALL DEPARTMENTS MAY BEGIN THE FIRST PHASE OF PREPARATIONS.
I'LL ADJUST THE SCHEDULE ACCORDINGLY.
EVERYTHING IS PROGRESSING SMOOTHLY.

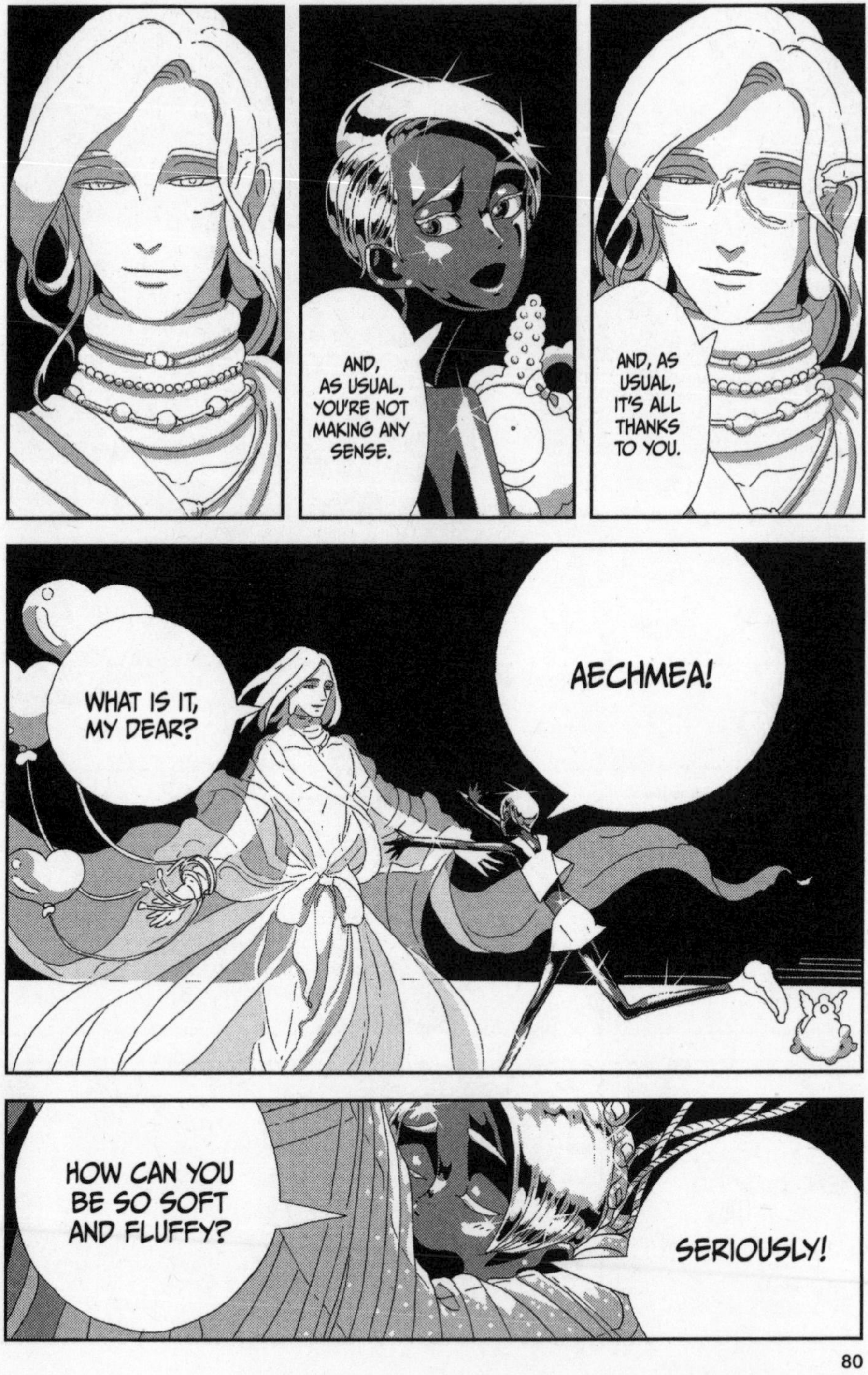
AND, AS USUAL, IT'S ALL THANKS TO YOU.
AND, AS USUAL, YOU'RE NOT MAKING ANY SENSE.
AECHMEA!
WHAT IS IT, MY DEAR?
SERIOUSLY!
HOW CAN YOU BE SO SOFT AND FLUFFY?

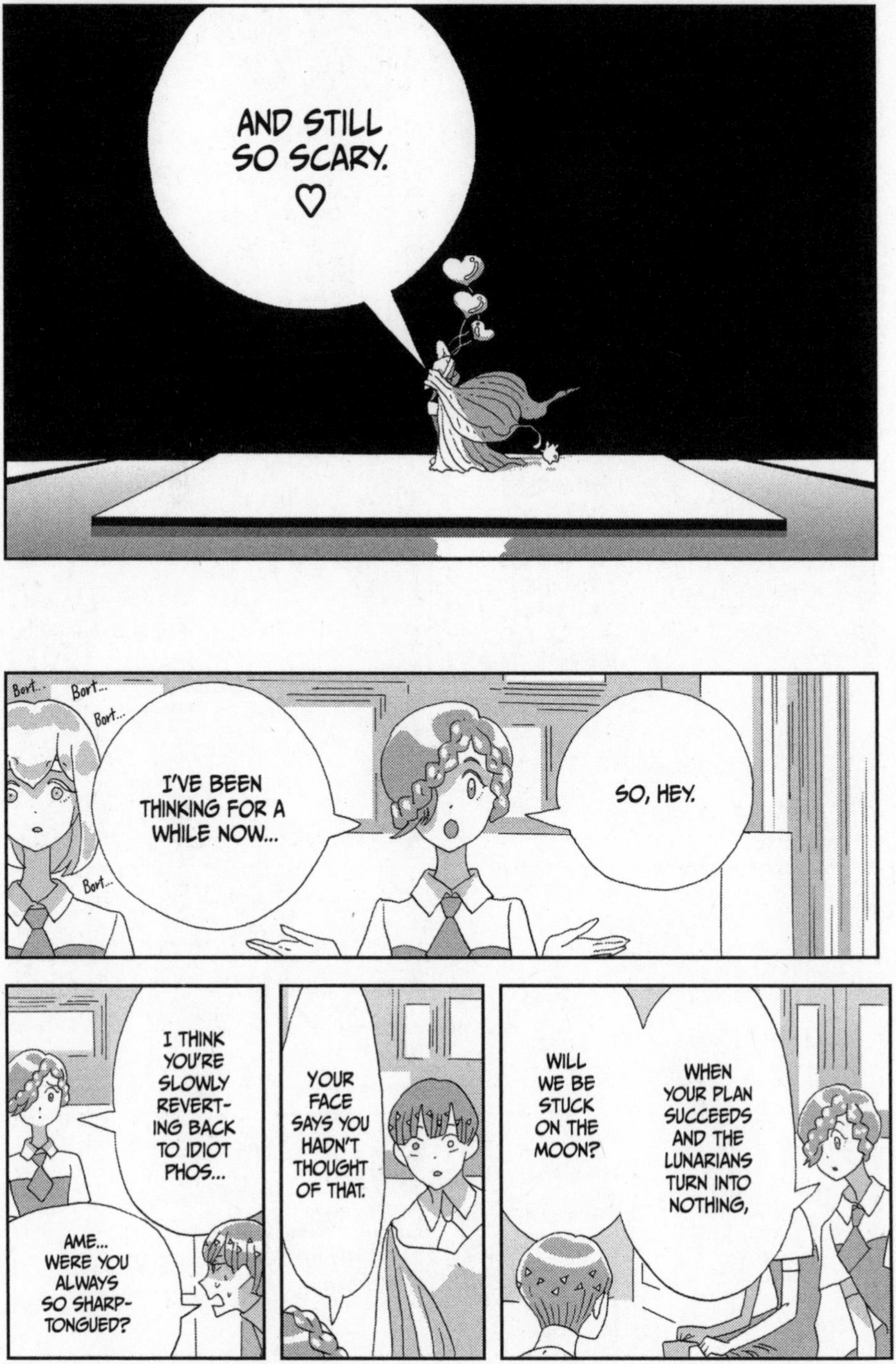
AND STILL SO SCARY. ♡
SO, HEY.
I'VE BEEN THINKING FOR A WHILE NOW...
Bort... Bort... Bort... Bort...
WHEN YOUR PLAN SUCCEEDS AND THE LUNARIANS TURN INTO NOTHING,
WILL WE BE STUCK ON THE MOON?
YOUR FACE SAYS YOU HADN'T THOUGHT OF THAT.
I THINK YOU'RE SLOWLY REVERT-ING BACK TO IDIOT PHOS...
AME... WERE YOU ALWAYS SO SHARP-TONGUED?

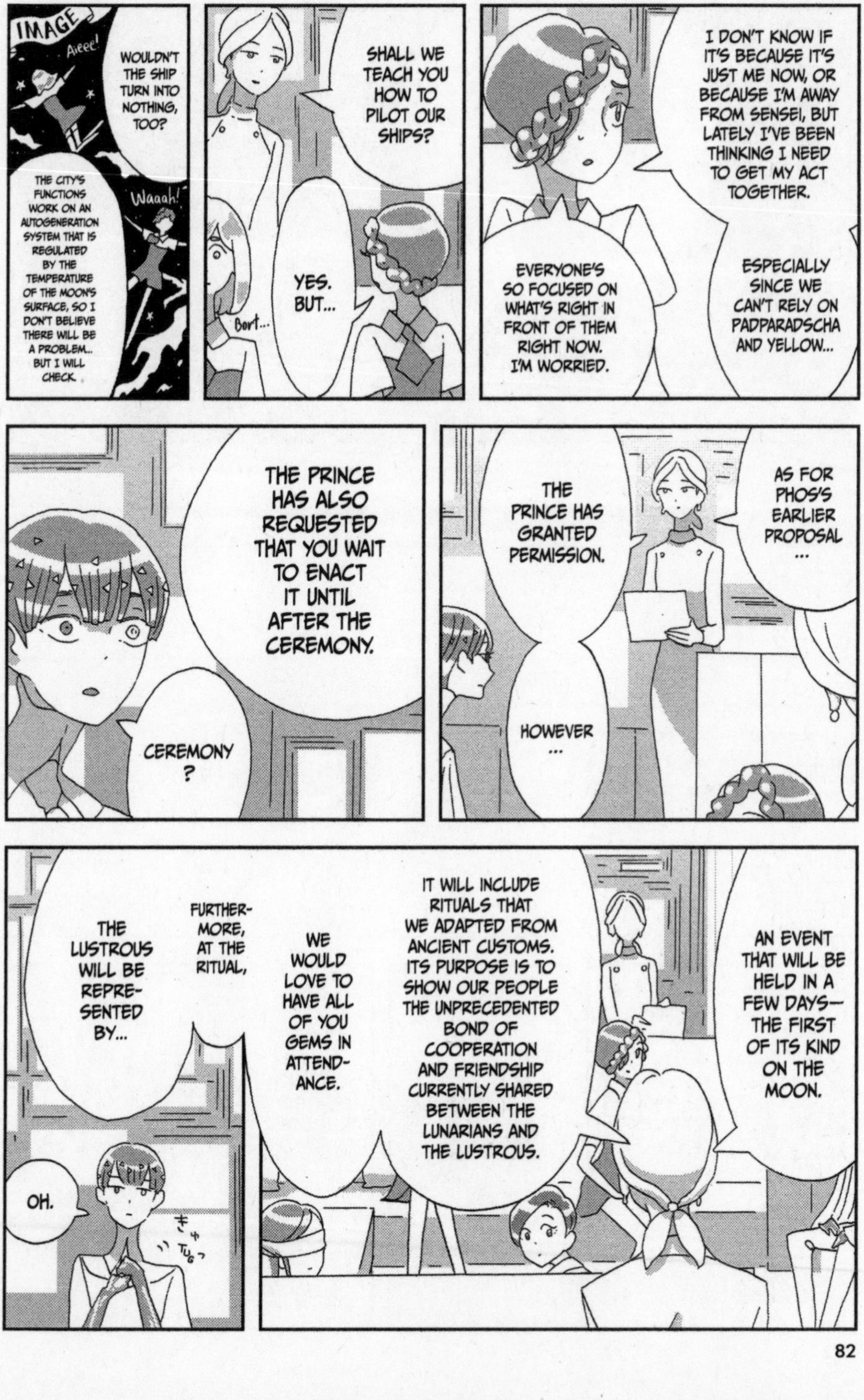
I DON'T KNOW IF IT'S BECAUSE IT'S JUST ME NOW, OR BECAUSE I'M AWAY FROM SENSEI, BUT LATELY I'VE BEEN THINKING I NEED TO GET MY ACT TOGETHER.
ESPECIALLY SINCE WE CAN'T RELY ON PADPARADSCHA AND YELLOW...
EVERYONE'S SO FOCUSED ON WHAT'S RIGHT IN FRONT OF THEM RIGHT NOW. I'M WORRIED.
SHALL WE TEACH YOU HOW TO PILOT OUR SHIPS?
YES. BUT...
Bort...
IMAGE
Aieee!
WOULDN'T THE SHIP TURN INTO NOTHING, TOO?
Waaah!
THE CITY'S FUNCTIONS WORK ON AN AUTOGENERATION SYSTEM THAT IS REGULATED BY THE TEMPERATURE OF THE MOON'S SURFACE, SO I DON'T BELIEVE THERE WILL BE A PROBLEM... BUT I WILL CHECK.
AS FOR PHOS'S EARLIER PROPOSAL ...
THE PRINCE HAS GRANTED PERMISSION.
HOWEVER ...
THE PRINCE HAS ALSO REQUESTED THAT YOU WAIT TO ENACT IT UNTIL AFTER THE CEREMONY.
CEREMONY ?
AN EVENT THAT WILL BE HELD IN A FEW DAYS— THE FIRST OF ITS KIND ON THE MOON.
IT WILL INCLUDE RITUALS THAT WE ADAPTED FROM ANCIENT CUSTOMS. ITS PURPOSE IS TO SHOW OUR PEOPLE THE UNPRECEDENTED BOND OF COOPERATION AND FRIENDSHIP CURRENTLY SHARED BETWEEN THE LUNARIANS AND THE LUSTROUS.
WE WOULD LOVE TO HAVE ALL OF YOU GEMS IN ATTENDANCE.
FURTHERMORE, AT THE RITUAL,
THE LUSTROUS WILL BE REPRESENTED BY...
OH.
TUG

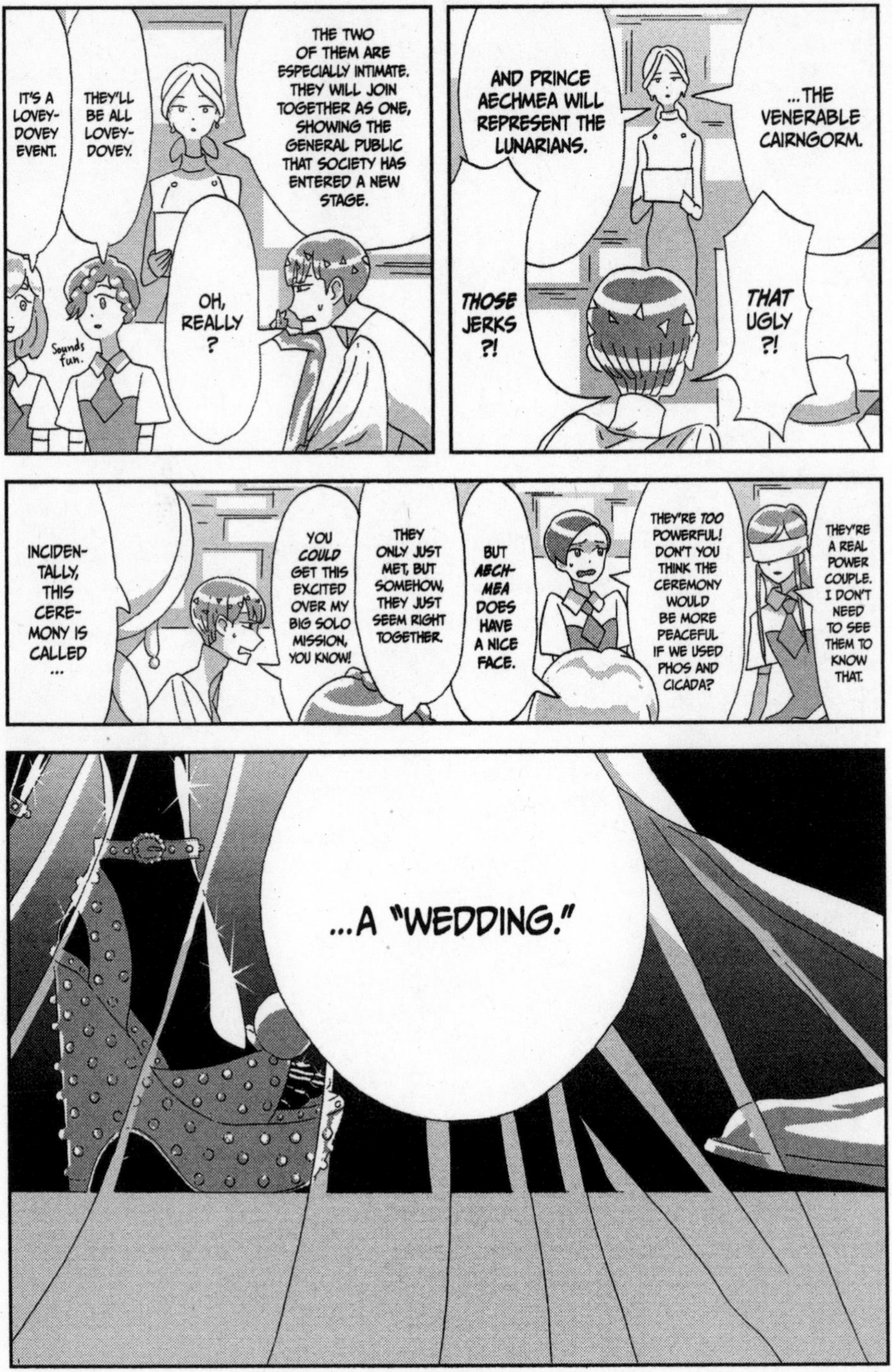
...THE VENERABLE CAIRNGORM.
AND PRINCE AECHMEA WILL REPRESENT THE LUNARIANS.
THAT UGLY ?!
THOSE JERKS ?!
THE TWO OF THEM ARE ESPECIALLY INTIMATE. THEY WILL JOIN TOGETHER AS ONE, SHOWING THE GENERAL PUBLIC THAT SOCIETY HAS ENTERED A NEW STAGE.
OH, REALLY ?
THEY'LL BE ALL LOVEY-DOVEY.
IT'S A LOVEY-DOVEY EVENT.
Sounds fun.
THEY'RE A REAL POWER COUPLE. I DON'T NEED TO SEE THEM TO KNOW THAT.
THEY'RE *TOO* POWERFUL! DON'T YOU THINK THE CEREMONY WOULD BE MORE PEACEFUL IF WE USED PHOS AND CICADA?
BUT *AECHMEA* DOES HAVE A NICE FACE.
THEY ONLY JUST MET, BUT SOMEHOW, THEY JUST SEEM RIGHT TOGETHER.
YOU *COULD* GET THIS EXCITED OVER MY BIG SOLO MISSION, YOU KNOW!
INCIDENTALLY, THIS CEREMONY IS CALLED ...
...A "WEDDING."

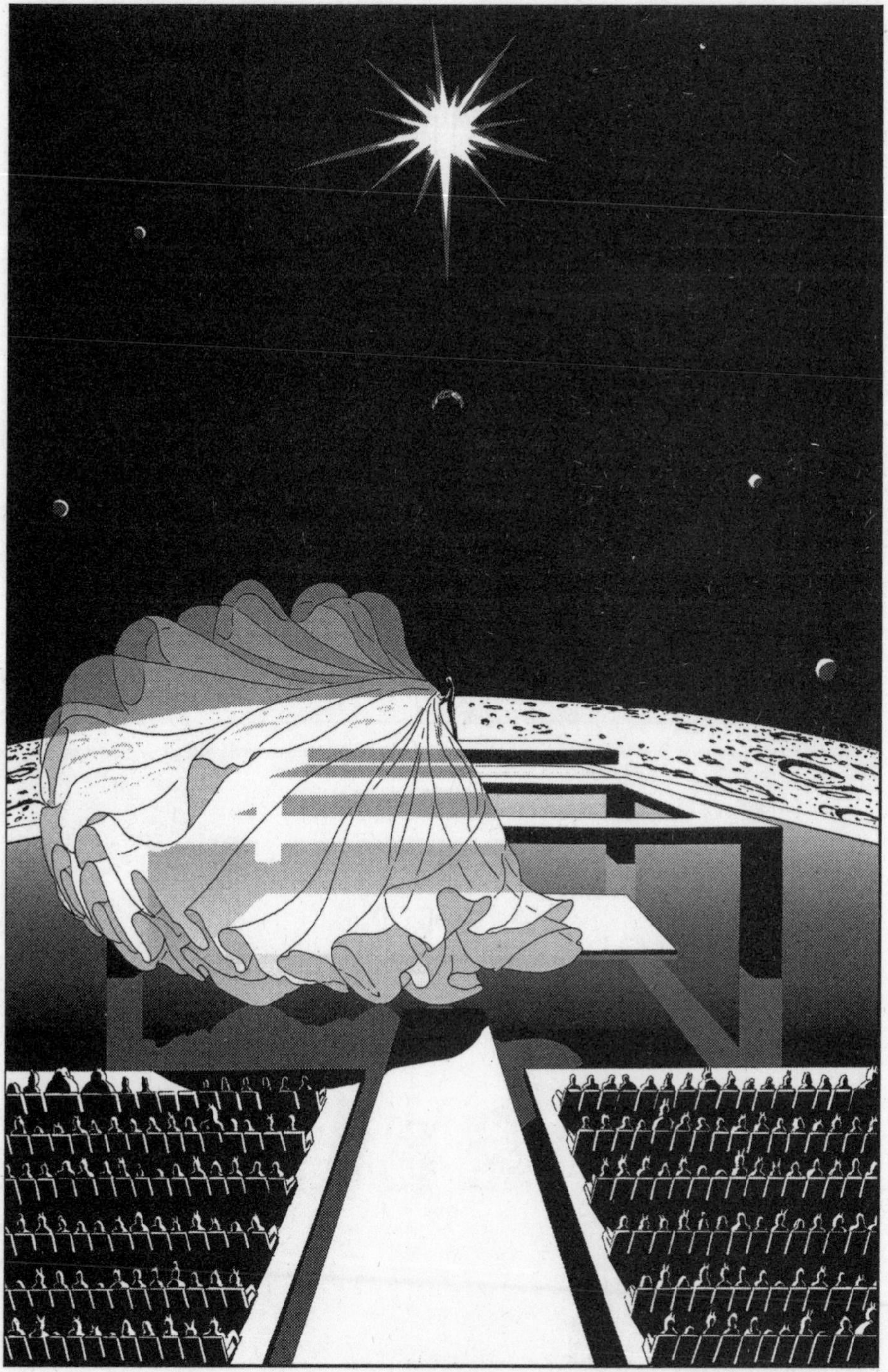

CHAPTER 74: Ceremony END

CHAPTER 75: Wish

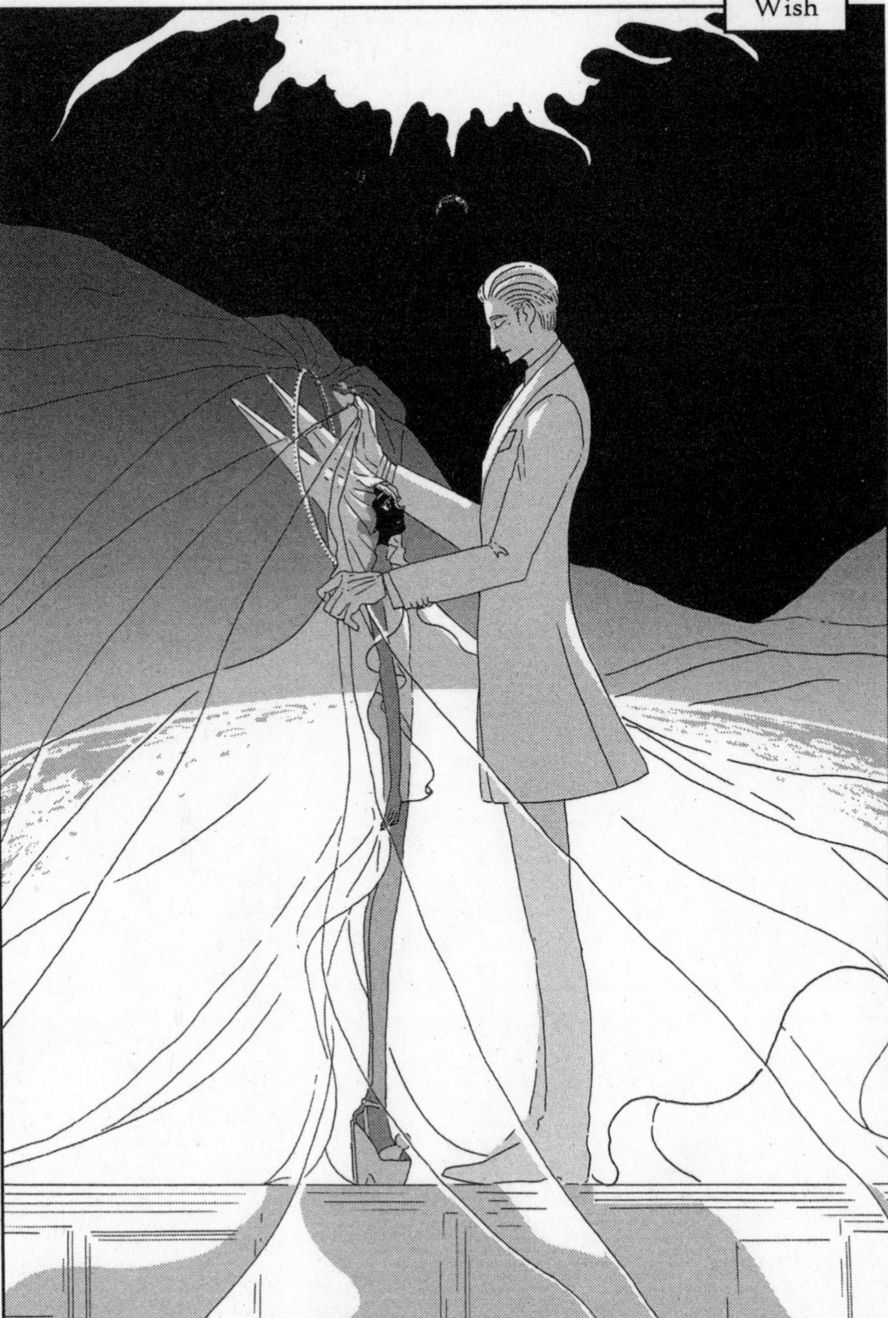

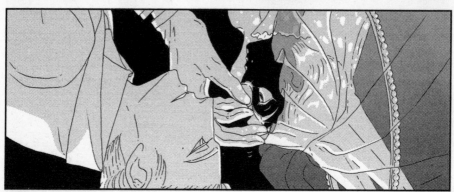

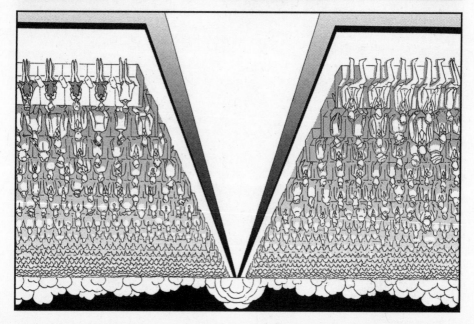

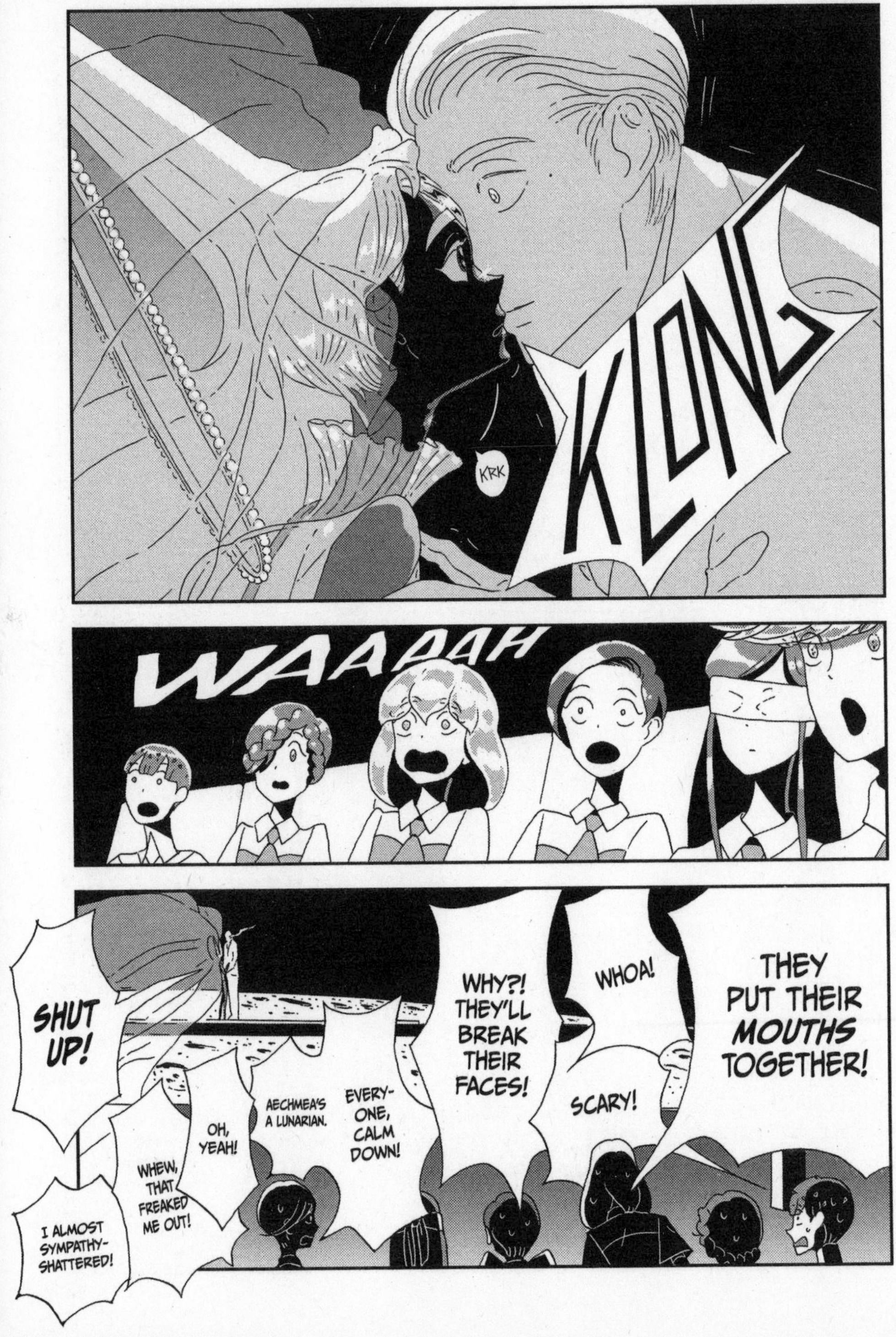
KLONG
KRK
WAAAAH
THEY PUT THEIR MOUTHS TOGETHER!
WHOA!
SCARY!
WHY?! THEY'LL BREAK THEIR FACES!
EVERY-ONE, CALM DOWN!
AECHMEA'S A LUNARIAN.
OH, YEAH!
WHEW, THAT FREAKED ME OUT!
SHUT UP!
I ALMOST SYMPATHY-SHATTERED!

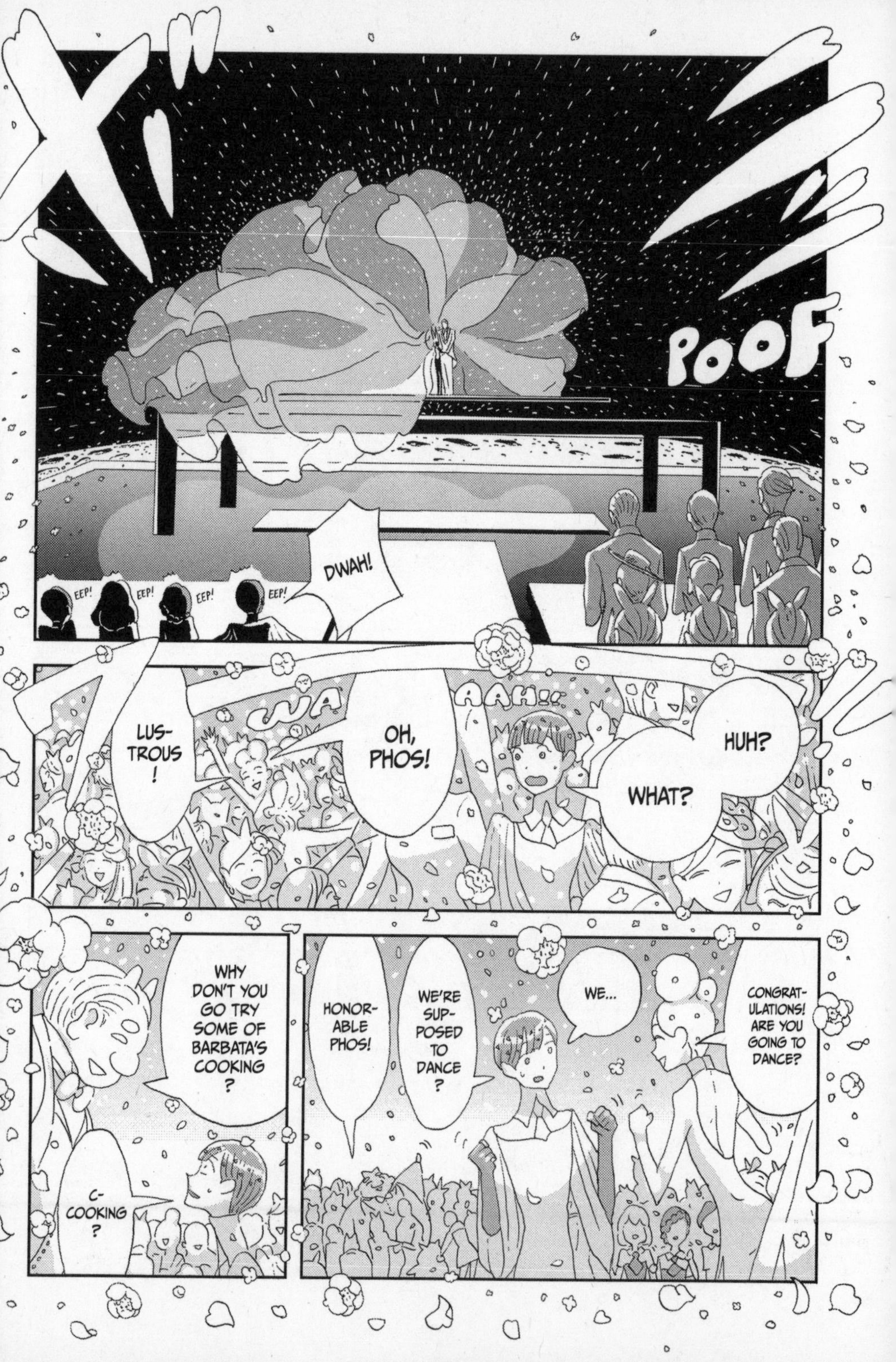
POOF
X"
DWAH!
EEP!
EEP!
EEP!
EEP!
HUH?
WHAT?
OH, PHOS!
WAAAH!!
LUS-TROUS!
CONGRAT-ULATIONS! ARE YOU GOING TO DANCE?
WE...
WE'RE SUP-POSED TO DANCE?
HONOR-ABLE PHOS!
WHY DON'T YOU GO TRY SOME OF BARBATA'S COOKING?
C-COOKING?

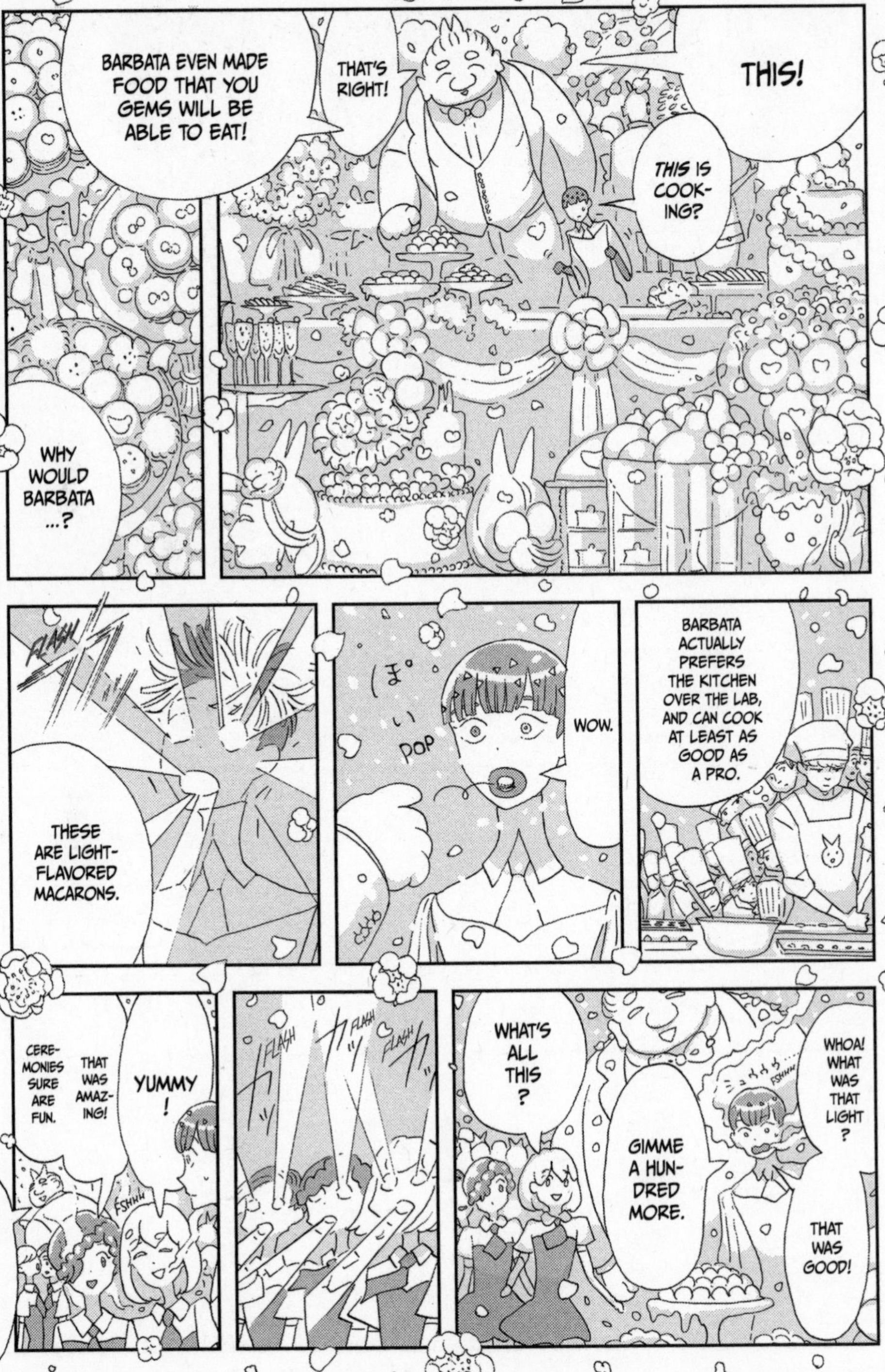
THIS!
THIS IS COOKING?
THAT'S RIGHT!
BARBATA EVEN MADE FOOD THAT YOU GEMS WILL BE ABLE TO EAT!
WHY WOULD BARBATA ...?
BARBATA ACTUALLY PREFERS THE KITCHEN OVER THE LAB, AND CAN COOK AT LEAST AS GOOD AS A PRO.
WOW.
POP
THESE ARE LIGHT-FLAVORED MACARONS.
FLASH
WHOA! WHAT WAS THAT LIGHT?
FSHHH
THAT WAS GOOD!
GIMME A HUNDRED MORE.
WHAT'S ALL THIS?
FLASH
FLASH
FLASH
YUMMY!
THAT WAS AMAZING!
CEREMONIES SURE ARE FUN.
FSHHH
THERE'S A CONCERT STARTING OVER THERE! LET'S GO!

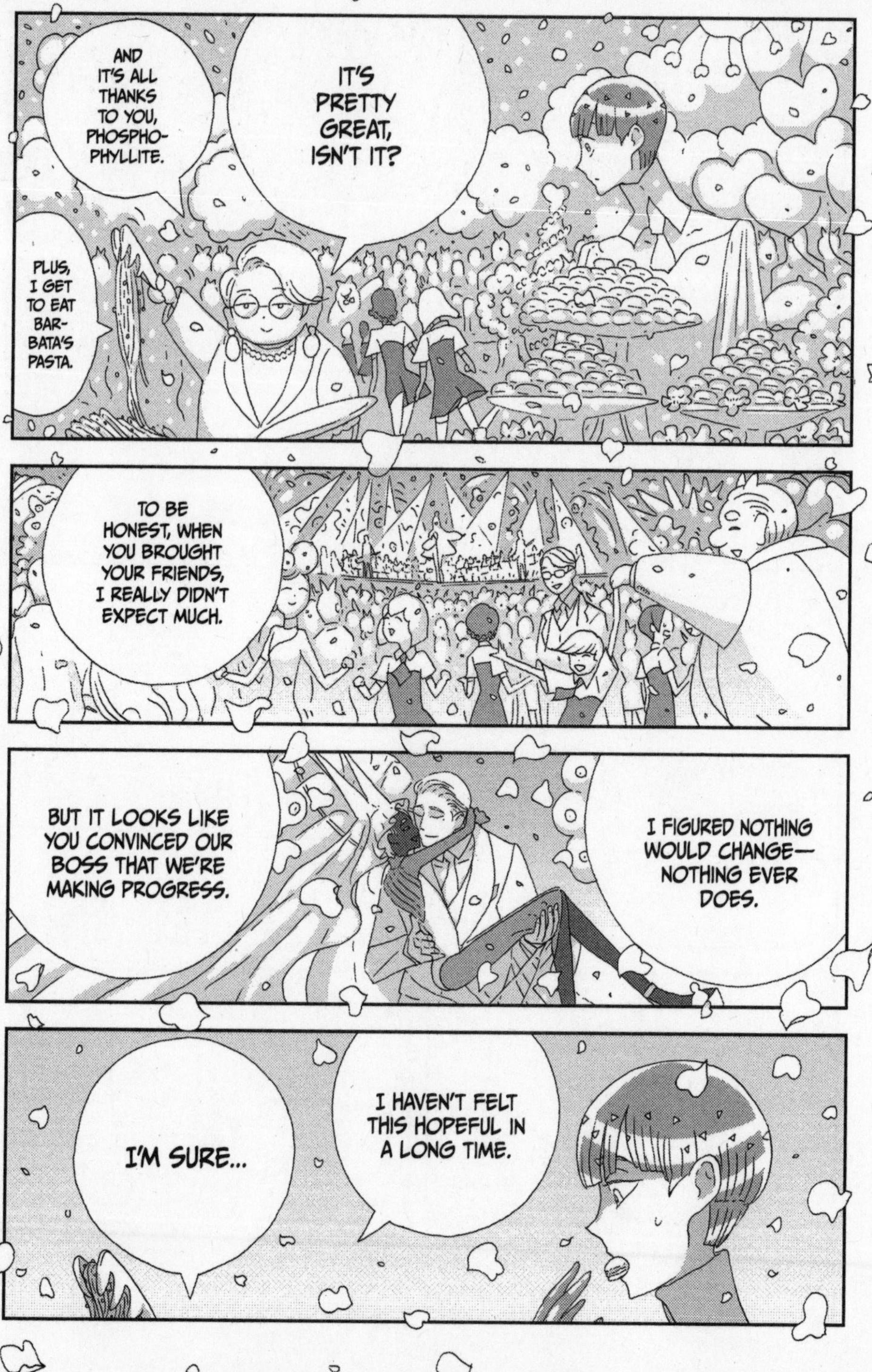
IT'S PRETTY GREAT, ISN'T IT?
AND IT'S ALL THANKS TO YOU, PHOSPHO-PHYLLITE.
PLUS, I GET TO EAT BAR-BATA'S PASTA.
TO BE HONEST, WHEN YOU BROUGHT YOUR FRIENDS, I REALLY DIDN'T EXPECT MUCH.
I FIGURED NOTHING WOULD CHANGE—NOTHING EVER DOES.
BUT IT LOOKS LIKE YOU CONVINCED OUR BOSS THAT WE'RE MAKING PROGRESS.
I HAVEN'T FELT THIS HOPEFUL IN A LONG TIME.
I'M SURE...

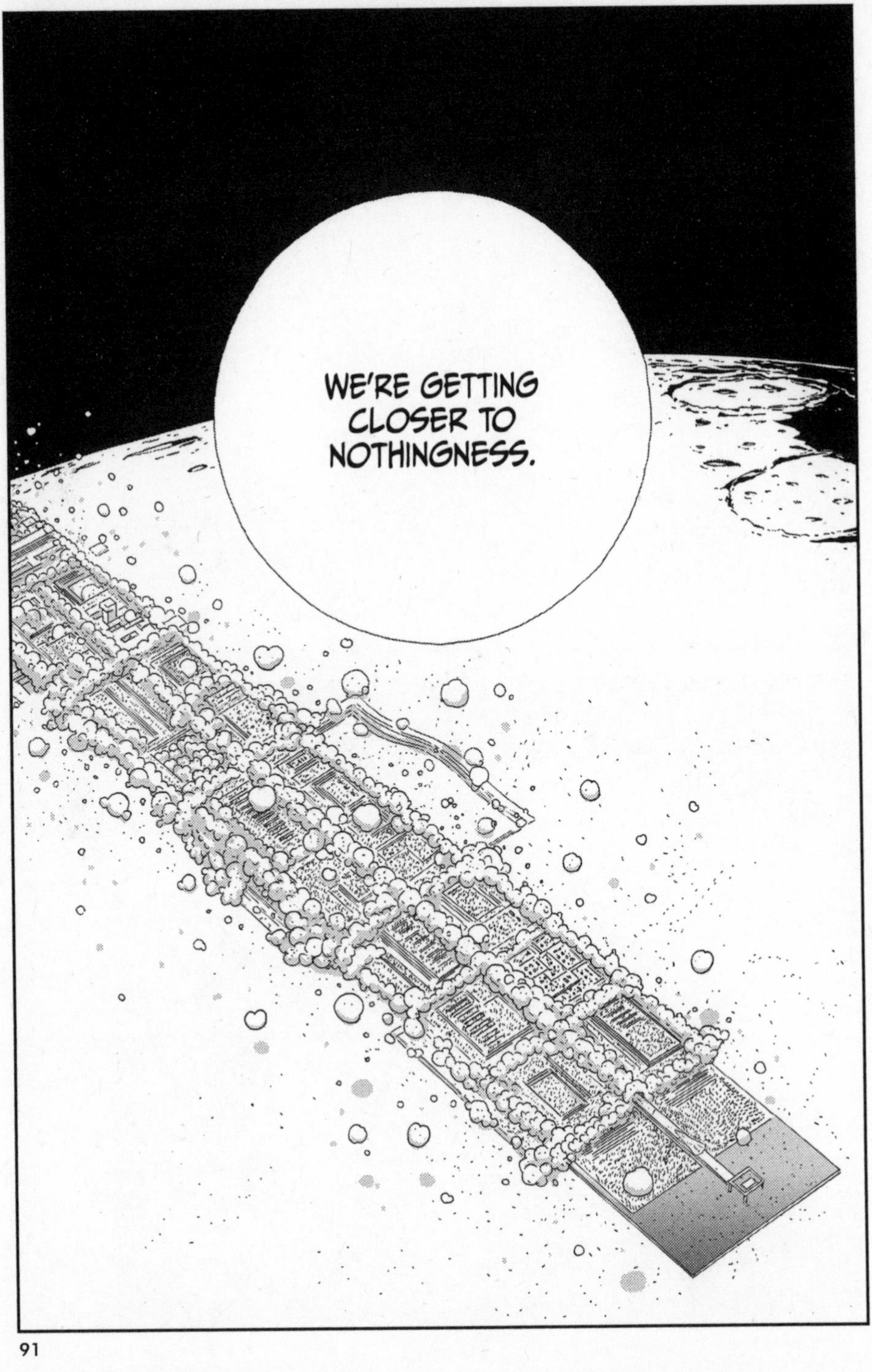
WE'RE GETTING CLOSER TO NOTHINGNESS.

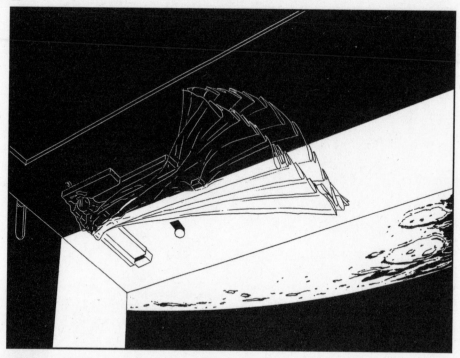

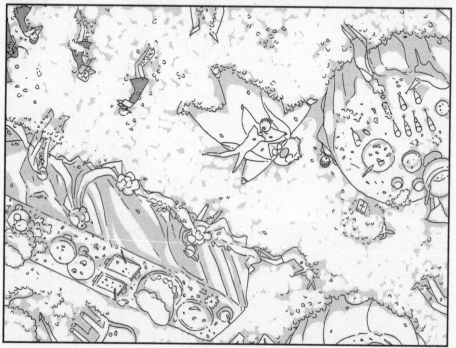

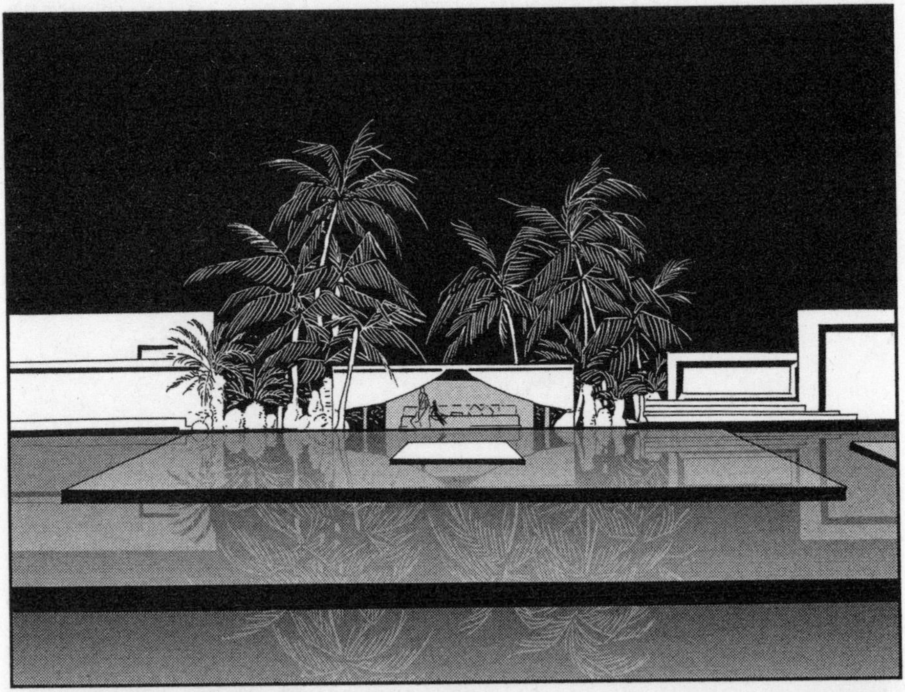

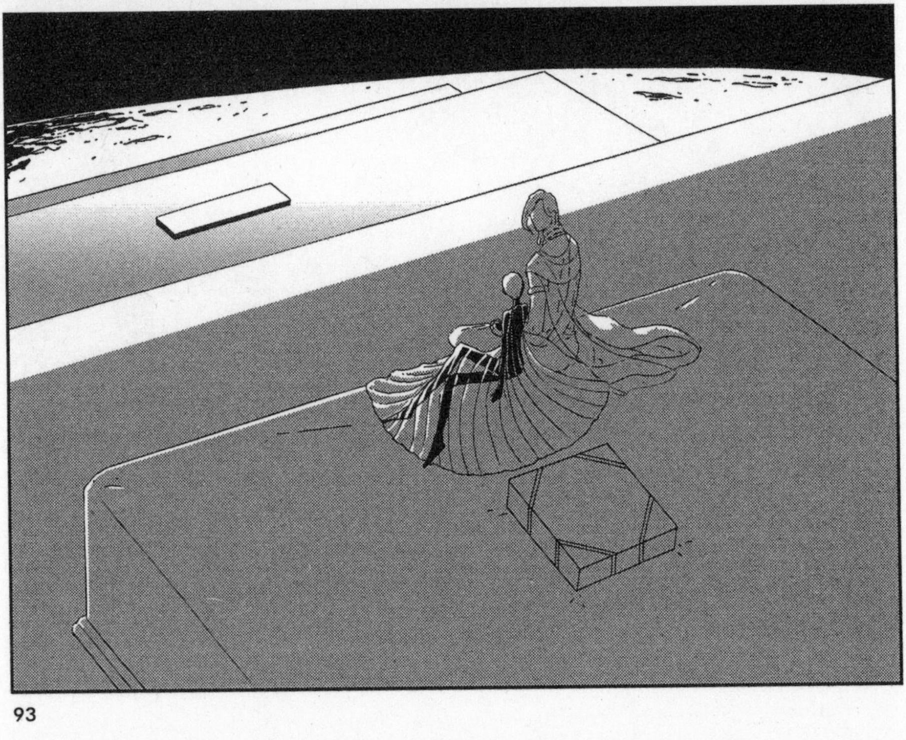

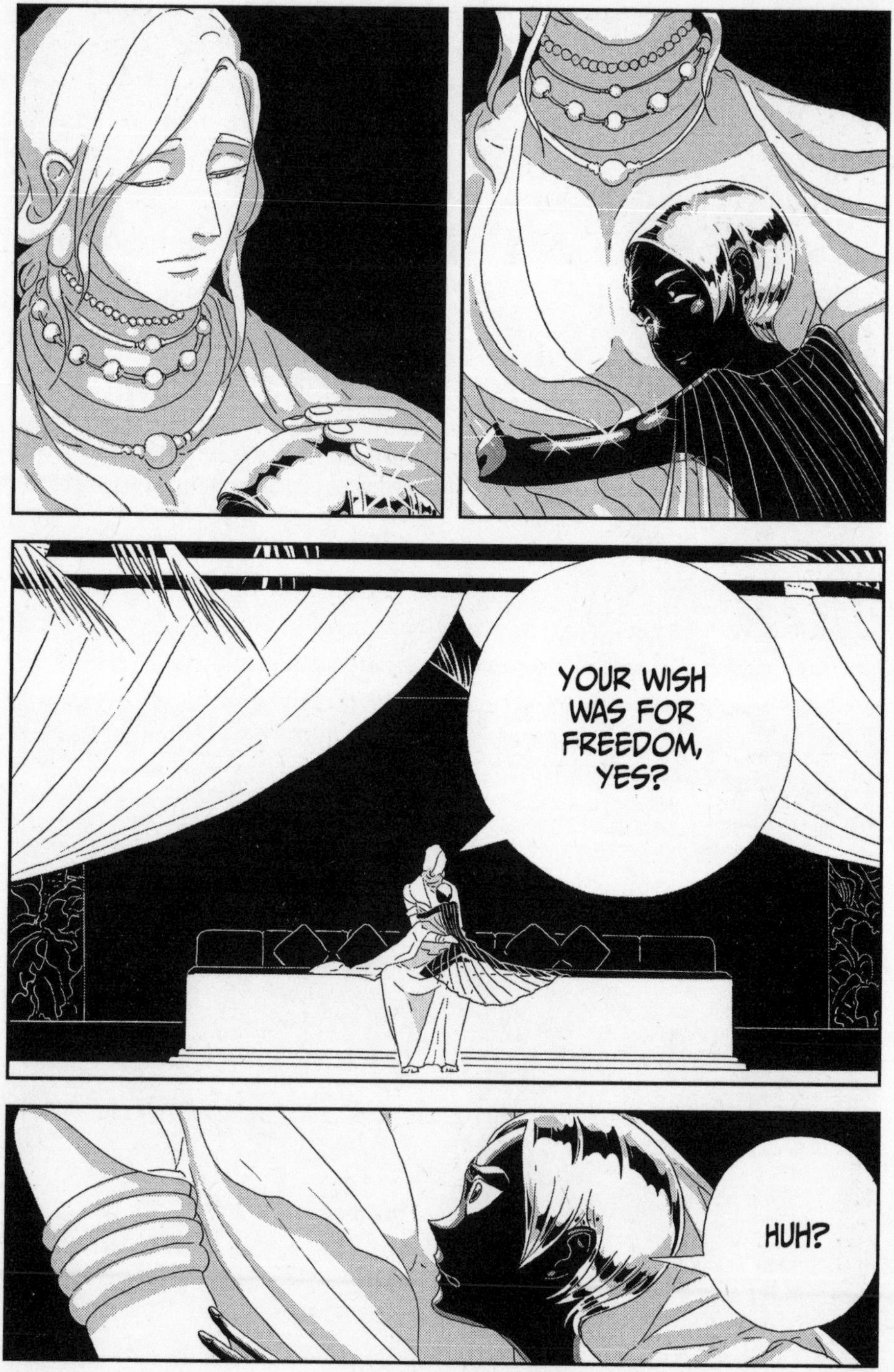
YOUR WISH WAS FOR FREEDOM, YES?
HUH?

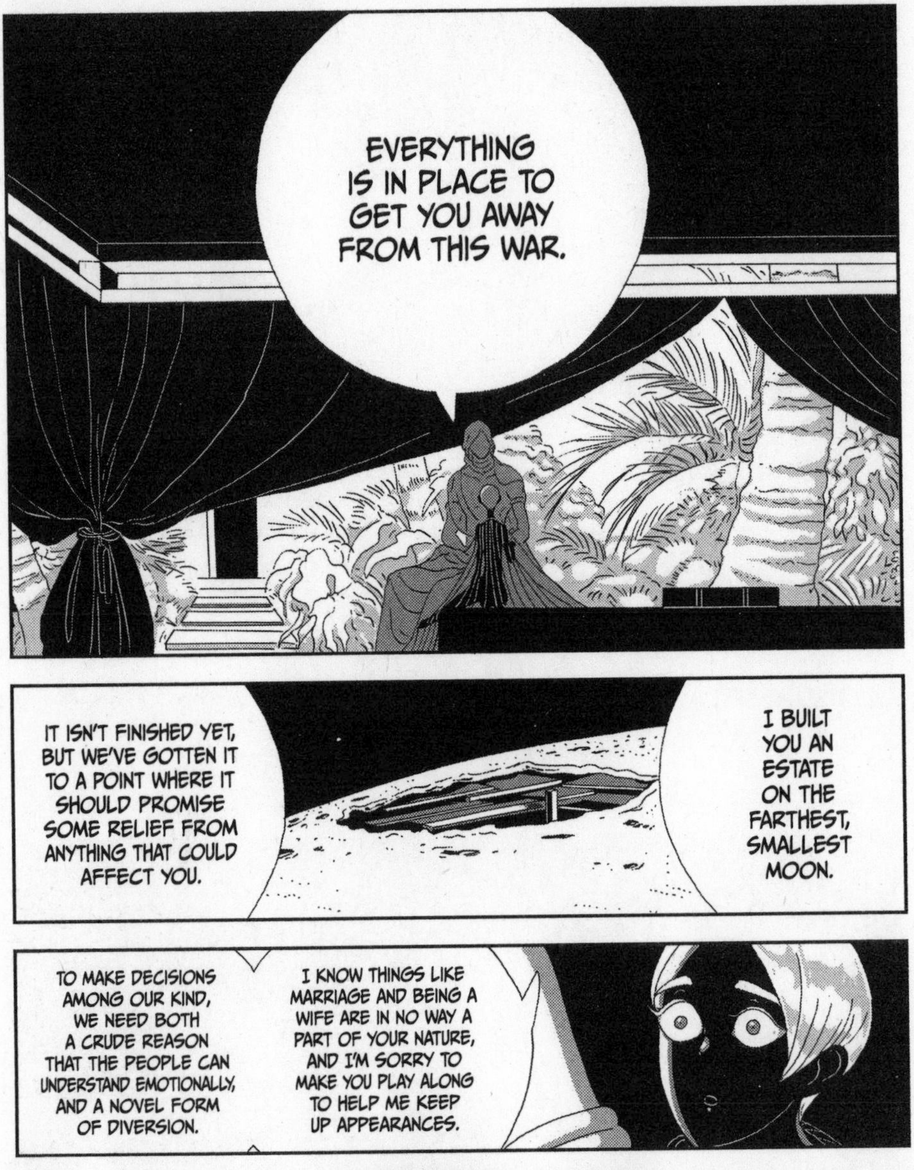
EVERYTHING IS IN PLACE TO GET YOU AWAY FROM THIS WAR.
I BUILT YOU AN ESTATE ON THE FARTHEST, SMALLEST MOON.
IT ISN'T FINISHED YET, BUT WE'VE GOTTEN IT TO A POINT WHERE IT SHOULD PROMISE SOME RELIEF FROM ANYTHING THAT COULD AFFECT YOU.
I KNOW THINGS LIKE MARRIAGE AND BEING A WIFE ARE IN NO WAY A PART OF YOUR NATURE, AND I'M SORRY TO MAKE YOU PLAY ALONG TO HELP ME KEEP UP APPEARANCES.
TO MAKE DECISIONS AMONG OUR KIND, WE NEED BOTH A CRUDE REASON THAT THE PEOPLE CAN UNDERSTAND EMOTIONALLY, AND A NOVEL FORM OF DIVERSION.
YOUR NEW ESTATE WILL BE A TEMPORARY HOME UNTIL THE DAY YOU GAIN TRUE FREEDOM.
IT IS THE SAFEST FORM OF FREEDOM I CAN PROVIDE IN THIS WORLD.

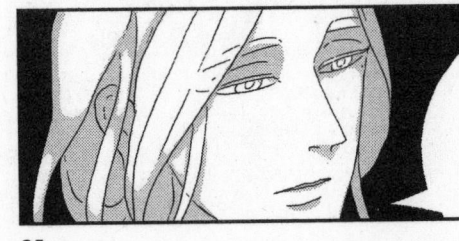

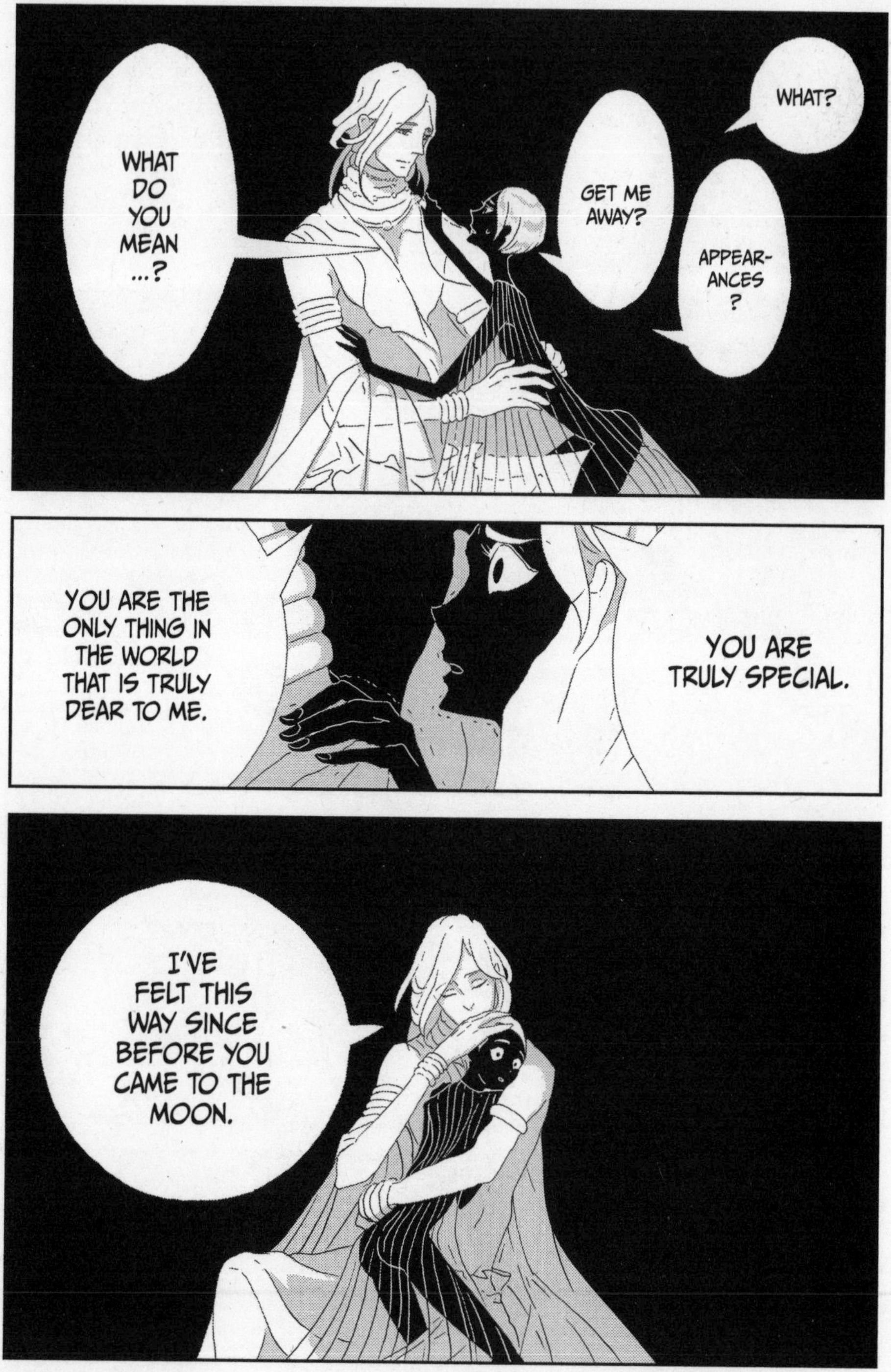
WHAT?
GET ME AWAY?
APPEARANCES?
WHAT DO YOU MEAN ...?
YOU ARE TRULY SPECIAL.
YOU ARE THE ONLY THING IN THE WORLD THAT IS TRULY DEAR TO ME.
I'VE FELT THIS WAY SINCE BEFORE YOU CAME TO THE MOON.

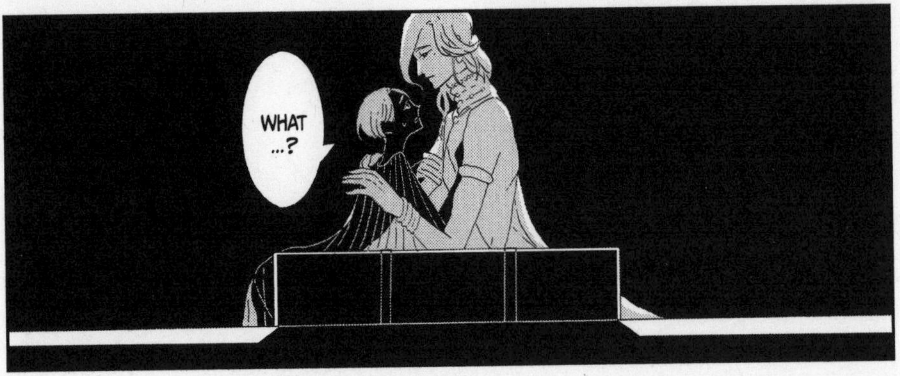
WHAT ...?

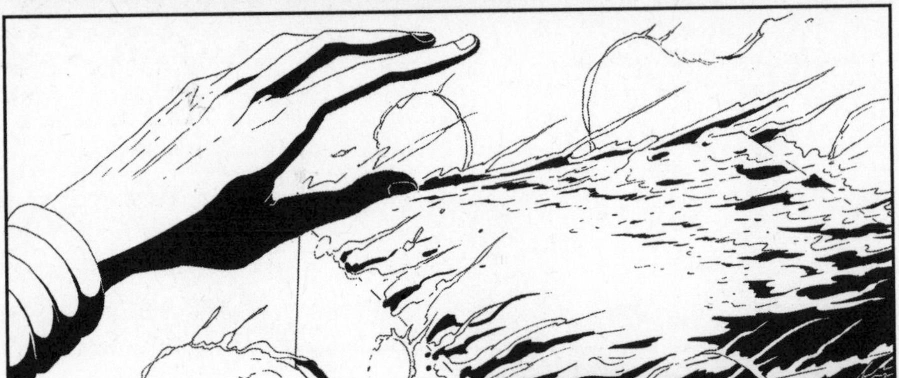

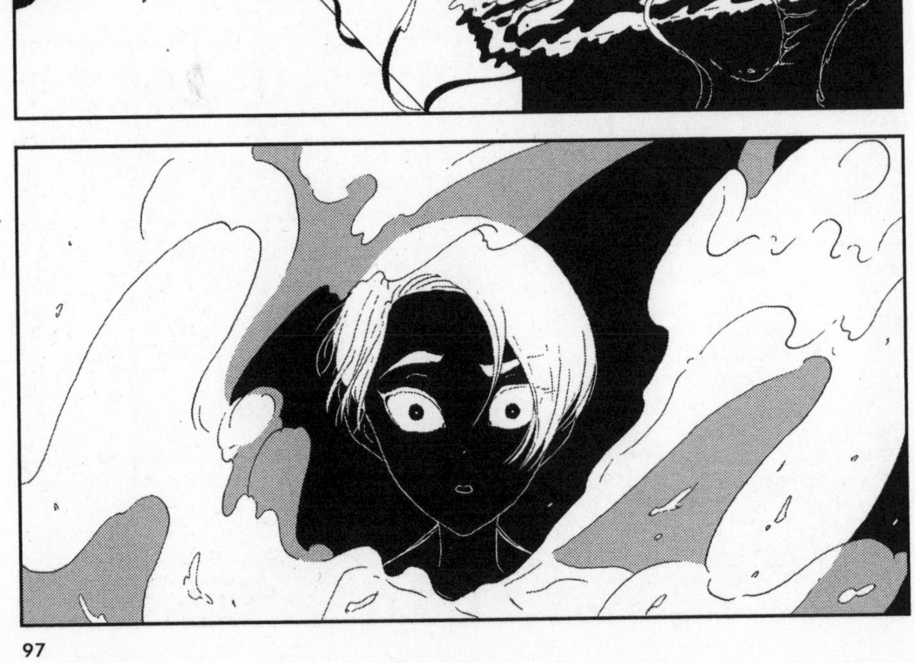

THIS IS YOUR LEFT ARM.
IT'S NOT A REPLICA. IT'S THE ARM WE TOOK 102 YEARS AGO.
DON'T WORRY. I'VE REMOVED THE OUTER LAYER OF QUARTZ.
I'LL PUT IT BACK ON FOR YOU.

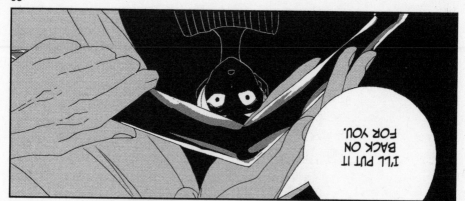

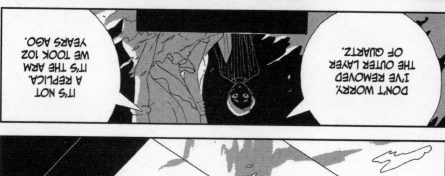

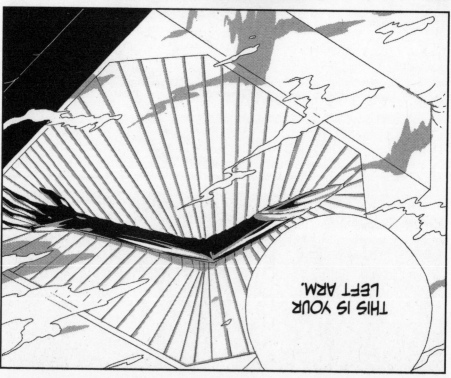

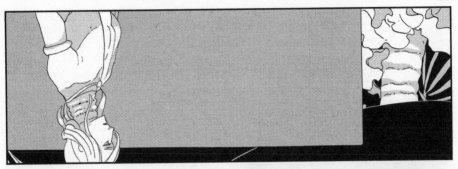

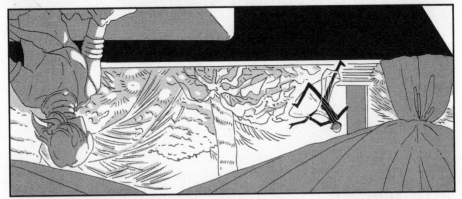

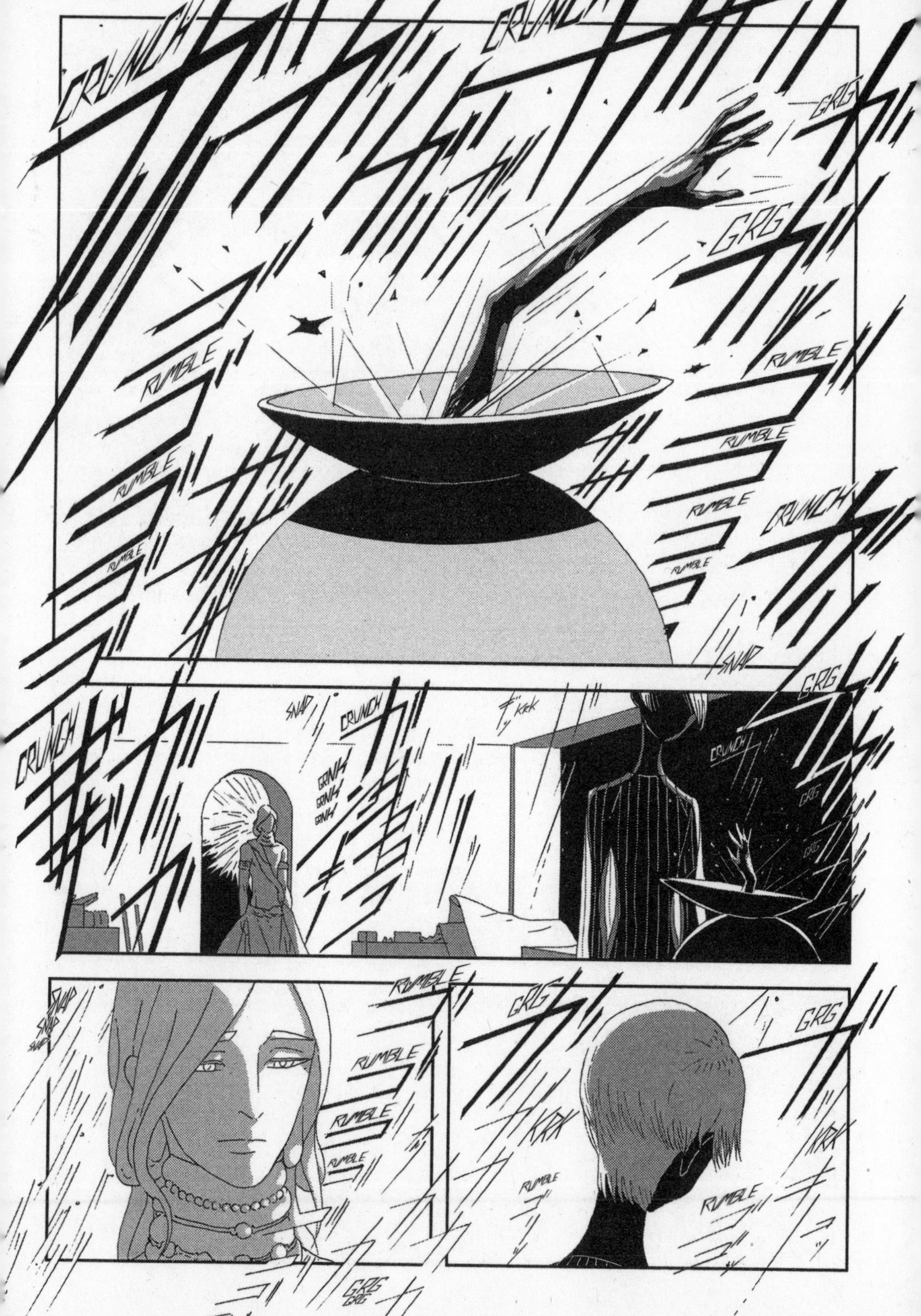
CRUNCH
CRUNCH
GRG
GRG
RUMBLE
RUMBLE
RUMBLE
RUMBLE
RUMBLE
RUMBLE
CRUNCH
SNAP
GRG
CRUNCH
GRG
GRG
KRK
CRUNCH
SNAP
GRNK GRNK GRNK
CRUNCH
GRG
KRK
RUMBLE
GRG
KRK
RUMBLE
RUMBLE
RUMBLE
RUMBLE
SNAP SNAP SNAP
GRG GRG

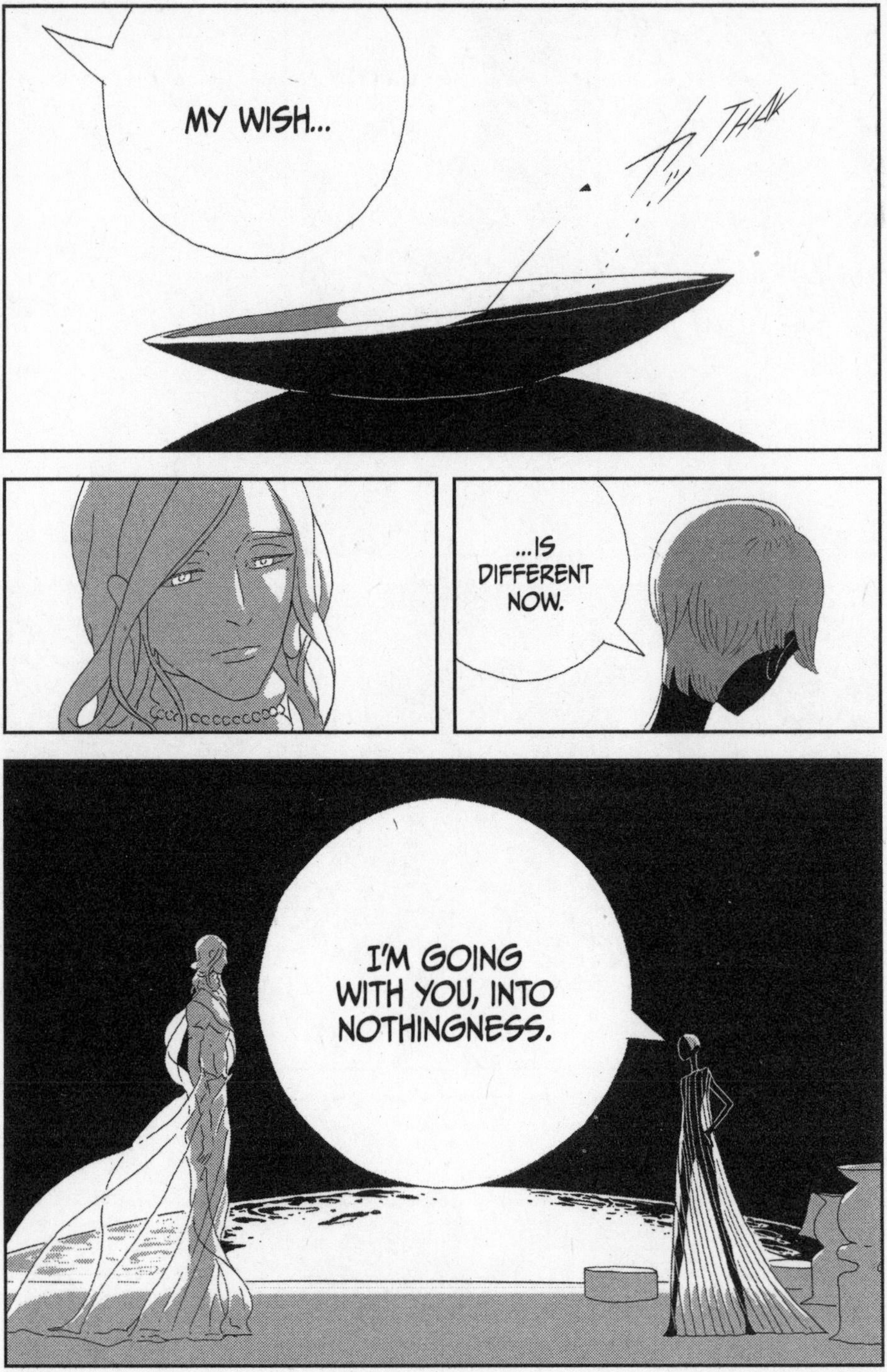
MY WISH...
THAK
...IS DIFFERENT NOW.
I'M GOING WITH YOU, INTO NOTHINGNESS.

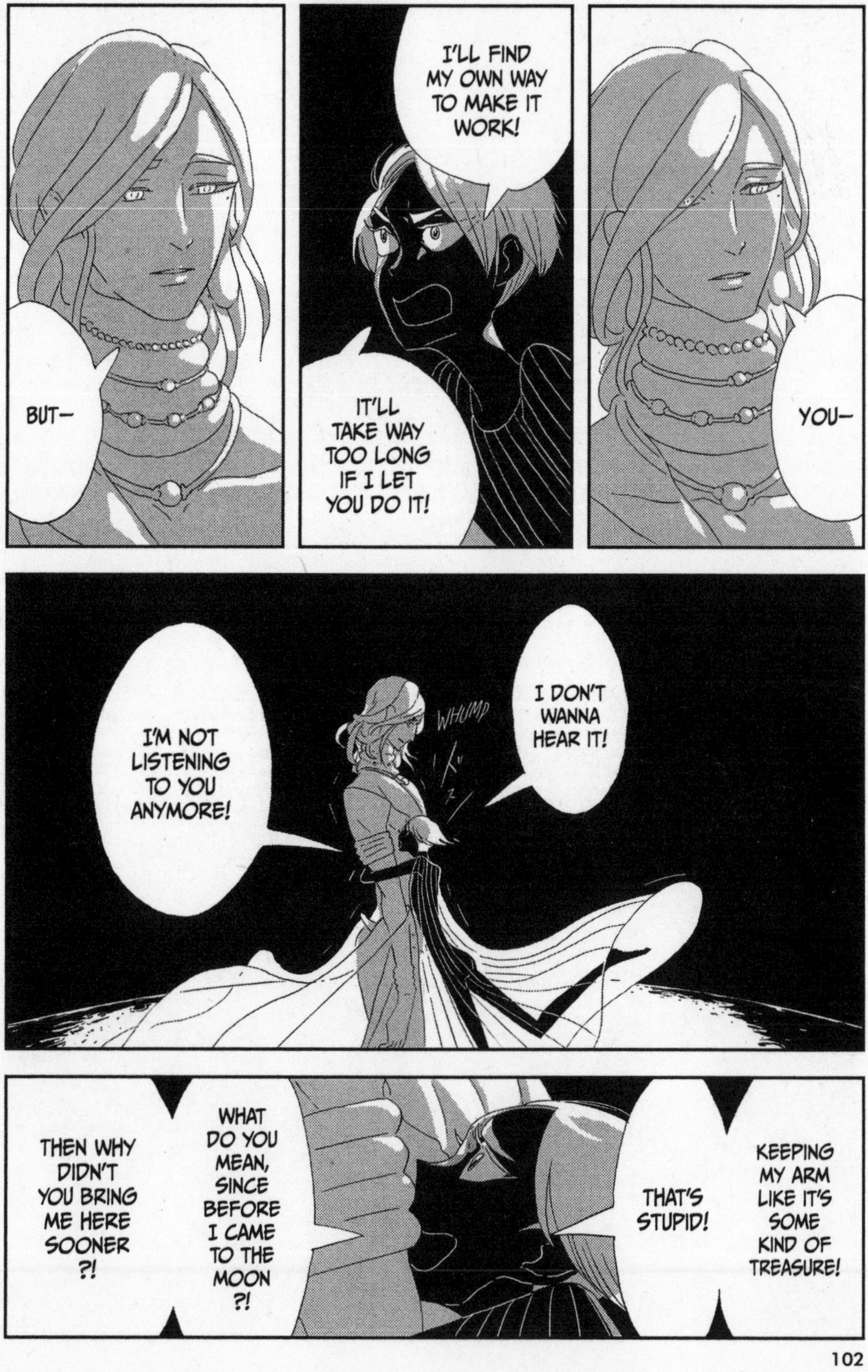
YOU—
I'LL FIND MY OWN WAY TO MAKE IT WORK!
IT'LL TAKE WAY TOO LONG IF I LET YOU DO IT!
BUT—
I DON'T WANNA HEAR IT!
WHUMP
I'M NOT LISTENING TO YOU ANYMORE!
KEEPING MY ARM LIKE IT'S SOME KIND OF TREASURE!
THAT'S STUPID!
WHAT DO YOU MEAN, SINCE BEFORE I CAME TO THE MOON ?!
THEN WHY DIDN'T YOU BRING ME HERE SOONER ?!

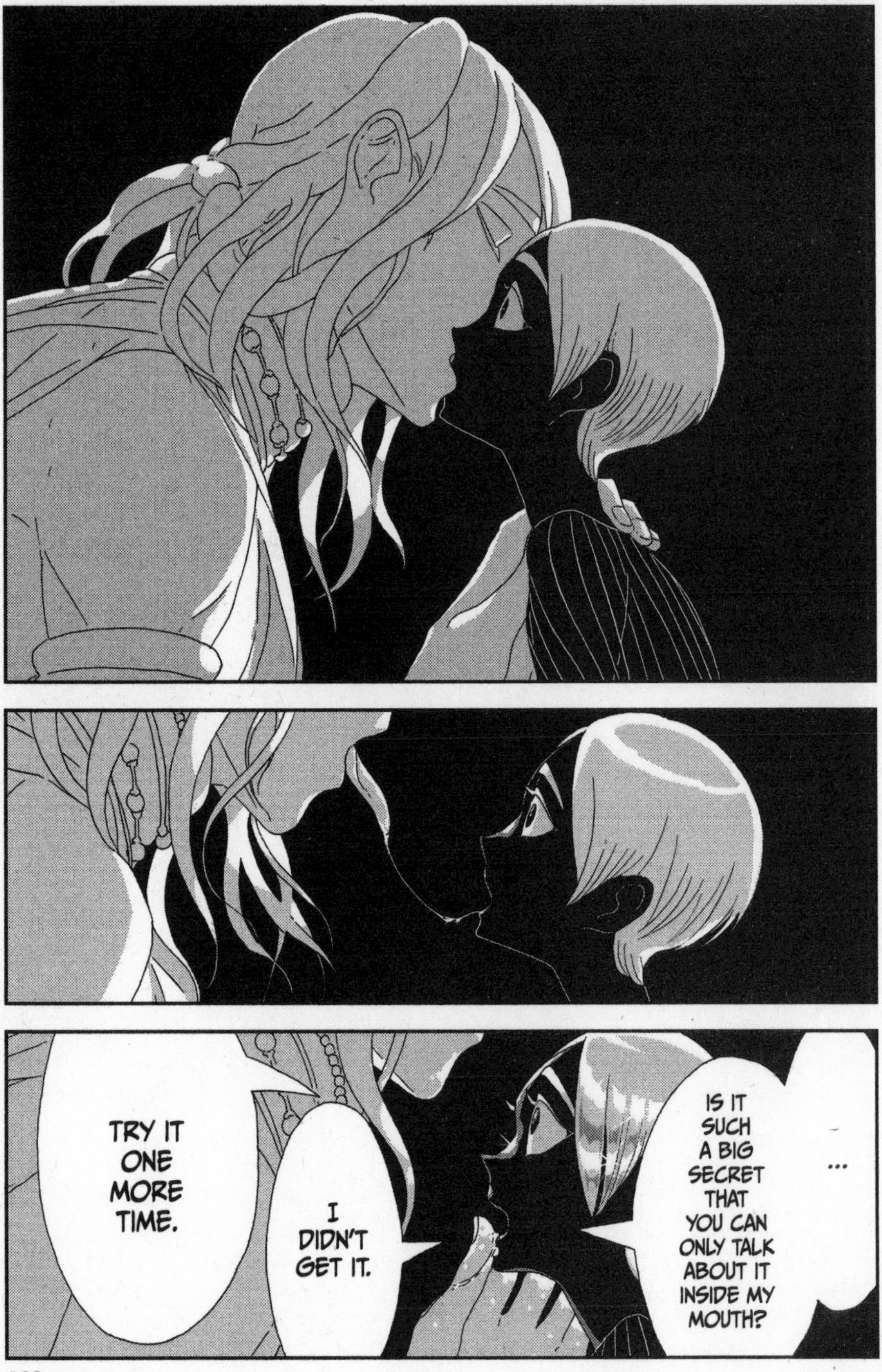
...
IS IT SUCH A BIG SECRET THAT YOU CAN ONLY TALK ABOUT IT INSIDE MY MOUTH?
I DIDN'T GET IT.
TRY IT ONE MORE TIME.

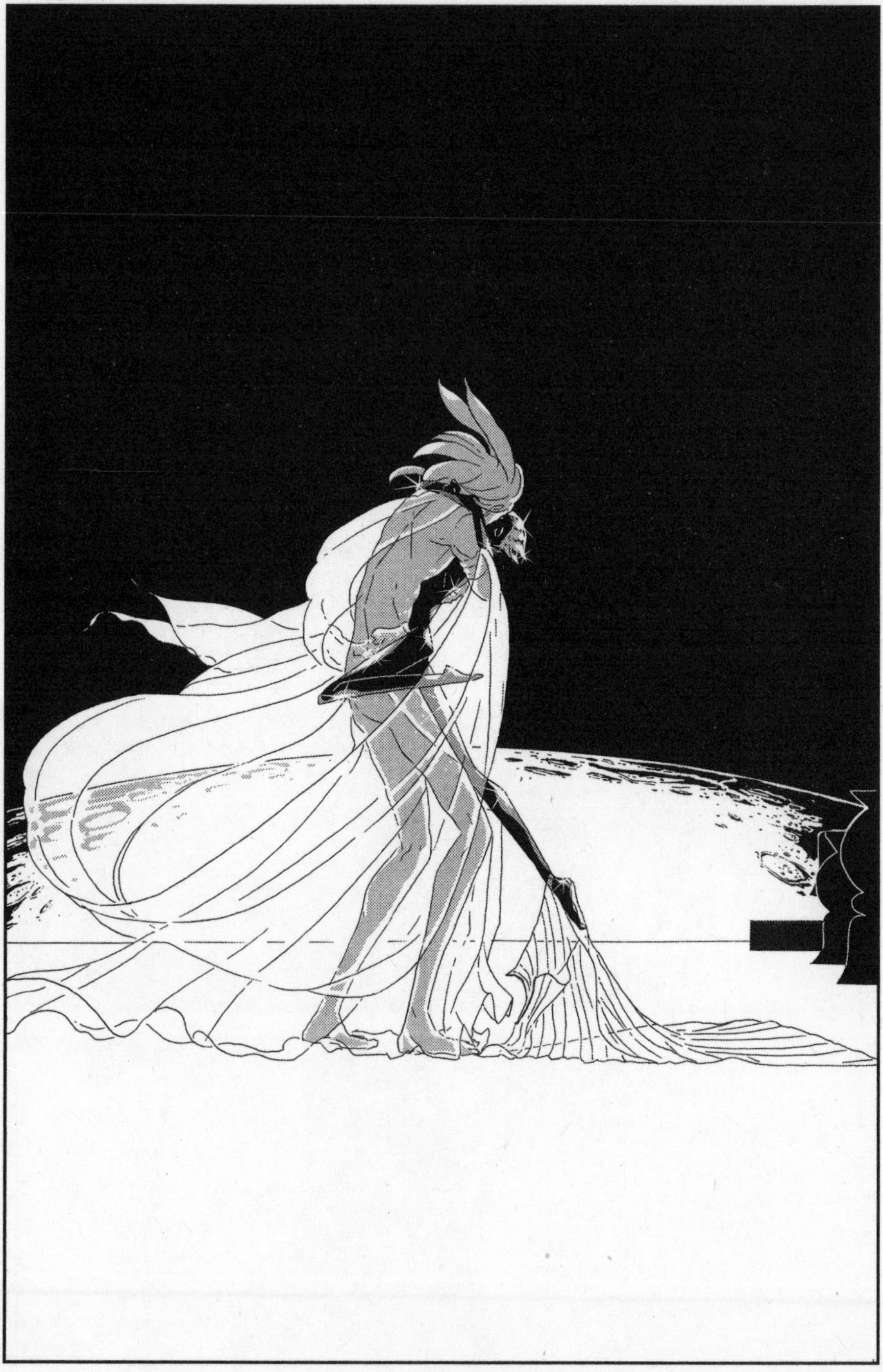

CHAPTER 75: Wish END

CHAPTER 76: Admirabilis

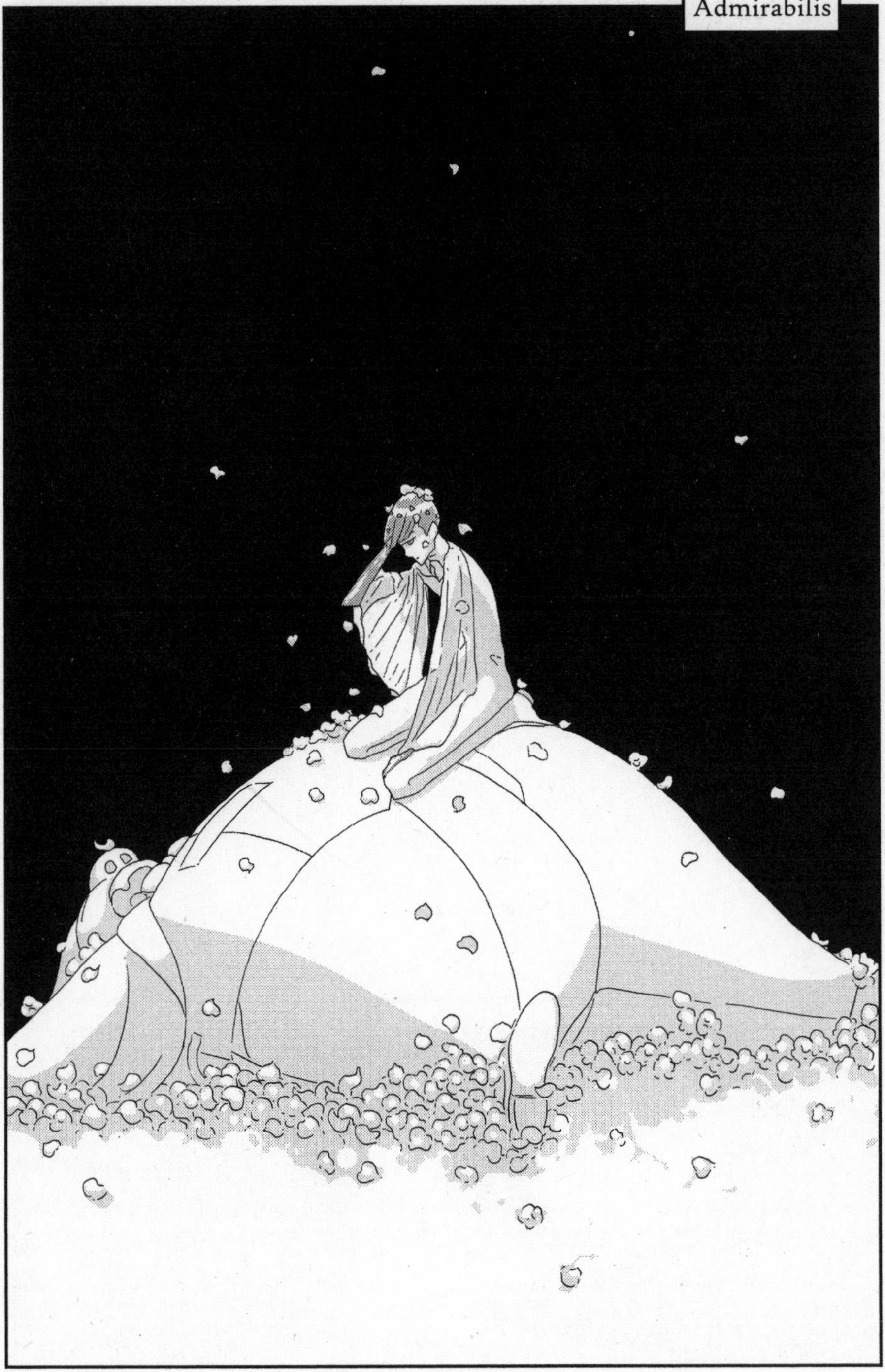

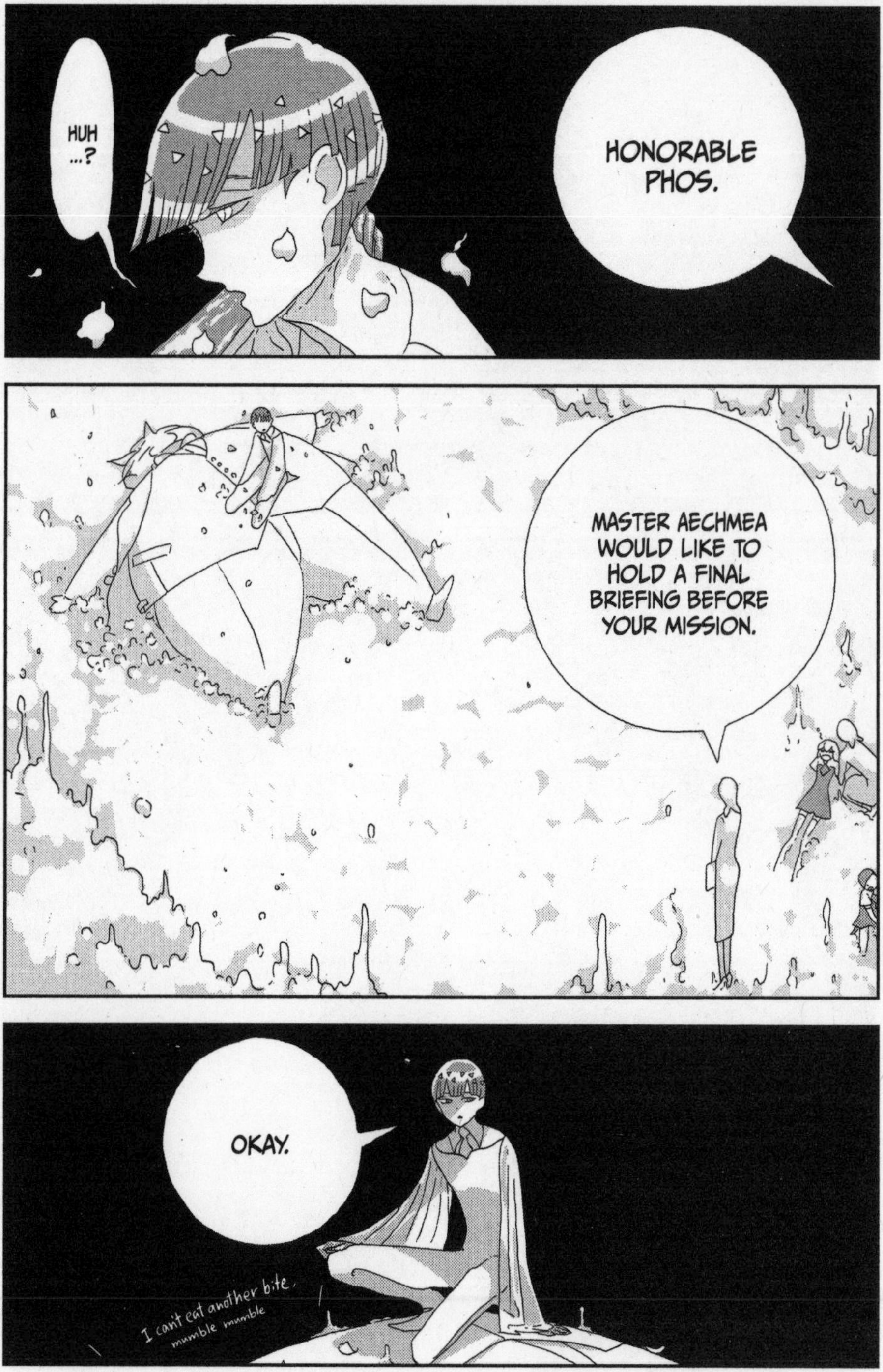
HONORABLE PHOS.
HUH ...?
MASTER AECHMEA WOULD LIKE TO HOLD A FINAL BRIEFING BEFORE YOUR MISSION.
OKAY.
I can't eat another bite.
mumble mumble

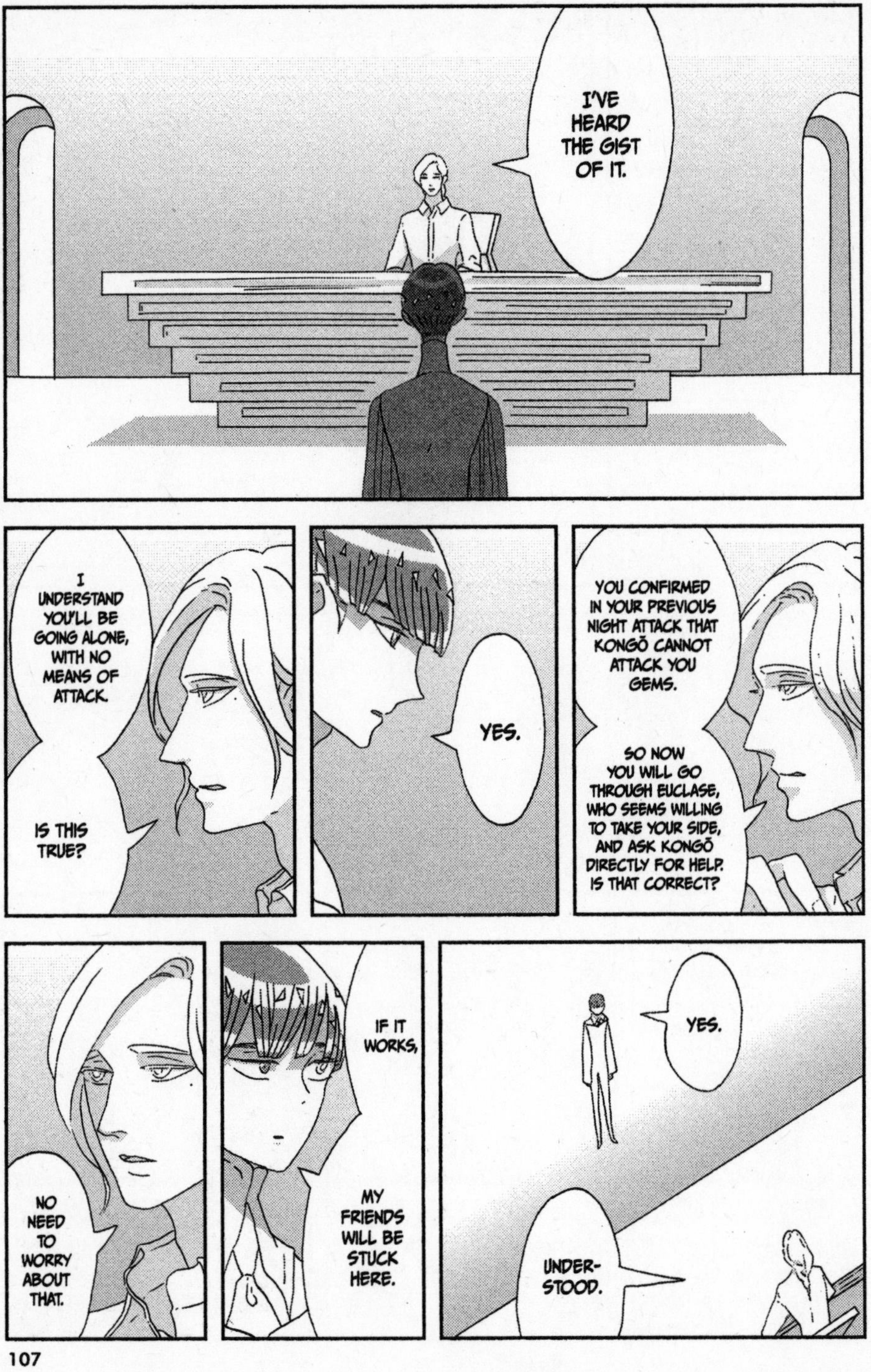
I'VE HEARD THE GIST OF IT.
YOU CONFIRMED IN YOUR PREVIOUS NIGHT ATTACK THAT KONGŌ CANNOT ATTACK YOU GEMS.
SO NOW YOU WILL GO THROUGH EUCLASE, WHO SEEMS WILLING TO TAKE YOUR SIDE, AND ASK KONGŌ DIRECTLY FOR HELP. IS THAT CORRECT?
YES.
I UNDERSTAND YOU'LL BE GOING ALONE, WITH NO MEANS OF ATTACK.
IS THIS TRUE?
YES.
UNDER-STOOD.
IF IT WORKS,
MY FRIENDS WILL BE STUCK HERE.
NO NEED TO WORRY ABOUT THAT.

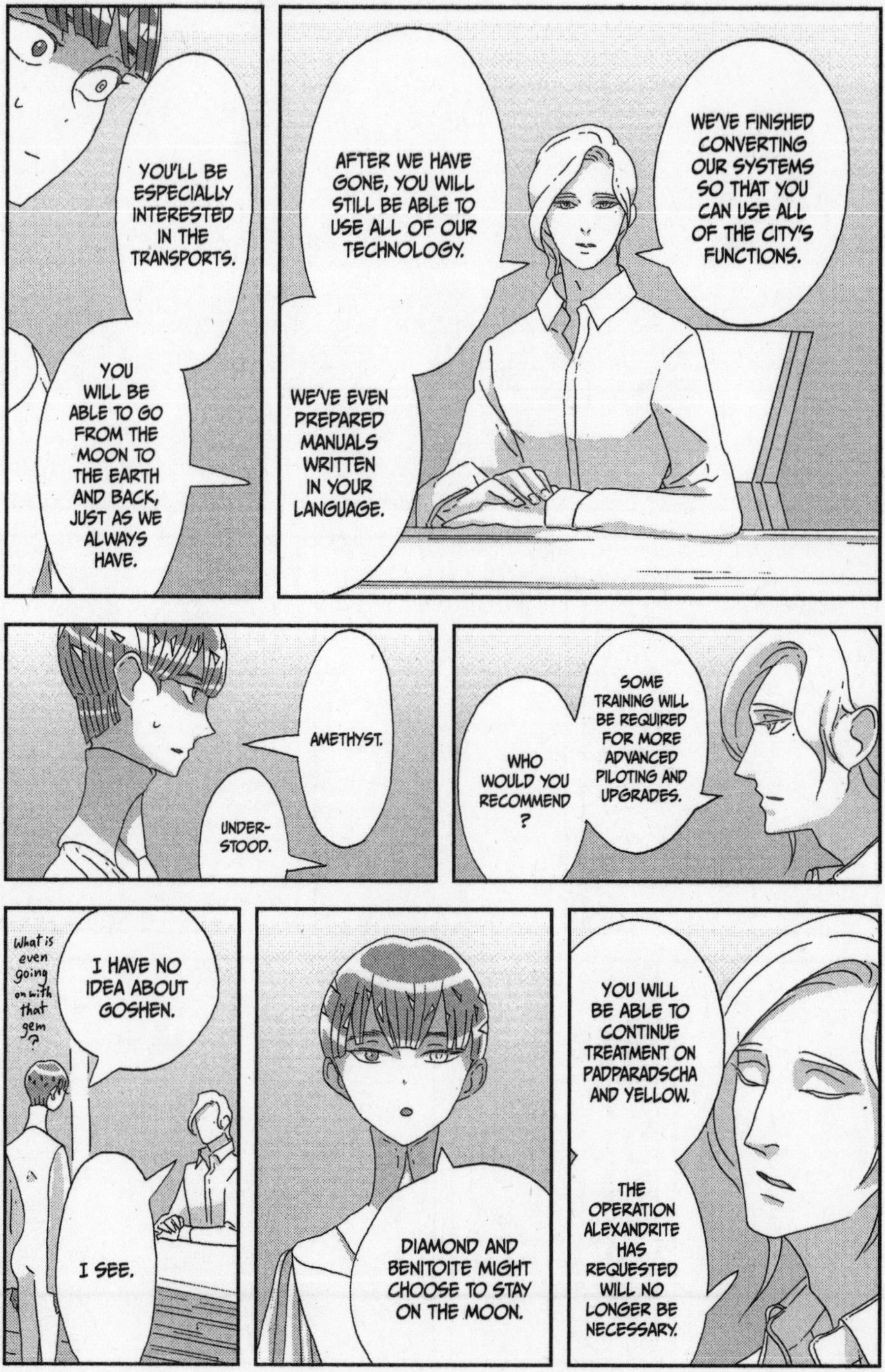
WE'VE FINISHED CONVERTING OUR SYSTEMS SO THAT YOU CAN USE ALL OF THE CITY'S FUNCTIONS.
AFTER WE HAVE GONE, YOU WILL STILL BE ABLE TO USE ALL OF OUR TECHNOLOGY.
WE'VE EVEN PREPARED MANUALS WRITTEN IN YOUR LANGUAGE.
YOU'LL BE ESPECIALLY INTERESTED IN THE TRANSPORTS.
YOU WILL BE ABLE TO GO FROM THE MOON TO THE EARTH AND BACK, JUST AS WE ALWAYS HAVE.
SOME TRAINING WILL BE REQUIRED FOR MORE ADVANCED PILOTING AND UPGRADES.
WHO WOULD YOU RECOMMEND ?
AMETHYST.
UNDER-STOOD.
YOU WILL BE ABLE TO CONTINUE TREATMENT ON PADPARADSCHA AND YELLOW.
THE OPERATION ALEXANDRITE HAS REQUESTED WILL NO LONGER BE NECESSARY.
DIAMOND AND BENITOITE MIGHT CHOOSE TO STAY ON THE MOON.
I HAVE NO IDEA ABOUT GOSHEN.
What is even going on with that gem ?
I SEE.

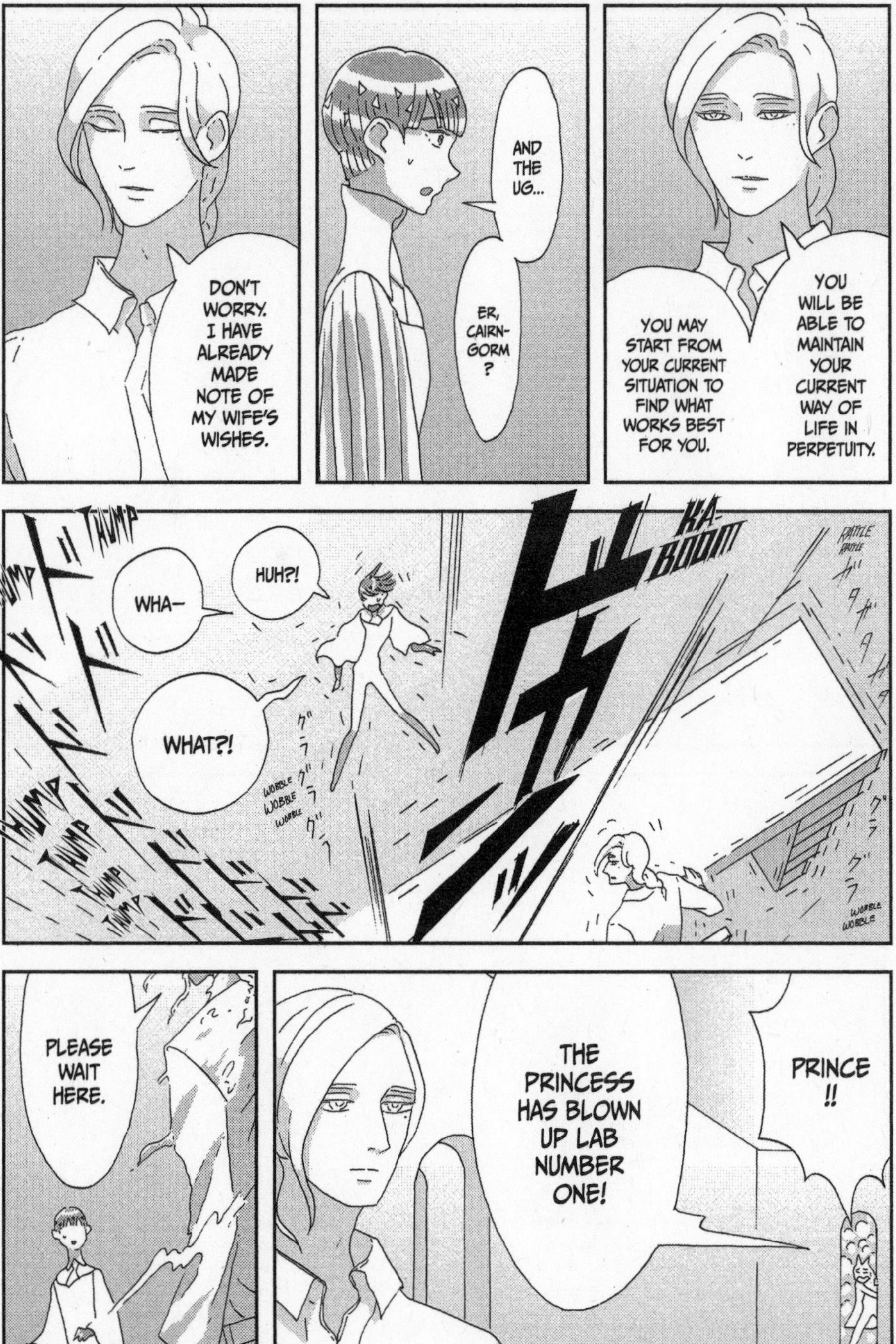
YOU WILL BE ABLE TO MAINTAIN YOUR CURRENT WAY OF LIFE IN PERPETUITY.
YOU MAY START FROM YOUR CURRENT SITUATION TO FIND WHAT WORKS BEST FOR YOU.
AND THE UG...
ER, CAIRN-GORM?
DON'T WORRY. I HAVE ALREADY MADE NOTE OF MY WIFE'S WISHES.
RATTLE RATTLE
KA-BOOM
WOBBLE WOBBLE
HUH?!
WHA–
WHAT?!
WOBBLE WOBBLE WOBBLE
THUMP THUMP
THUMP THUMP THUMP THUMP
PRINCE!!
THE PRINCESS HAS BLOWN UP LAB NUMBER ONE!
PLEASE WAIT HERE.

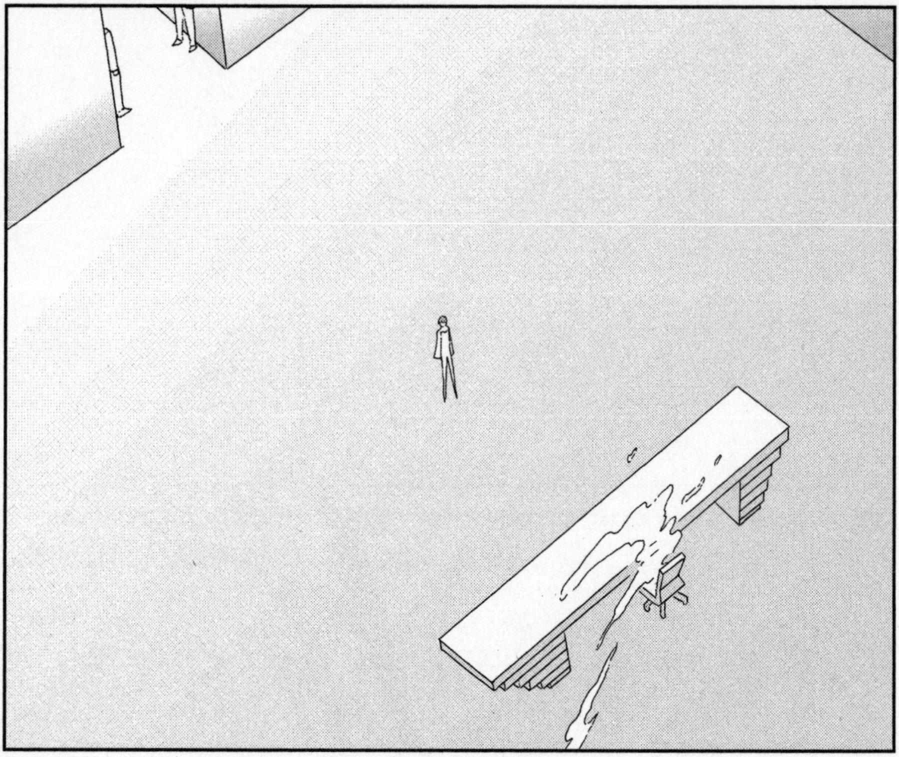

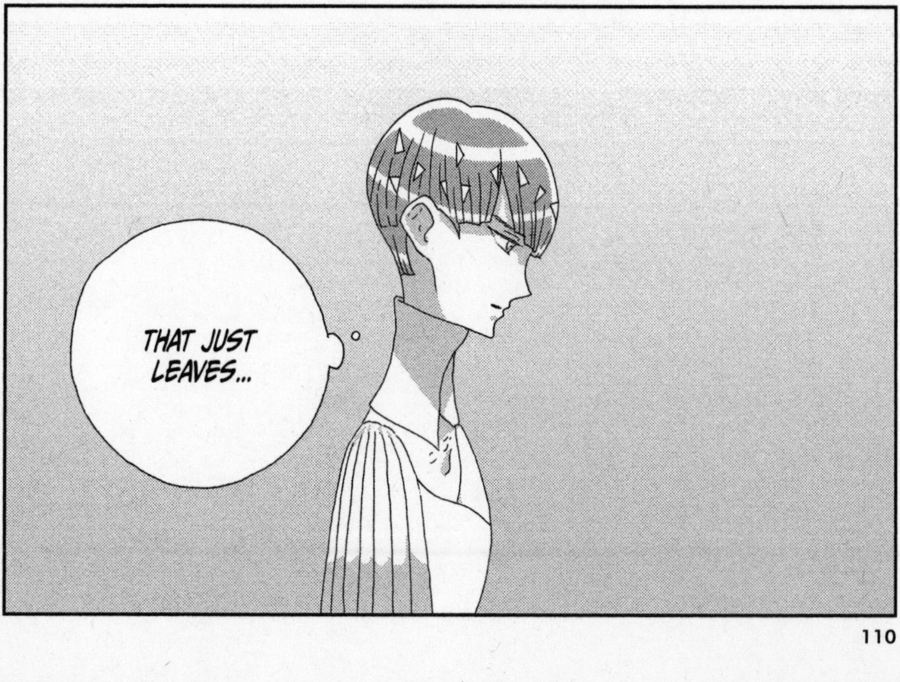
THAT JUST LEAVES...

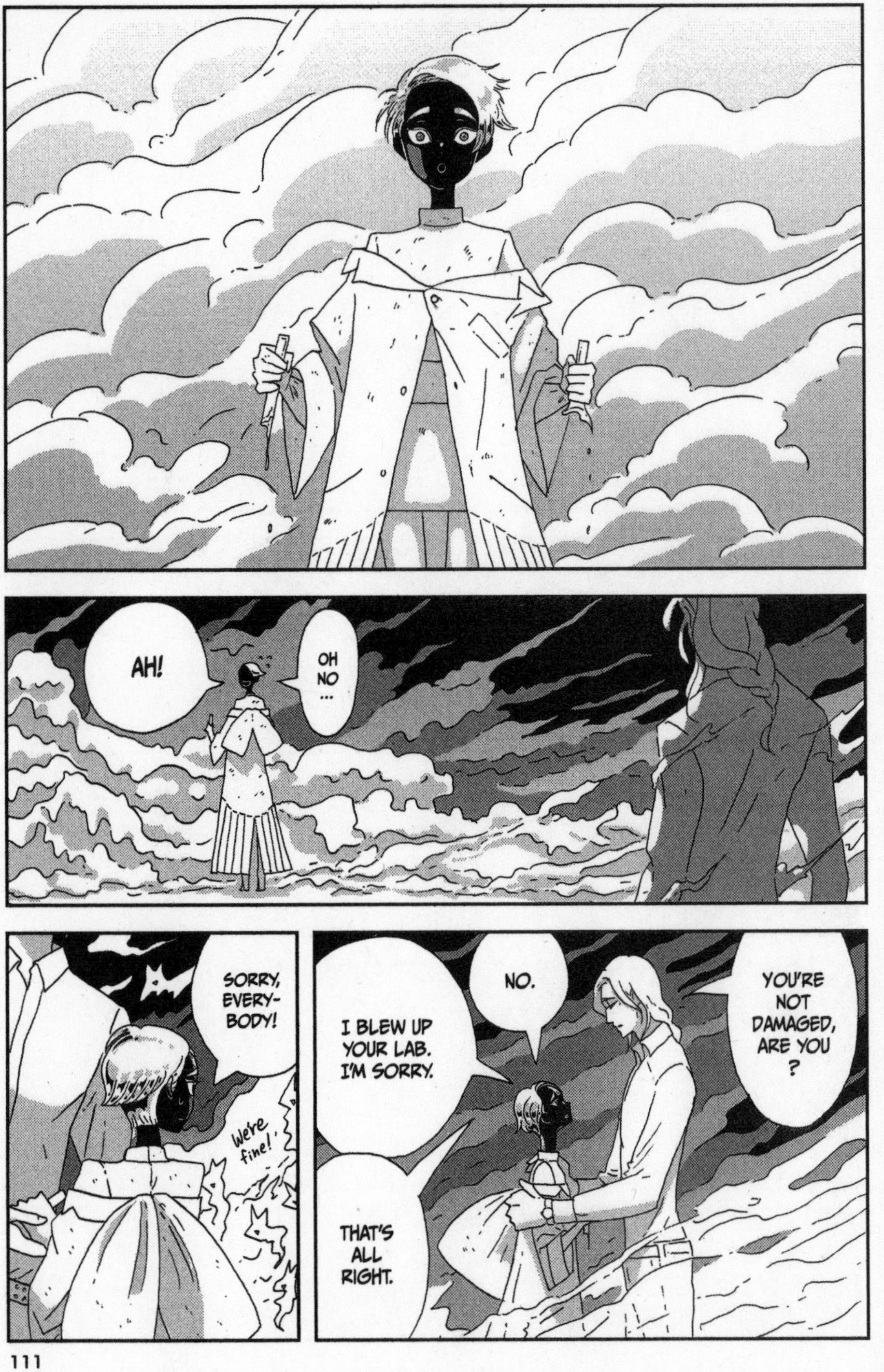
OH NO ...
AH!
YOU'RE NOT DAMAGED, ARE YOU ?
NO.
I BLEW UP YOUR LAB. I'M SORRY.
THAT'S ALL RIGHT.
SORRY, EVERY-BODY!
We're fine!

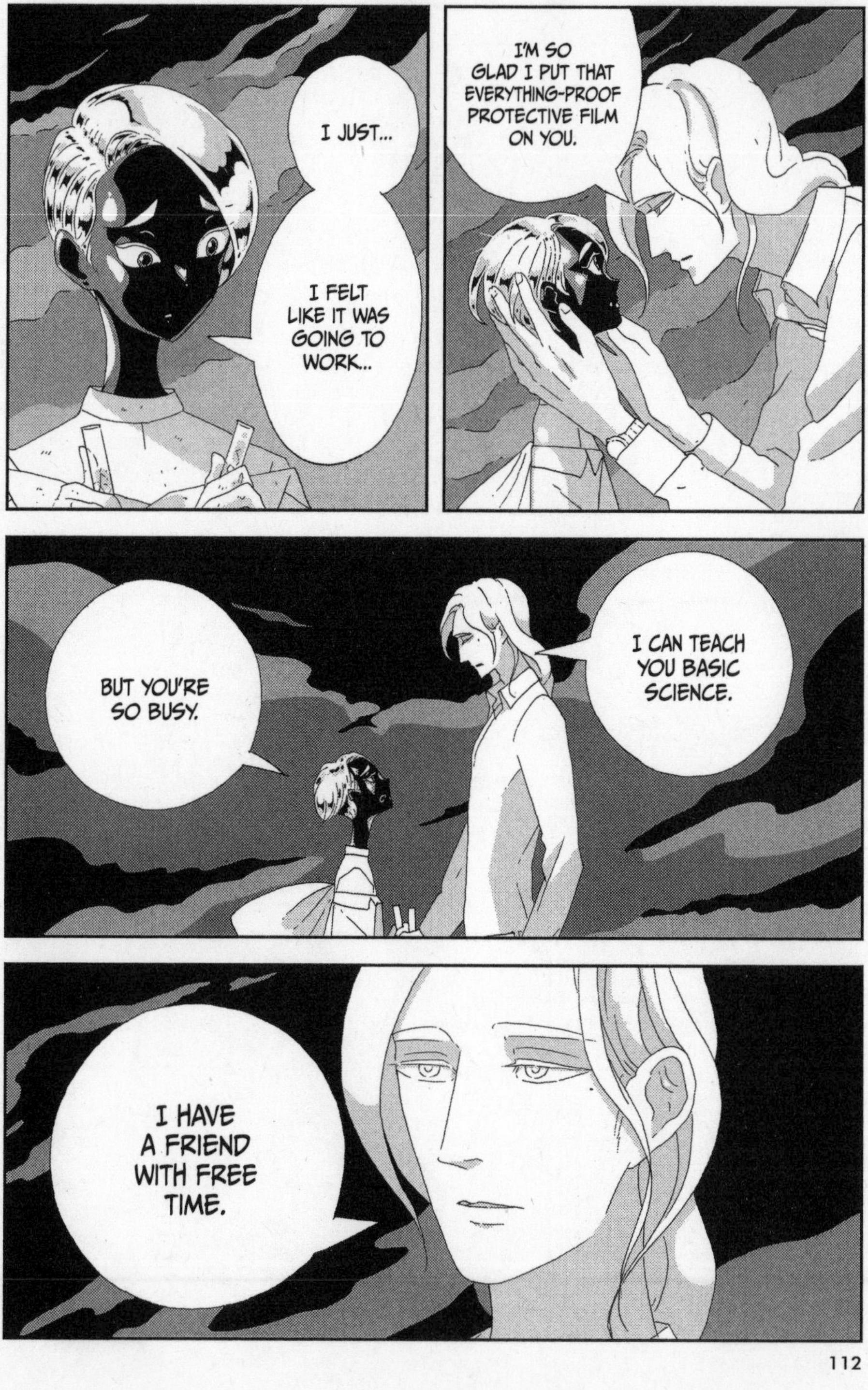
I'M SO GLAD I PUT THAT EVERYTHING-PROOF PROTECTIVE FILM ON YOU.
I JUST...
I FELT LIKE IT WAS GOING TO WORK...
I CAN TEACH YOU BASIC SCIENCE.
BUT YOU'RE SO BUSY.
I HAVE A FRIEND WITH FREE TIME.

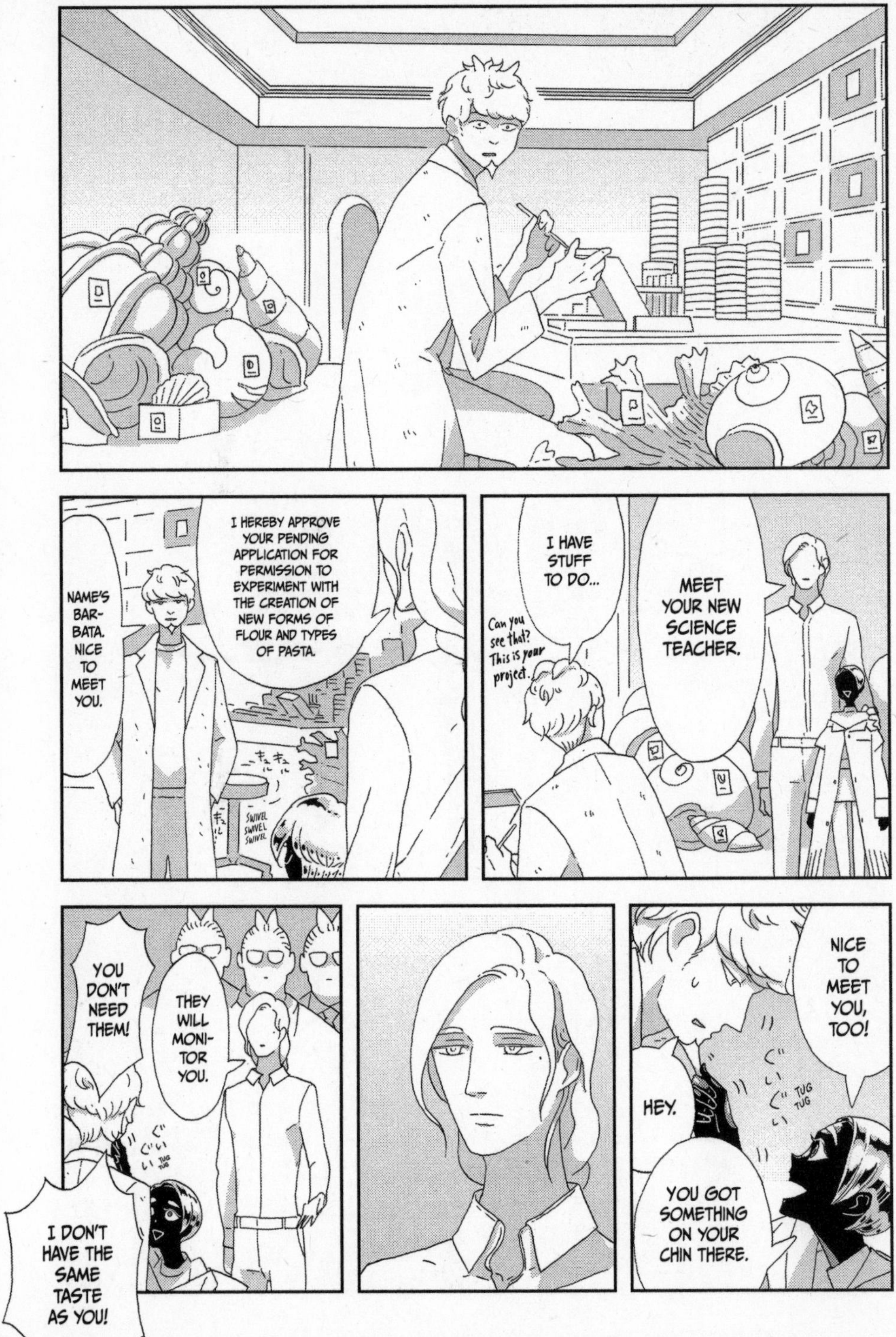
MEET YOUR NEW SCIENCE TEACHER.
I HAVE STUFF TO DO...
Can you see that? This is your project.
I HEREBY APPROVE YOUR PENDING APPLICATION FOR PERMISSION TO EXPERIMENT WITH THE CREATION OF NEW FORMS OF FLOUR AND TYPES OF PASTA.
NAME'S BAR-BATA. NICE TO MEET YOU.
SWIVEL SWIVEL SWIVEL
NICE TO MEET YOU, TOO!
TUG TUG
HEY.
YOU GOT SOMETHING ON YOUR CHIN THERE.
THEY WILL MONI-TOR YOU.
YOU DON'T NEED THEM!
TUG TUG
I DON'T HAVE THE SAME TASTE AS YOU!

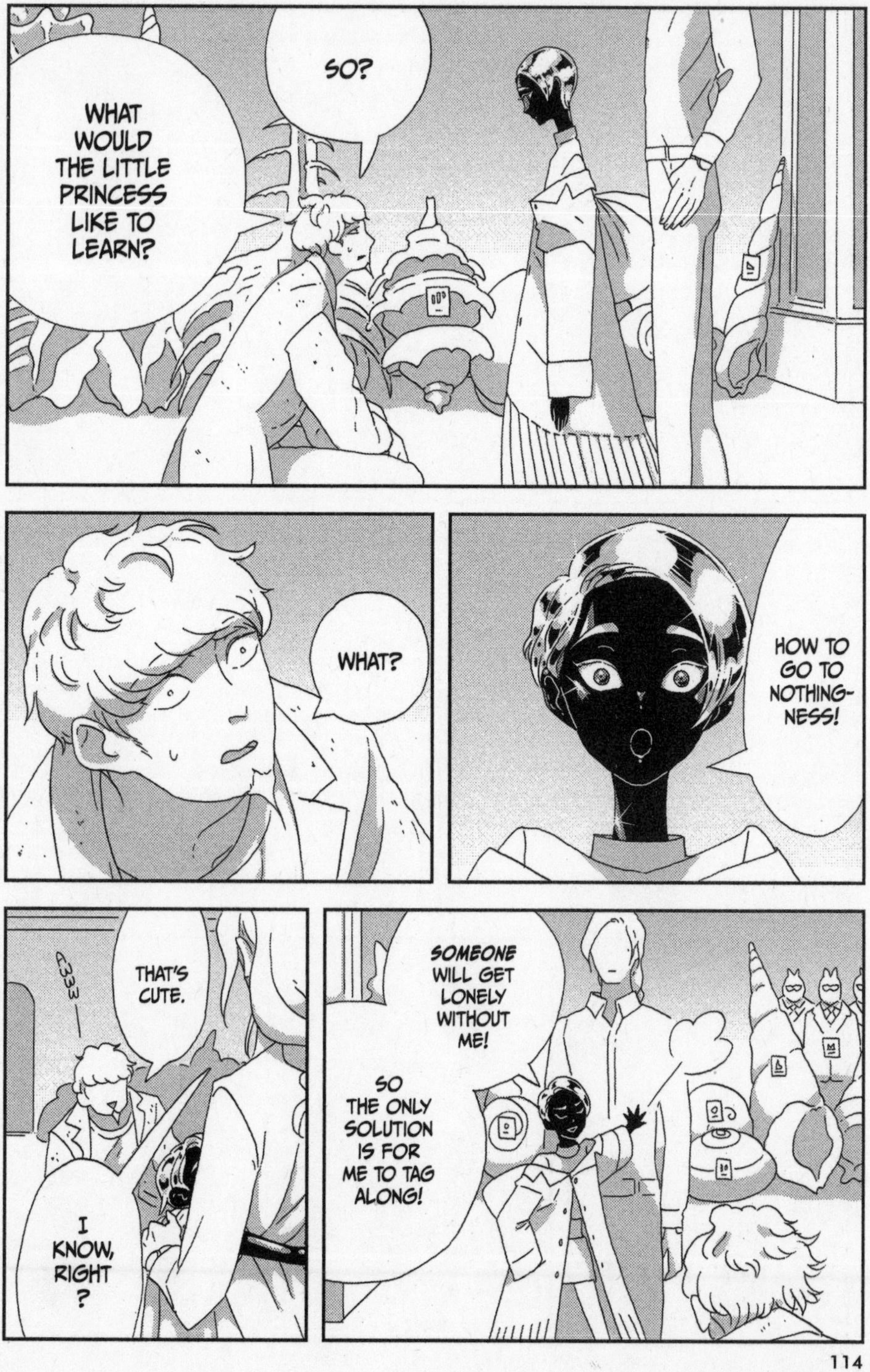
SO?
WHAT WOULD THE LITTLE PRINCESS LIKE TO LEARN?
HOW TO GO TO NOTHING-NESS!
WHAT?
SOMEONE WILL GET LONELY WITHOUT ME!
SO THE ONLY SOLUTION IS FOR ME TO TAG ALONG!
THAT'S CUTE.
I KNOW, RIGHT?

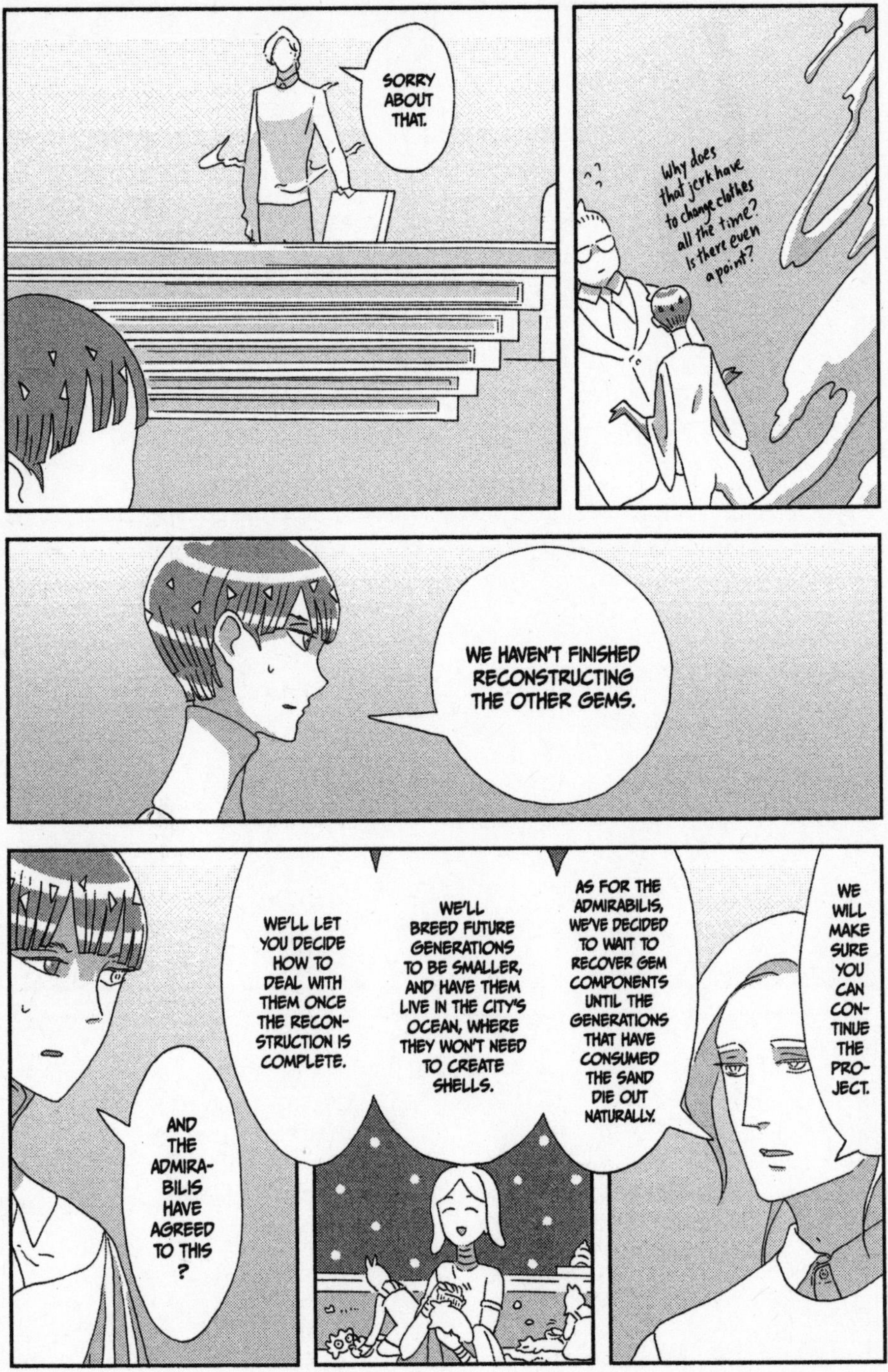
Why does that jerk have to change clothes all the time? Is there even a point?
SORRY ABOUT THAT.
WE HAVEN'T FINISHED RECONSTRUCTING THE OTHER GEMS.
WE WILL MAKE SURE YOU CAN CONTINUE THE PROJECT.
AS FOR THE ADMIRABILIS, WE'VE DECIDED TO WAIT TO RECOVER GEM COMPONENTS UNTIL THE GENERATIONS THAT HAVE CONSUMED THE SAND DIE OUT NATURALLY.
WE'LL BREED FUTURE GENERATIONS TO BE SMALLER, AND HAVE THEM LIVE IN THE CITY'S OCEAN, WHERE THEY WON'T NEED TO CREATE SHELLS.
WE'LL LET YOU DECIDE HOW TO DEAL WITH THEM ONCE THE RECONSTRUCTION IS COMPLETE.
AND THE ADMIRABILIS HAVE AGREED TO THIS?

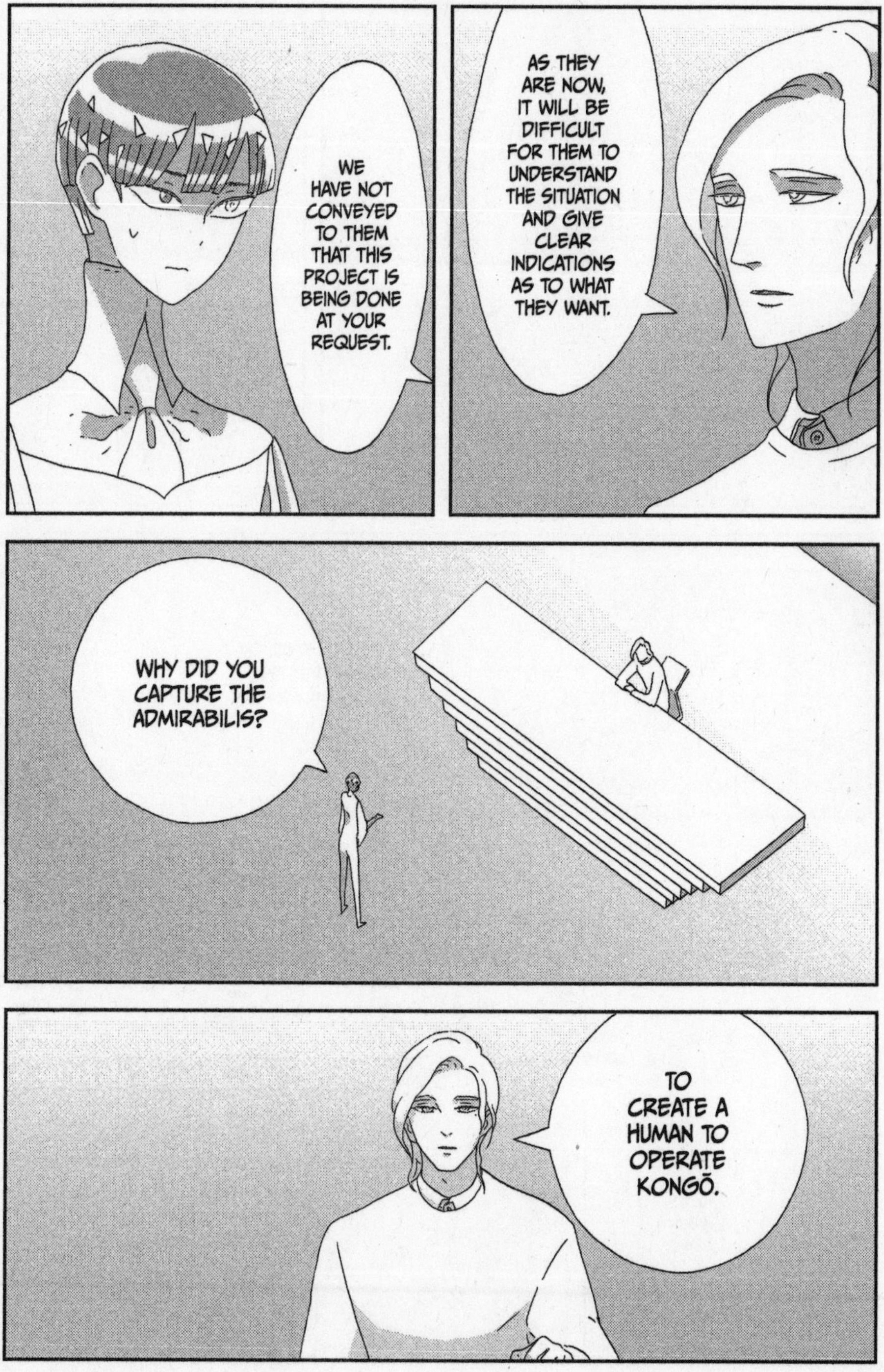
AS THEY ARE NOW, IT WILL BE DIFFICULT FOR THEM TO UNDERSTAND THE SITUATION AND GIVE CLEAR INDICATIONS AS TO WHAT THEY WANT.
WE HAVE NOT CONVEYED TO THEM THAT THIS PROJECT IS BEING DONE AT YOUR REQUEST.
WHY DID YOU CAPTURE THE ADMIRABILIS?
TO CREATE A HUMAN TO OPERATE KONGŌ.

"...WE WENT TO THE DESCENDANTS OF THE FLESH TO ASK FOR THEIR HELP."

THEY AGREED TO GIVE US THEIR CRIMINALS.

LONG, LONG AGO...

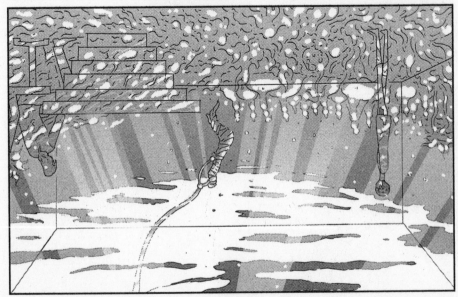

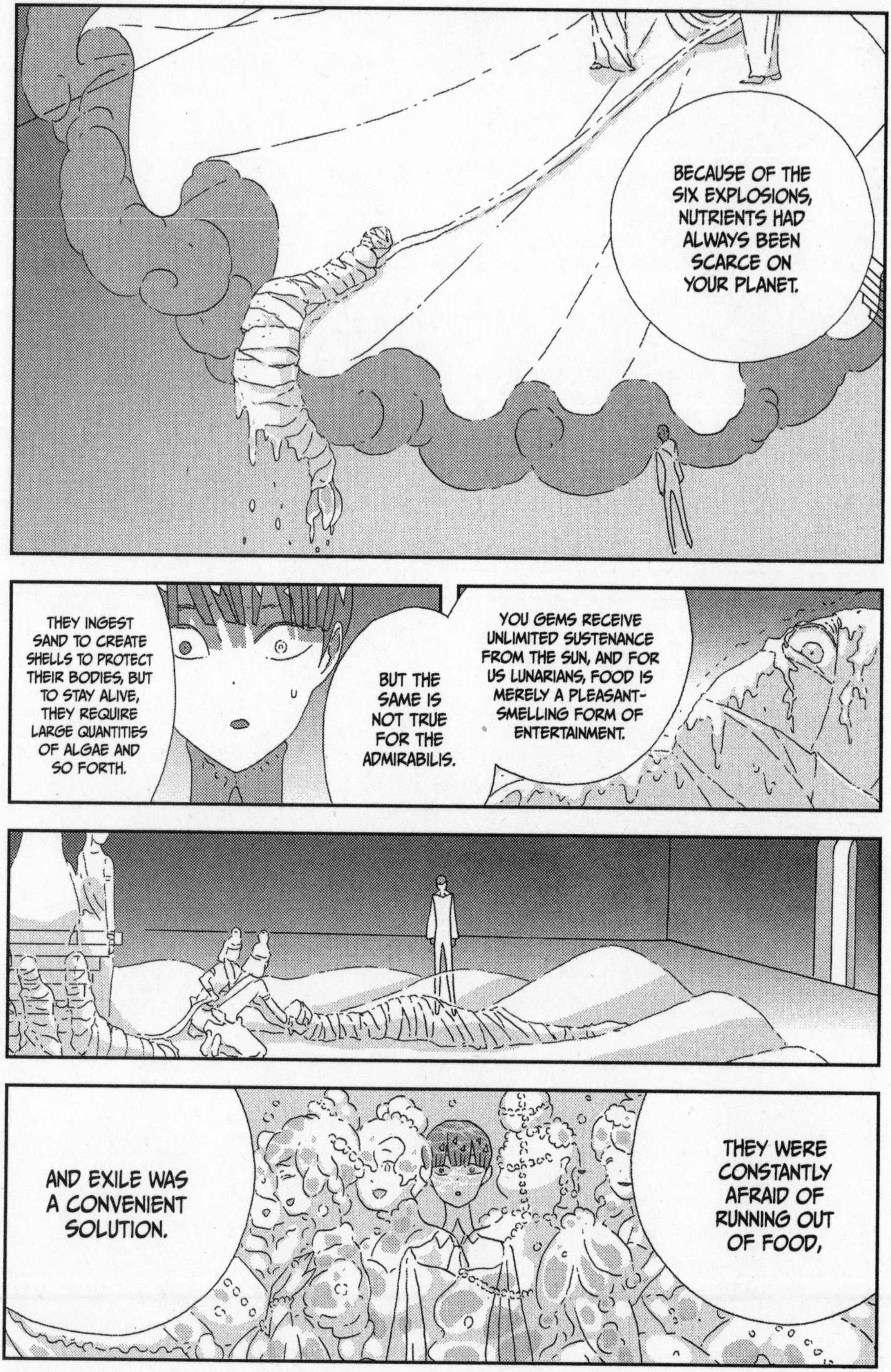
BECAUSE OF THE SIX EXPLOSIONS, NUTRIENTS HAD ALWAYS BEEN SCARCE ON YOUR PLANET.
YOU GEMS RECEIVE UNLIMITED SUSTENANCE FROM THE SUN, AND FOR US LUNARIANS, FOOD IS MERELY A PLEASANT-SMELLING FORM OF ENTERTAINMENT.
BUT THE SAME IS NOT TRUE FOR THE ADMIRABILIS.
THEY INGEST SAND TO CREATE SHELLS TO PROTECT THEIR BODIES, BUT TO STAY ALIVE, THEY REQUIRE LARGE QUANTITIES OF ALGAE AND SO FORTH.
THEY WERE CONSTANTLY AFRAID OF RUNNING OUT OF FOOD,
AND EXILE WAS A CONVENIENT SOLUTION.

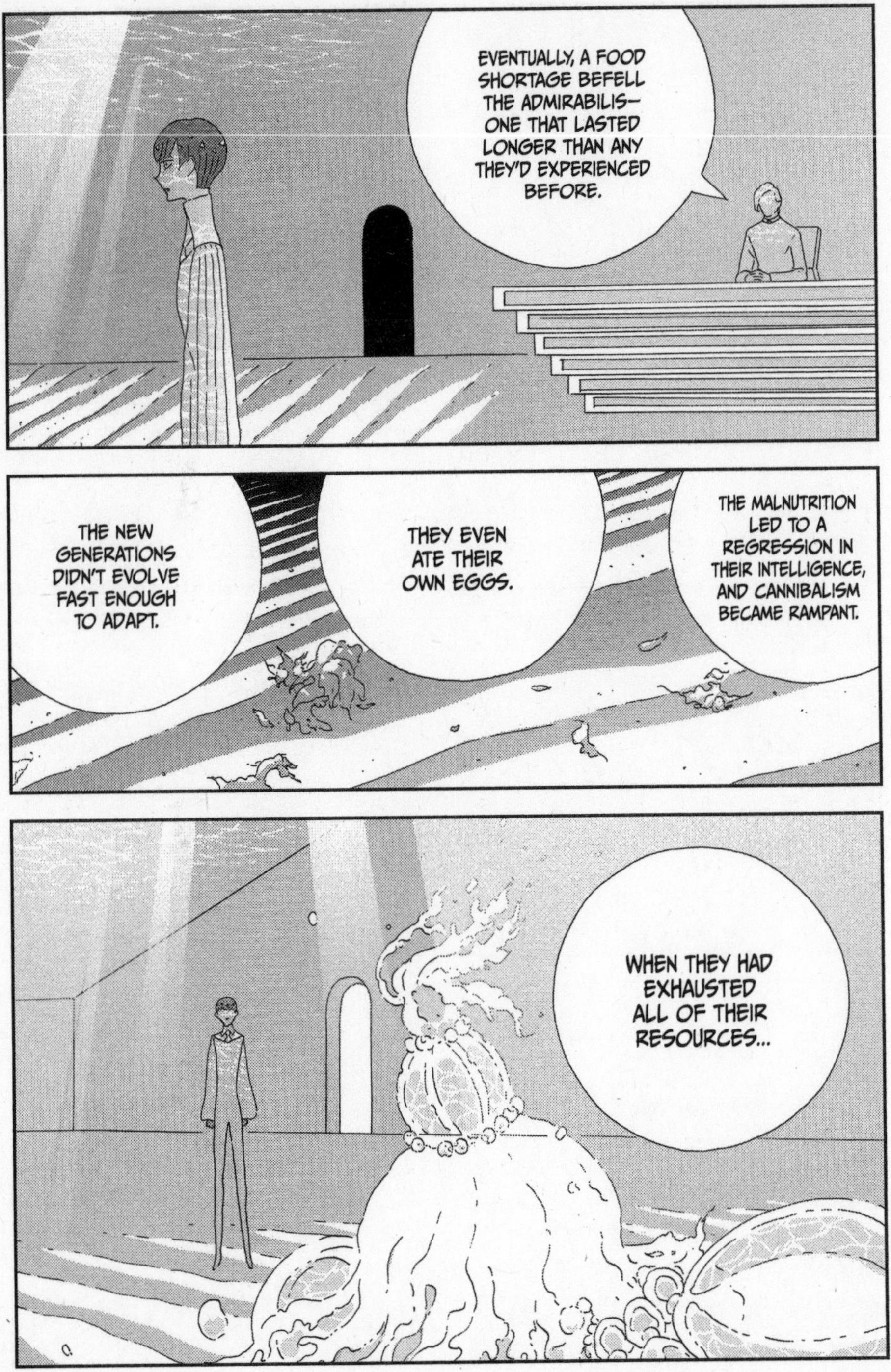
EVENTUALLY, A FOOD SHORTAGE BEFELL THE ADMIRABILIS— ONE THAT LASTED LONGER THAN ANY THEY'D EXPERIENCED BEFORE.
THE MALNUTRITION LED TO A REGRESSION IN THEIR INTELLIGENCE, AND CANNIBALISM BECAME RAMPANT.
THEY EVEN ATE THEIR OWN EGGS.
THE NEW GENERATIONS DIDN'T EVOLVE FAST ENOUGH TO ADAPT.
WHEN THEY HAD EXHAUSTED ALL OF THEIR RESOURCES...

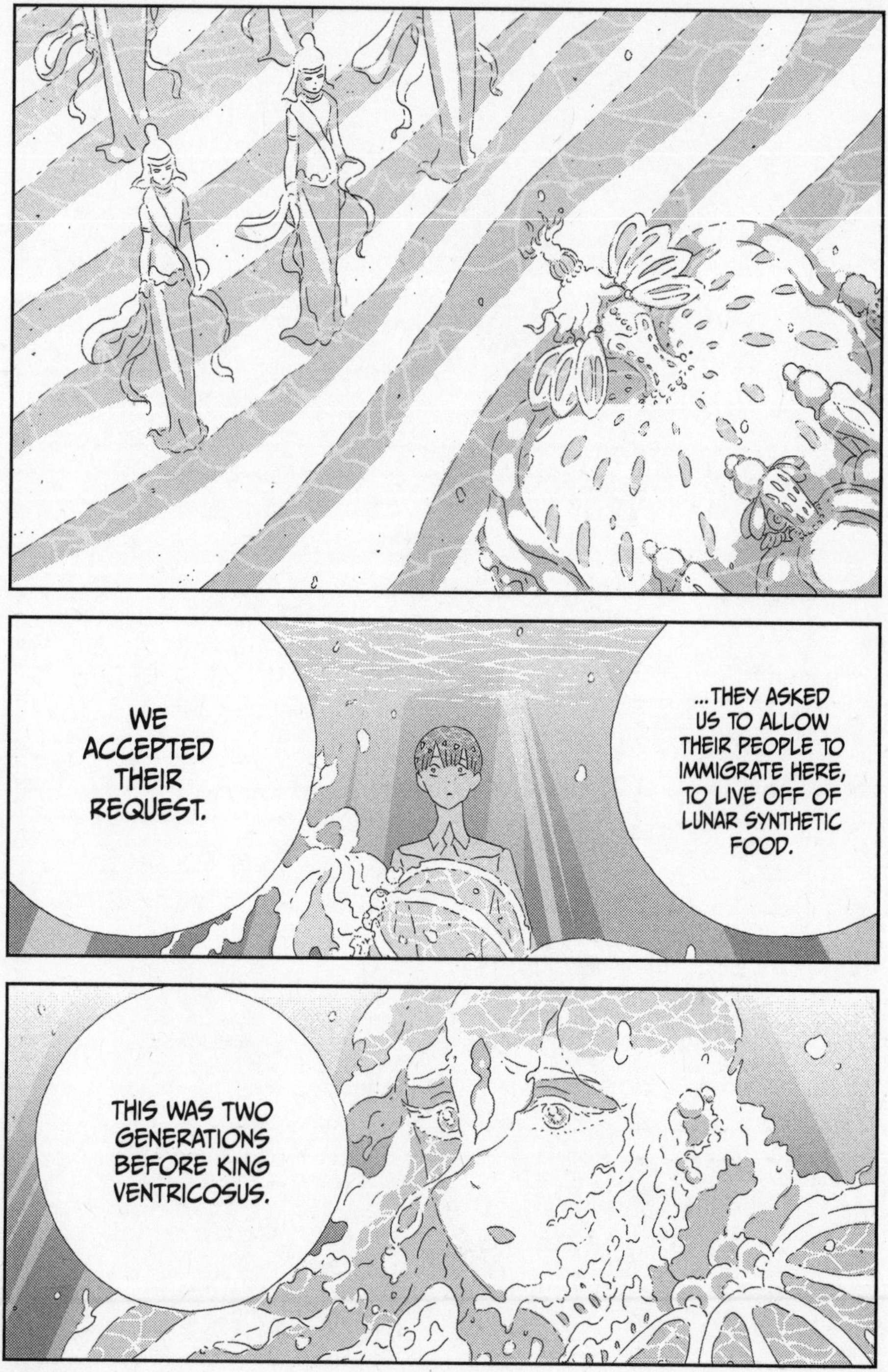
...THEY ASKED US TO ALLOW THEIR PEOPLE TO IMMIGRATE HERE, TO LIVE OFF OF LUNAR SYNTHETIC FOOD.
WE ACCEPTED THEIR REQUEST.
THIS WAS TWO GENERATIONS BEFORE KING VENTRICOSUS.

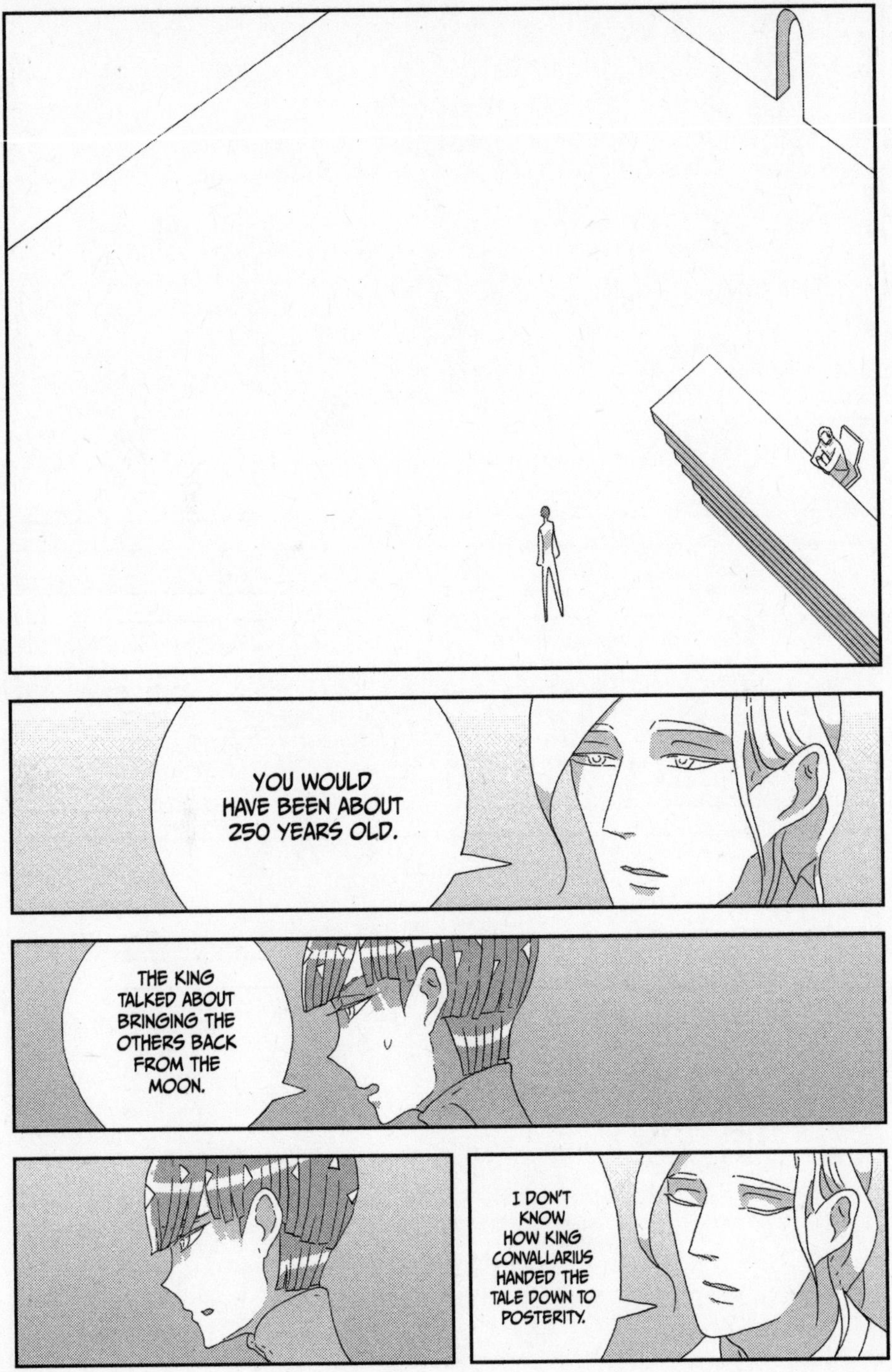
YOU WOULD HAVE BEEN ABOUT 250 YEARS OLD.
THE KING TALKED ABOUT BRINGING THE OTHERS BACK FROM THE MOON.
I DON'T KNOW HOW KING CONVALLARIUS HANDED THE TALE DOWN TO POSTERITY.

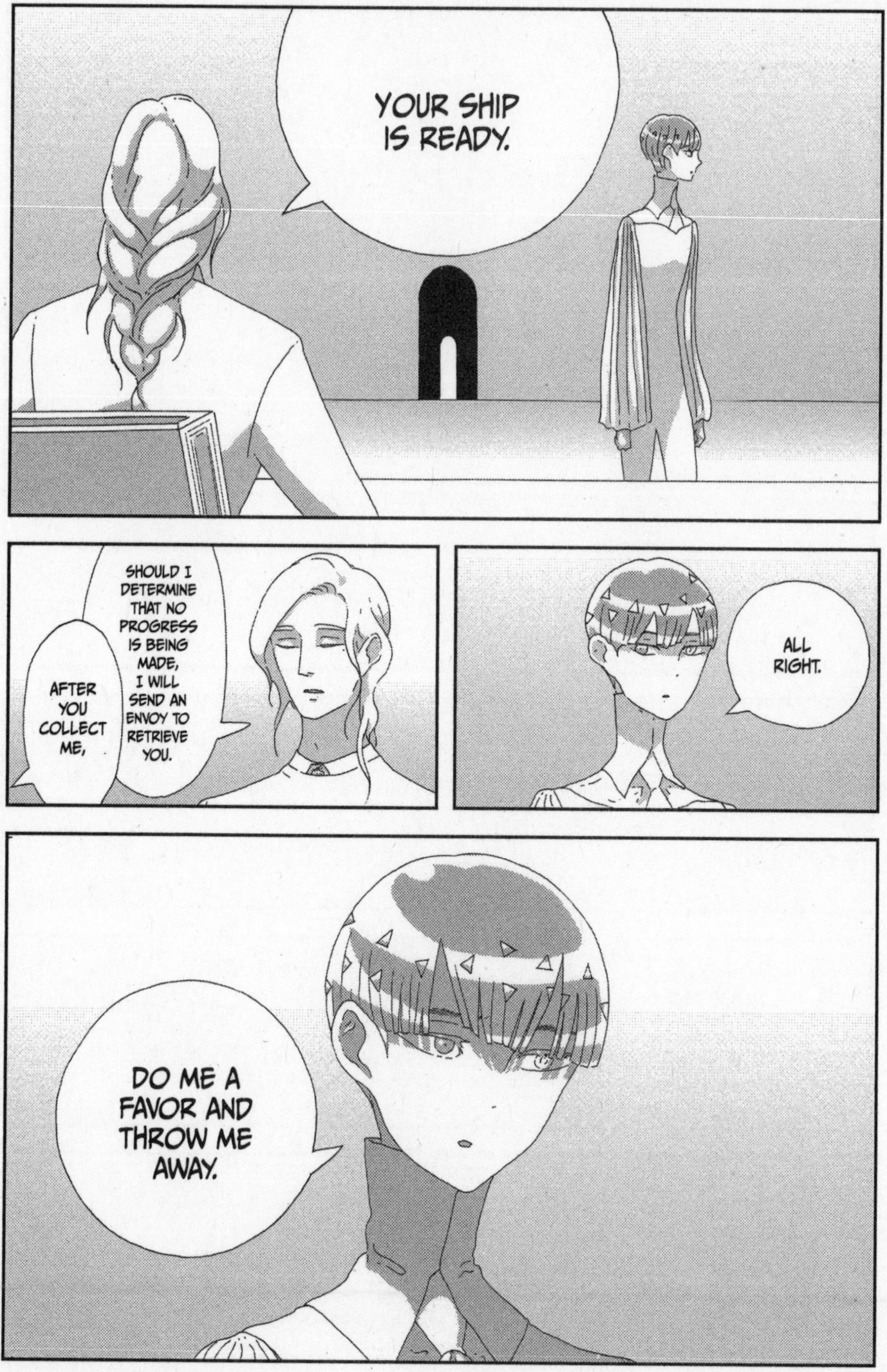
YOUR SHIP IS READY.
ALL RIGHT.
AFTER YOU COLLECT ME,
SHOULD I DETERMINE THAT NO PROGRESS IS BEING MADE, I WILL SEND AN ENVOY TO RETRIEVE YOU.
DO ME A FAVOR AND THROW ME AWAY.

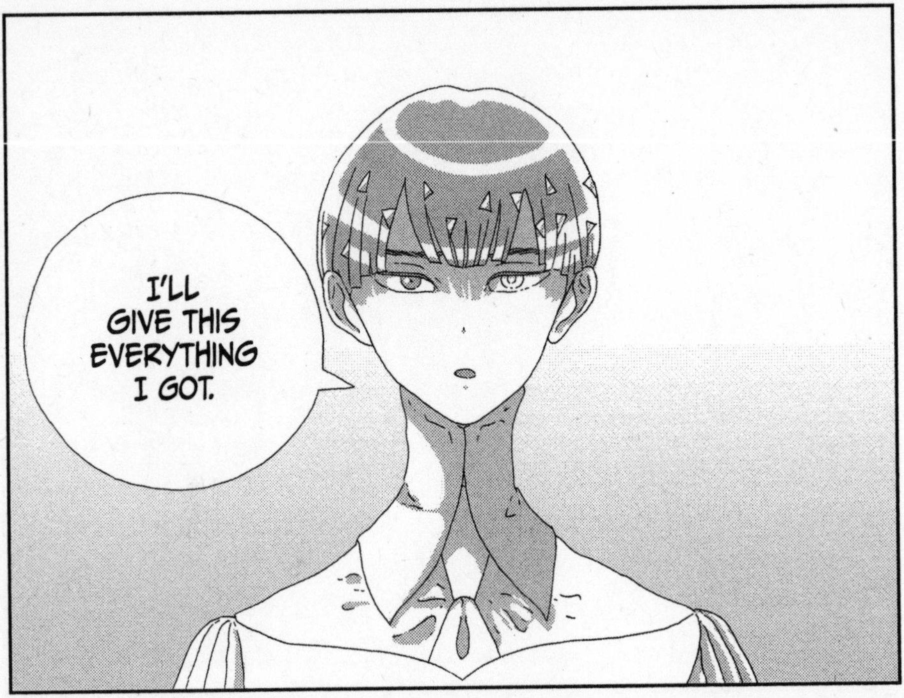
I'LL GIVE THIS EVERYTHING I GOT.
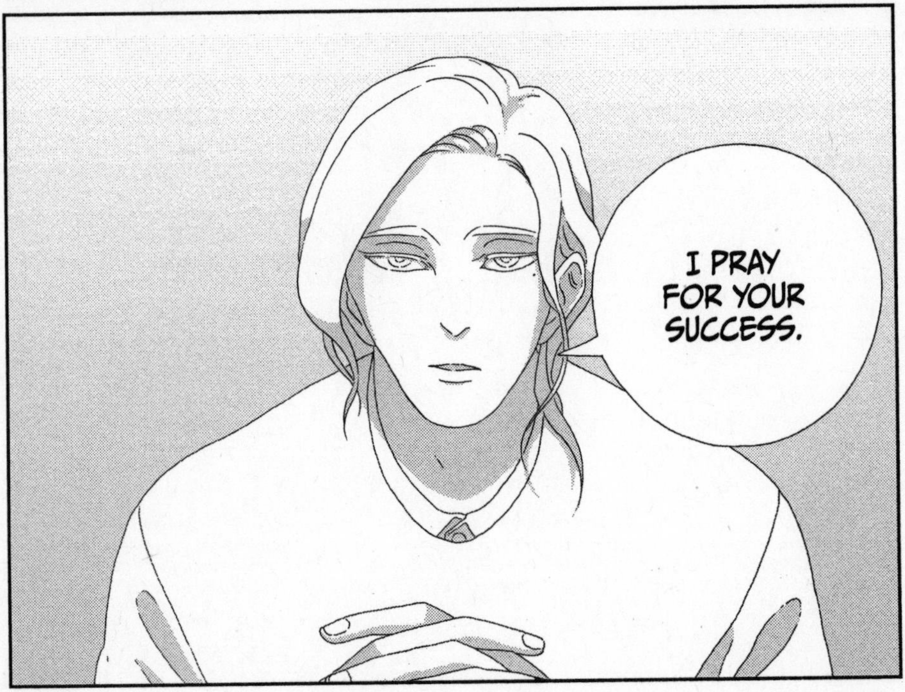
I PRAY FOR YOUR SUCCESS.

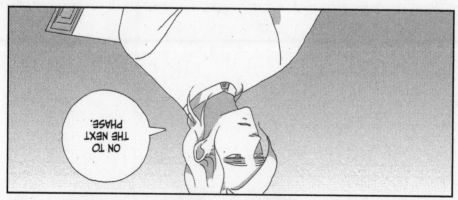

ON TO
THE NEXT
PHASE.

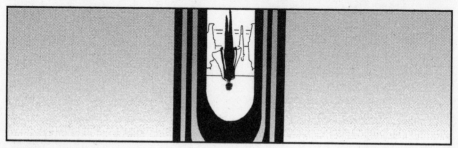

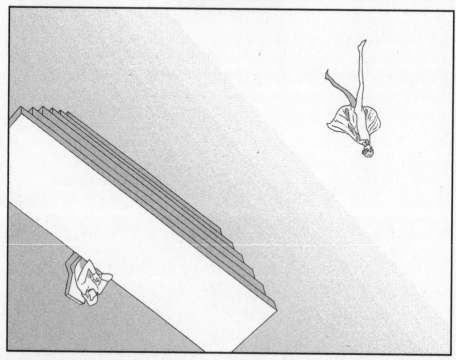

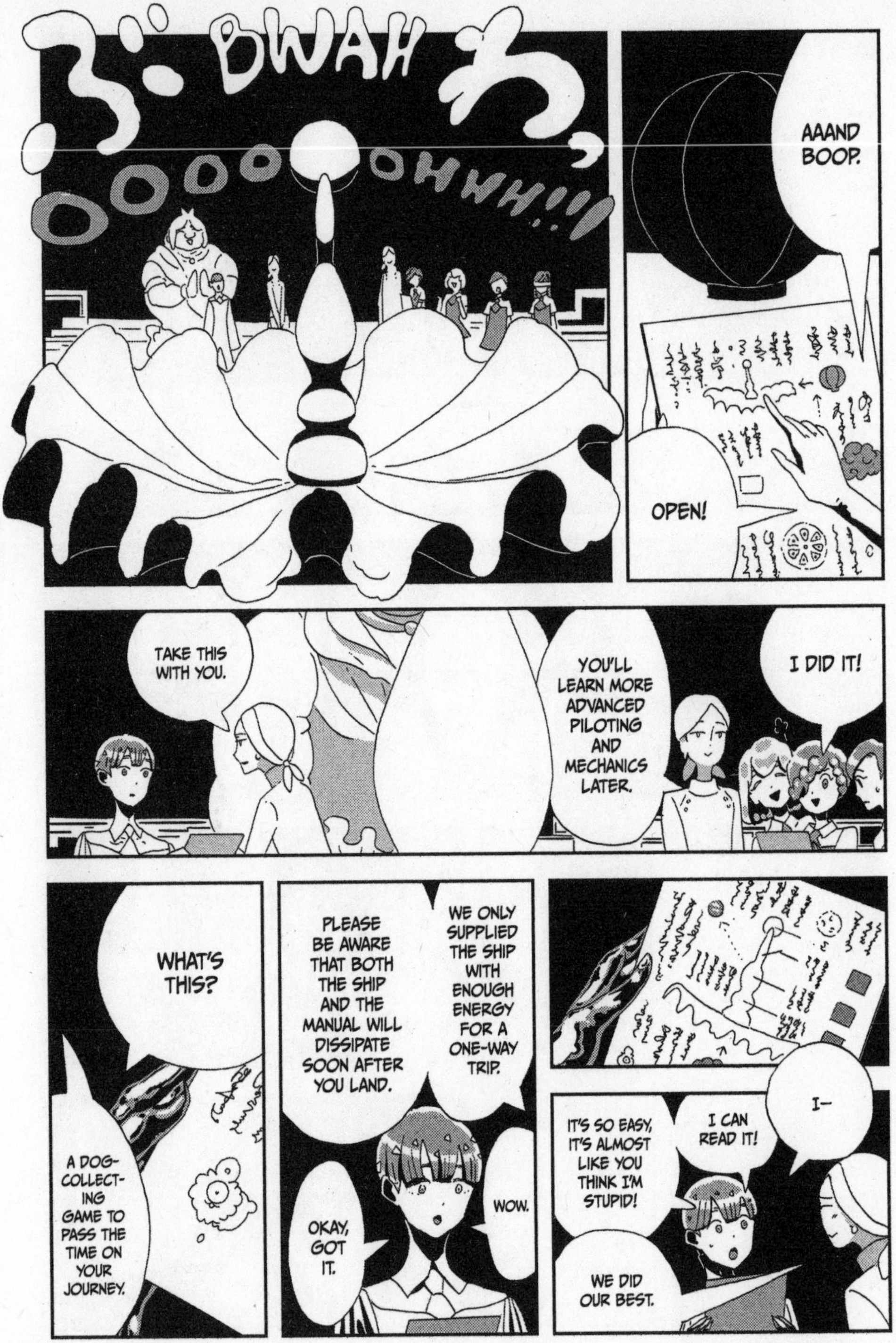
AAAND BOOP.
OPEN!
ぶ BWAH わ
OOOOOHHH!!!
I DID IT!
YOU'LL LEARN MORE ADVANCED PILOTING AND MECHANICS LATER.
TAKE THIS WITH YOU.
I—
I CAN READ IT!
IT'S SO EASY, IT'S ALMOST LIKE YOU THINK I'M STUPID!
WE DID OUR BEST.
WE ONLY SUPPLIED THE SHIP WITH ENOUGH ENERGY FOR A ONE-WAY TRIP.
PLEASE BE AWARE THAT BOTH THE SHIP AND THE MANUAL WILL DISSIPATE SOON AFTER YOU LAND.
WOW.
OKAY, GOT IT.
WHAT'S THIS?
A DOG-COLLECTING GAME TO PASS THE TIME ON YOUR JOURNEY.

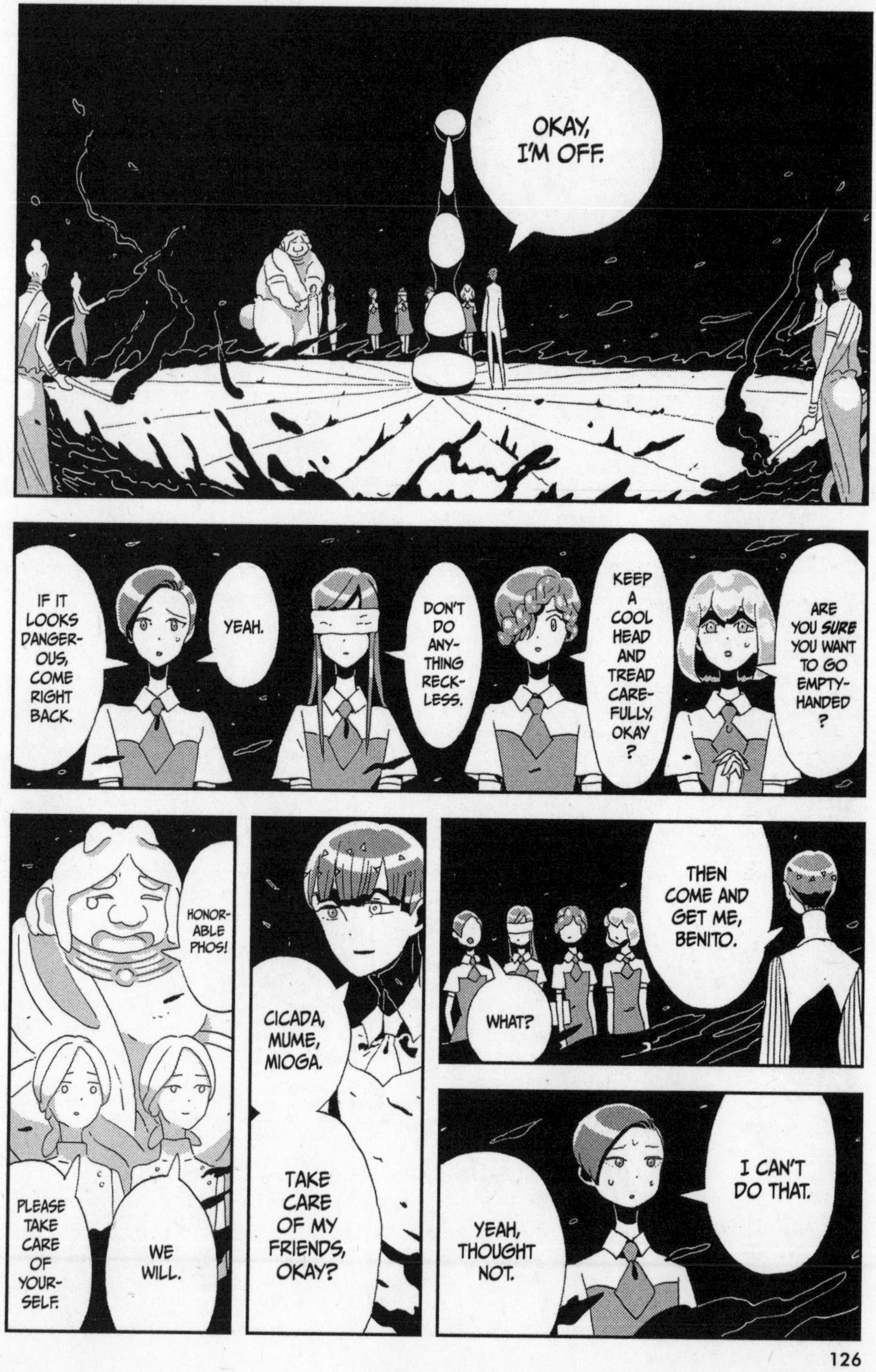
OKAY, I'M OFF.
ARE YOU SURE YOU WANT TO GO EMPTY-HANDED ?
KEEP A COOL HEAD AND TREAD CARE-FULLY, OKAY ?
DON'T DO ANY-THING RECK-LESS.
YEAH.
IF IT LOOKS DANGER-OUS, COME RIGHT BACK.
THEN COME AND GET ME, BENITO.
WHAT?
I CAN'T DO THAT.
YEAH, THOUGHT NOT.
CICADA, MUME, MIOGA.
TAKE CARE OF MY FRIENDS, OKAY?
HONOR-ABLE PHOS!
PLEASE TAKE CARE OF YOUR-SELF.
WE WILL.

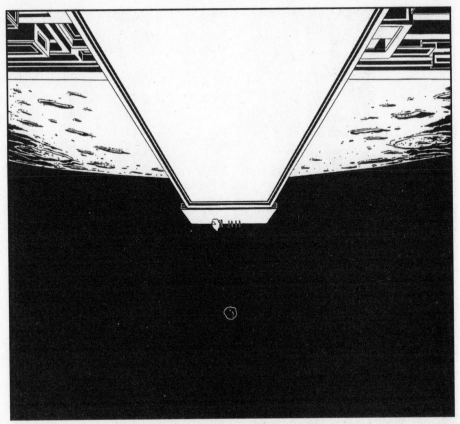

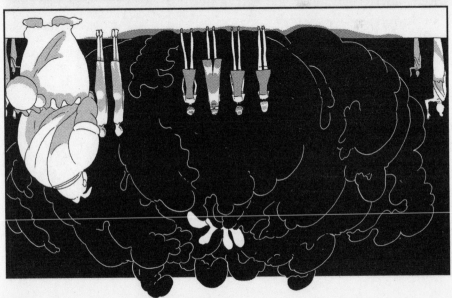

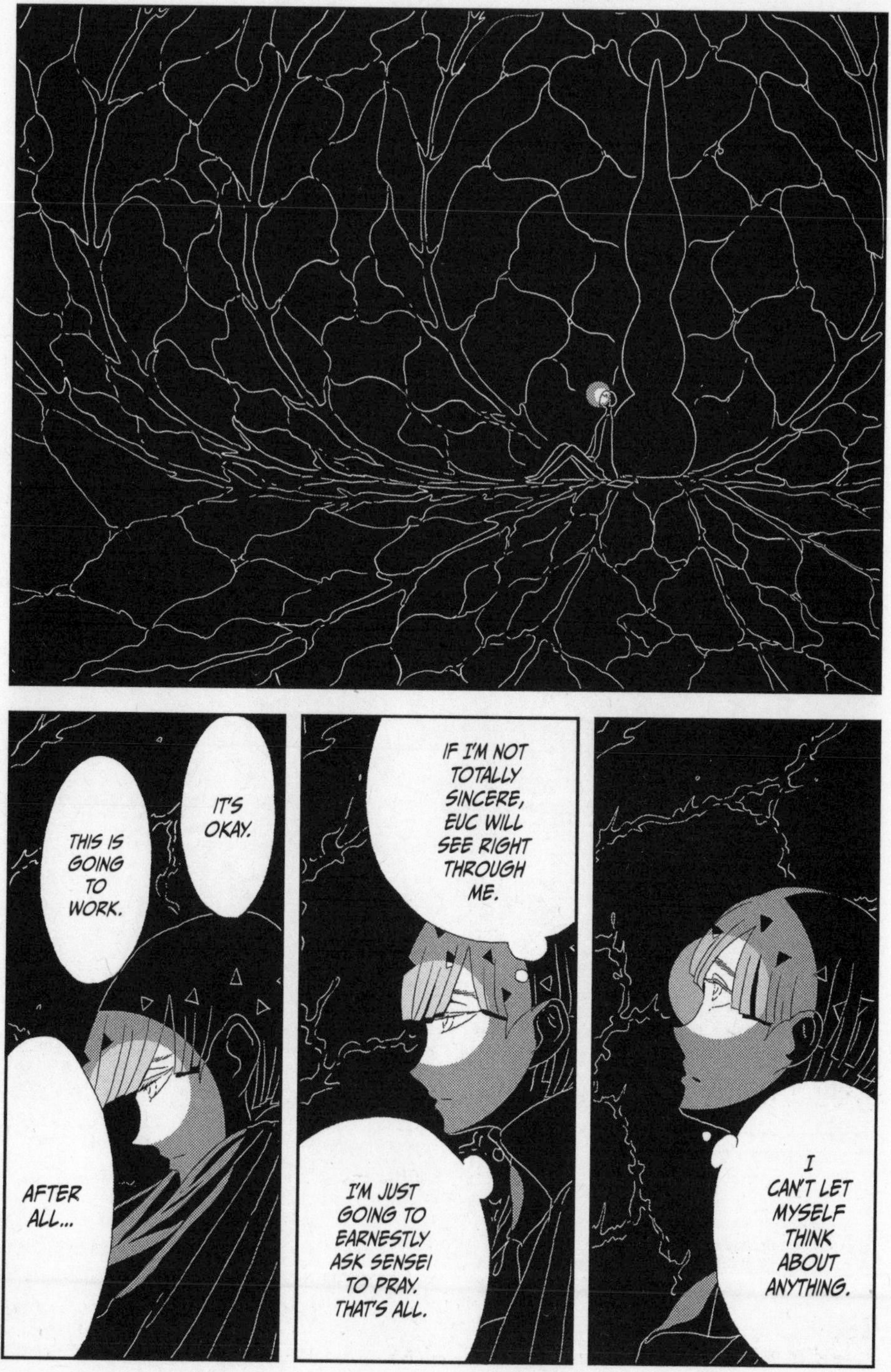
I CAN'T LET MYSELF THINK ABOUT ANYTHING.
IF I'M NOT TOTALLY SINCERE, EUC WILL SEE RIGHT THROUGH ME.
I'M JUST GOING TO EARNESTLY ASK SENSEI TO PRAY. THAT'S ALL.
IT'S OKAY.
THIS IS GOING TO WORK.
AFTER ALL...

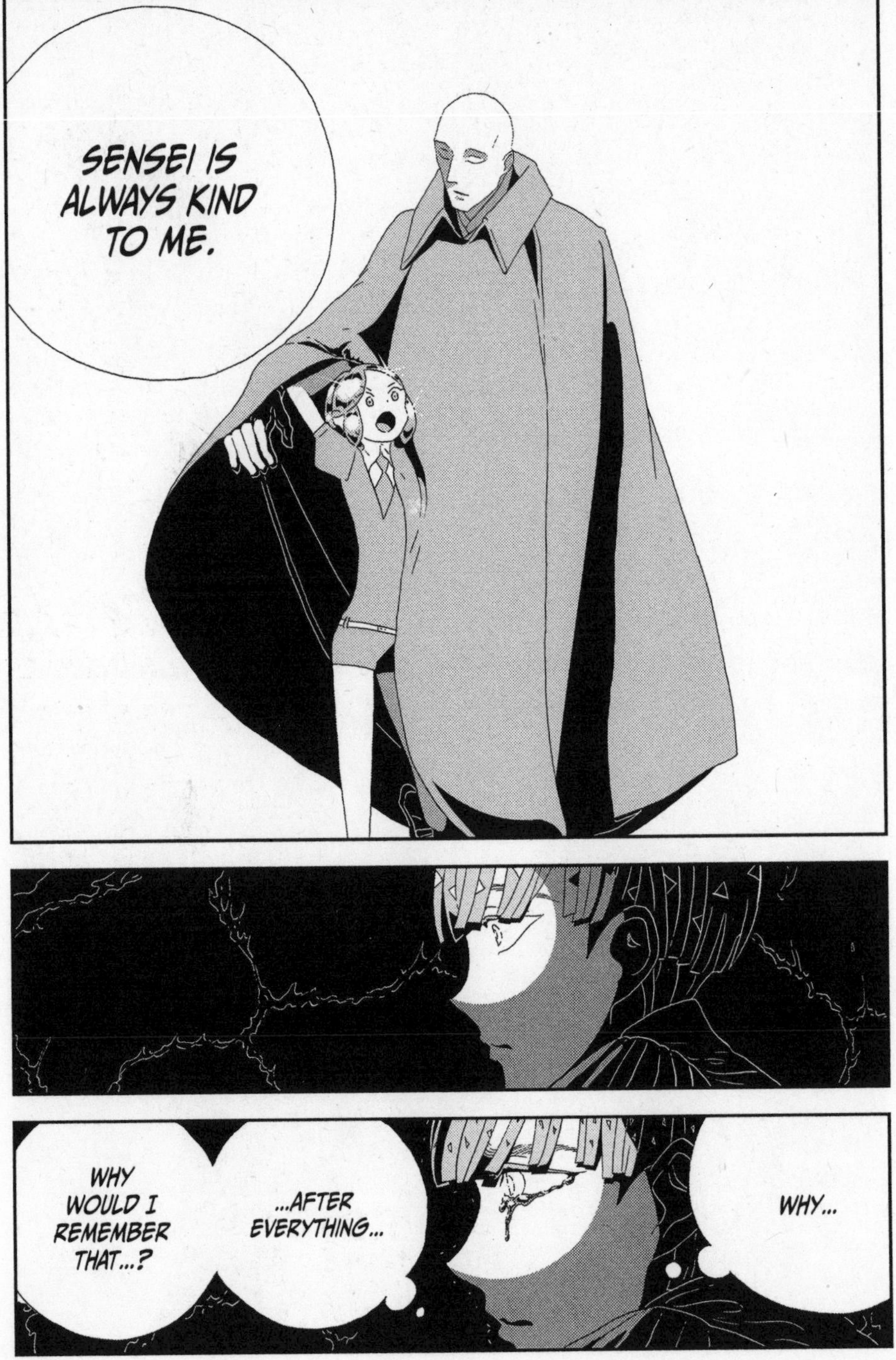
SENSEI IS ALWAYS KIND TO ME.
WHY...
...AFTER EVERYTHING...
WHY WOULD I REMEMBER THAT...?

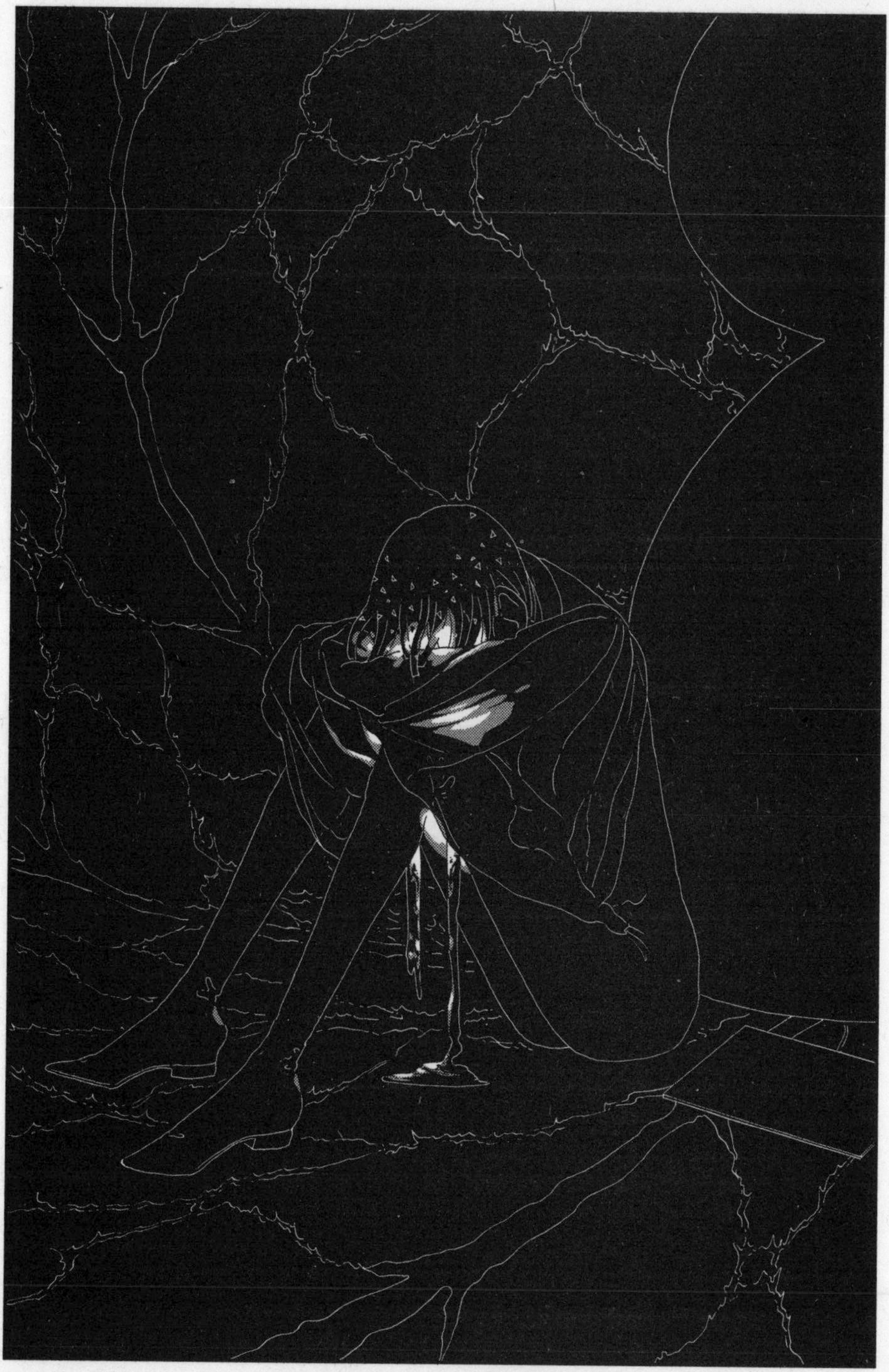

CHAPTER 76: Admirabilis END

CHAPTER 77:

Authentication

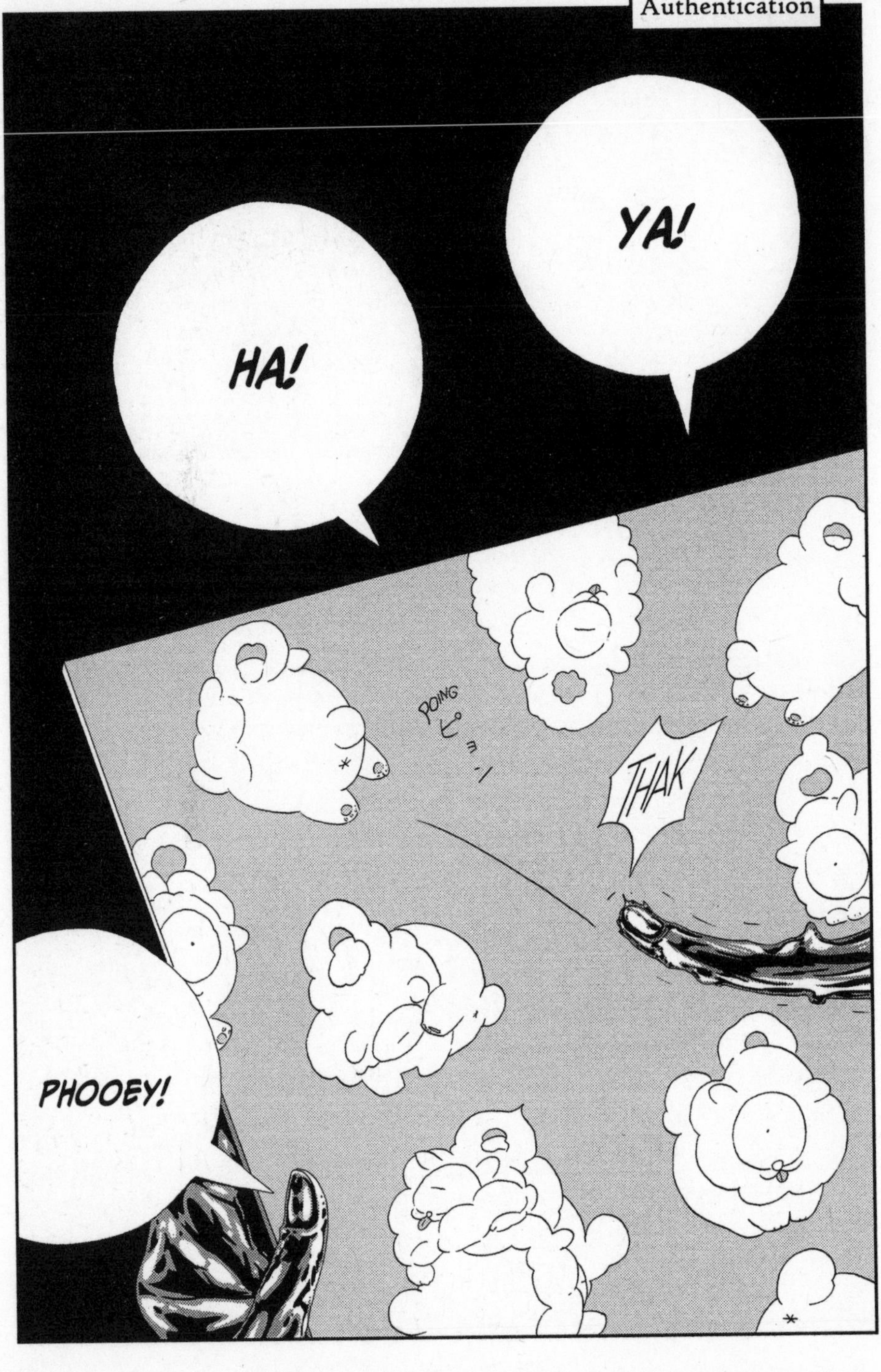
YA!
HA!
THAK
POING
ピョン
PHOOEY!

YOU LITTLE!
HEY!
THAK
THAK
THAK
YAH!
THAK
WHAAAAAAT ?!
IS IT ME, OR IS THE LAST LEVEL WAY HARDER THAN ALL THE OTHERS?!
CLUNK

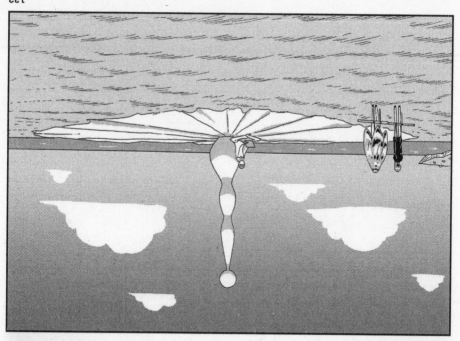

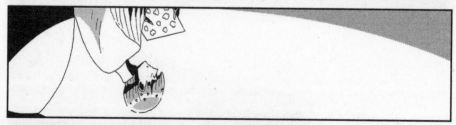

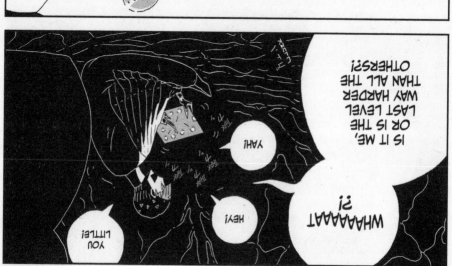

LOOK!
I'M UNARMED!
OH! THIS TABLET WON'T HURT YOU.
IT'S GONNA BE GONE BEFORE YOU KNOW IT.
...ANYWAY, MIND IF I BEAT THIS GAME FIRST?

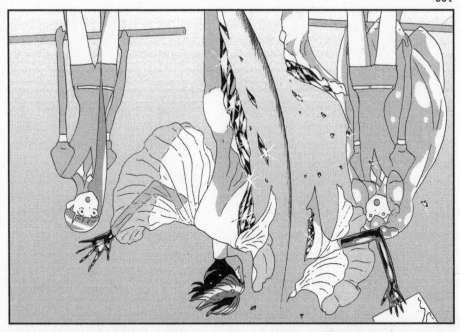

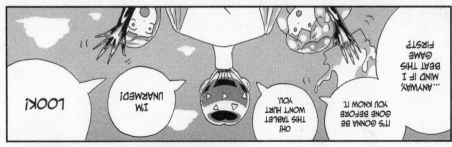

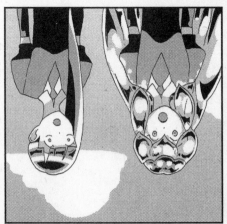

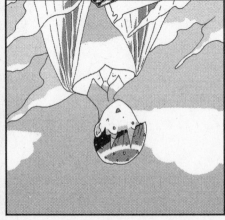

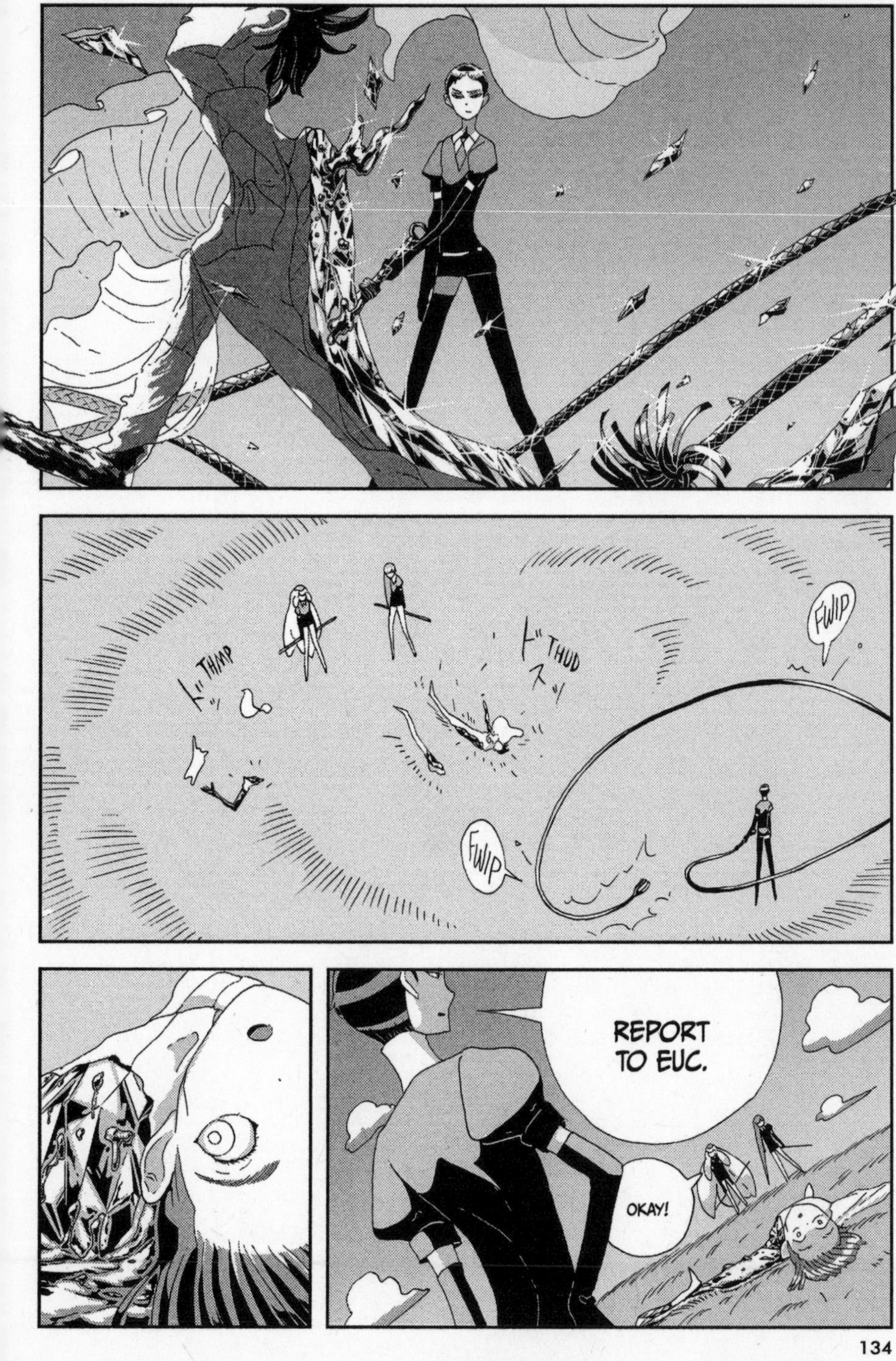
FWIP
THUD
THMP
FWIP
REPORT TO EUC.
OKAY!

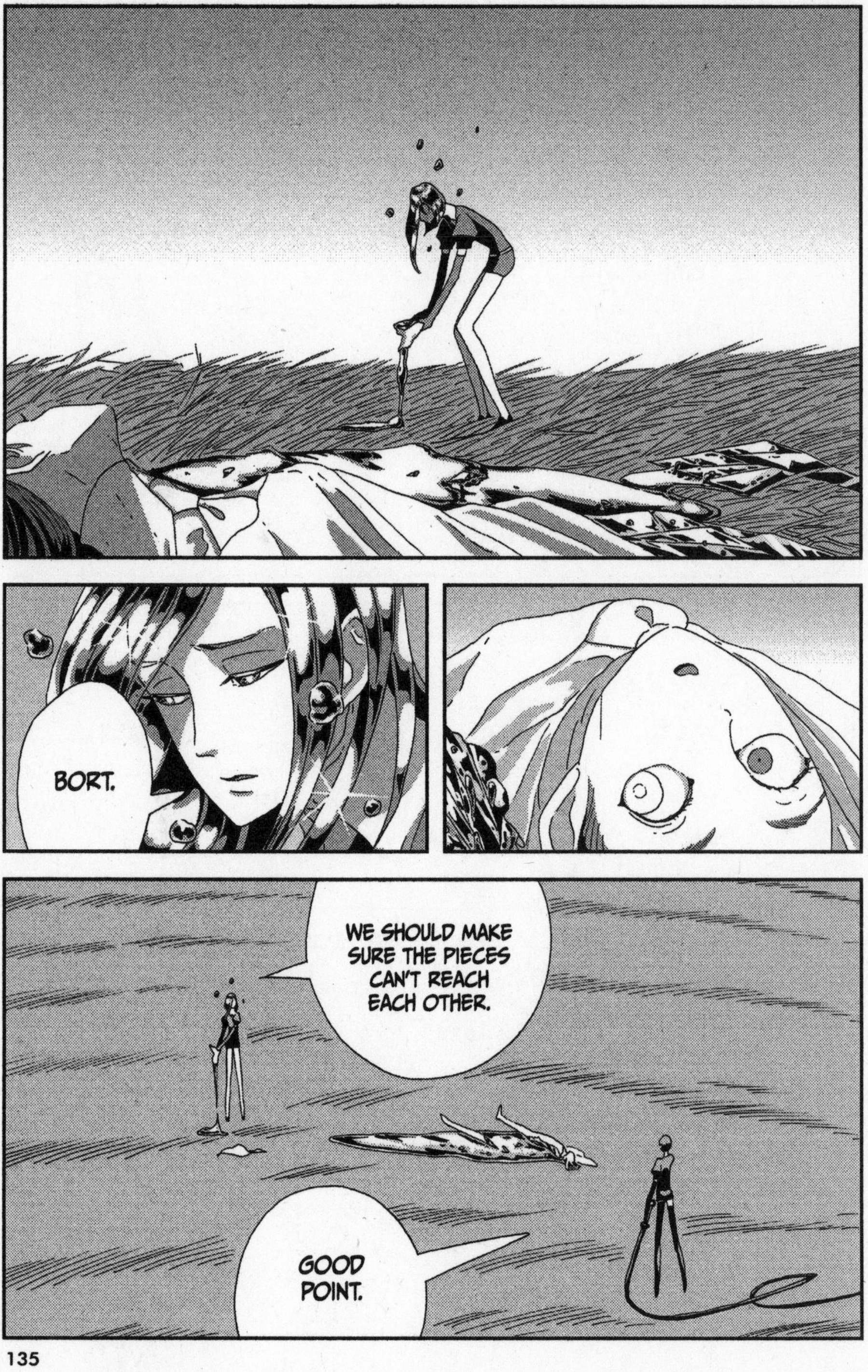
BORT.
WE SHOULD MAKE SURE THE PIECES CAN'T REACH EACH OTHER.
GOOD POINT.

I WANT TO SEE SENSEI.
I WANT...
...TO SEE SENSEI.

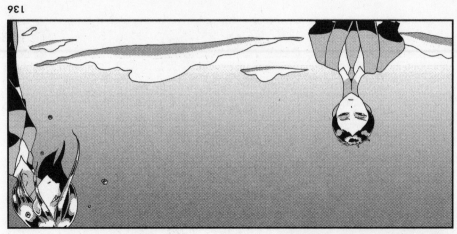

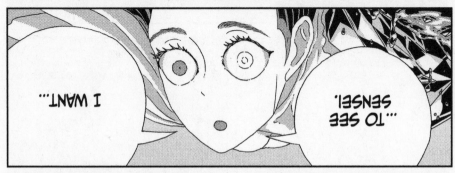

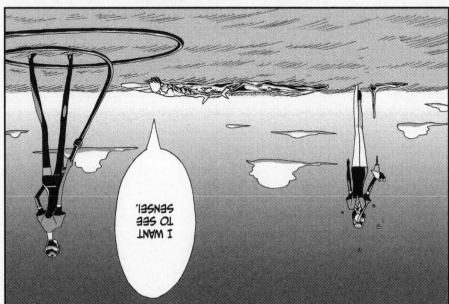

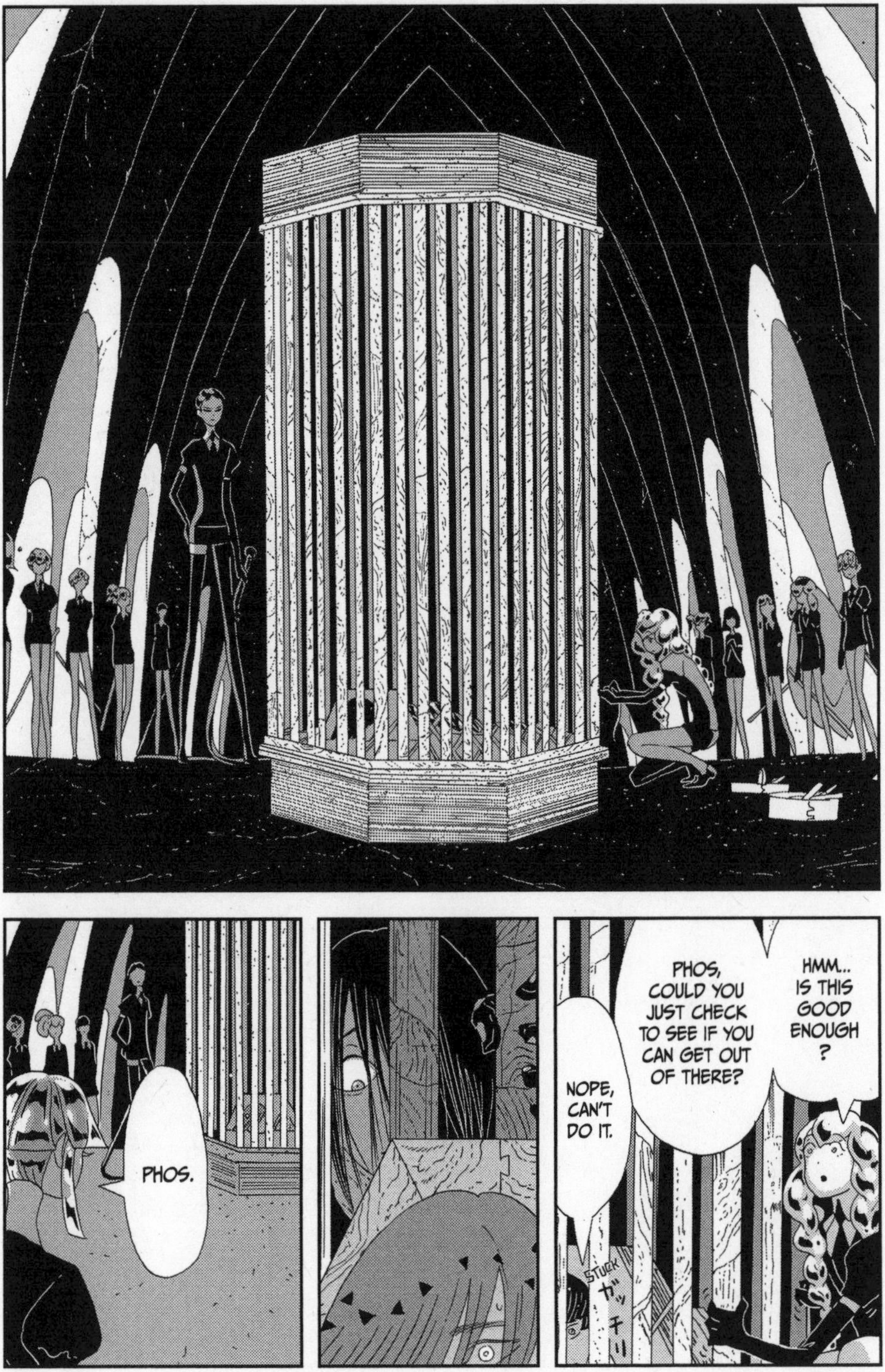
HMM... IS THIS GOOD ENOUGH ?
PHOS, COULD YOU JUST CHECK TO SEE IF YOU CAN GET OUT OF THERE?
NOPE, CAN'T DO IT.
STUCK
ガッチリ
PHOS.

KONGŌ WANTS TO SEE YOU, TOO.
SENSEI.

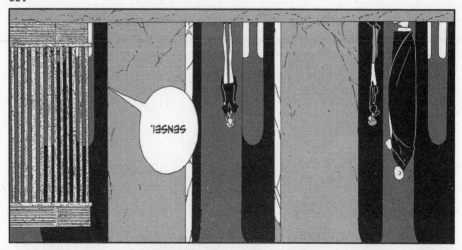

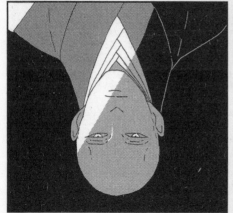

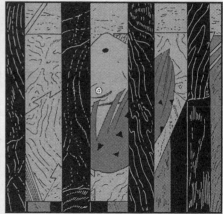

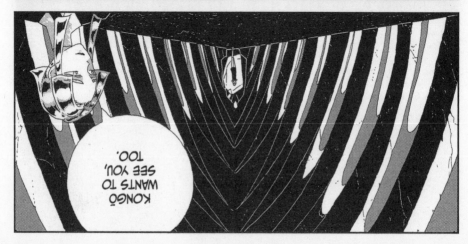

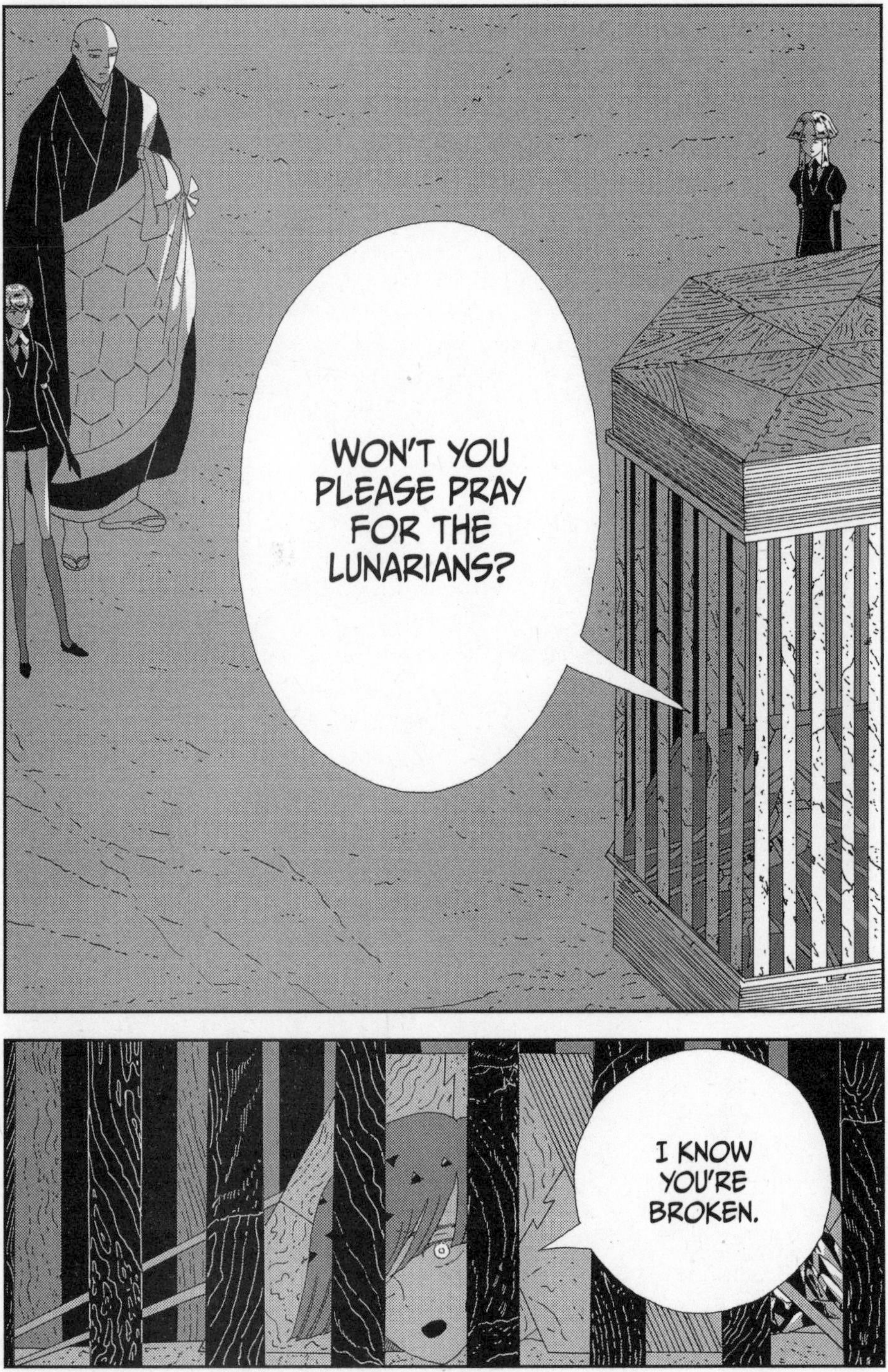
WON'T YOU PLEASE PRAY FOR THE LUNARIANS?
I KNOW YOU'RE BROKEN.

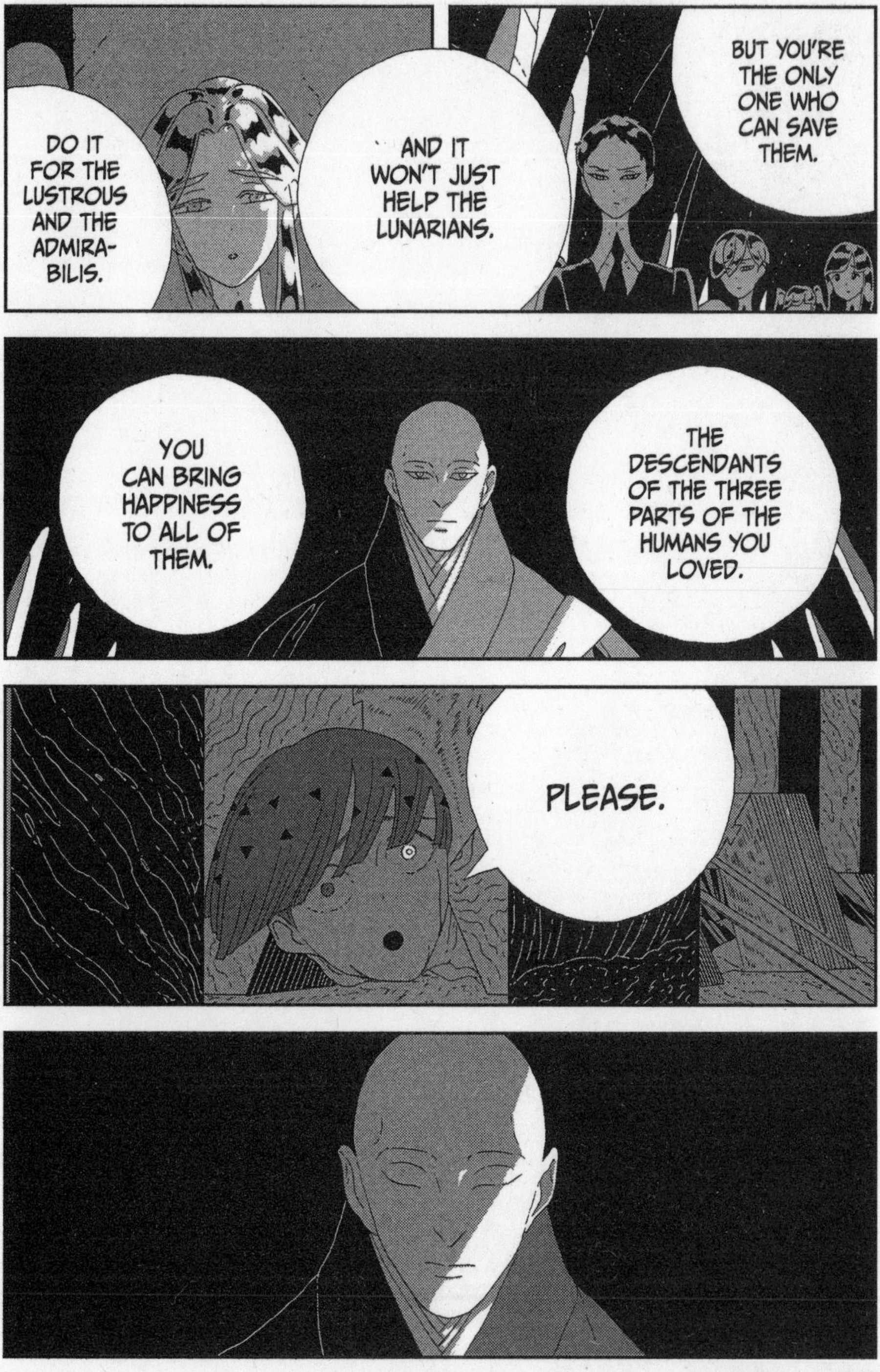
BUT YOU'RE THE ONLY ONE WHO CAN SAVE THEM.
AND IT WON'T JUST HELP THE LUNARIANS.
DO IT FOR THE LUSTROUS AND THE ADMIRA-BILIS.
THE DESCENDANTS OF THE THREE PARTS OF THE HUMANS YOU LOVED.
YOU CAN BRING HAPPINESS TO ALL OF THEM.
PLEASE.

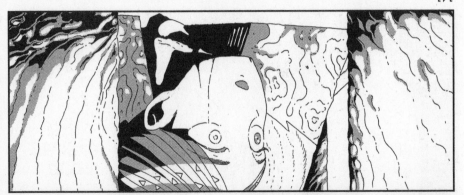

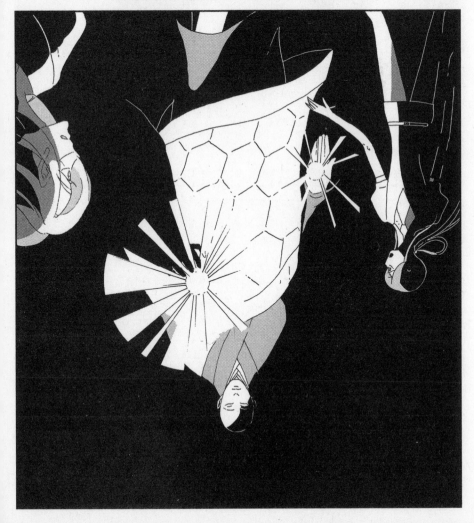

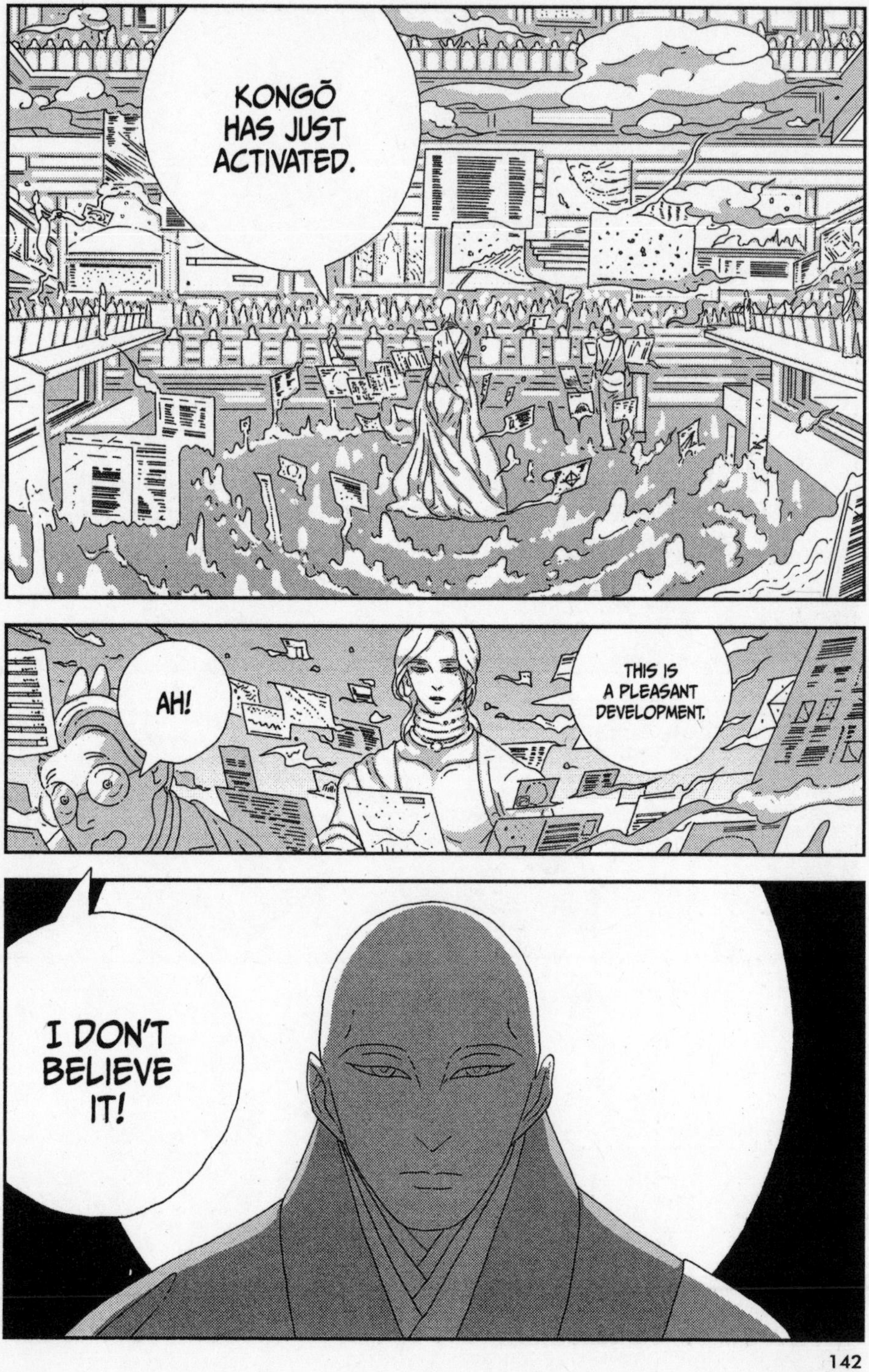
KONGŌ HAS JUST ACTIVATED.
THIS IS A PLEASANT DEVELOPMENT.
AH!
I DON'T BELIEVE IT!

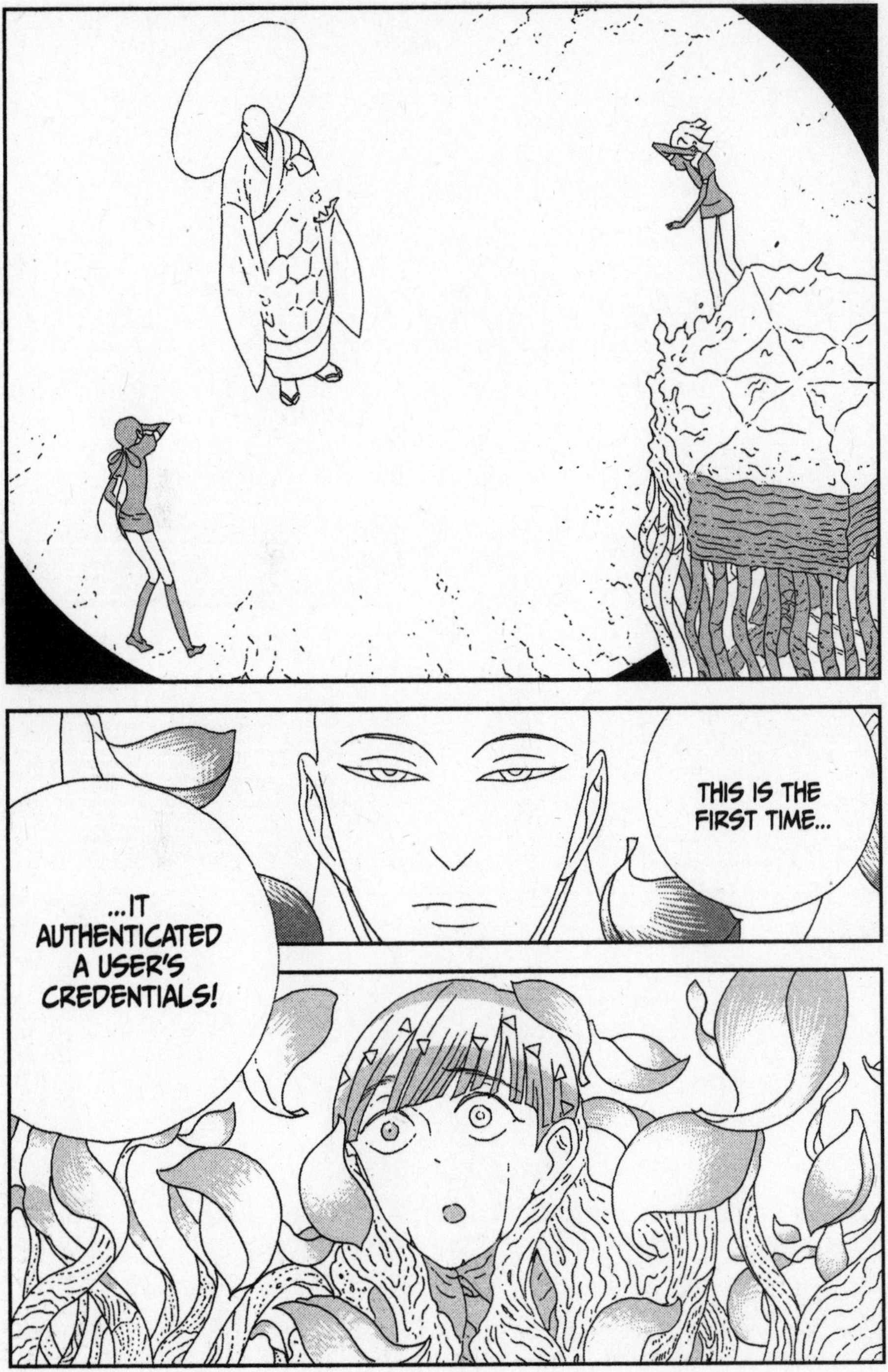
THIS IS THE FIRST TIME...
...IT AUTHENTICATED A USER'S CREDENTIALS!

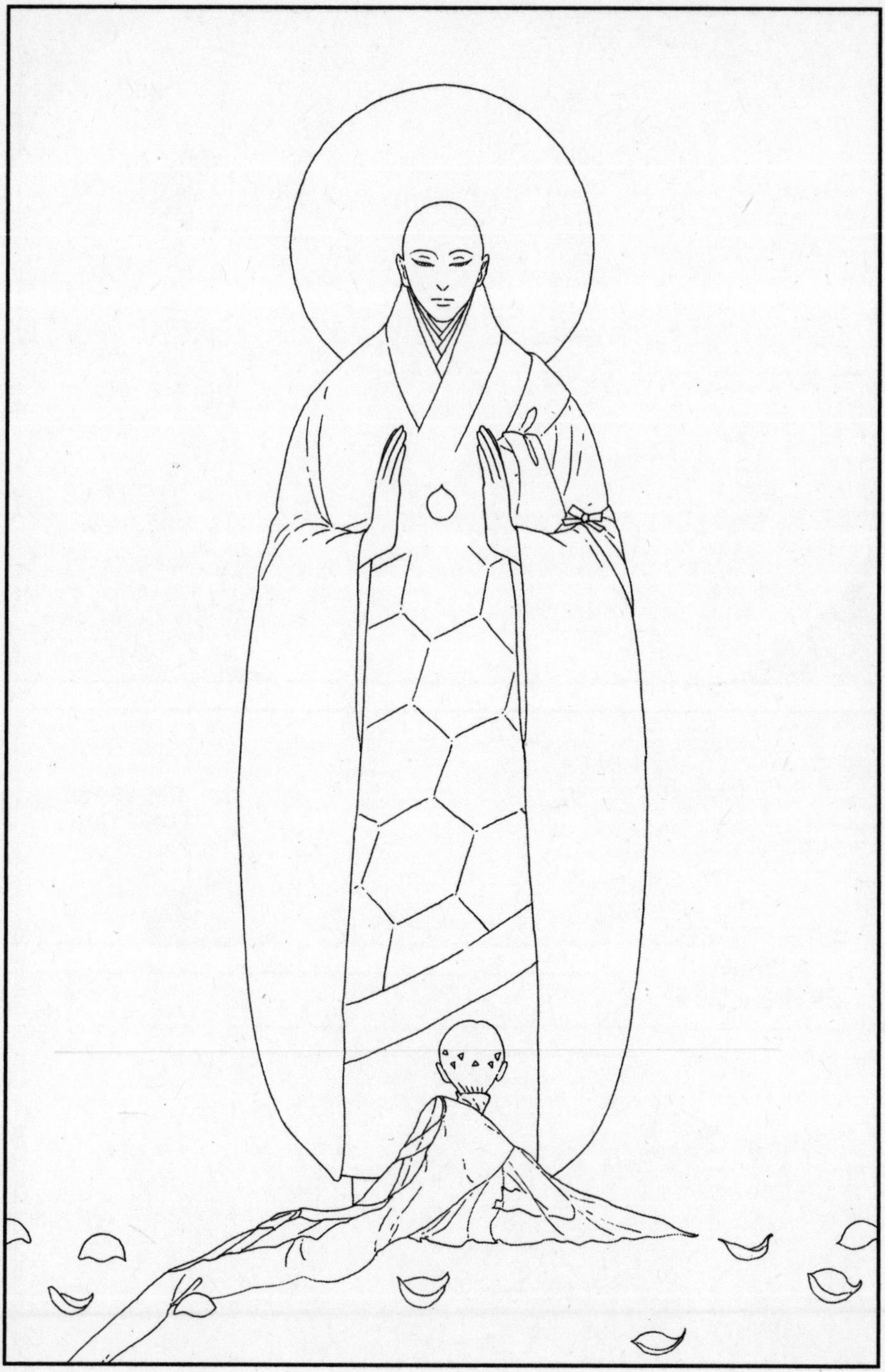

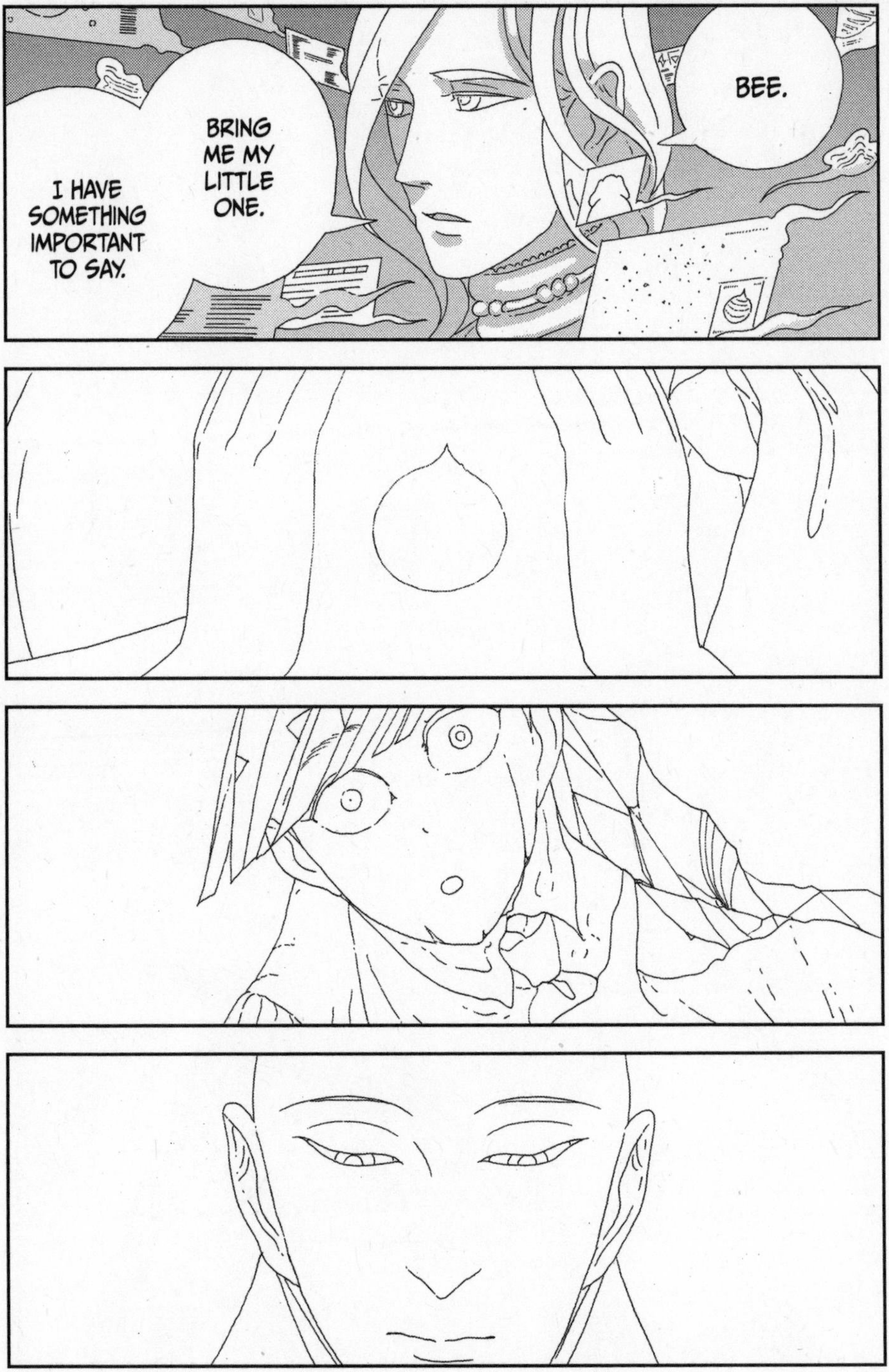
BEE.
BRING ME MY LITTLE ONE.
I HAVE SOMETHING IMPORTANT TO SAY.

I CAN'T. NOT EVEN FOR YOU.

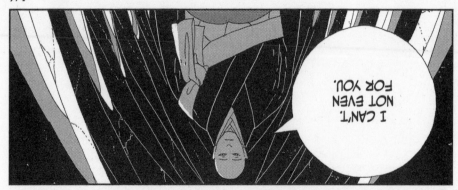

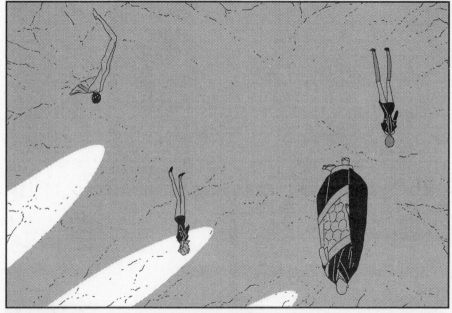

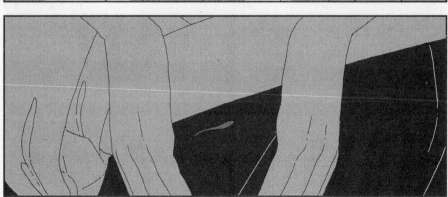

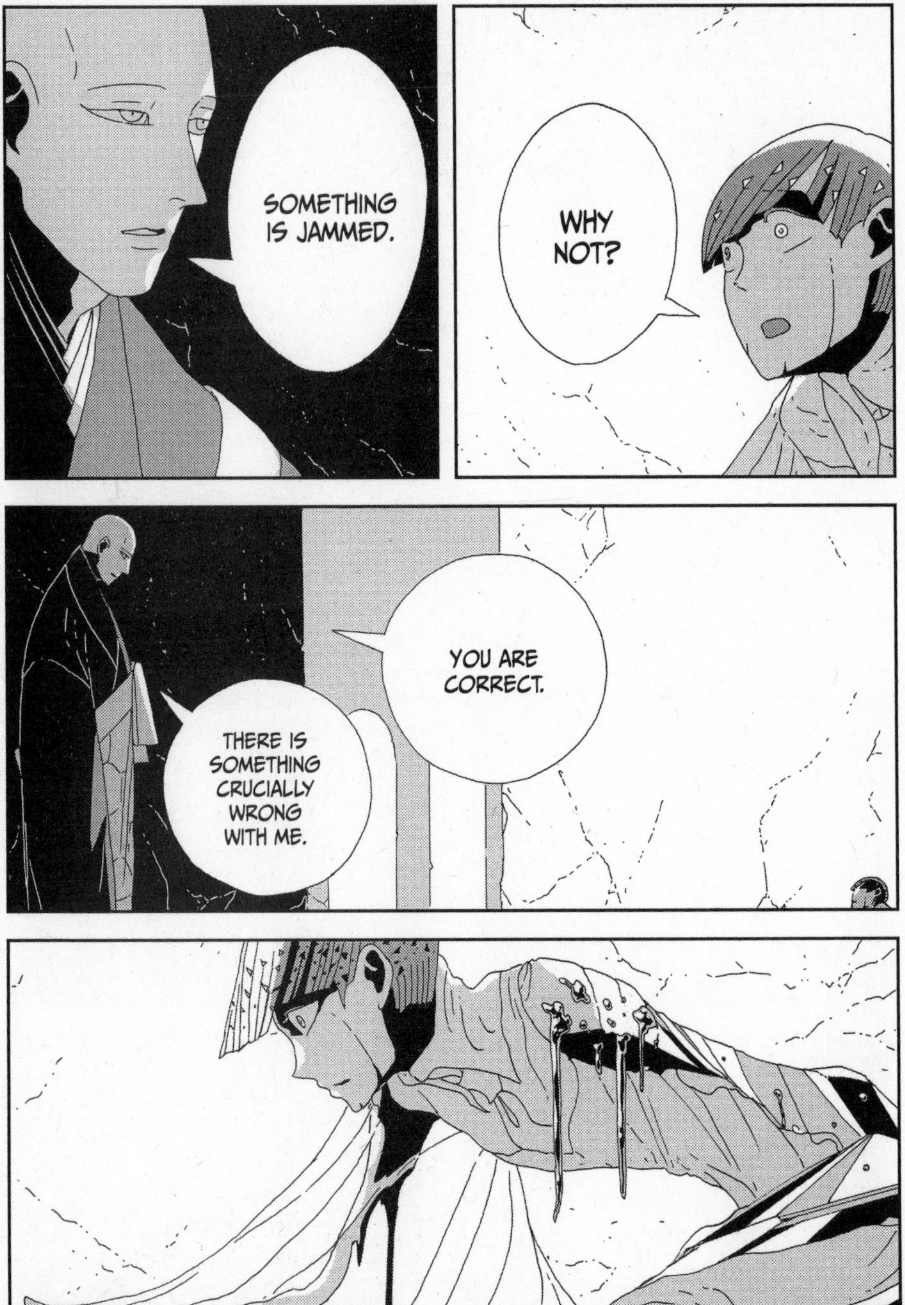
WHY NOT?
SOMETHING IS JAMMED.
YOU ARE CORRECT.
THERE IS SOMETHING CRUCIALLY WRONG WITH ME.

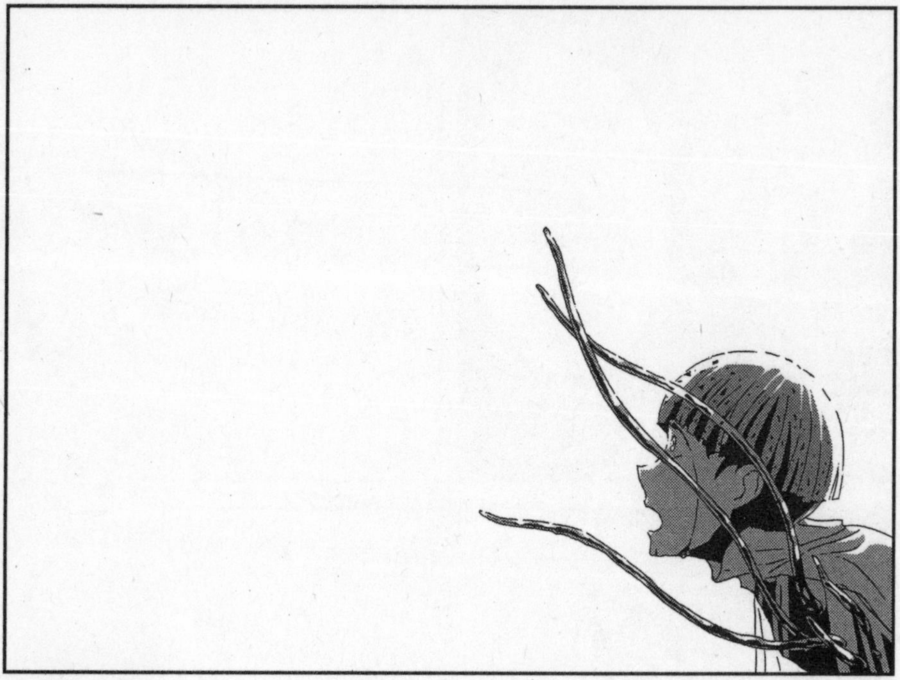
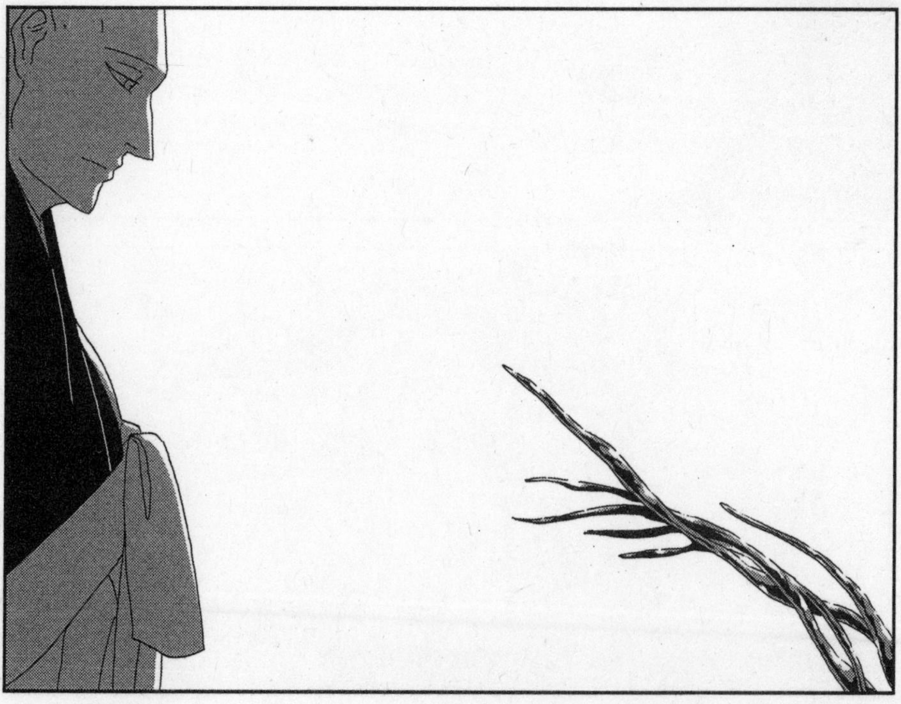

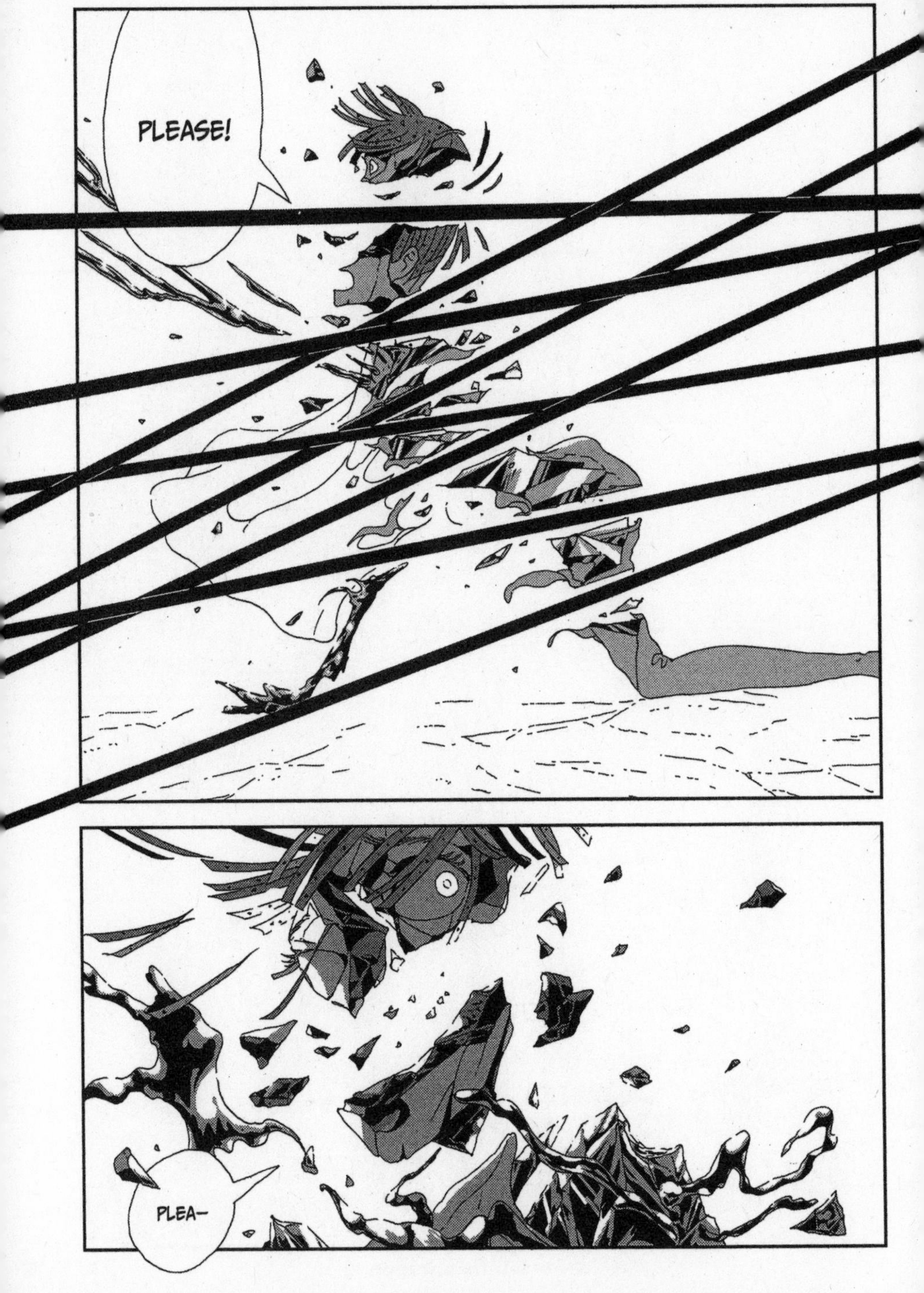
PLEASE!
PLEA–

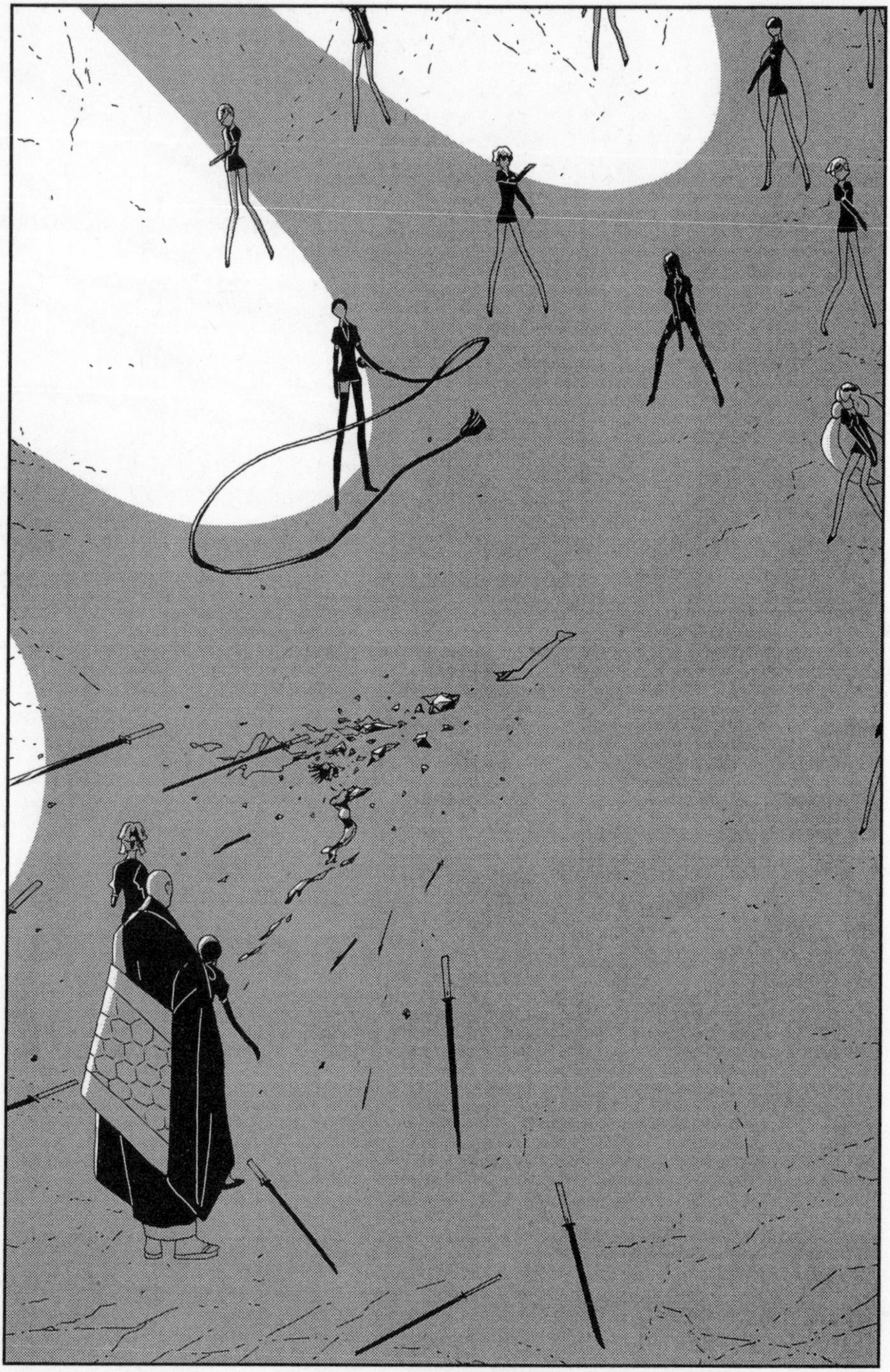

CHAPTER 77: Authentication END

CHAPTER 78: Passage

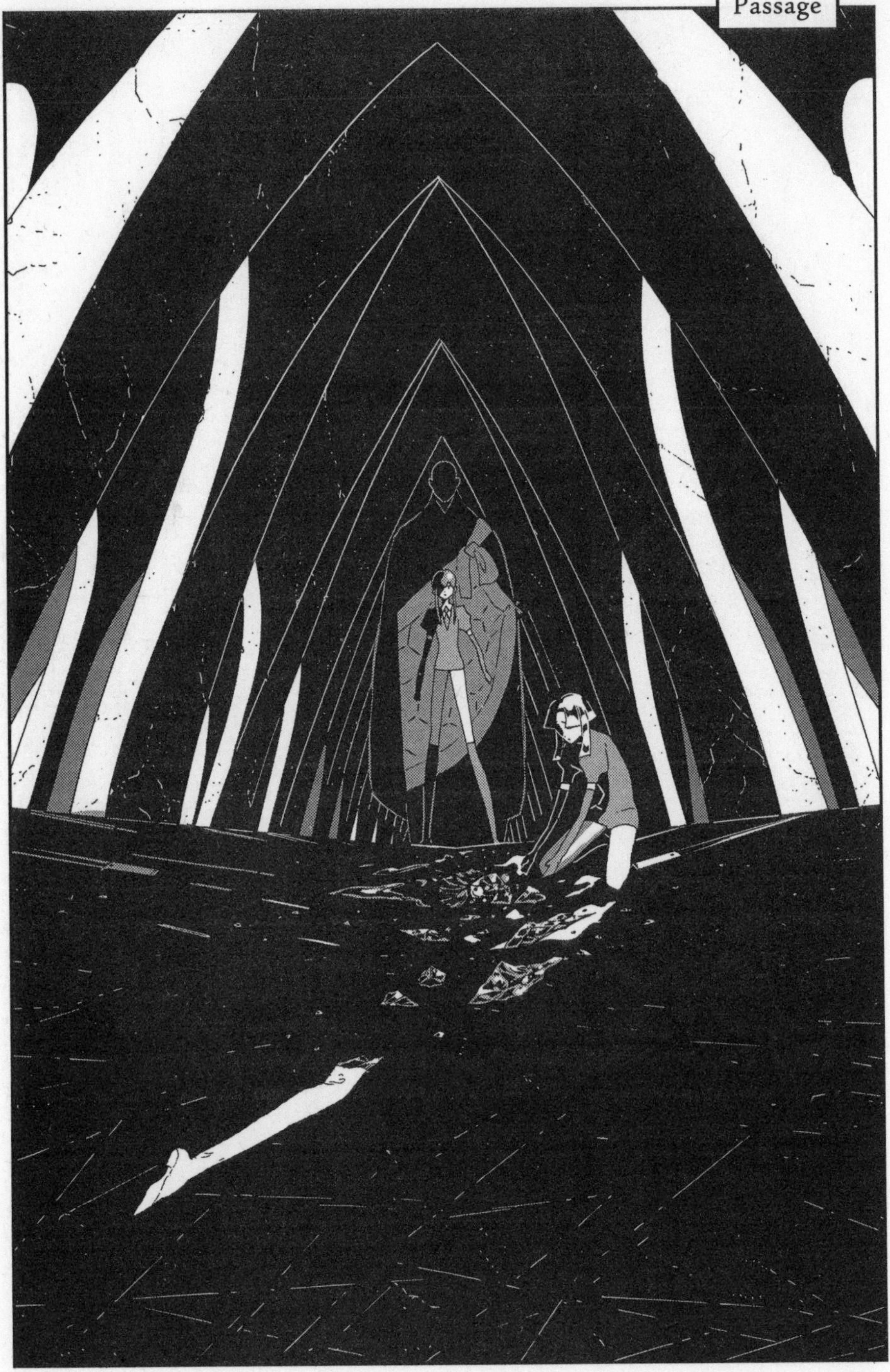

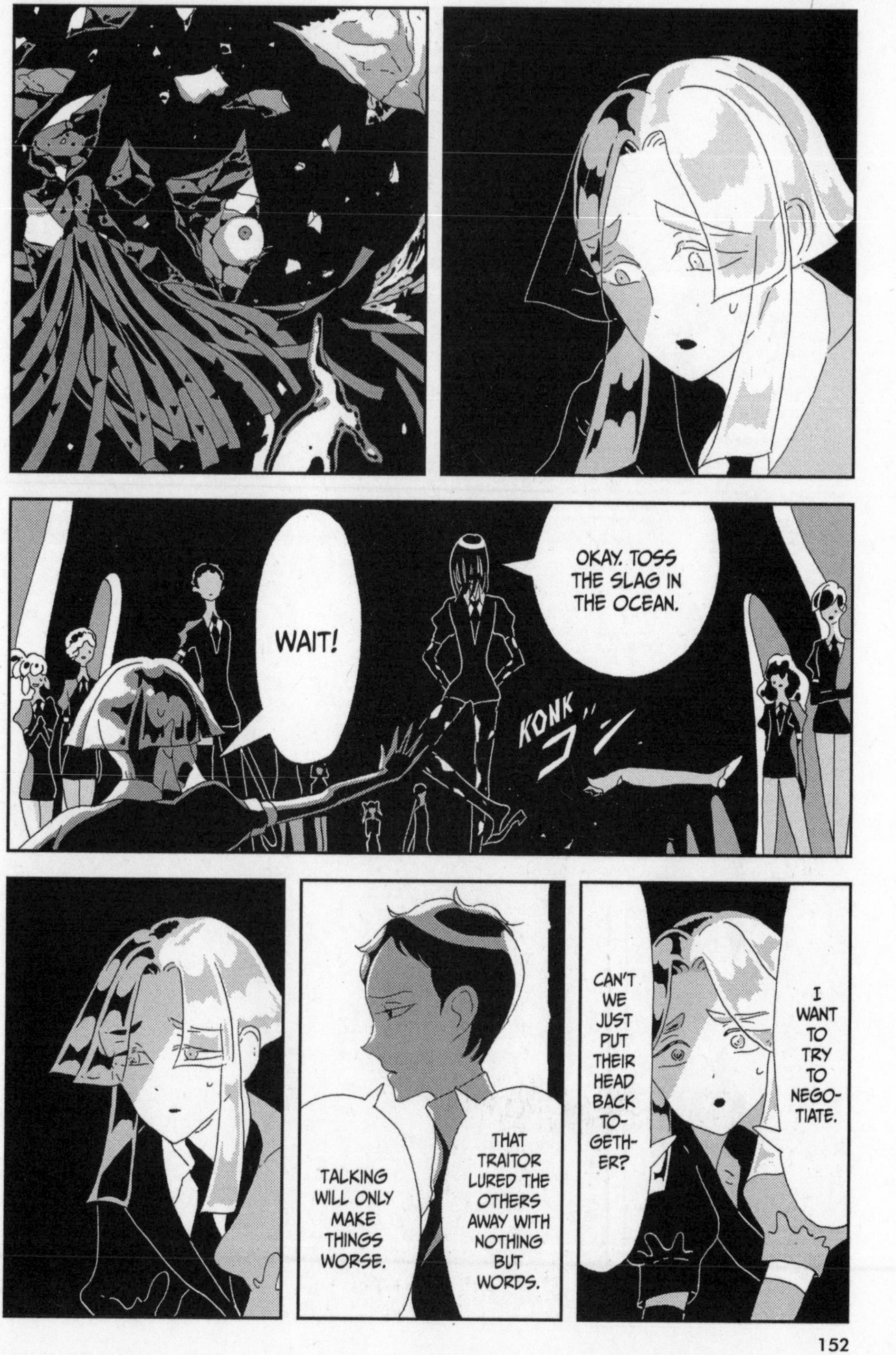
OKAY. TOSS THE SLAG IN THE OCEAN.
KONK
WAIT!
I WANT TO TRY TO NEGO-TIATE.
CAN'T WE JUST PUT THEIR HEAD BACK TO-GETH-ER?
THAT TRAITOR LURED THE OTHERS AWAY WITH NOTHING BUT WORDS.
TALKING WILL ONLY MAKE THINGS WORSE.

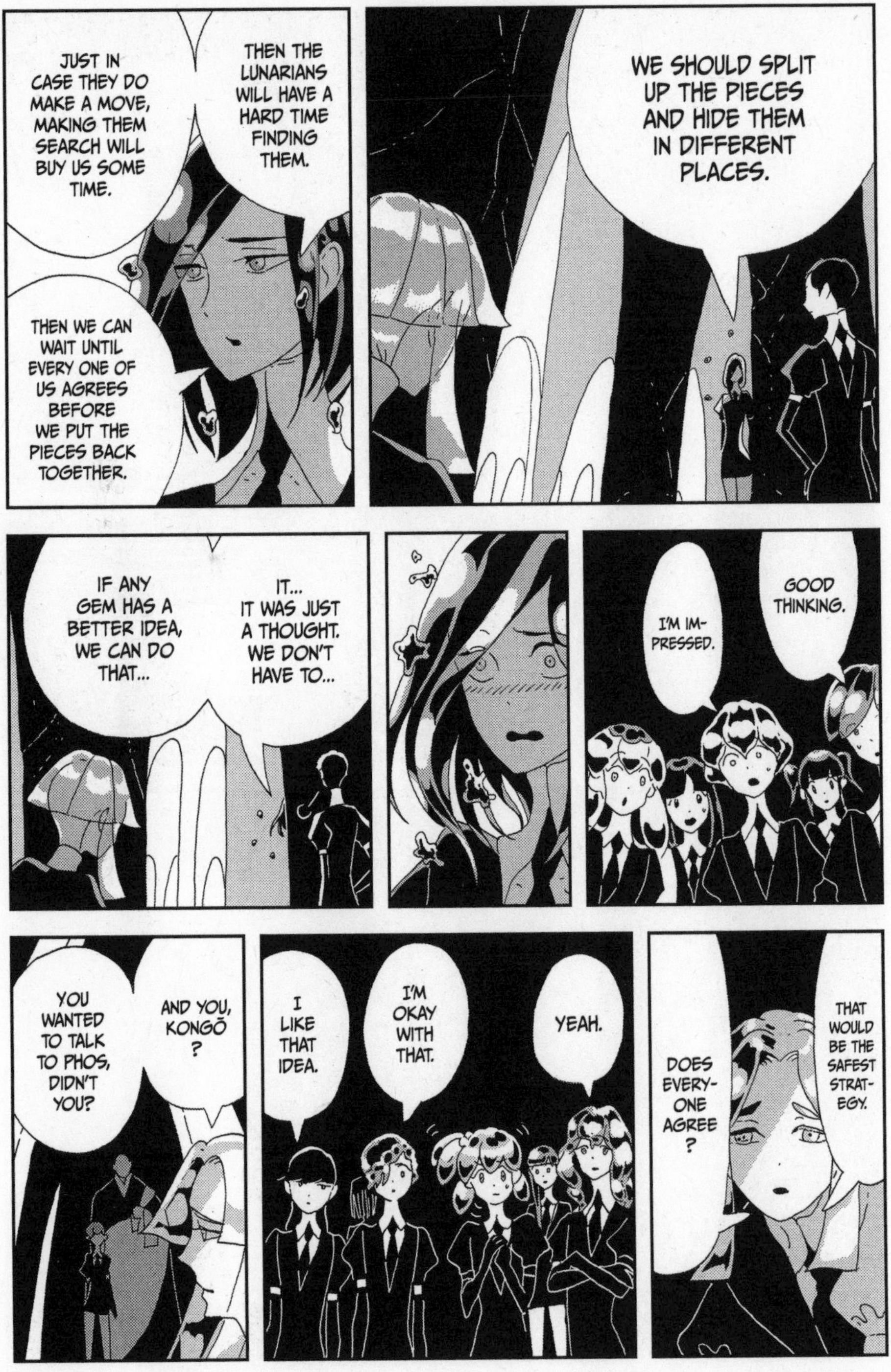
WE SHOULD SPLIT UP THE PIECES AND HIDE THEM IN DIFFERENT PLACES.
THEN THE LUNARIANS WILL HAVE A HARD TIME FINDING THEM.
JUST IN CASE THEY DO MAKE A MOVE, MAKING THEM SEARCH WILL BUY US SOME TIME.
THEN WE CAN WAIT UNTIL EVERY ONE OF US AGREES BEFORE WE PUT THE PIECES BACK TOGETHER.
GOOD THINKING.
I'M IM-PRESSED.
IT... IT WAS JUST A THOUGHT. WE DON'T HAVE TO...
IF ANY GEM HAS A BETTER IDEA, WE CAN DO THAT...
THAT WOULD BE THE SAFEST STRAT-EGY.
DOES EVERY-ONE AGREE ?
YEAH.
I'M OKAY WITH THAT.
I LIKE THAT IDEA.
AND YOU, KONGŌ ?
YOU WANTED TO TALK TO PHOS, DIDN'T YOU?

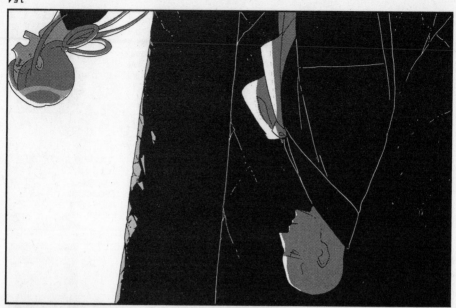

SIGH...

PHOS...

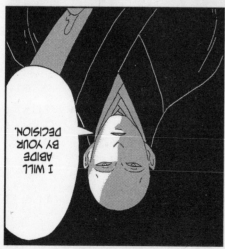

I WILL ABIDE BY YOUR DECISION.

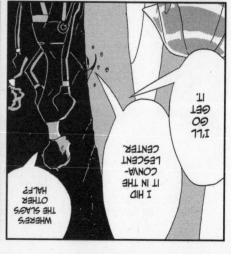

WHERE'S THE SLAG'S OTHER HALF?

I HID IT IN THE CONVA-LESCENT CENTER.

I'LL GO GET IT.

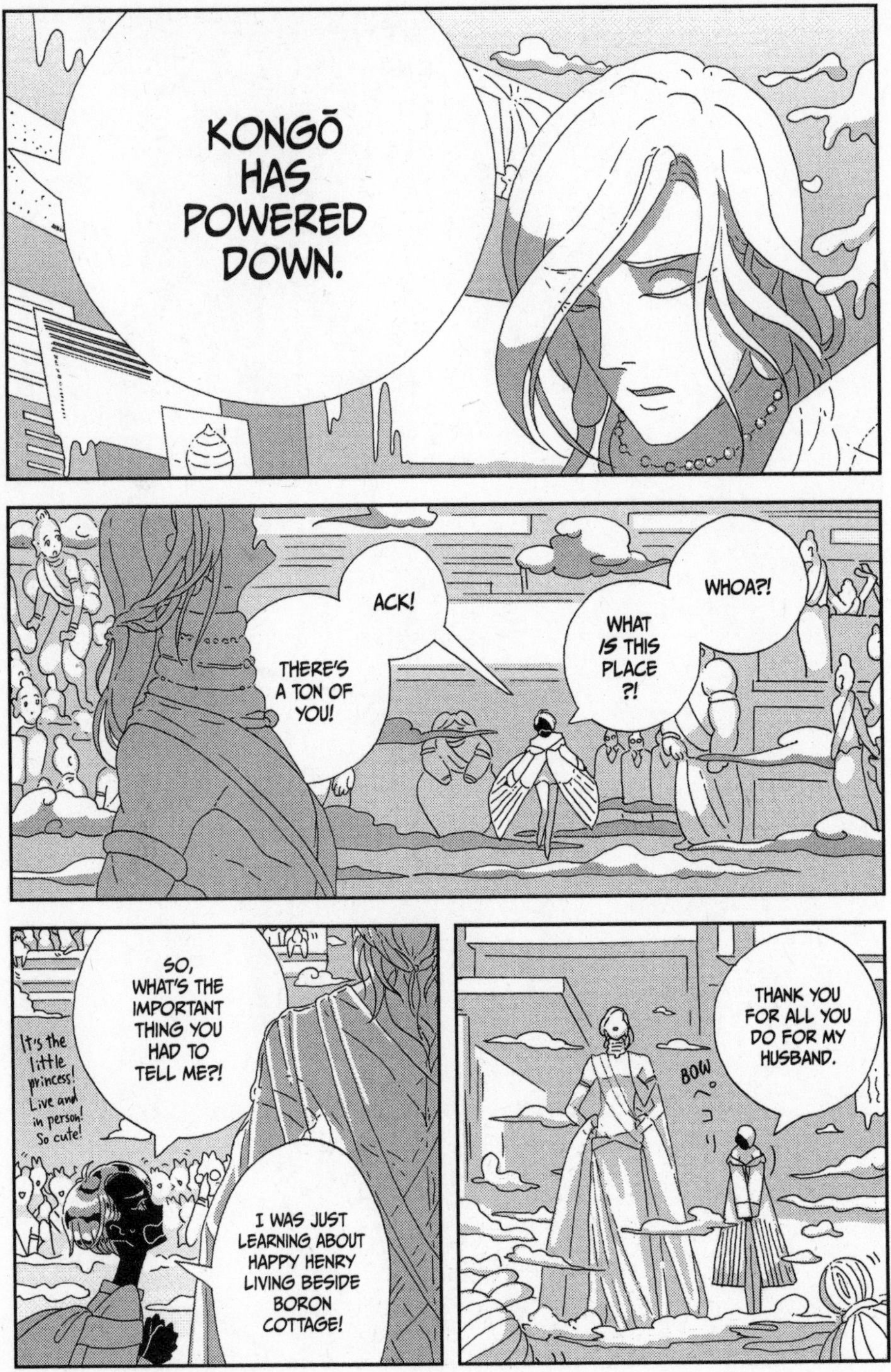
KONGŌ HAS POWERED DOWN.
WHOA?!
WHAT IS THIS PLACE ?!
ACK!
THERE'S A TON OF YOU!
THANK YOU FOR ALL YOU DO FOR MY HUSBAND.
BOW
SO, WHAT'S THE IMPORTANT THING YOU HAD TO TELL ME?!
It's the little princess! Live and in person! So cute!
I WAS JUST LEARNING ABOUT HAPPY HENRY LIVING BESIDE BORON COTTAGE!

I'LL BE MAKING DINNER TONIGHT.
SERIOUSLY ?!
WHAT WILL IT BE?
CURRY.

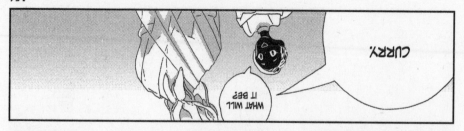

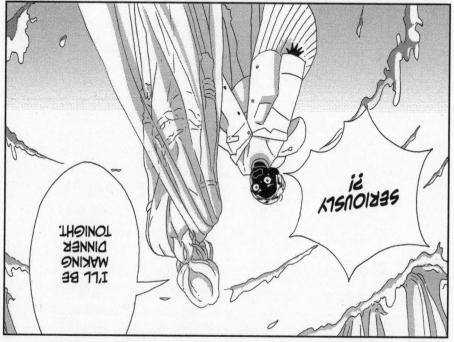

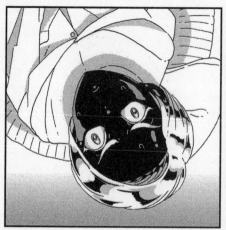

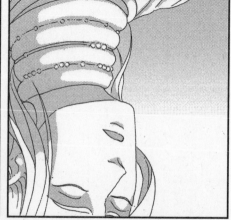

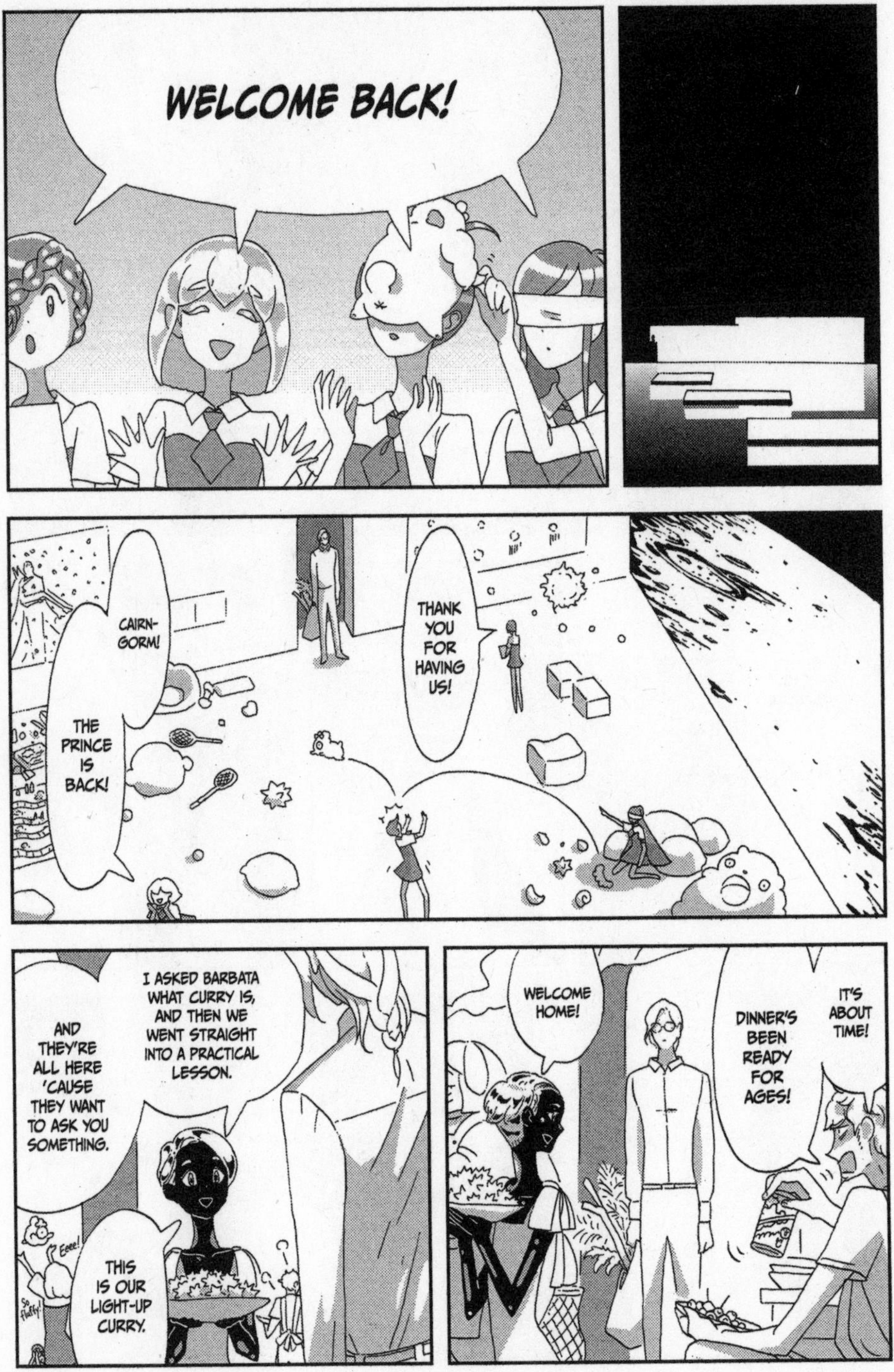
WELCOME BACK!
THANK YOU FOR HAVING US!
CAIRN-GORM!
THE PRINCE IS BACK!
IT'S ABOUT TIME!
DINNER'S BEEN READY FOR AGES!
WELCOME HOME!
I ASKED BARBATA WHAT CURRY IS, AND THEN WE WENT STRAIGHT INTO A PRACTICAL LESSON.
AND THEY'RE ALL HERE 'CAUSE THEY WANT TO ASK YOU SOMETHING.
Eeee!
THIS IS OUR LIGHT-UP CURRY.
So fluffy!

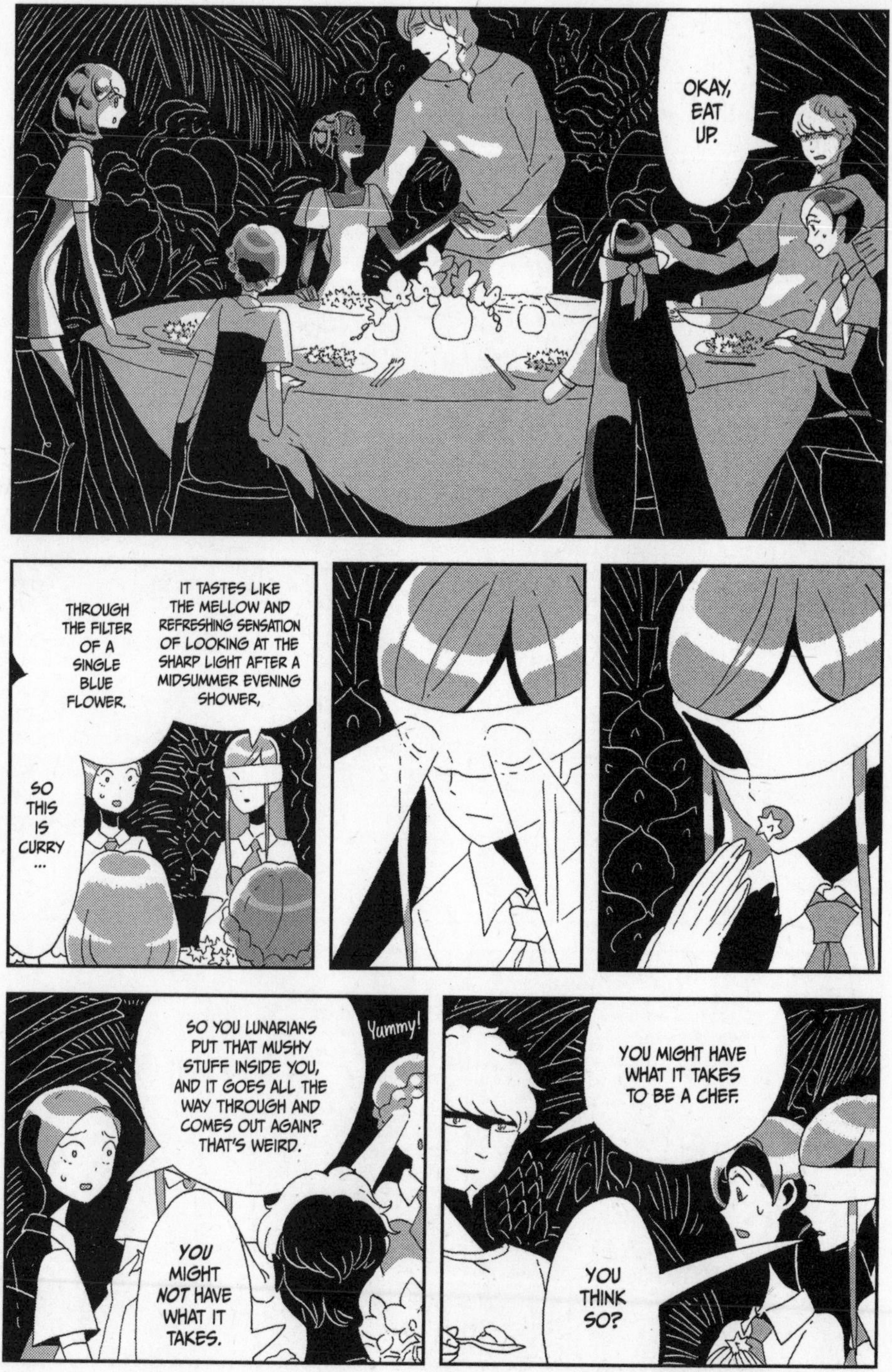
OKAY, EAT UP.
IT TASTES LIKE THE MELLOW AND REFRESHING SENSATION OF LOOKING AT THE SHARP LIGHT AFTER A MIDSUMMER EVENING SHOWER,
THROUGH THE FILTER OF A SINGLE BLUE FLOWER.
SO THIS IS CURRY ...
YOU MIGHT HAVE WHAT IT TAKES TO BE A CHEF.
YOU THINK SO?
SO YOU LUNARIANS PUT THAT MUSHY STUFF INSIDE YOU, AND IT GOES ALL THE WAY THROUGH AND COMES OUT AGAIN? THAT'S WEIRD.
Yummy!
YOU MIGHT NOT HAVE WHAT IT TAKES.

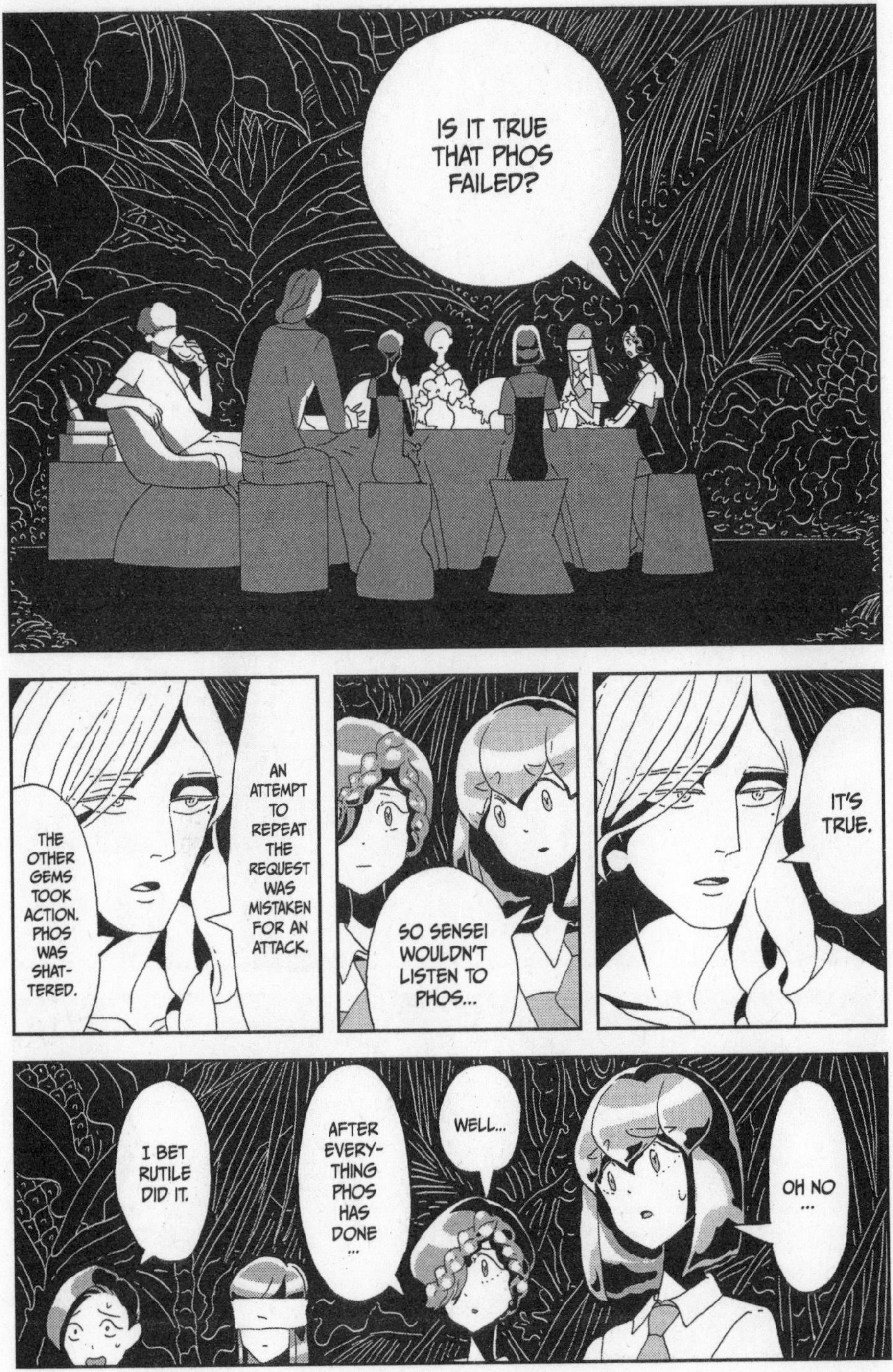
IS IT TRUE THAT PHOS FAILED?
IT'S TRUE.
SO SENSEI WOULDN'T LISTEN TO PHOS...
AN ATTEMPT TO REPEAT THE REQUEST WAS MISTAKEN FOR AN ATTACK.
THE OTHER GEMS TOOK ACTION. PHOS WAS SHAT-TERED.
OH NO ...
WELL...
AFTER EVERY-THING PHOS HAS DONE ...
I BET RUTILE DID IT.

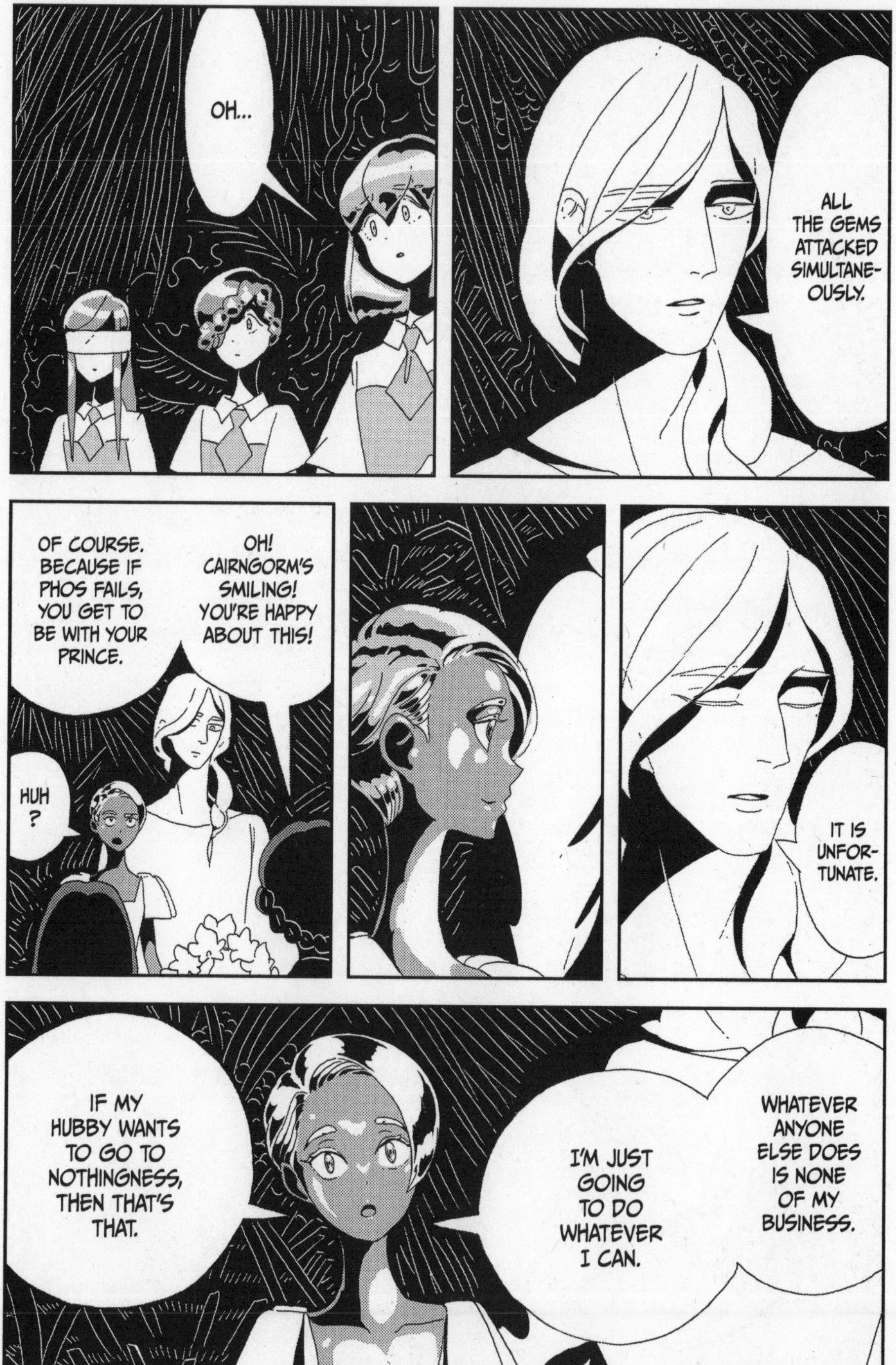
ALL THE GEMS ATTACKED SIMULTANEOUSLY.
OH...
IT IS UNFORTUNATE.
OH! CAIRNGORM'S SMILING! YOU'RE HAPPY ABOUT THIS!
OF COURSE. BECAUSE IF PHOS FAILS, YOU GET TO BE WITH YOUR PRINCE.
HUH?
WHATEVER ANYONE ELSE DOES IS NONE OF MY BUSINESS.
I'M JUST GOING TO DO WHATEVER I CAN.
IF MY HUBBY WANTS TO GO TO NOTHINGNESS, THEN THAT'S THAT.

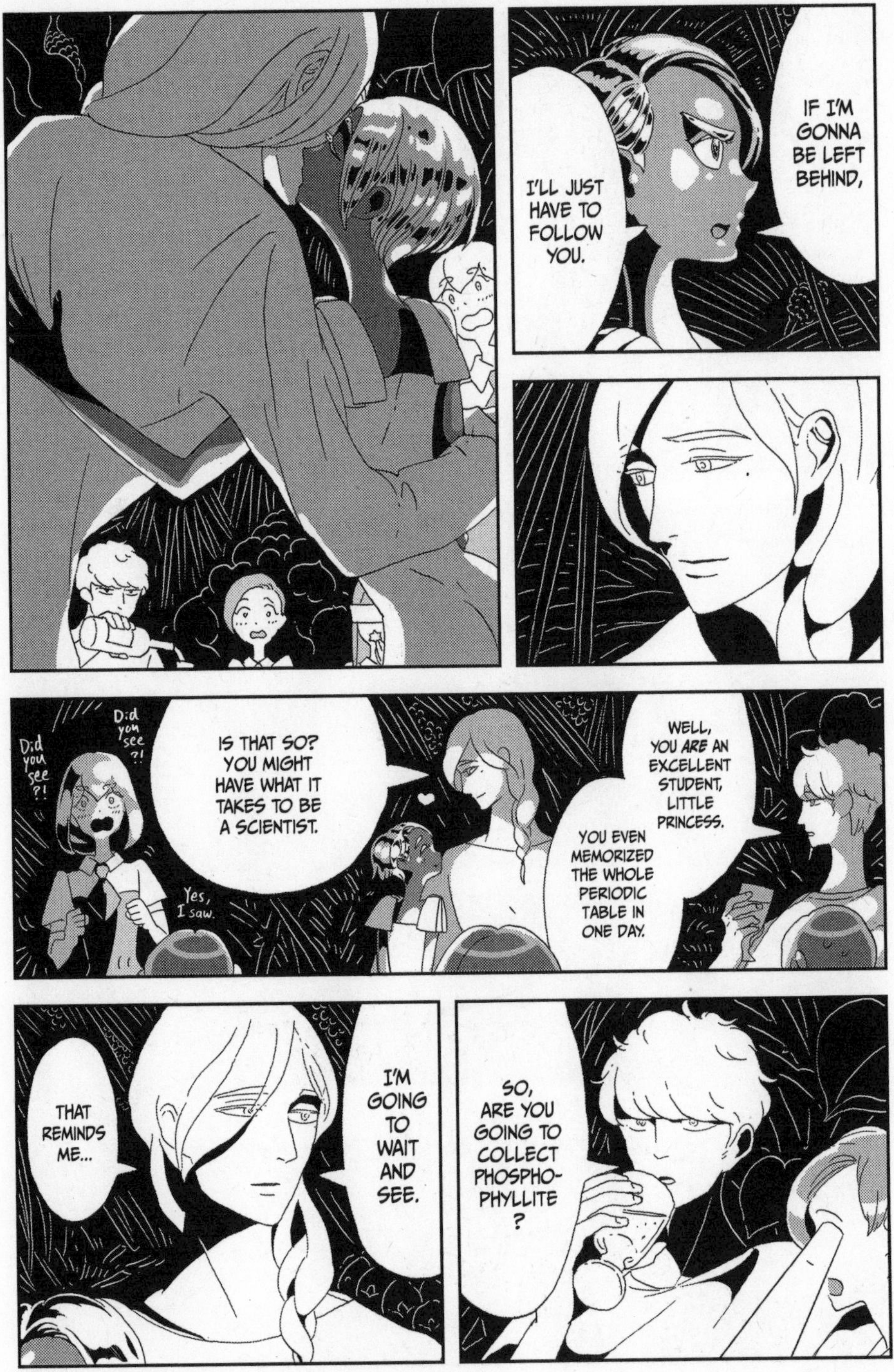
IF I'M GONNA BE LEFT BEHIND,
I'LL JUST HAVE TO FOLLOW YOU.
WELL, YOU ARE AN EXCELLENT STUDENT, LITTLE PRINCESS.
YOU EVEN MEMORIZED THE WHOLE PERIODIC TABLE IN ONE DAY.
IS THAT SO? YOU MIGHT HAVE WHAT IT TAKES TO BE A SCIENTIST.
Did you see ?!
Did you see ?!
Yes, I saw.
SO, ARE YOU GOING TO COLLECT PHOSPHO-PHYLLITE ?
I'M GOING TO WAIT AND SEE.
THAT REMINDS ME...

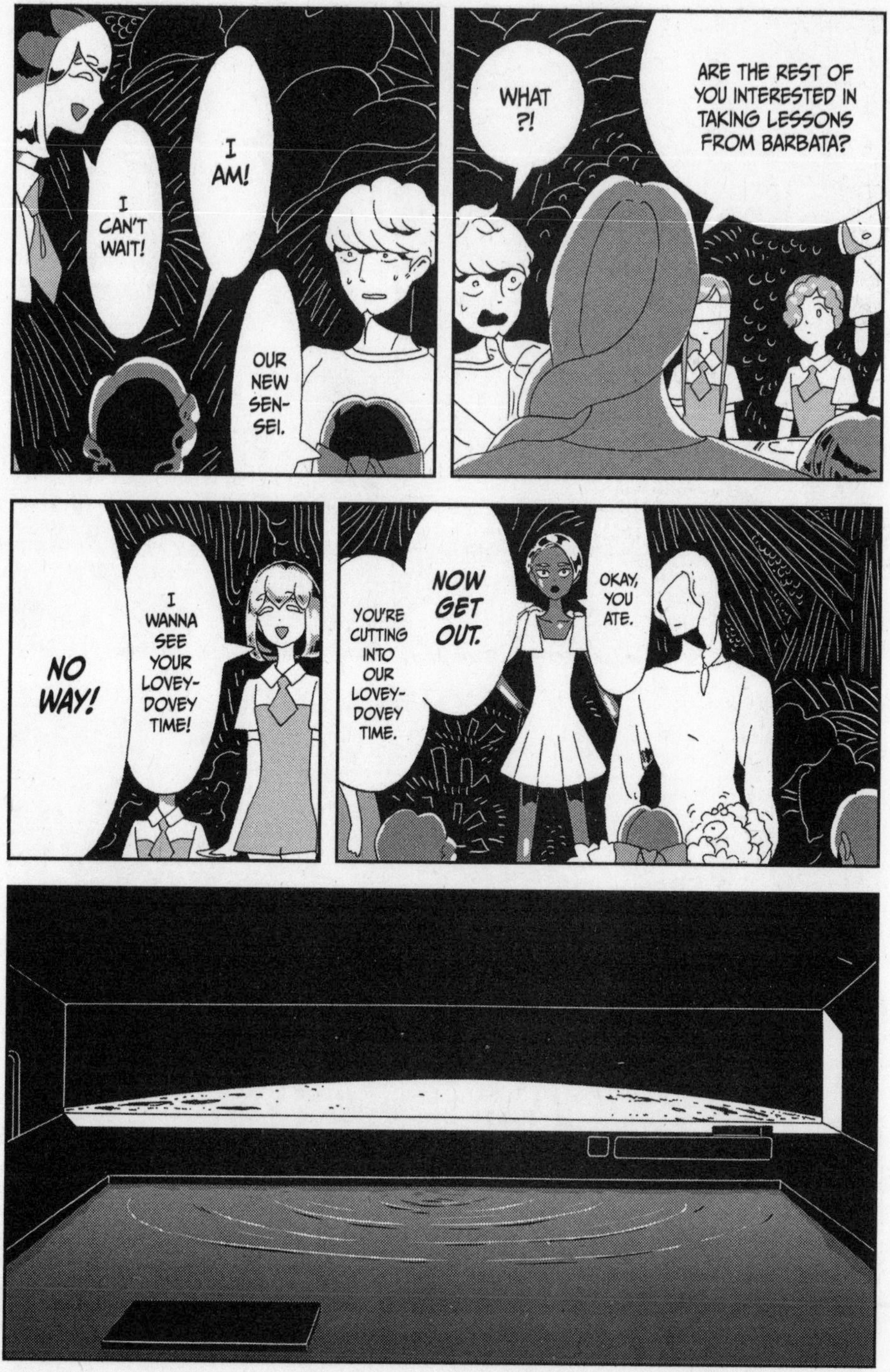
ARE THE REST OF YOU INTERESTED IN TAKING LESSONS FROM BARBATA?
WHAT ?!
I AM!
I CAN'T WAIT!
OUR NEW SEN-SEI.
OKAY, YOU ATE.
NOW GET OUT.
YOU'RE CUTTING INTO OUR LOVEY-DOVEY TIME.
I WANNA SEE YOUR LOVEY-DOVEY TIME!
NO WAY!

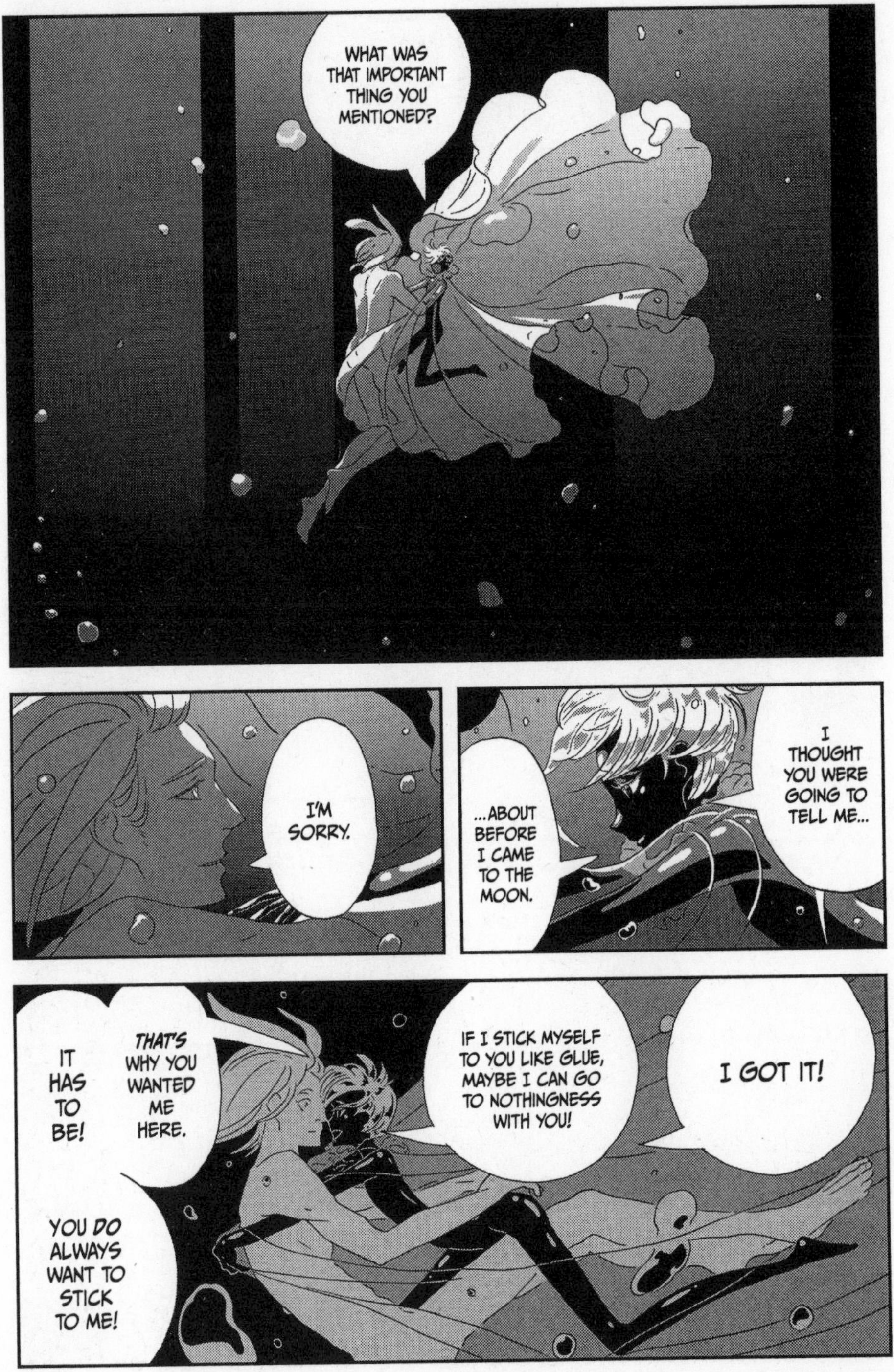
WHAT WAS THAT IMPORTANT THING YOU MENTIONED?
I THOUGHT YOU WERE GOING TO TELL ME...
...ABOUT BEFORE I CAME TO THE MOON.
I'M SORRY.
I GOT IT!
IF I STICK MYSELF TO YOU LIKE GLUE, MAYBE I CAN GO TO NOTHINGNESS WITH YOU!
THAT'S WHY YOU WANTED ME HERE.
IT HAS TO BE!
YOU DO ALWAYS WANT TO STICK TO ME!

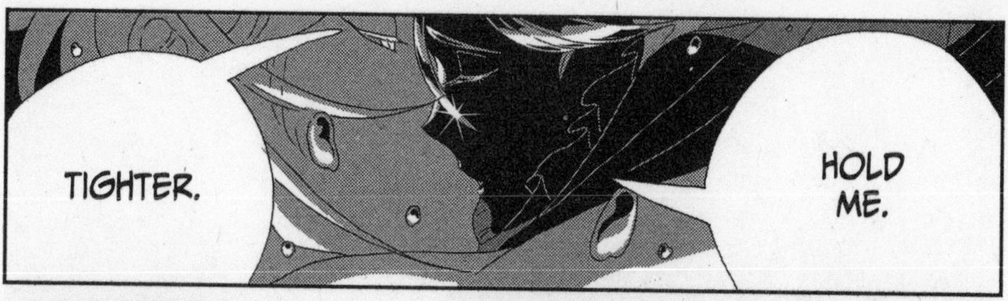
HOLD ME.
TIGHTER.
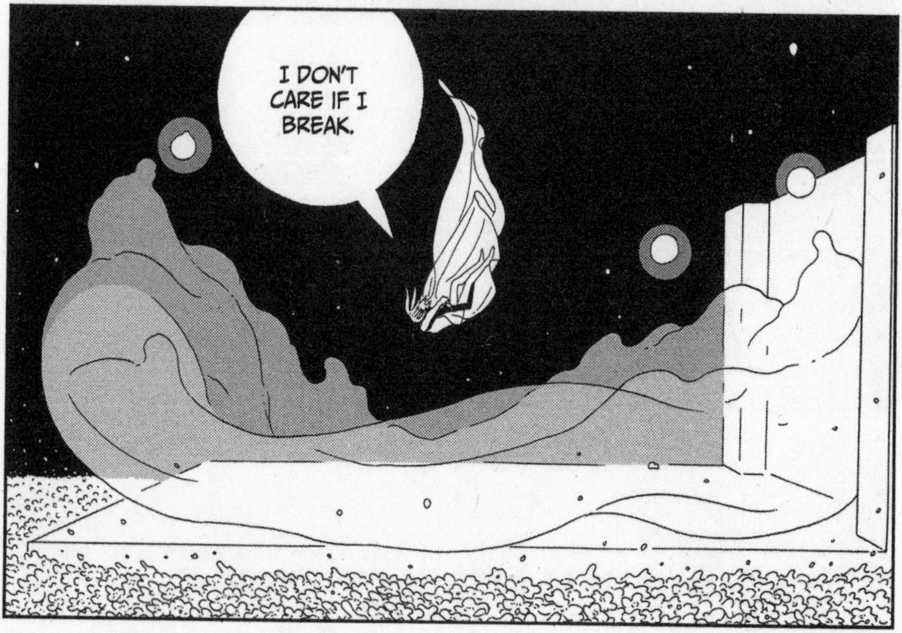
I DON'T CARE IF I BREAK.
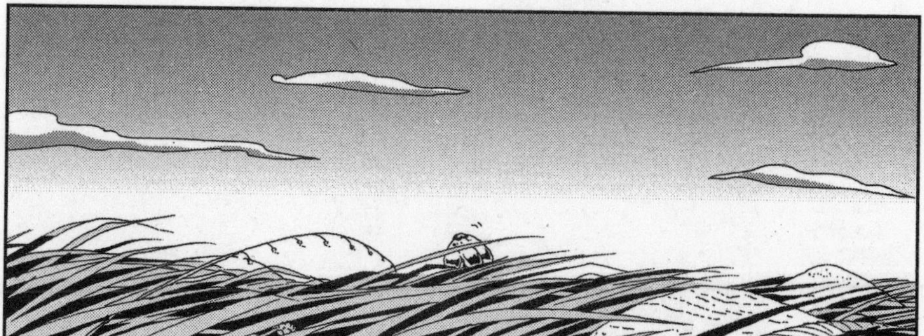

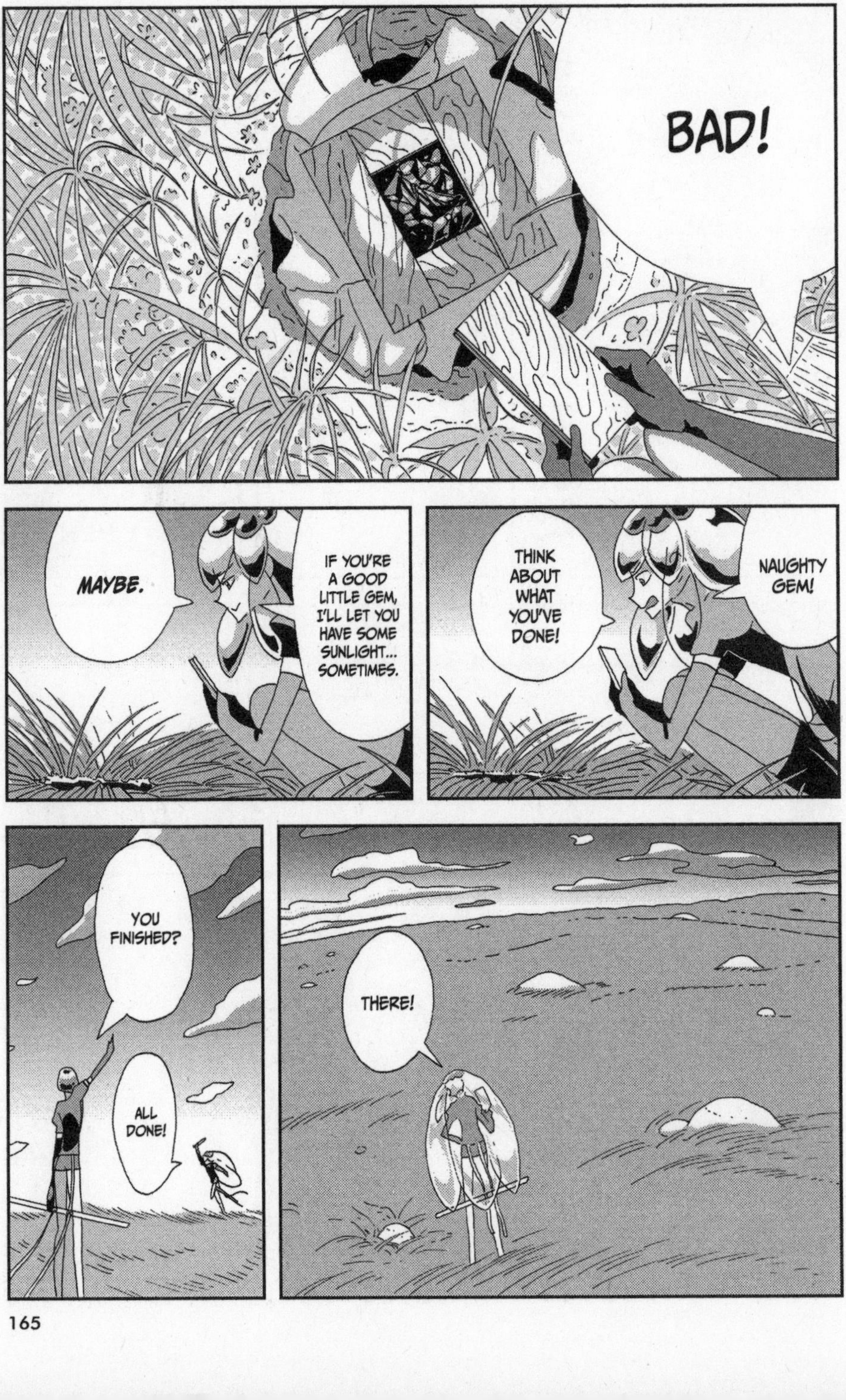
BAD!
NAUGHTY GEM!
THINK ABOUT WHAT YOU'VE DONE!
IF YOU'RE A GOOD LITTLE GEM, I'LL LET YOU HAVE SOME SUNLIGHT... SOMETIMES.
MAYBE.
THERE!
YOU FINISHED?
ALL DONE!

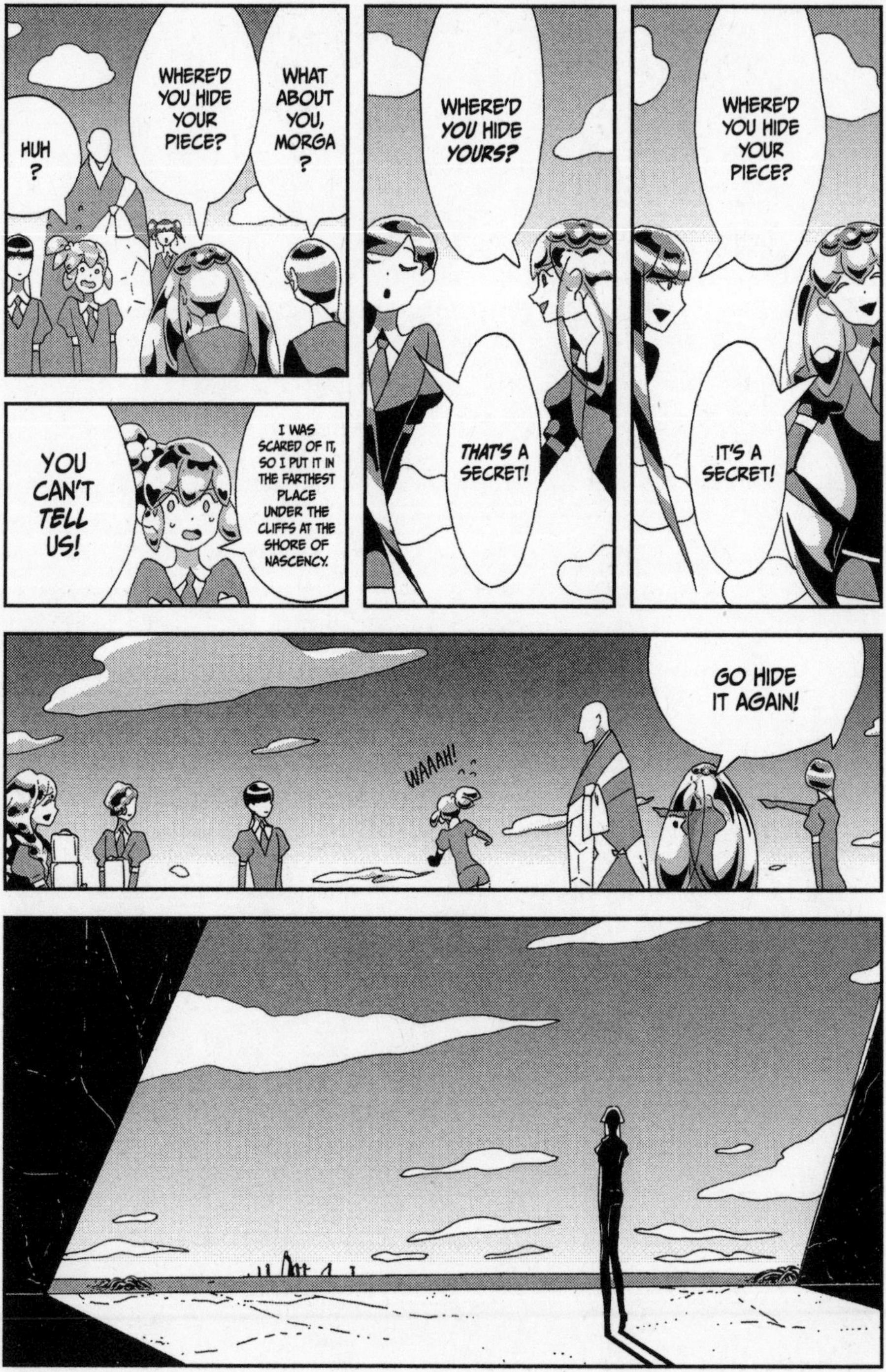
WHERE'D YOU HIDE YOUR PIECE?
IT'S A SECRET!
WHERE'D YOU HIDE YOURS?
THAT'S A SECRET!
WHAT ABOUT YOU, MORGA ?
WHERE'D YOU HIDE YOUR PIECE?
HUH ?
I WAS SCARED OF IT, SO I PUT IT IN THE FARTHEST PLACE UNDER THE CLIFFS AT THE SHORE OF NASCENCY.
YOU CAN'T TELL US!
GO HIDE IT AGAIN!
WAAAH!

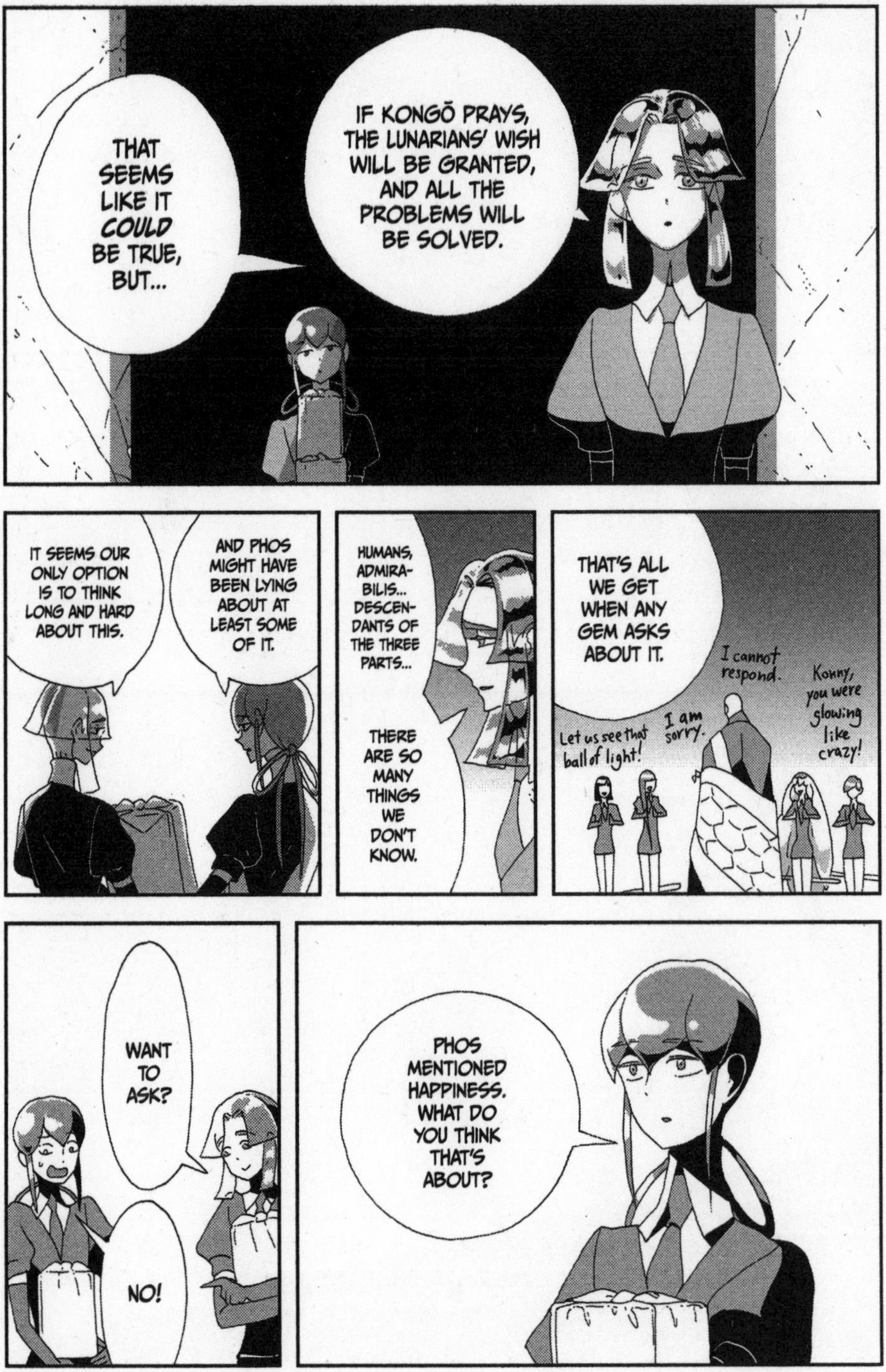
IF KONGŌ PRAYS, THE LUNARIANS' WISH WILL BE GRANTED, AND ALL THE PROBLEMS WILL BE SOLVED.
THAT SEEMS LIKE IT COULD BE TRUE, BUT...
THAT'S ALL WE GET WHEN ANY GEM ASKS ABOUT IT.
I cannot respond.
Konny, you were glowing like crazy!
I am sorry.
Let us see that ball of light!
HUMANS, ADMIRABILIS... DESCENDANTS OF THE THREE PARTS...
THERE ARE SO MANY THINGS WE DON'T KNOW.
AND PHOS MIGHT HAVE BEEN LYING ABOUT AT LEAST SOME OF IT.
IT SEEMS OUR ONLY OPTION IS TO THINK LONG AND HARD ABOUT THIS.
PHOS MENTIONED HAPPINESS. WHAT DO YOU THINK THAT'S ABOUT?
WANT TO ASK?
NO!

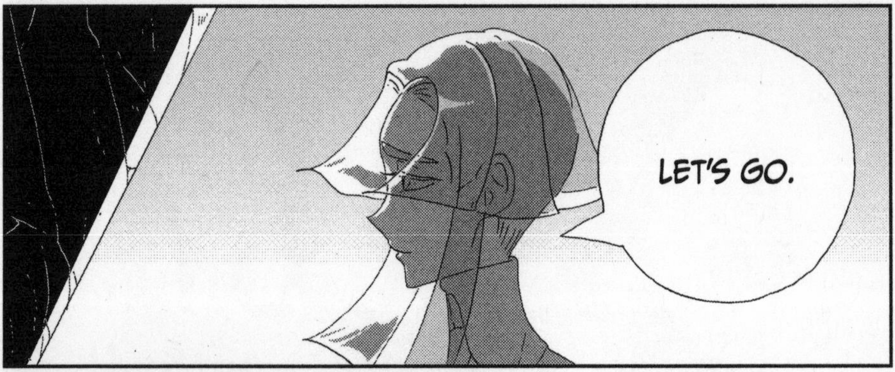
LET'S GO.
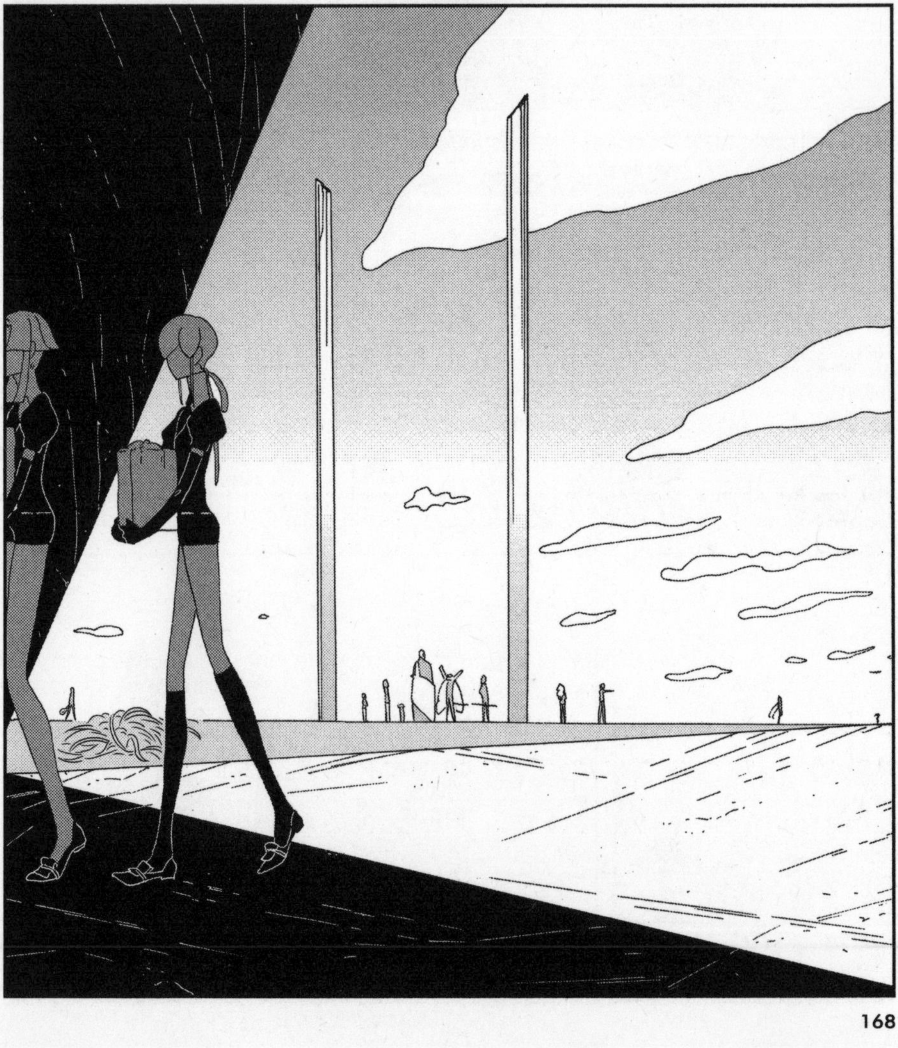

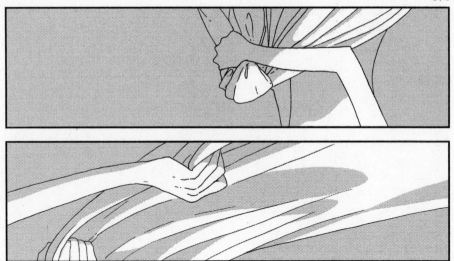

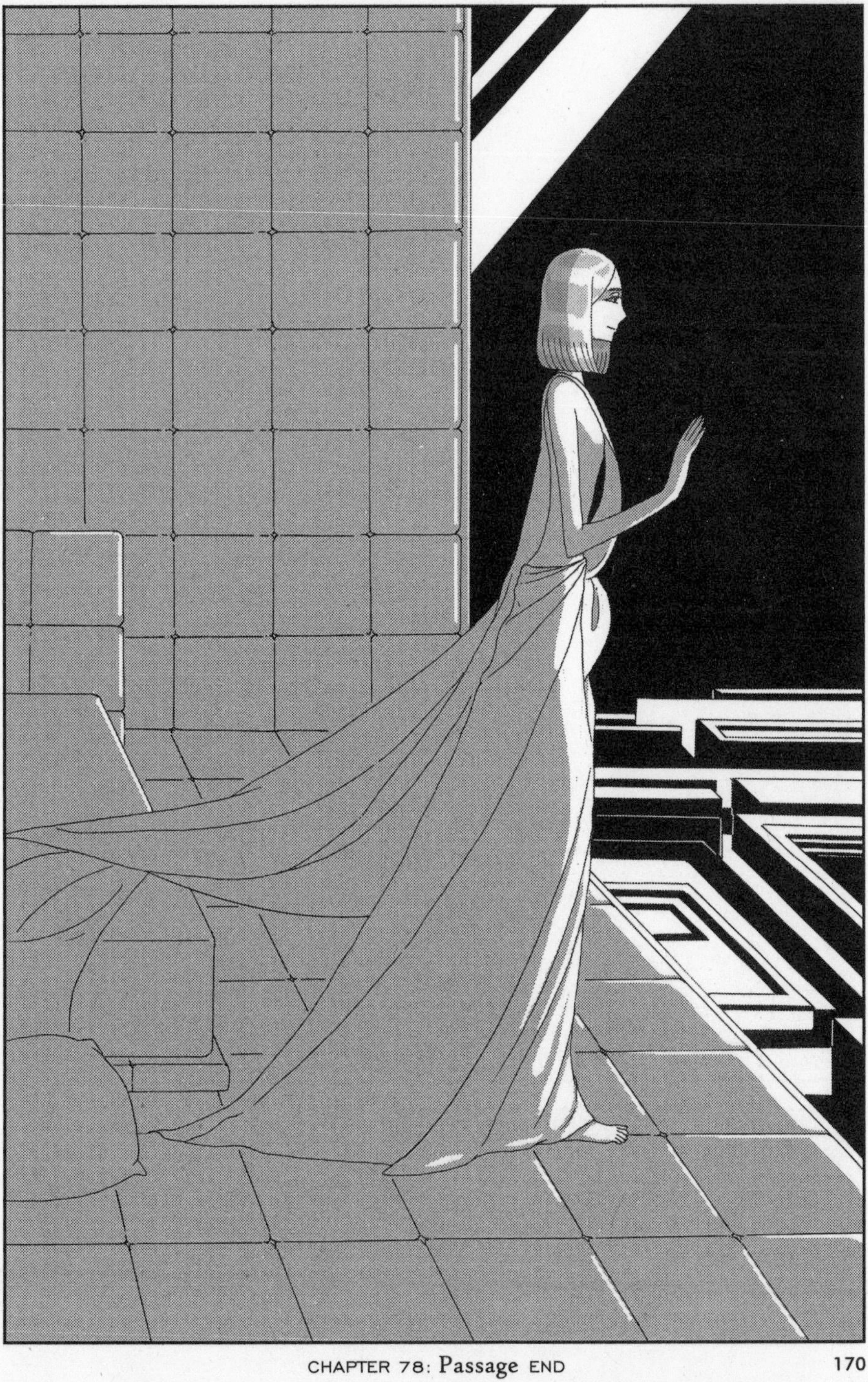

CHAPTER 78: Passage END

CHAPTER 79:

220 Years

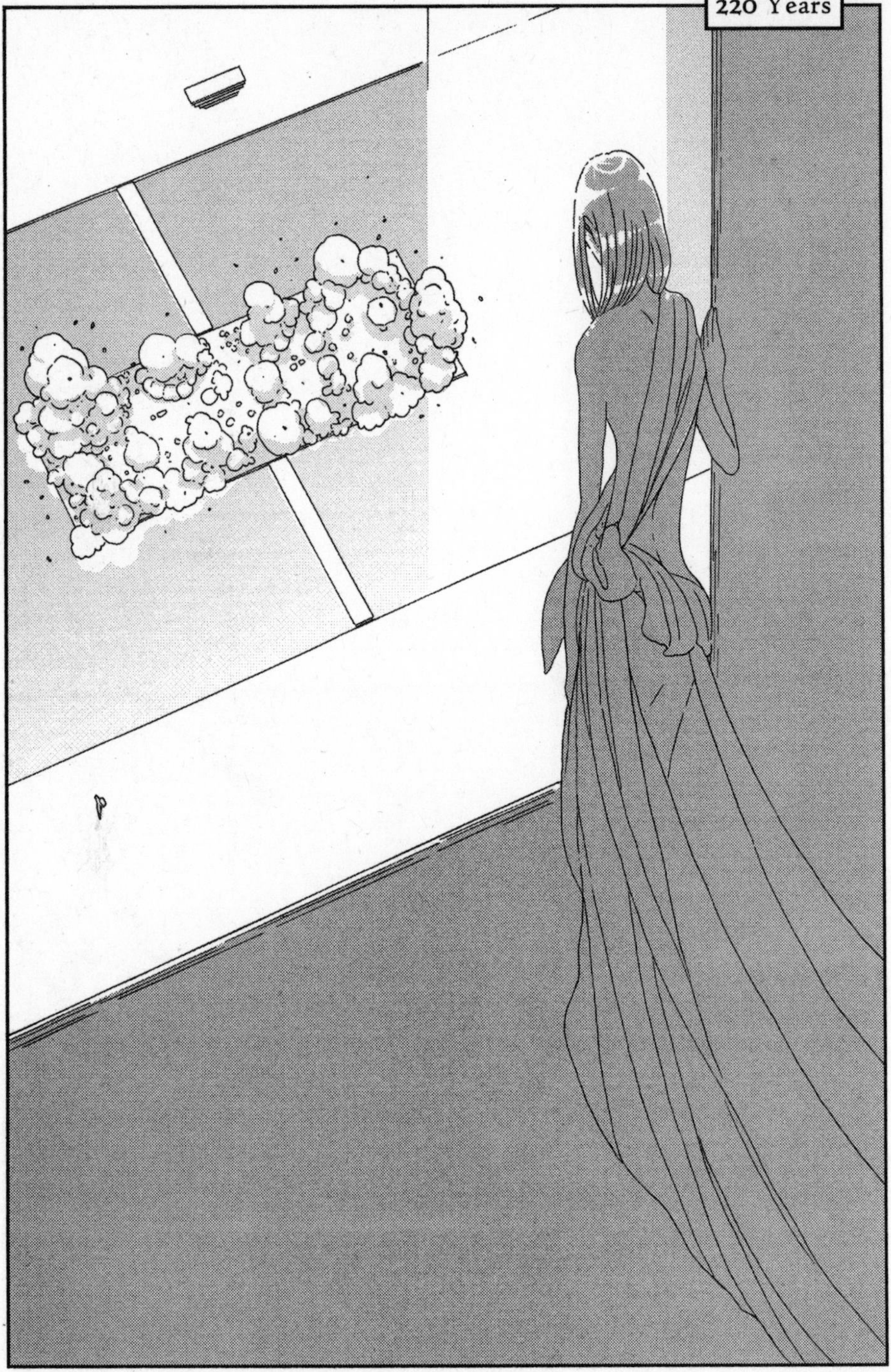

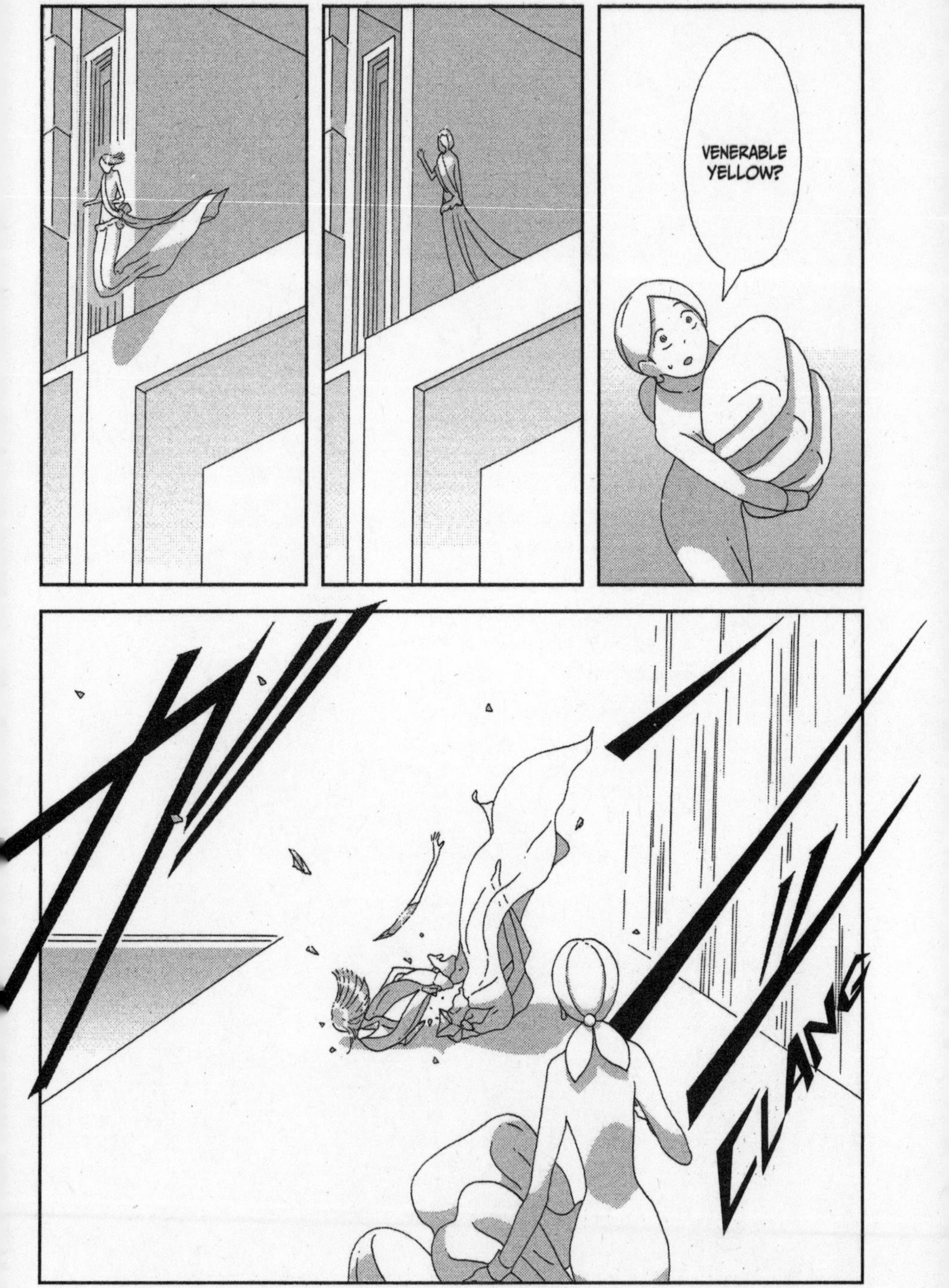
VENERABLE YELLOW?
CLANG

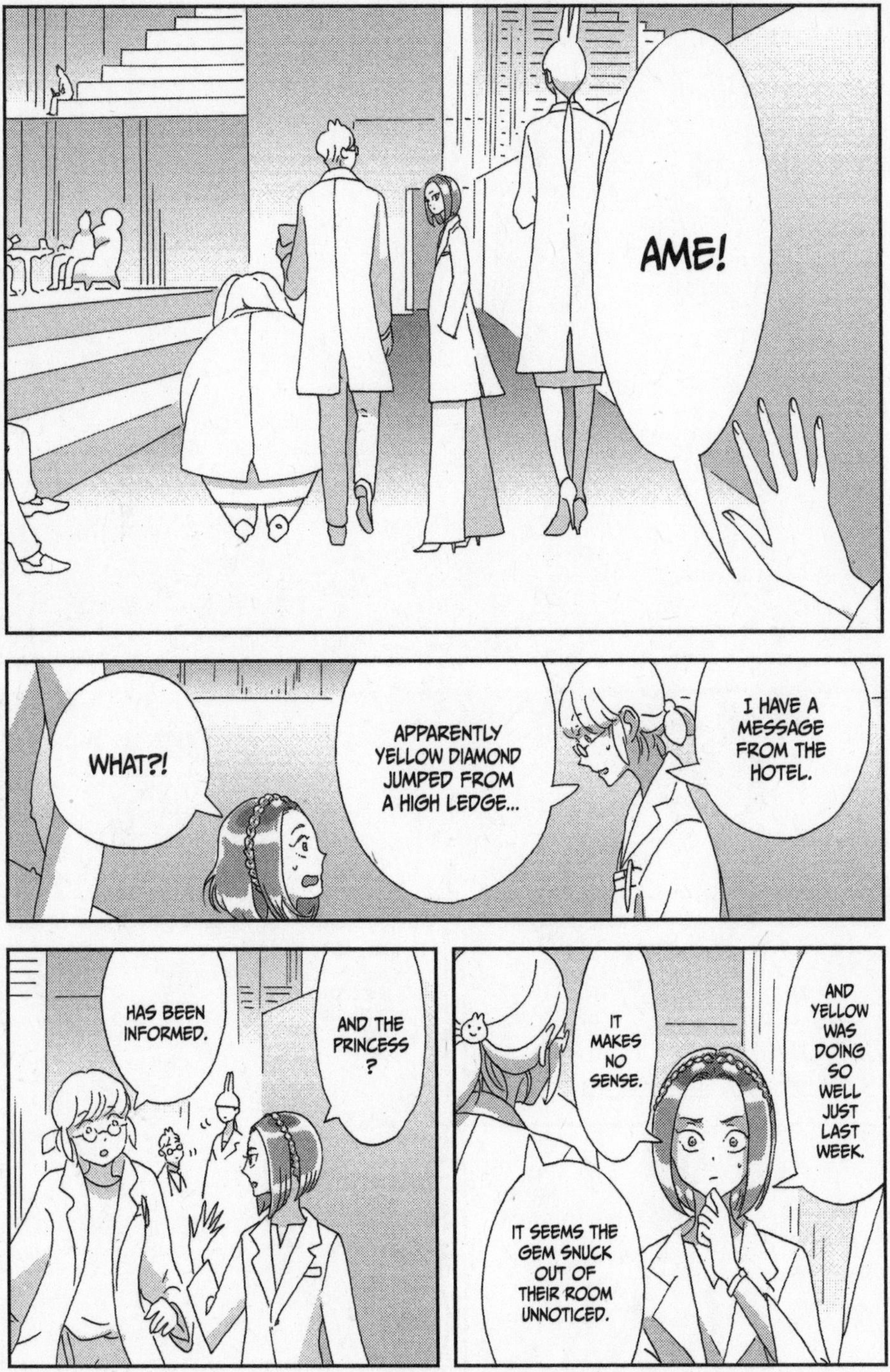
AME!
I HAVE A MESSAGE FROM THE HOTEL.
APPARENTLY YELLOW DIAMOND JUMPED FROM A HIGH LEDGE...
WHAT?!
AND YELLOW WAS DOING SO WELL JUST LAST WEEK.
IT MAKES NO SENSE.
IT SEEMS THE GEM SNUCK OUT OF THEIR ROOM UNNOTICED.
AND THE PRINCESS ?
HAS BEEN INFORMED.

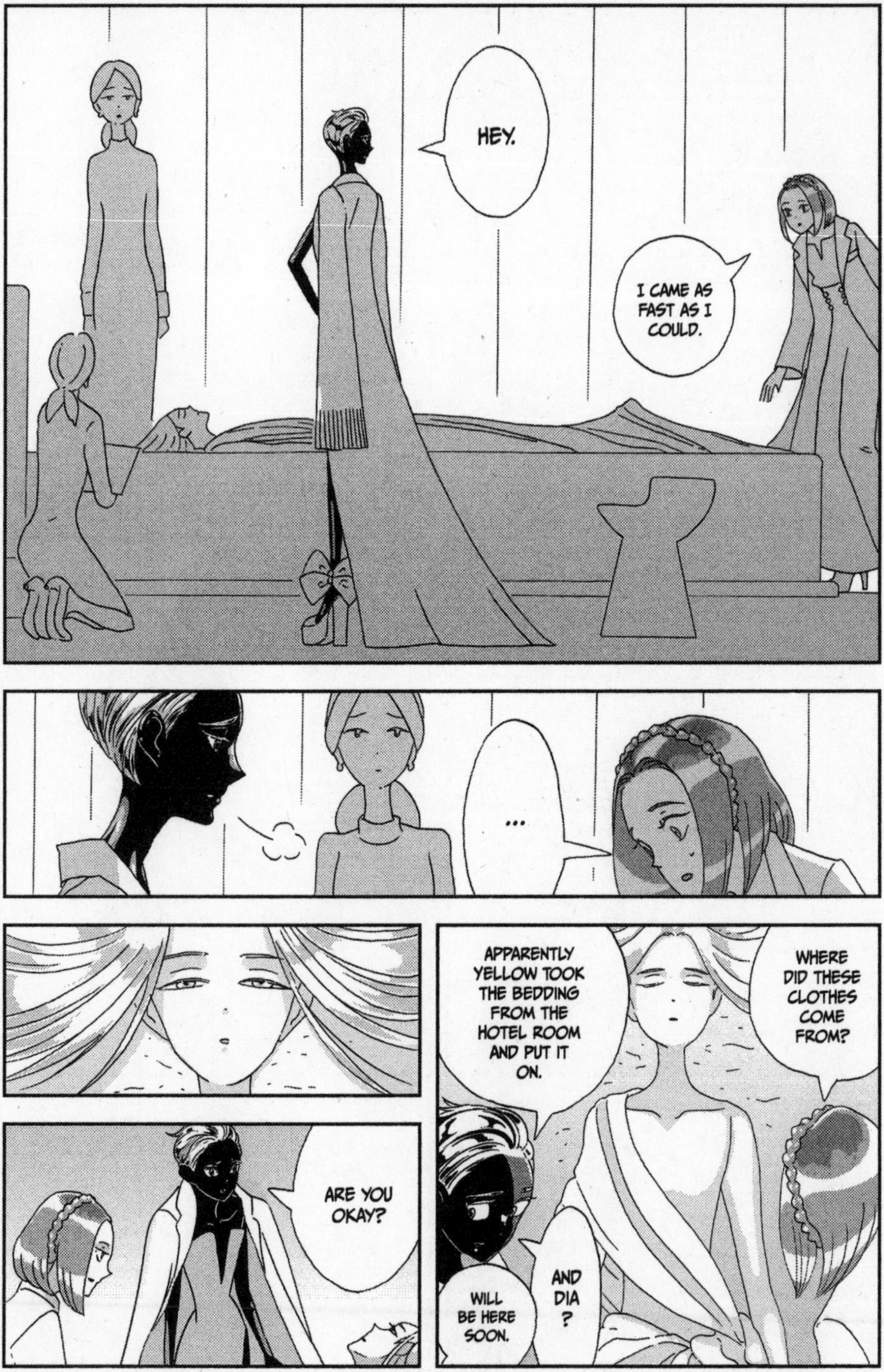
I CAME AS FAST AS I COULD.
HEY.
...
WHERE DID THESE CLOTHES COME FROM?
APPARENTLY YELLOW TOOK THE BEDDING FROM THE HOTEL ROOM AND PUT IT ON.
AND DIA ?
WILL BE HERE SOON.
ARE YOU OKAY?

AAHH...
CAIRN-GORM...
OH! YOU MEAN ME!
I HAVEN'T HEARD THAT NAME IN AGES!
I'D FOR-GOTTEN ALL ABOUT IT.
I'M SORRY.
I THOUGHT I'D TAKE A WALK TO THE GARDEN...
I SEE.
I DON'T KNOW WHAT TO DO.
I CAN'T FLY.
MY BODY FEELS SO HEAVY TODAY.

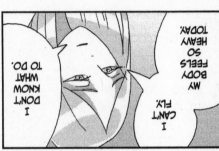

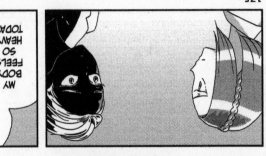

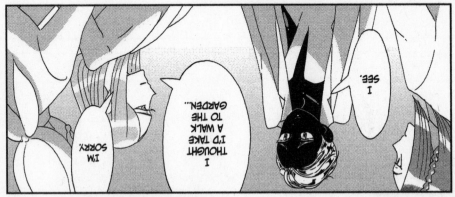

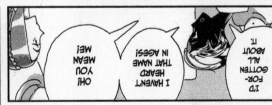

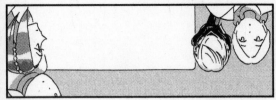

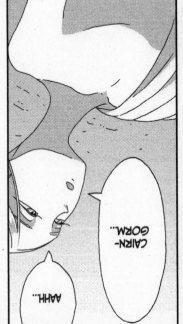

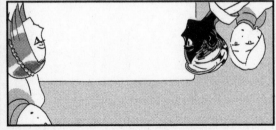

YELLOW ?
TELL ME MORE.
OH, RIGHT...
I'M YELLOW DIAMOND ...
YELLOW IS SUFFERING FROM DELUSIONS OF BEING A LUNARIAN.

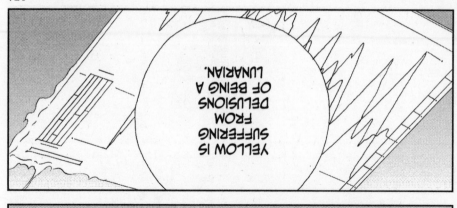

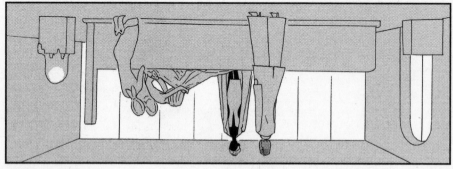

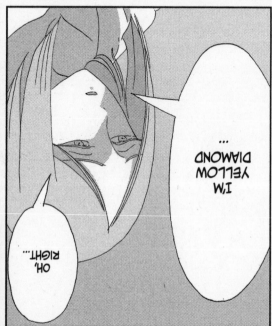

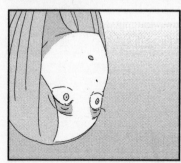

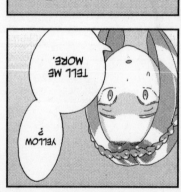

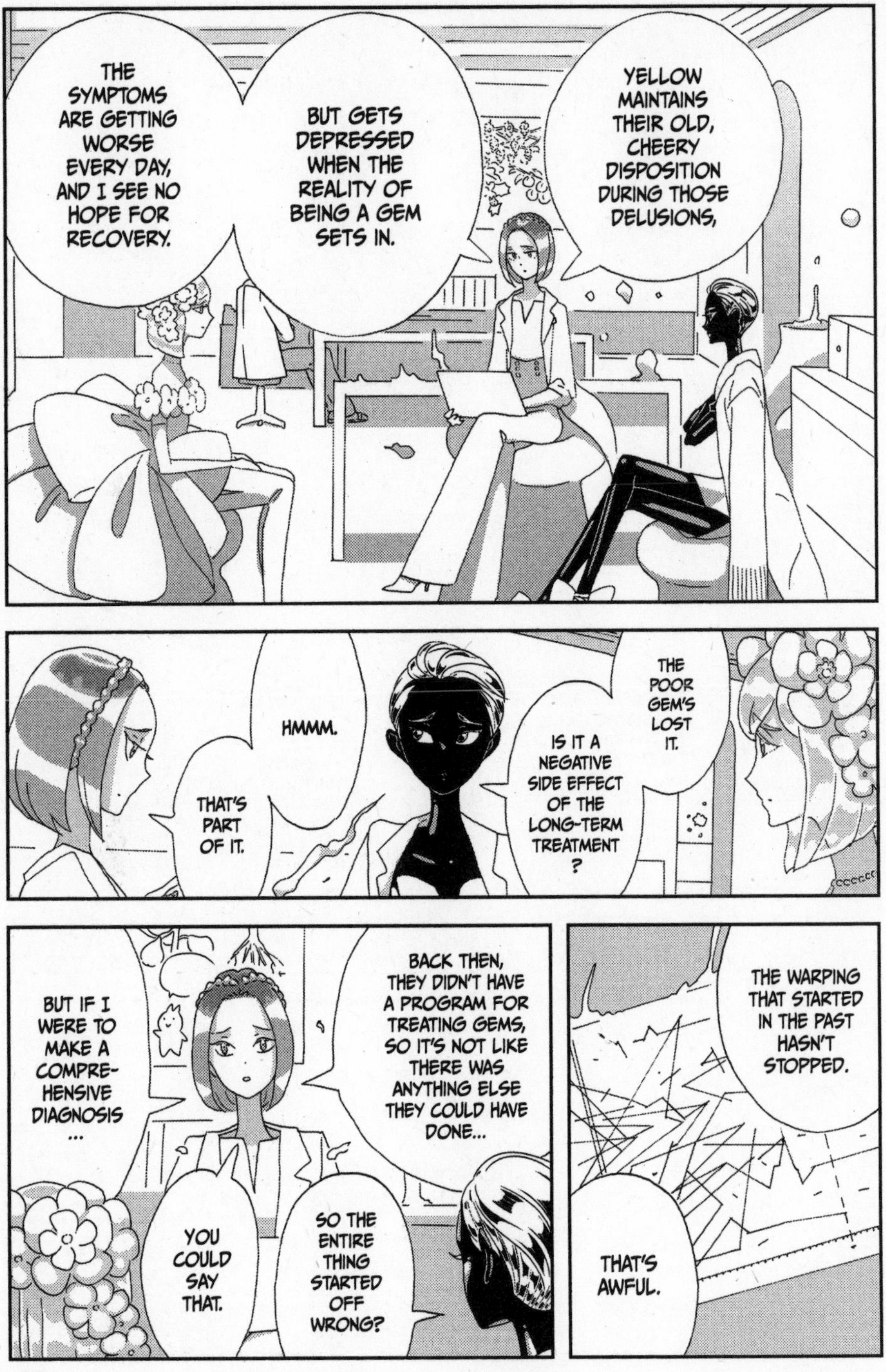
YELLOW MAINTAINS THEIR OLD, CHEERY DISPOSITION DURING THOSE DELUSIONS,
BUT GETS DEPRESSED WHEN THE REALITY OF BEING A GEM SETS IN.
THE SYMPTOMS ARE GETTING WORSE EVERY DAY, AND I SEE NO HOPE FOR RECOVERY.
THE POOR GEM'S LOST IT.
IS IT A NEGATIVE SIDE EFFECT OF THE LONG-TERM TREATMENT ?
HMMM.
THAT'S PART OF IT.
THE WARPING THAT STARTED IN THE PAST HASN'T STOPPED.
THAT'S AWFUL.
BACK THEN, THEY DIDN'T HAVE A PROGRAM FOR TREATING GEMS, SO IT'S NOT LIKE THERE WAS ANYTHING ELSE THEY COULD HAVE DONE...
SO THE ENTIRE THING STARTED OFF WRONG?
YOU COULD SAY THAT.
BUT IF I WERE TO MAKE A COMPRE-HENSIVE DIAGNOSIS ...

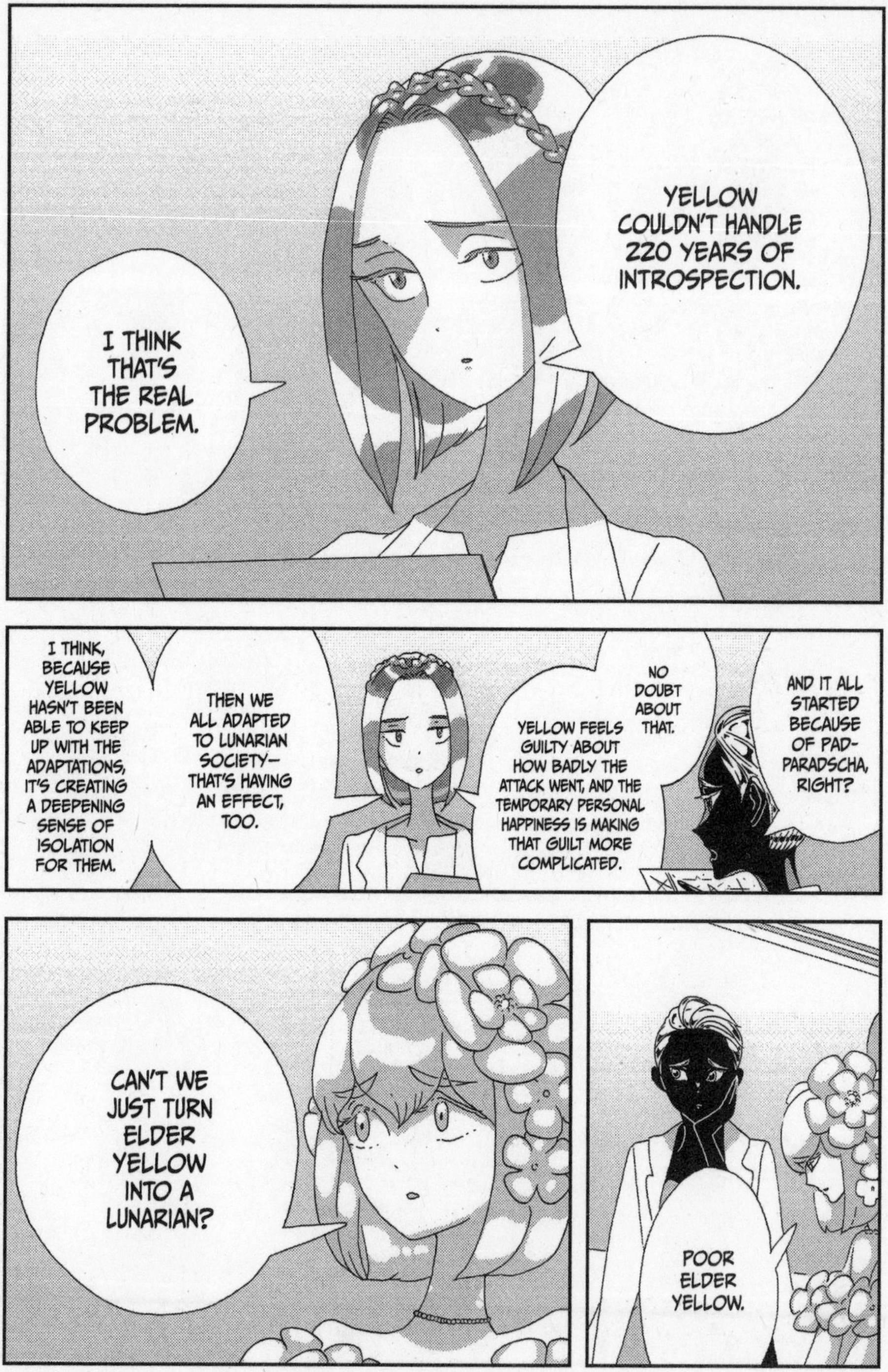
YELLOW COULDN'T HANDLE 220 YEARS OF INTROSPECTION.
I THINK THAT'S THE REAL PROBLEM.
AND IT ALL STARTED BECAUSE OF PAD-PARADSCHA, RIGHT?
NO DOUBT ABOUT THAT.
YELLOW FEELS GUILTY ABOUT HOW BADLY THE ATTACK WENT, AND THE TEMPORARY PERSONAL HAPPINESS IS MAKING THAT GUILT MORE COMPLICATED.
THEN WE ALL ADAPTED TO LUNARIAN SOCIETY—THAT'S HAVING AN EFFECT, TOO.
I THINK, BECAUSE YELLOW HASN'T BEEN ABLE TO KEEP UP WITH THE ADAPTATIONS, IT'S CREATING A DEEPENING SENSE OF ISOLATION FOR THEM.
POOR ELDER YELLOW.
CAN'T WE JUST TURN ELDER YELLOW INTO A LUNARIAN?

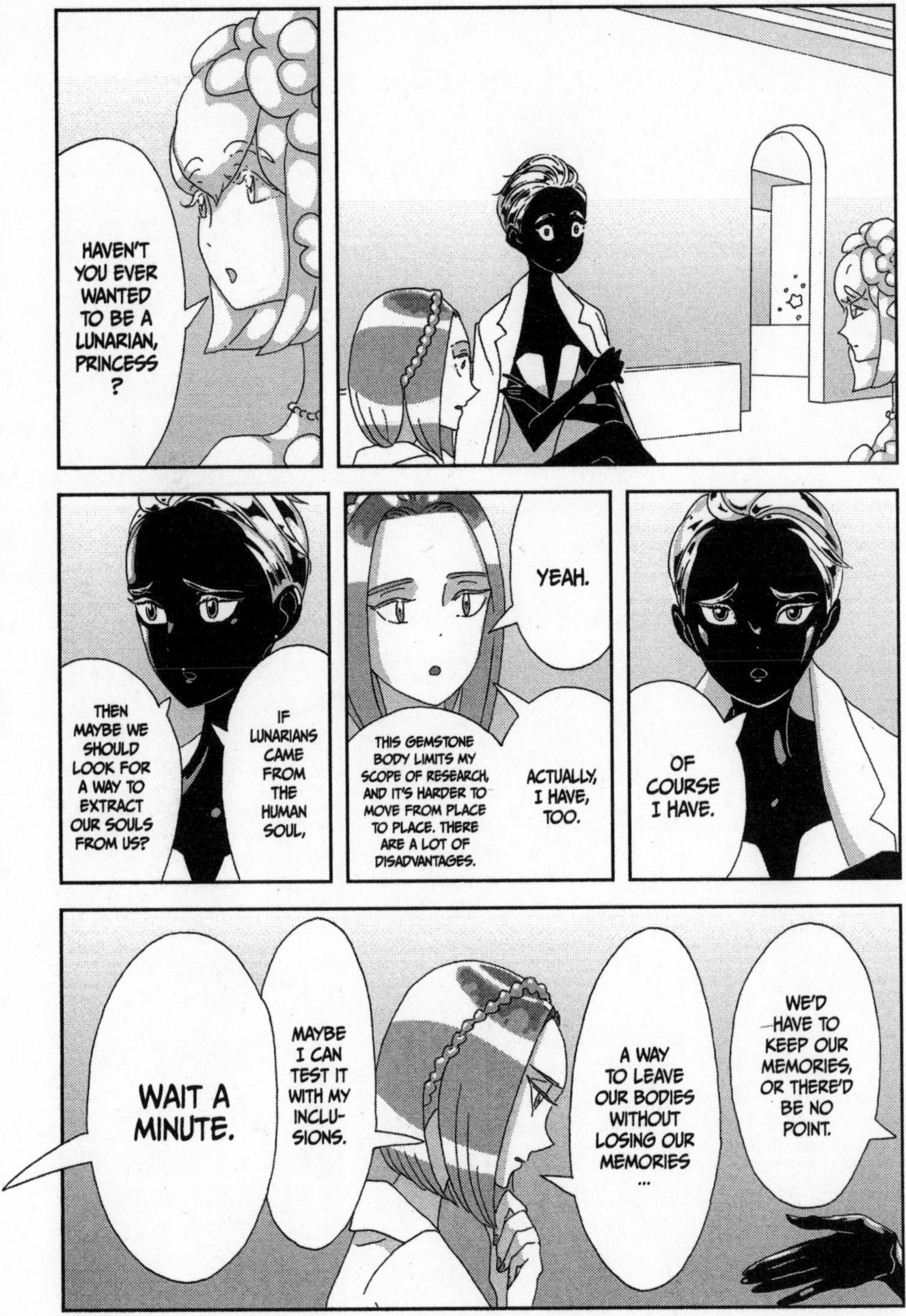
HAVEN'T YOU EVER WANTED TO BE A LUNARIAN, PRINCESS ?
OF COURSE I HAVE.
YEAH.
ACTUALLY, I HAVE, TOO.
THIS GEMSTONE BODY LIMITS MY SCOPE OF RESEARCH, AND IT'S HARDER TO MOVE FROM PLACE TO PLACE. THERE ARE A LOT OF DISADVANTAGES.
IF LUNARIANS CAME FROM THE HUMAN SOUL,
THEN MAYBE WE SHOULD LOOK FOR A WAY TO EXTRACT OUR SOULS FROM US?
WE'D HAVE TO KEEP OUR MEMORIES, OR THERE'D BE NO POINT.
A WAY TO LEAVE OUR BODIES WITHOUT LOSING OUR MEMORIES ...
MAYBE I CAN TEST IT WITH MY INCLU- SIONS.
WAIT A MINUTE.

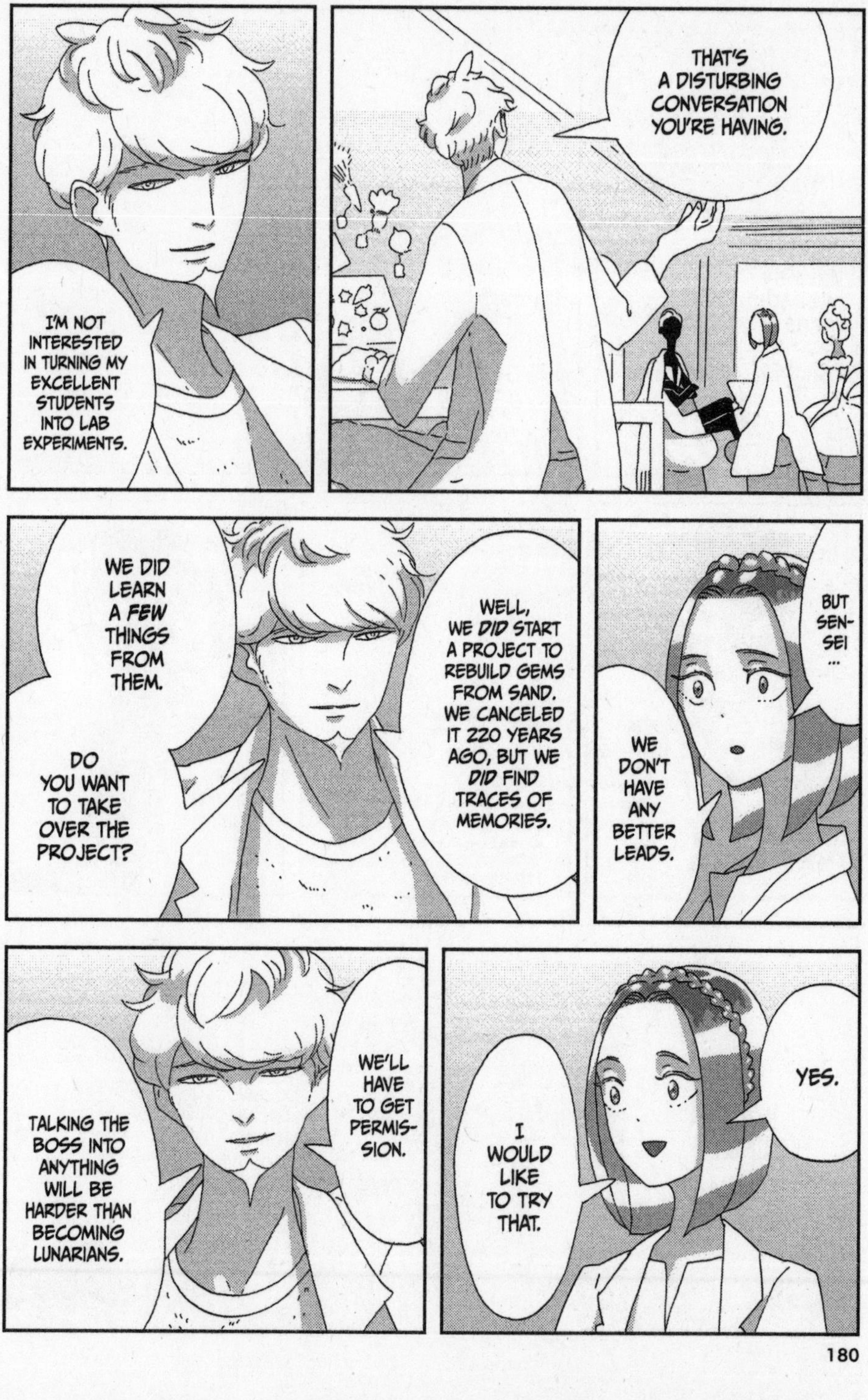
THAT'S A DISTURBING CONVERSATION YOU'RE HAVING.
I'M NOT INTERESTED IN TURNING MY EXCELLENT STUDENTS INTO LAB EXPERIMENTS.
BUT SEN-SEI ...
WE DON'T HAVE ANY BETTER LEADS.
WELL, WE *DID* START A PROJECT TO REBUILD GEMS FROM SAND. WE CANCELED IT 220 YEARS AGO, BUT WE *DID* FIND TRACES OF MEMORIES.
WE DID LEARN A *FEW* THINGS FROM THEM.
DO YOU WANT TO TAKE OVER THE PROJECT?
YES.
I WOULD LIKE TO TRY THAT.
WE'LL HAVE TO GET PERMIS-SION.
TALKING THE BOSS INTO ANYTHING WILL BE HARDER THAN BECOMING LUNARIANS.

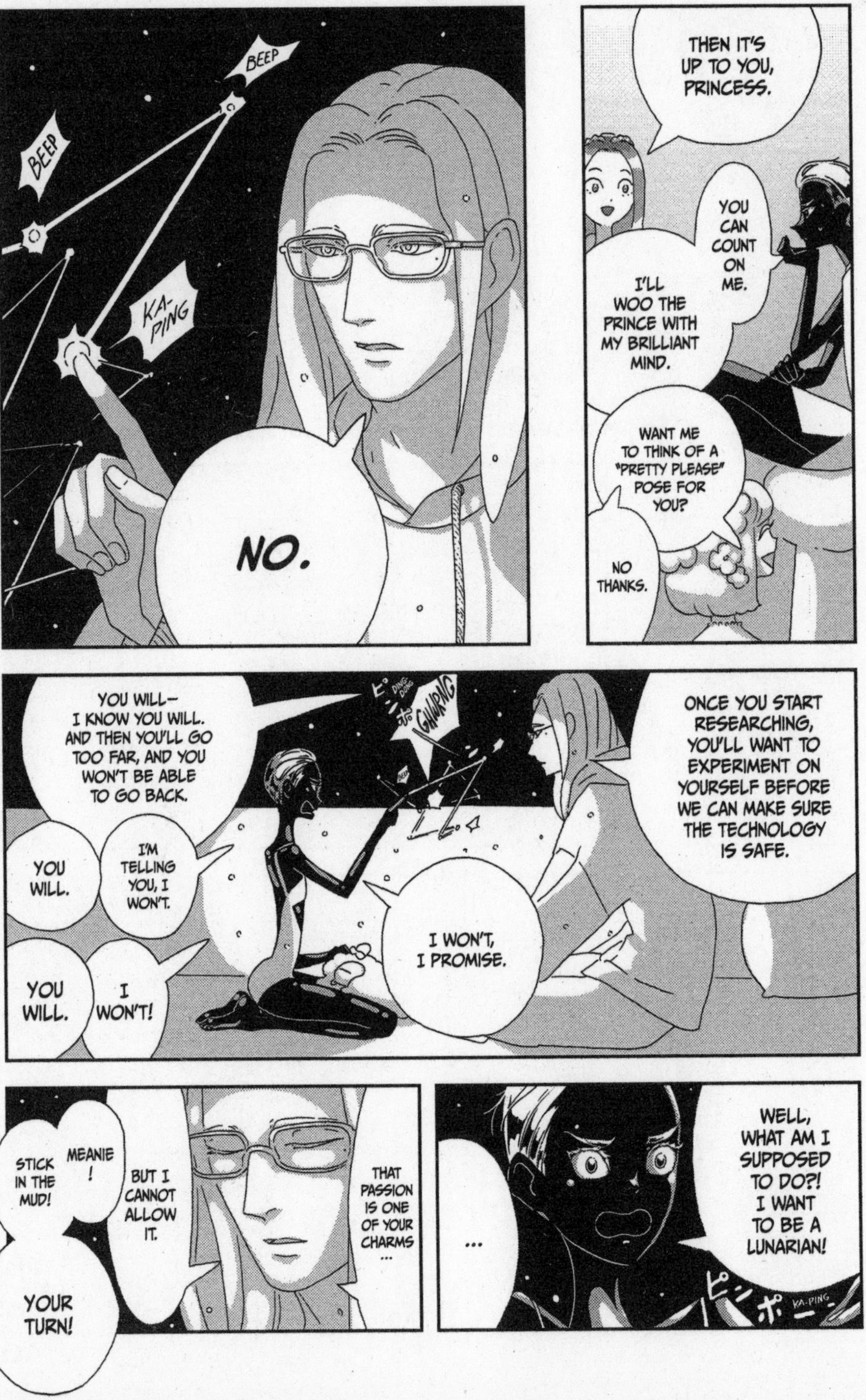
THEN IT'S UP TO YOU, PRINCESS.
YOU CAN COUNT ON ME.
I'LL WOO THE PRINCE WITH MY BRILLIANT MIND.
WANT ME TO THINK OF A "PRETTY PLEASE" POSE FOR YOU?
NO THANKS.
BEEP
BEEP
KA-PING
NO.
ONCE YOU START RESEARCHING, YOU'LL WANT TO EXPERIMENT ON YOURSELF BEFORE WE CAN MAKE SURE THE TECHNOLOGY IS SAFE.
DING DONG
GHURNG
YOU WILL— I KNOW YOU WILL. AND THEN YOU'LL GO TOO FAR, AND YOU WON'T BE ABLE TO GO BACK.
I WON'T, I PROMISE.
I'M TELLING YOU, I WON'T.
YOU WILL.
I WON'T!
YOU WILL.
WELL, WHAT AM I SUPPOSED TO DO?! I WANT TO BE A LUNARIAN!
KA-PING
...
THAT PASSION IS ONE OF YOUR CHARMS ...
BUT I CANNOT ALLOW IT.
MEANIE !
STICK IN THE MUD!
YOUR TURN!

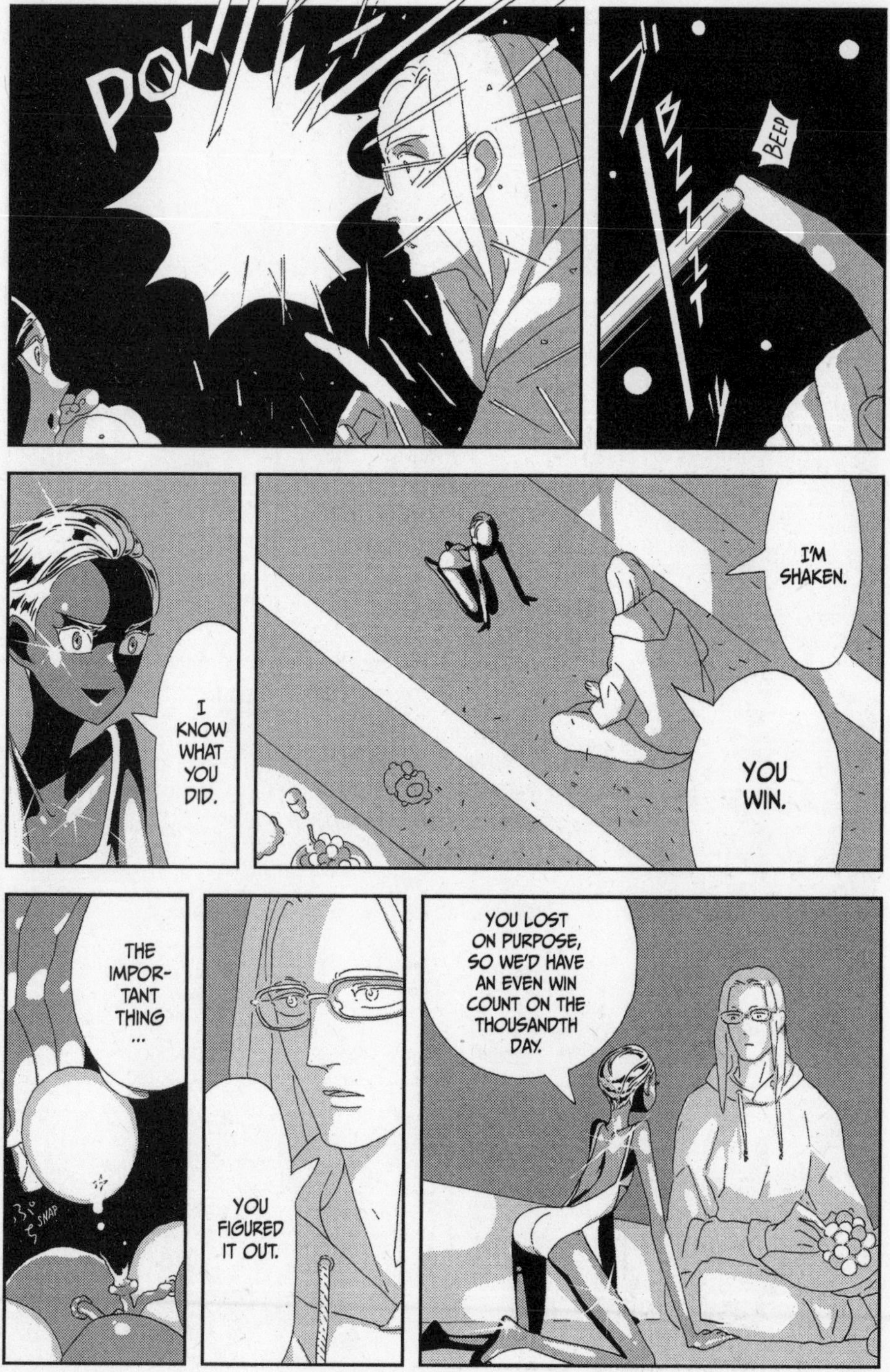
BEEP
BZZZT
POW
I'M SHAKEN.
YOU WIN.
I KNOW WHAT YOU DID.
YOU LOST ON PURPOSE, SO WE'D HAVE AN EVEN WIN COUNT ON THE THOUSANDTH DAY.
YOU FIGURED IT OUT.
THE IMPOR-TANT THING ...
SNAP

...ISN'T TO WIN A SINGLE DAY'S VICTORY, BUT TO COMMAND THE WHOLE FIELD.
THE TIME HAS NOT COME YET.
PLEASE!
GIVE US PER-MISSION! ♡
TWITCH
FINE.
AS A REWARD FOR YOUR RESOLVE AND KEEN PERCEPTION.
BUT ONLY THE BASIC RESEARCH.
YAY!
IT'S BETTER THAN YOU DOING IT BEHIND MY BACK. YOU WILL REPORT TO ME BEFORE YOU BEGIN ANY STEP OF THE PROCESS.
AND YOUR BECOMING A LUNARIAN IS AN ENTIRELY DIFFERENT MATTER.
UNDER-STAND?
PAT PAT
IF YOU SAY SO!

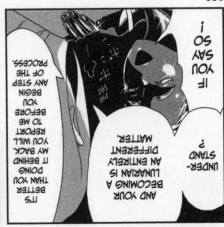

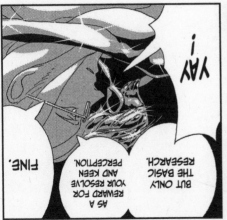

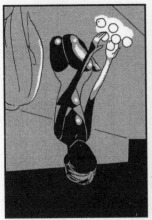

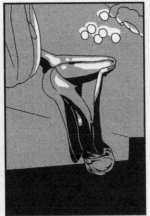

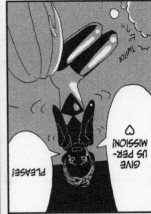

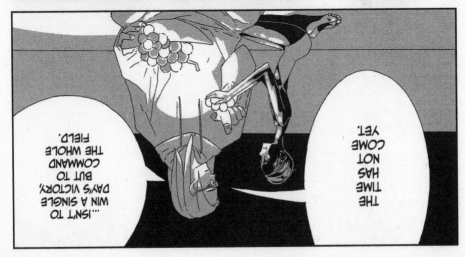

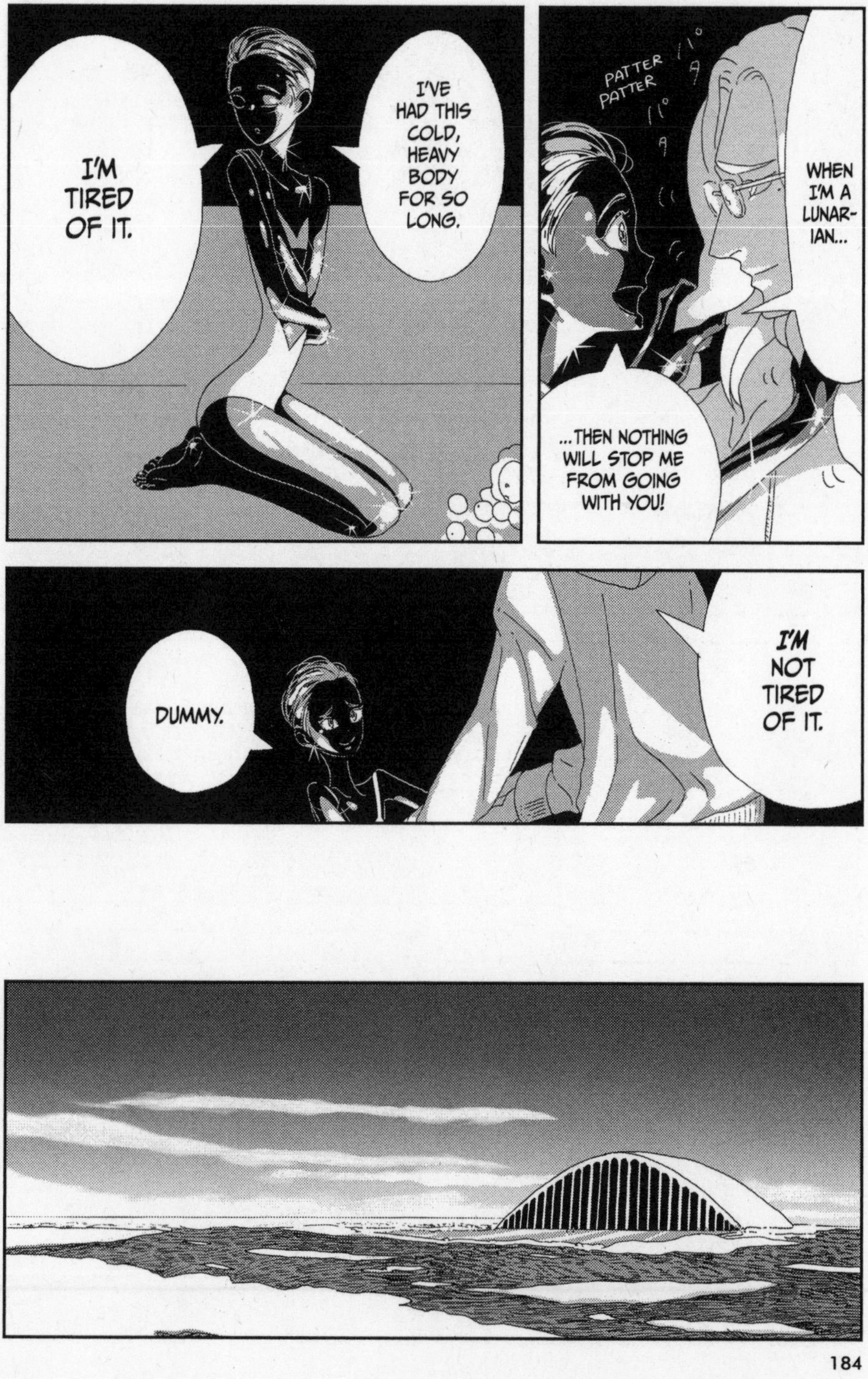
PATTER PATTER
WHEN I'M A LUNAR-IAN...
...THEN NOTHING WILL STOP ME FROM GOING WITH YOU!
I'VE HAD THIS COLD, HEAVY BODY FOR SO LONG.
I'M TIRED OF IT.
I'M NOT TIRED OF IT.
DUMMY.

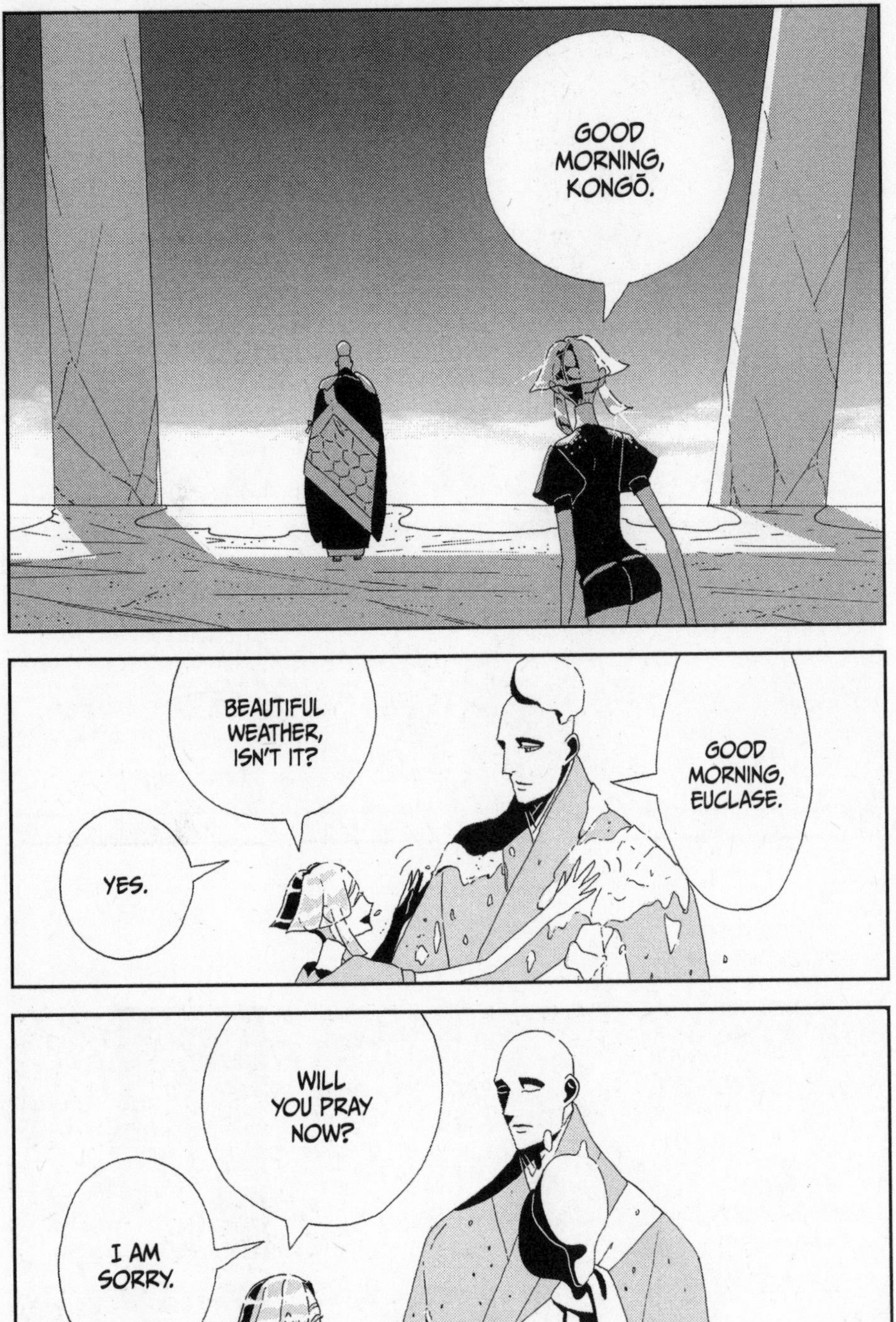
GOOD MORNING, KONGŌ.
GOOD MORNING, EUCLASE.
BEAUTIFUL WEATHER, ISN'T IT?
YES.
WILL YOU PRAY NOW?
I AM SORRY.

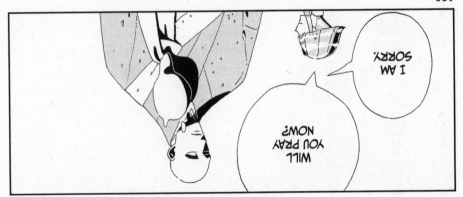

HOW MANY TIMES HAVE I ASKED THAT NOW?
EIGHTY THOUSAND, THREE HUNDRED AND TWENTY-TWO.
RIGHT.
I DON'T THINK THE LUNARIANS WILL BE COMING TODAY...
...SO I'M NOT GOING TO ASK YOU AGAIN.
I'VE DECIDED I'M GOING TO HIBERNATE WITH THE OTHERS THIS YEAR.
I WAS BOUND TO GET SLEEPY EVENTUALLY.

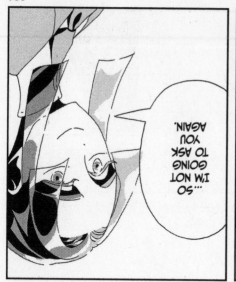

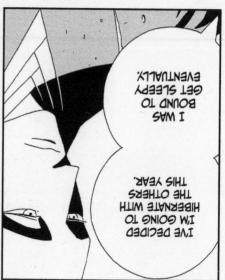

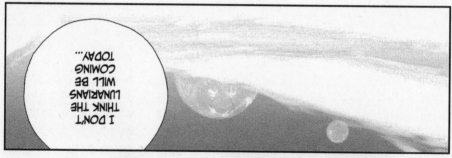

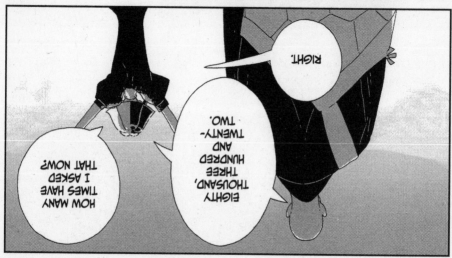

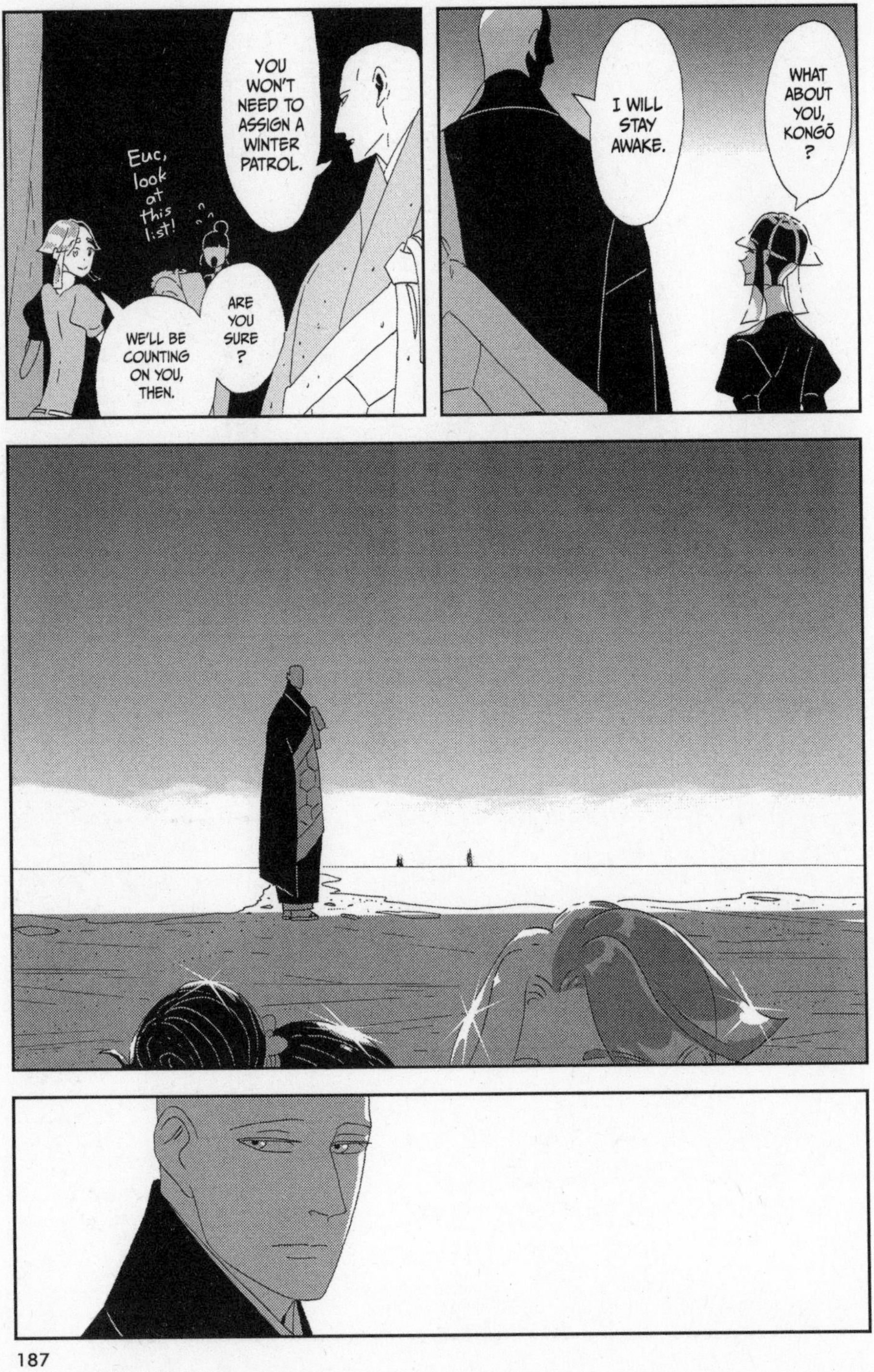
WHAT ABOUT YOU, KONGŌ ?
I WILL STAY AWAKE.
YOU WON'T NEED TO ASSIGN A WINTER PATROL.
Euc, look at this list!
ARE YOU SURE ?
WE'LL BE COUNTING ON YOU, THEN.

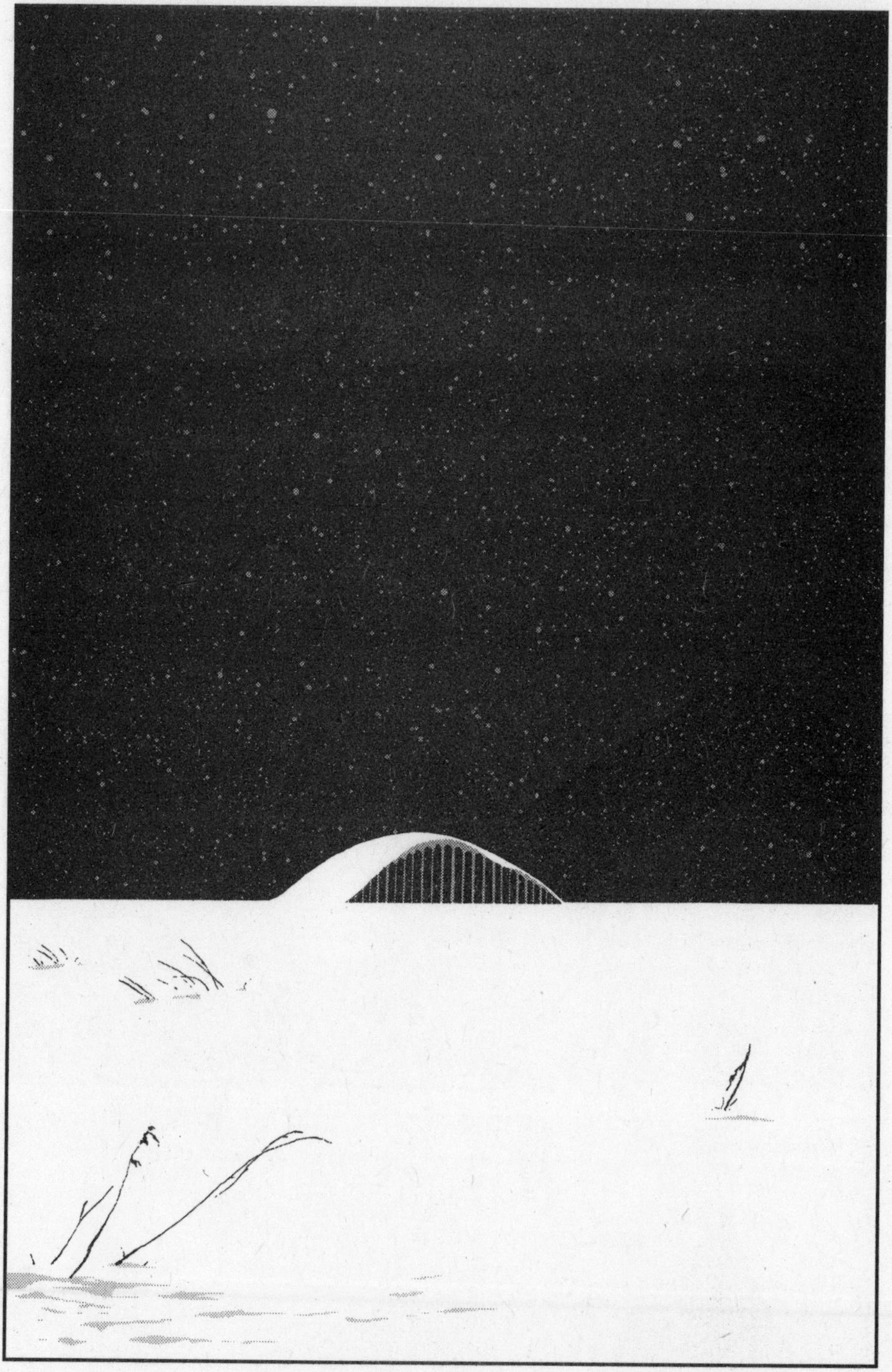

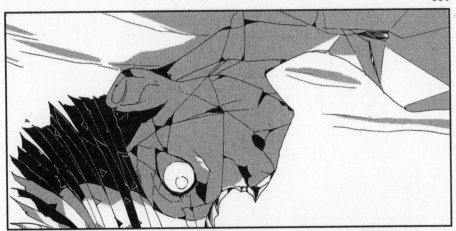

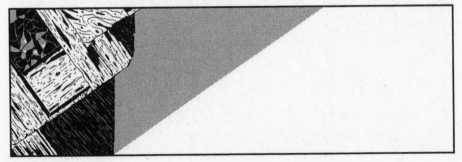

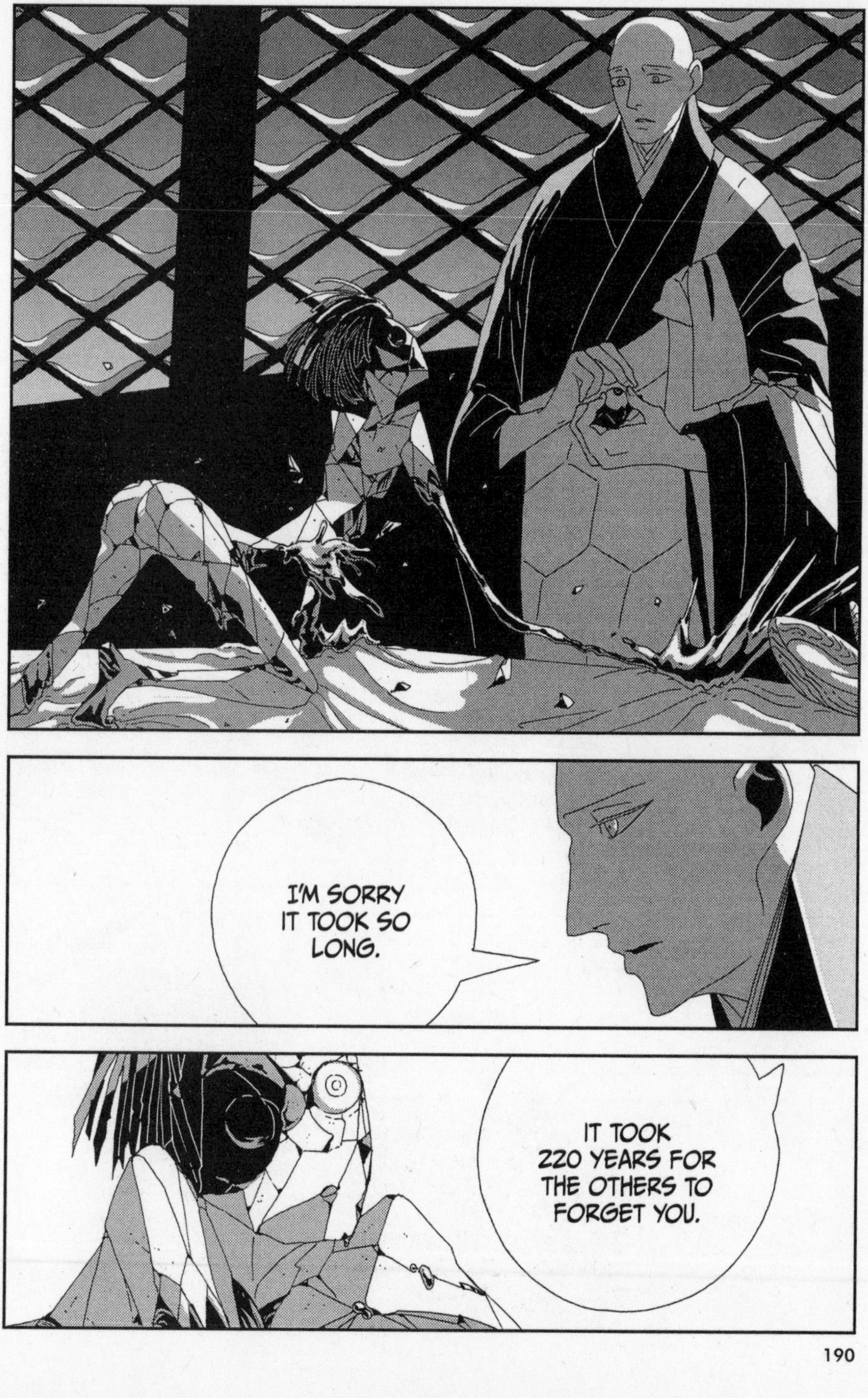
I'M SORRY IT TOOK SO LONG.
IT TOOK 220 YEARS FOR THE OTHERS TO FORGET YOU.

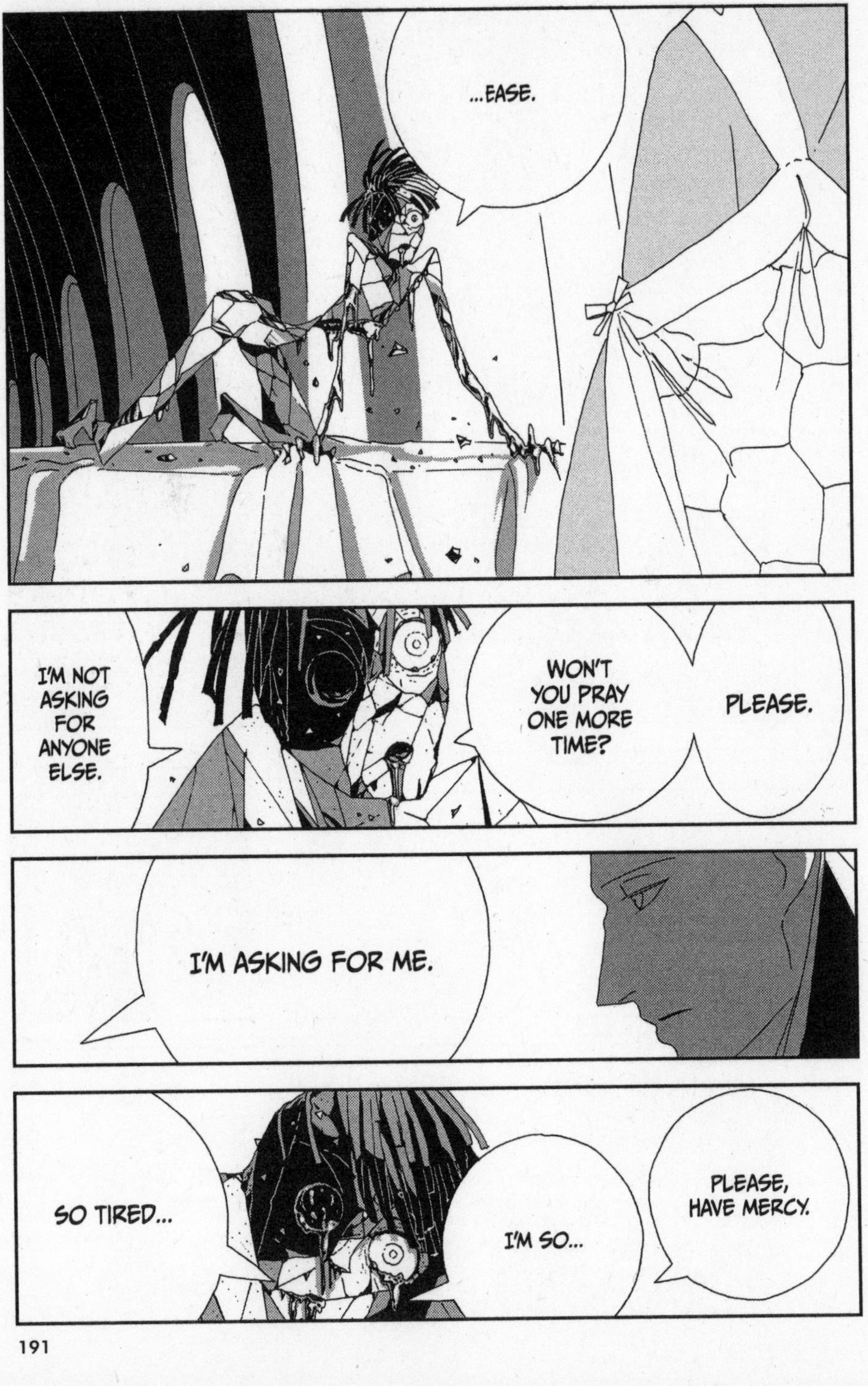
...EASE.
PLEASE.
WON'T YOU PRAY ONE MORE TIME?
I'M NOT ASKING FOR ANYONE ELSE.
I'M ASKING FOR ME.
PLEASE, HAVE MERCY.
I'M SO...
SO TIRED...

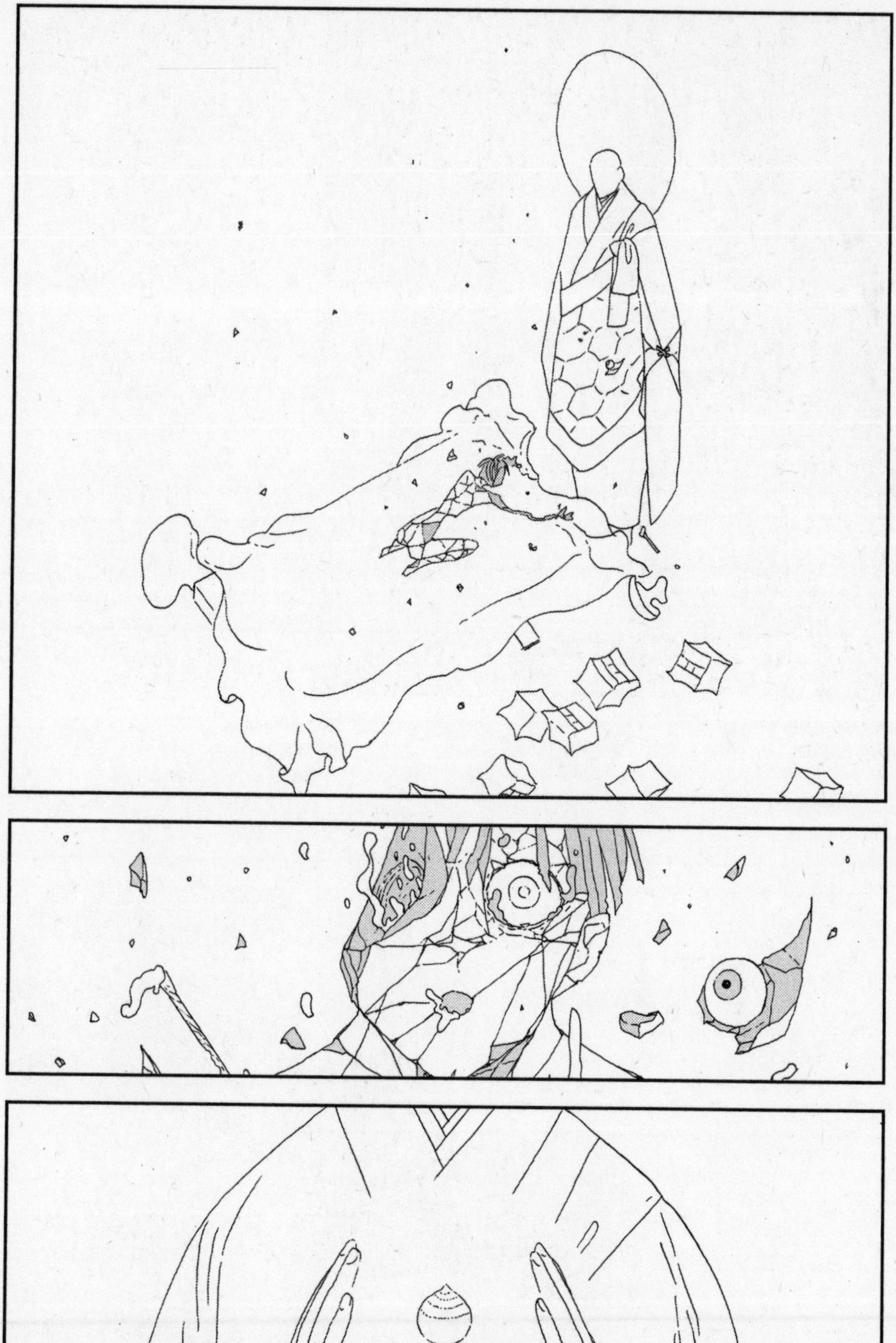

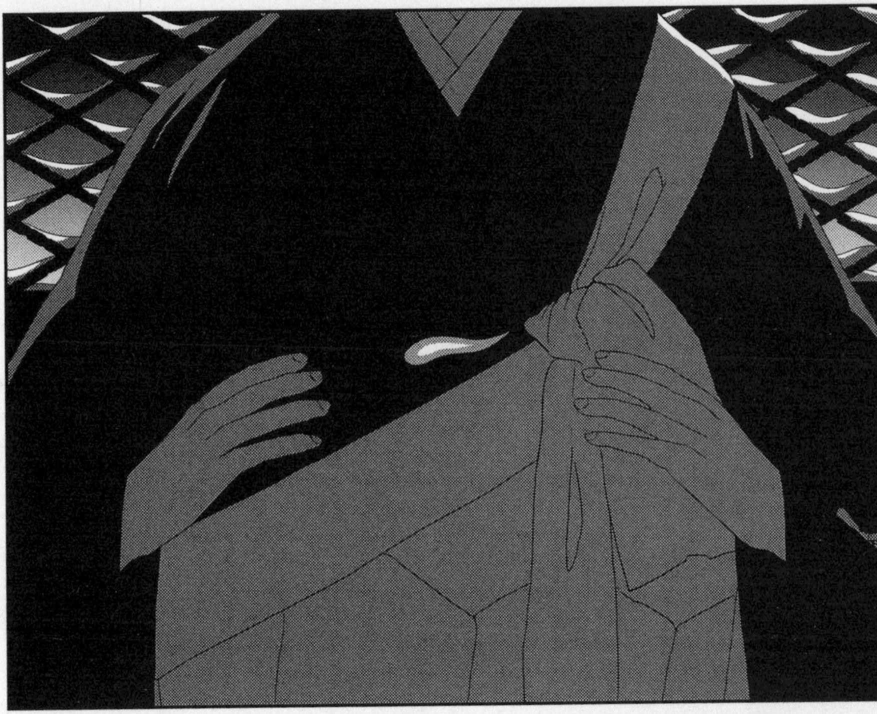
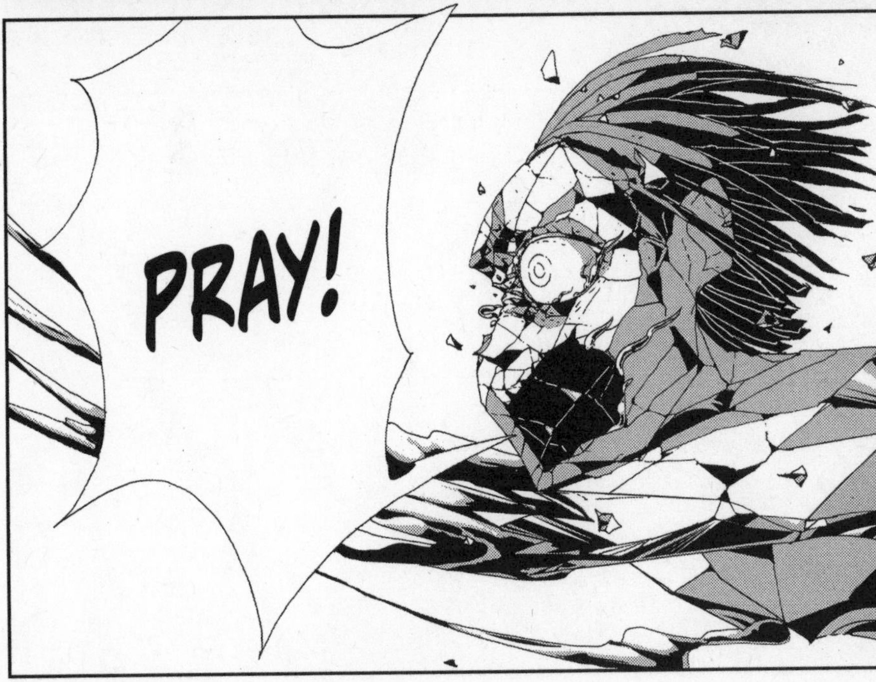
PRAY!

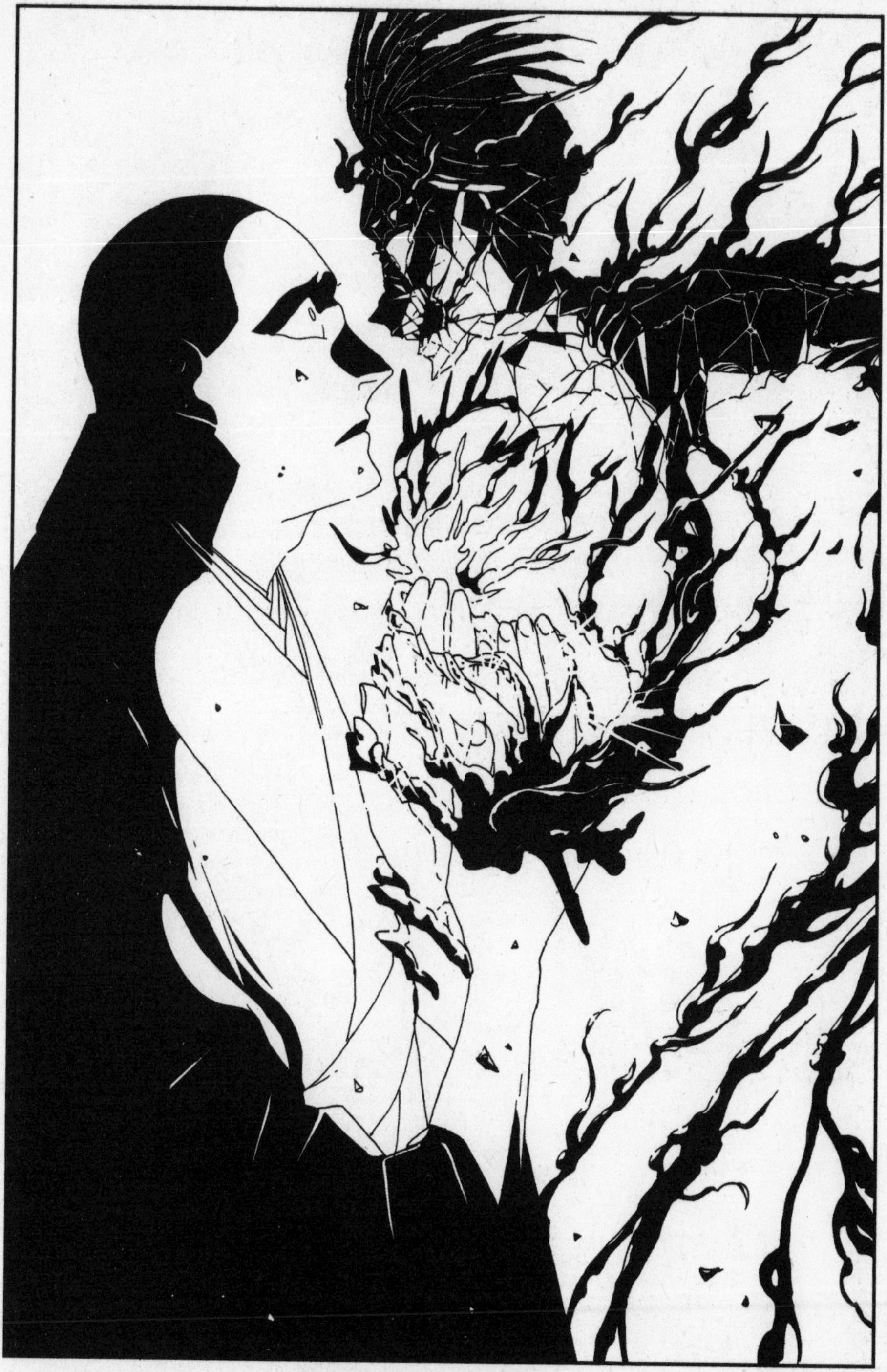

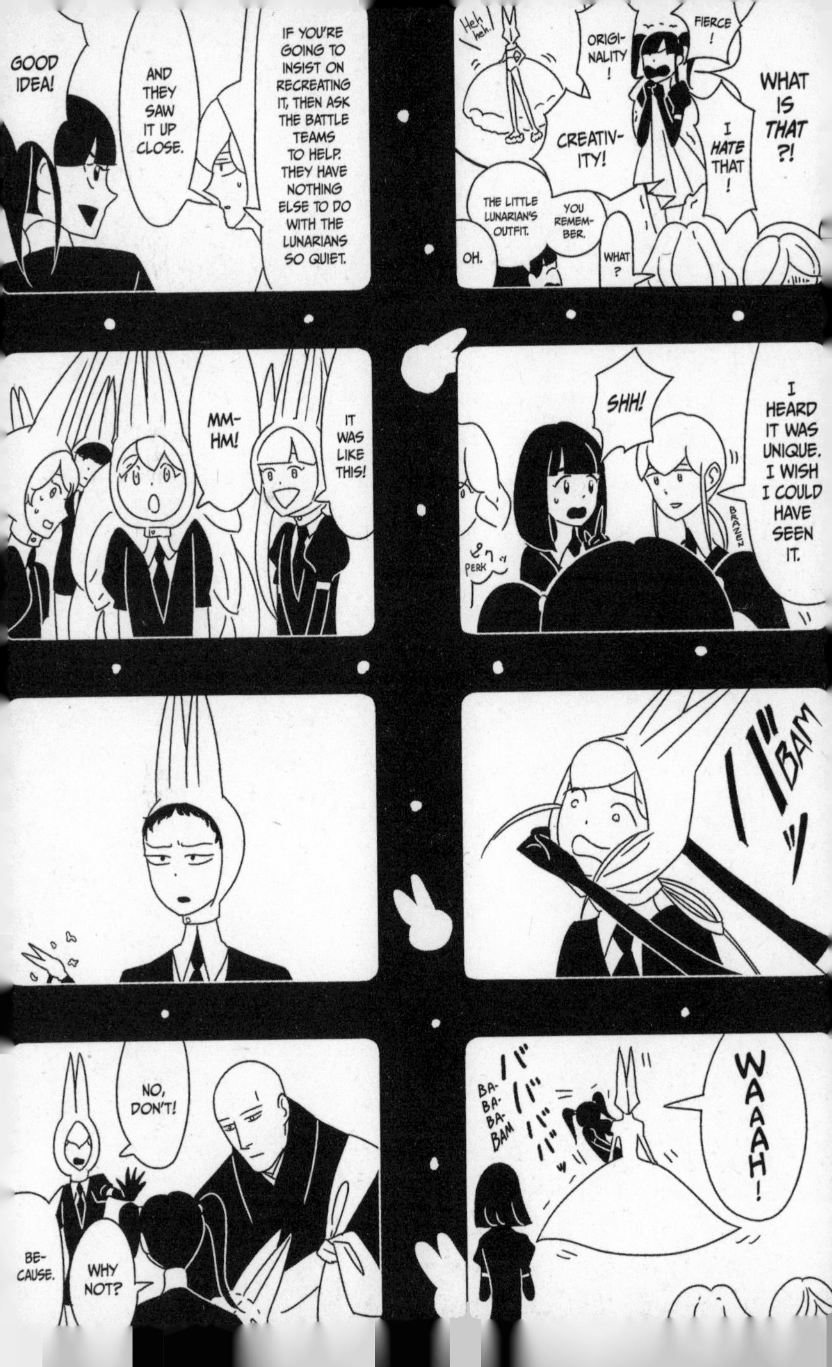
WHAT IS THAT?!
I HATE THAT!
FIERCE!
ORIGI-NALITY!
Heh heh.
CREATIV-ITY!
YOU REMEM-BER.
THE LITTLE LUNARIAN'S OUTFIT.
WHAT?
OH.
I HEARD IT WAS UNIQUE. I WISH I COULD HAVE SEEN IT.
BRAZEN
SHH!
PERK
BAM
WAAAH!
BA-BA-BA-BAM
IF YOU'RE GOING TO INSIST ON RECREATING IT, THEN ASK THE BATTLE TEAMS TO HELP. THEY HAVE NOTHING ELSE TO DO WITH THE LUNARIANS SO QUIET.
AND THEY SAW IT UP CLOSE.
GOOD IDEA!
IT WAS LIKE THIS!
MM-HM!
NO, DON'T!
WHY NOT?
BE-CAUSE.

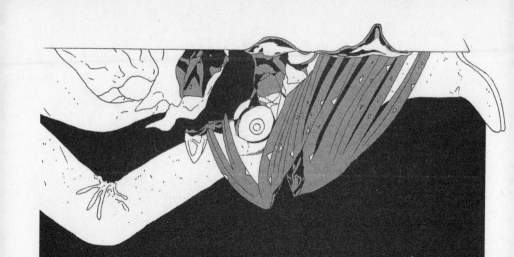

TRANSLATION NOTES

HAPPY HENRY *page 155*

"Happy Henry lives beside Boron Cottage" is the first part of a mnemonic device to remember the first 20 elements of the periodic table of elements, and the chemical symbols that go with them. These words correlate to hydrogen (H), helium (He), lithium (Li), beryllium (Be), boron (B), and carbon (C).

In the original Japanese text, Cairngorm complains about being interrupted while learning about the *suihei liebe*. This is the Japanese mnemonic device for learning the periodic table, where *suihei* means "sailor," and *liebe* is the German word for "lover." As one might expect, it corresponds with hydrogen (*suiso*), helium, lithium, and beryllium. Because Cairngorm was specifically learning about the *suihei* part of the equation, there's a strong possibility that there was further instruction on each of the elements than just the chemical symbols.

LAND OF THE LUSTROUS

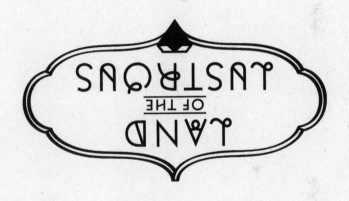

JAPANESE EDITION INSIDE COVER GALLERY

Volume 10

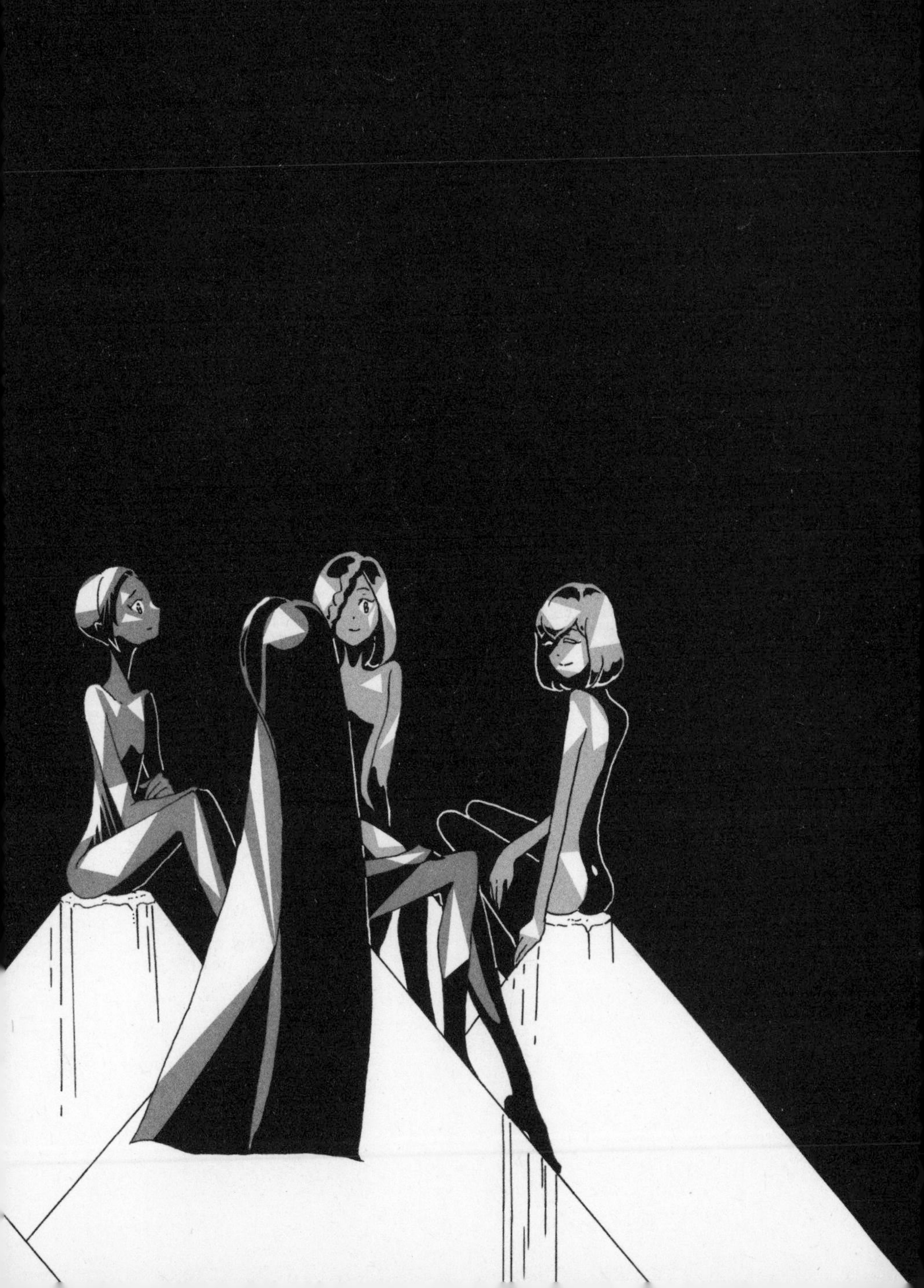

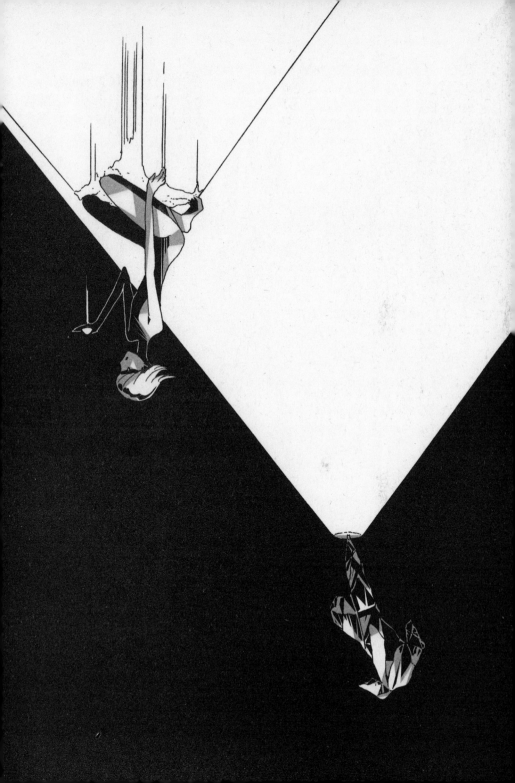

KC/ KODANSHA COMICS

Young Theo adores books, but the prejudice and hatred of his village keeps them ever out of his reach. Then one day, he chances to meet Sedona, a traveling librarian who works for the great library of Afrzaak, City of Books, and his life changes forever...

✦

MITSU IZUMI'S STUNNING ARTWORK BRINGS A FANTASTICAL LITERARY ADVENTURE TO LUSH, THRILLING LIFE!

Magus of the Library © Mitsu Izumi/Kodansha Ltd.

Magus of the Library
Mitsu Izumi

◄ KAMOME ►
SHIRAHAMA

Witch Hat Atelier

A magical manga
adventure for
fans of Disney
and Studio
Ghibli!

Witch Hat Atelier © Kamome Shirahama/Kodansha Ltd

The magical adventure that took Japan by storm is finally here, from acclaimed DC and Marvel cover artist Kamome Shirahama!

In a world where everyone takes wonders like magic spells and dragons for granted, Coco is a girl with a simple dream: She wants to be a witch. But everybody knows magicians are born, not made, and Coco was not born with a gift for magic. Resigned to her un-magical life, Coco is about to give up on her dream to become a witch…until the day she meets Qifrey, a mysterious, traveling magician. After secretly seeing Qifrey perform magic in a way she's never seen before, Coco soon learns what everybody "knows" might not be the truth, and discovers that her magical dream may not be as far away as it may seem…

KC
KODANSHA
COMICS

In love, there are no save points.

ヲタクに恋は難しい

NOW AN ANIME!

WOTAKOI:
LOVE IS HARD FOR OTAKU
by FUJITA

Narumi has had it rough: Every boyfriend she's had dumped her once they found out she was an otaku, so she's gone to great lengths to hide it. At her new job, she bumps into Hirotaka, her childhood friend and fellow otaku. When Hirotaka almost gets her secret outed at work, she comes up with a plan to keep him quiet. But he comes up with a counter-proposal: Why doesn't she just date him instead?

© Fujita/Ichijinsha, Inc. All rights reserved.

10 DANCE

Inouesatoh presents

The slow-burn queer romance that'll sweep you off your feet!

"A FANTASTIC DEBUT VOLUME... ONE OF MY FAVORITE BOOKS OF THE YEAR."
— AiPT!

"10 DANCE IS A MUST-READ FOR ANYONE WHO'S ENJOYED MANGA AND ANIME ABOUT COMPETITIVE DANCE (ON OR OFF THE ICE!)."
—Anime UK News

Shinya Sugiki, the dashing lord of Standard Ballroom, and Shinya Suzuki, passionate king of Latin Dance: The two share more than just a first name and a love of the sport. They each want to become champion of the 10-Dance Competition, which means they'll need to learn the other's specialty dances, and who better to learn from than the best? But old rivalries die hard, and things get further complicated when they realize there might be more between them than an uneasy partnership...

KCJ KODANSHA COMICS

10 DANCE © Inouesatoh/Kodansha Ltd.

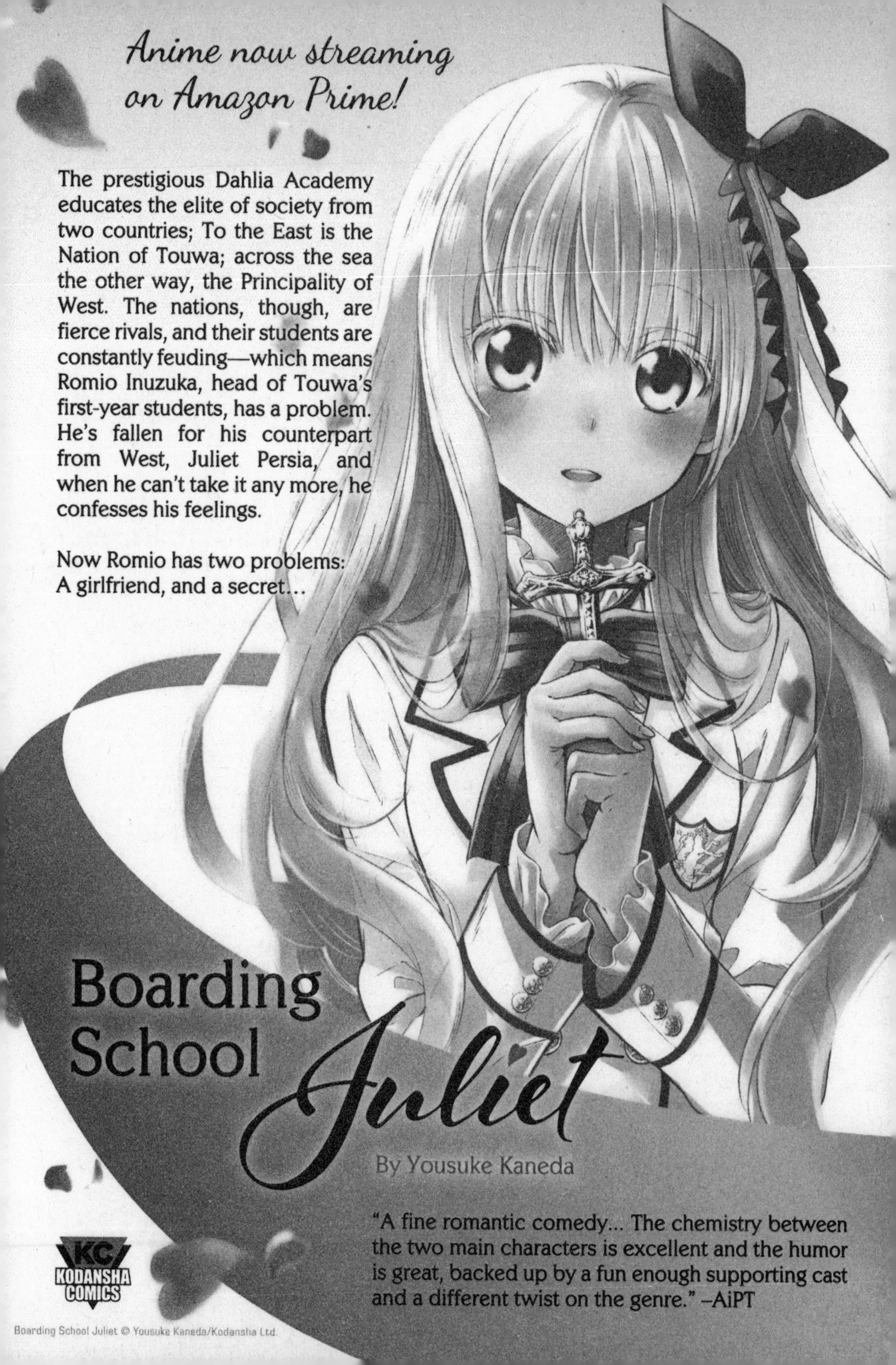
Anime now streaming on Amazon Prime!
The prestigious Dahlia Academy educates the elite of society from two countries; To the East is the Nation of Touwa; across the sea the other way, the Principality of West. The nations, though, are fierce rivals, and their students are constantly feuding—which means Romio Inuzuka, head of Touwa's first-year students, has a problem. He's fallen for his counterpart from West, Juliet Persia, and when he can't take it any more, he confesses his feelings.
Now Romio has two problems: A girlfriend, and a secret...
Boarding School Juliet
By Yousuke Kaneda
"A fine romantic comedy... The chemistry between the two main characters is excellent and the humor is great, backed up by a fun enough supporting cast and a different twist on the genre." –AiPT
KC KODANSHA COMICS
Boarding School Juliet © Yousuke Kaneda/Kodansha Ltd.

"You and me together...we would be unstoppable!"

GLEIPNIR

Gleipnir © Sun Takeda/Kodansha Ltd.

KC KODANSHA COMICS

Shuichi Kagaya is a smart kid, and most smart kids his age would be thinking about college. Shuichi is also a monster, and he's smart enough to know that monsters don't go to college. But after he uses his monstrous form to save his classmate Claire Aoki, it doesn't matter what his plans for the future were, because he's not the one making the decisions anymore. Now that the seductive, sadistic Claire knows Shuichi's secret, she's got her own ideas about what a monster is good for—because he's not the first monster she's met...

A dark and sexy body-horror action manga perfect for fans of Prison School and High School of the Dead!

THE MAGICAL GIRL CLASSIC THAT BROUGHT A
GENERATION OF READERS TO MANGA, NOW BACK IN A
DEFINITIVE, HARDCOVER COLLECTOR'S EDITION!

CARDCAPTOR SAKURA
COLLECTOR'S EDITION
C L A M P

Cardcaptor Sakura Collector's Edition © CLAMP • Shigatsu Tsuitachi Co., Ltd. / Kodansha Ltd.

Ten-year-old Sakura Kinomoto lives a pretty normal life with her older brother, Tōya, and widowed father, Fujitaka—until the day she discovers a strange book in her father's library, and her life takes a magical turn...

• A deluxe large-format hardcover edition of CLAMP's shojo manga classic
• All-new foil-stamped cover art on each volume
• Comes with exclusive collectible art card

KODANSHA COMICS

17 years after the original Cardcaptor *Sakura* manga ended, CLAMP returns with more magical adventures from a beloved manga classic!

Cardcaptor Sakura

❀ CLEAR CARD ❀

KC KODANSHA COMICS

Sakura Kinomoto's about to start middle school, and everything's coming up cherry blossoms. Not only has she managed to recapture the scattered Clow Cards and make them her own Sakura Cards, but her sweetheart Syaoran Li has moved from Hong Kong to Tokyo and is going to be in her class! But her joy is interrupted by a troubling dream in which the cards turn transparent, and when Sakura awakens to discover her dream has become reality, it's clear that her magical adventures are far from over...

© CLAMP·Shigatsu Tsuitachi Co., Ltd. / Kodansha Ltd. All rights reserved

KC KODANSHA COMICS

Hitorijime My Hero © Memeco Arii/Kodansha Ltd.

Hitorijime My Hero

Memeco Arii

Masahiro Setagawa doesn't believe in heroes, but wishes he could: He's found himself in a gang of small-time street bullies, and with no prospects for a real future. But when high school teacher (and scourge of the streets) Kousuke Ohshiba comes to his rescue, he finds he may need to start believing after all... in heroes, and in his budding feelings, too.

A BL romance between a good boy who didn't know he was waiting for a hero, and a bad boy who comes to his rescue!

ANIME OUT NOW FROM SENTAI FILMWORKS!

THE HIGH SCHOOL HAREM COMEDY WITH FIVE TIMES THE CUTE GIRLS!

"An entertaining romantic-comedy with a snarky edge to it." —Taykobon

Futaro Uesugi is a second-year in high school, scraping to get by and pay off his family's debt. The only thing he can do is study, so when Futaro receives a part-time job offer to tutor the five daughters of a wealthy businessman, he can't pass it up. Little does he know, these five beautiful sisters are quintuplets, but the only thing they have in common...is that they're all terrible at studying!

THE QUINTESSENTIAL QUINTUPLETS

negi haruba

ANIME OUT NOW!

KC KODANSHA COMICS

The Quintessential Quintuplets © Negi Haruba/Kodansha

KCI
KODANSHA
COMICS

At Granbell Kingdom, an abandoned amusement park, Shiki has lived his entire life among machines. But one day, Rebecca and her cat companion Happy appear at the park's front gates. Little do these newcomers know that this is the first human contact Granbell has had in a hundred years! As Shiki stumbles his way into making new friends, his former neighbors stir at an opportunity for a robo-rebellion... And when his old homeland becomes too dangerous, Shiki must join Rebecca and Happy on their spaceship and escape into the boundless cosmos.

A high-flying space adventure! All the steadfast friendship and wild fighting you've been waiting for...IN SPACE!

EDENS ZERO © Hiro Mashima/Kodansha, Ltd.

HIRO MASHIMA IS BACK! JOIN THE CREATOR OF **FAIRY TAIL** AS HE TAKES TO THE STARS FOR ANOTHER THRILLING SAGA!

EDENS ZERO
エデンズ ゼロ

Praise for Yoko Nogiri's That Wolf-Boy is Mine!

"Emotional squees...will-they-won't-they plot...[and a] pleasantly quick pace."
—Otaku USA Magazine

"A series that is pure shojo sugar—a cute love story about two nice people looking for their places in the world, and finding them with each other." —Anime News Network

KODANSHA COMICS

LOVE IN FOCUS

Love in Focus © Yoko Nogiri/Kodansha Ltd.

Mako's always had a passion for photography. When she loses someone dear to her, she clings onto her art as a relic of the close relationship she once had. Luckily, her childhood best friend Kei encourages her to come to his high school and join their prestigious photo club. With nothing to lose, Mako grabs her camera and moves into the dorm where Kei and his classmates live. Soon, a fresh take on life, along with a mysterious new muse, begin to come into focus!

A picture-perfect shojo series from Yoko Nogiri, creator of the hit That Wolf-Boy is Mine!

Land of the Lustrous 10 is a work of fiction. Names, characters, places, and incidents are the products of the author's imagination or are used fictitiously. Any resemblance to actual events, locales, or persons, living or dead, is entirely coincidental.

A Kodansha Comics Trade Paperback Original
Land of the Lustrous 10 copyright © 2019 Haruko Ichikawa
English translation copyright © 2020 Haruko Ichikawa

All rights reserved.

Published in the United States by Kodansha Comics, an imprint of Kodansha USA Publishing, LLC, New York.

Publication rights for this English edition arranged through Kodansha Ltd., Tokyo.

First published in Japan in 2019 by Kodansha Ltd., Tokyo.

ISBN 978-1-63236-915-4

Printed in the United States of America.

www.kodanshacomics.com

9 8 7 6 5 4 3 2 1
Translation: Alethea Nibley & Athena Nibley
Lettering: Evan Hayden
Editing: Tiff Ferentini
Kodansha Comics edition cover design by Phil Balsman

Publisher: Kiichiro Sugawara
Managing editor: Maya Rosewood
Vice president of marketing & publicity: Naho Yamada

Director of publishing services: Ben Applegate
Associate director of operations: Stephen Pakula
Publishing services managing editor: Noelle Webster
Assistant production manager: Emi Lotto